PRAISE FOR
TARGET: PATTON

★ ★ ★ ★

"Robert Wilcox's *Target: Patton* has enough twists and turns to satisfy the most demanding murder-mystery fan with the added bonus of historical possibility. Populated with legendary real-life characters, Wilcox introduces the world to Douglas Bazata: a man of action as improbably true as Lawrence of Arabia. With a screenwriter's gift for picture images and a military historian's discipline for detail, Wilcox peels back the decades to the chaotic final chords of World War II and the opening act of the Cold War by asking the heretofore unanswered question: was General George S. Patton murdered?"
—DOUG MCINTYRE, KABC Radio/*Los Angeles Daily News*

"*Target: Patton* is a terrific book investigating the mysterious death of one of America's greatest military heroes: General George S. Patton, Jr. Reporter Robert Wilcox takes the reader into the mystery: from Patton's suspicious car crash in Occupied Germany in 1945 to his unexpected death two weeks later, bringing to light new evidence and raising serious questions, all of which makes for a fascinating read."
—PAUL E. VALLELY, Major General, U.S. Army (Ret.),
Chairman, Stand Up America USA
Co-author of *Endgame: The Blueprint for Victory in the War on Terror*

"I am most surprised to learn in Robert Wilcox's highly readable book that there is a reasonable doubt and more that George Patton's death in Germany in December 1945 was not the result of a car crash but possibly foul play by hired assassins. Certainly there was motive and opportunity, but was there method? Over the years, I had heard a version of this tale based upon German villainy, but never with the detail and matter-of-fact persuasion in *Target: Patton*. I don't know if he was murdered, but I am no longer sure he wasn't. Exhume the corpse. End the debate."
—JOHN BATCHELOR, host WABC, WMAL, KSFO, KFI

TARGET: PATTON

★ ★ ★ ★ ★ ★ ★ ★ ★ ★ ★ ★ ★ ★ ★ ★ ★ ★ ★

TARGET: PATTON

★ ★ ★ ★ ★ ★ ★ ★ ★ ★ ★ ★ ★ ★ ★ ★ ★ ★ ★ ★

THE PLOT TO ASSASSINATE
GENERAL GEORGE S. PATTON

ROBERT K. WILCOX

Since 1947
REGNERY
PUBLISHING, INC.
An Eagle Publishing Company • Washington, DC

Cataloging-in-Publication data on file with the Library of Congress

ISBN 978-1-59698-579-7 (hard cover)
ISBN 978-1-59698-606-0 (paperback)
First paperback edition published in 2010

Published in the United States by
Regnery Publishing, Inc.
One Massachusetts Avenue, NW
Washington, DC 20001
www.regnery.com

Manufactured in the United States of America

10 9 8 7 6 5 4 3 2 1

Books are available in quantity for promotional or premium use. Write to Director of Special Sales, Regnery Publishing, Inc., One Massachusetts Avenue NW, Washington, DC 20001, for information on discounts and terms or call (202) 216-0600.

Distributed to the trade by:
Perseus Distribution
387 Park Avenue South
New York, NY 10016

To Bego

CONTENTS

★ ★ ★ ★

★ ★ ★ ★

INTRODUCTION

Almost since the day General George S. Patton, Jr. died, there have been persistent rumors that he was murdered. Not just murdered, though—assassinated. It has been repeated relentlessly that he was killed because he was hated by his superior officers due to jealousy and fear. Jealousy of him because he was, in fact, the best general in the United States Army. Fear of him because they thought he was going to expose many of the cowardly, incompetent, and corrupt things done by the Allied High Command during World War II. If that were not enough, there have been persistent claims that the Russians were also trying to assassinate him because Stalin hated him.

Robert K. Wilcox has taken on a major story in his quest for the truth of the matter. One thing is for certain in Mr. Wilcox's book: he has obviously worked for years on this project and has done a great deal of homework concerning this issue. His research and story are highly detailed and comprehensive. The book is thoroughly researched and well written. It is a story of intrigue, deceit, obfuscations, and politics (both civil and military).

Does Mr. Wilcox find the trail to the truth? Does he prove his assertions? Well, the thing is... if I tell that, I will be giving away the entire story, and I certainly can't do that. It will be up to the reader to decide for himself once he has read this worthwhile book. It is, indeed, a good read.

Charles M. Province
The George S. Patton, Jr. Historical Society
17010 S. Potter Road
Oregon City OR 97045
http://www.pattonhq.com

★ ★ ★ ★

CAST OF PRINCIPAL CHARACTERS AND SOURCES

ALLEN, Colonel Robert S.—World War II Patton aide, author, and journalist

ANDREW, Christopher—professor, author who has written on Soviet assassination

"ANGELA"—pseudonym for Joe Scruce's (aka "Spruce") daughter

AYER, Fred, Jr.—Patton's nephew and FBI agent in charge of the bureau's European operations during World War II

BABALAS, Lieutenant Peter K.—Military policeman who was one of the first at the scene of Patton's accident on December 9, 1945

BALL, Colonel Lawrence C.—commander of 130th Station Hospital, Heidelberg, where General Patton was taken after his December 9, 1945 accident on December 9, 1945

BANDERA, Stepan—Ukrainian nationalist leader and one of three important sources who informed Counter Intelligence Corps (CIC) agent Stephen Skubik that General Patton was on a Soviet hit list

BAZATA, Douglas deWitt—former OSS "Jedburgh" agent who claimed involvement in a plot to assassinate General Patton

BAZATA, Marie-Pierre—Douglas Bazata's wife

BENTLEY, Elizabeth—U.S.-born NKVD spy who first blew the whistle to the FBI about extensive Soviet spying during World War II in America

BILLINGTON, Joy—Washington, D.C. journalist who wrote about Bazata

BLUMENSON, Martin—author, Patton historian

BRADLEY, General Omar—General Patton's contemporary and immediate boss as Patton commanded the Third Army in France and Germany

BREINDEL, Eric—author, journalist who has written on Soviet espionage

CAIRNS, Brigadier Hugh—British neurosurgeon who first attended General Patton at the 130th Station Hospital, Heidelberg, Germany

CAVE-BROWN, Anthony—author, Donovan biographer

CHURCHILL, Winston—Prime minister of Britain and one of the Allied "Big Three" leaders

CIC—Counter Intelligence Corps, an army intelligence agency in World War II

COBB, General Nicholas B.—mentioned by General Gay as arriving at the scene of the December 9, 1945 accident and helping out

COLBY, William "Bill"—former OSS Jedburgh agent and Bazata friend who later became head of the CIA

CURRAN, Major— soldier mentioned by General Gay as being one of the first on the scene of Patton's accident

DAVIDOV, General Alexander M (aka "Davidow," "Davidoff")—Soviet chief of repatriation in post-war Germany and Soviet spymaster believed by CIC's Stephen Skubik to have been involved in General Patton's death

D'ESTE, Carlo—author, historian, Patton biographer

DECRESCENZO, Sergeant Armando— said to have arrived at the accident scene with three other soldiers

DONOVAN, General William J. "Wild Bill"—head of the Office of Strategic Services (OSS), the U.S.'s World War II spy agency, forerunner to the CIA

DUGGAN, Laurence—State Department official who spied for the NKVD

EISENHOWER, General Dwight D.—Supreme Allied Commander in Europe later to become president of the United States

FARAGO, Ladislas—Hungarian-born former U.S. naval intelligence officer, author, and historian who was the first to write on Patton's accident using interviews extensively with eyewitnesses and visiting the site

FITIN, General Pavel M.—head of the Soviet intelligence service, the NKVD (later to become the KGB) during World War II

FUGATE, Denver—historian who has written in-depth about General Patton's injury and death

GAVIN, General James M.—World War II parachute troop commander and author

GAY, General Hobart "Hap"—close aide to Patton who was with him when he was injured in the car accident December 9, 1945

GILLESPIE, First Lieutenant William L.—Stephen Skubik's immediate CIC boss in post-war Germany

GINGOLD, Lester—Memphis, Tennessee enlisted man who took rare photos, including of Robert L. Thompson, at the Patton accident scene December 9, 1945

HADDEN, Lieutenant John A.—General Gay's aide-de-camp at the time of the December 9, 1945 accident

HAYNES, John Earl—historian, author who has written on Soviet espionage

HENDRIKX, Peter J. K.—Patton researcher in the Netherlands

HILL, Lieutenant Colonel Paul S., Jr.—Head physician attending General Patton when he first arrived at the 130th Station Hospital in Heidelberg, Germany

HIRSHSON, Stanley P.—professor, Patton historian, author

HISS, Alger—State Department official identified by Russian officials and Venona decrypts as a Soviet spy

HOETTL, Major Wilhelm—high-placed German intelligence officer who offered after World War II his Balkan spy network to the U.S. for use against the Soviets

HOPKINS, Harry—One of the "New Deal" architects and Soviet sympathizer who became President Roosevelt's closest advisor

IRVING, David—author, World War II historian

IRZYK, General Albin F.—World War II tank commander, author

KENT, Doctor Gerald T. Kent—junior physician who attended injured General Patton when he first arrived at the 130th Station Hospital, Heidelberg, Germany

KEYES, General Geoffrey—Commander of Seventh Army in whose jurisdiction Patton's December 9, 1945 accident occurred. A friend of Patton's, he conducted an investigation into the accident which is missing.

KLEHR, Harvey—professor, historian, author who has written on Soviet espionage

KRUMMER, Frank—alleged to have been one of possibly two passengers in the truck that collided with General Patton's Cadillac on December 9, 1945

LARSON, Matt—General Motors Cadillac expert

LAYTON, Lieutenant Hugh O.—Military policeman said to have been at the December 9, 1945 accident scene

LEE, Duncan—trusted aide to OSS chief William Donovan and NKVD spy

MACINTOSH, Colonel—OSS officer (possibly fictitiously named) who dealt with Stephen Skubik's intelligence about death threats to General Patton

MARSHALL, General George C.—head of the U.S. Army, General Eisenhower's immediate boss, answerable only to the president

MAY, Technical Sergeant Ralph E.—one of two CIC agents partnering with Stephen Skubik in their 970th Detachment office

METZ, Lieutenant John—Military policeman and partner of Babalas who arrived at the accident scene

MILLAR, George—British Special Operations Executive (SOE) agent, codenamed "Emile," whom Bazata aided while in Occupied France. Millar later wrote *Maquis*, one of the more famous books about the French Resistance. Bazata is one of those featured in the book.

MITROKHIN, Vasili—KGB archivist whose smuggled notes and copies of documents have been the basis for intelligence revelations about Soviet spying

MONTGOMERY, Field Marshall Bernard—high-ranking British general and World War II Patton rival

MORGANTHAU, Treasury Secretary Henry—vehemently anti-German New Deal cabinet member and friend of both President Roosevelt and OSS chief, Wild Bill Donovan. Author of the "Morganthau Plan" to prostrate Germany after the war.

MURPHY, Robert D.—diplomat and special representative of President Roosevelt, sent to aid Eisenhower and the Allies in the World War II invasion of North Africa

NOLAN, Frederick—British writer and novelist who authored fictional account of General Patton's injury and death

OGDEN, Sergeant Leroy—said by Woodring to have been at the scene of the accident and to have helped stop Patton's bleeding

OSS—Office of Strategic Services, forerunner of the CIA

PATTERSON, Robert P.—One of President Roosevelt's "Wise men" and Under Secretary of War to whom Patton expressed his wish to fight the Soviets

PATTON, Beatrice Ayer—General Patton's wife

PATTON, General George S., Jr.—famed fighting commander who died in a German hospital December 21, 1945 after being injured in a mysterious accident on December 9

PROVINCE, Charles M.—Patton historian, author

RODIN, Colonel Leo—CIC or OSS officer (possibly a fictitious name) to whom Stephen Skubik reported threats against General Patton

ROMERSTEIN, Herbert—author, intelligence expert

ROOSEVELT, Franklin Delano—"FDR," Democratic president of the U.S. throughout World War II and, as such, supreme commander until his death in April 1945

SHANAHAN, Lieutenant Joseph—military policeman (MP) said to have been at the scene of the December 9, 1945 accident in which General Patton was injured

SHANDRUK, General Pavlo—Ukrainian military leader and one of three sources who warned Stephen Skubik that General Patton was on a Soviet hit list

SHELTON, Suzy—authored an article with a lengthy interview of Horace Woodring about the December 9, 1945 accident

SKUBIK, Stephen J.—CIC agent attached to Patton's armies in Germany whose Ukrainian sources told him of a Soviet plot to assassinate the controversial general. He later wrote a book about the plot

SNYDER, Captain Ned—doctor at scene of December 9, 1945 accident who attended General Patton's injuries and, along with his commanding officer, Major Charles Tucker, helped transport Patton to a Heidelberg hospital

SMAL-STOCKI, Professor Roman—Ukrainian scholar and diplomat and one of three sources who told Stephen Skubik that General Patton was on a Soviet hit list

SMITH, Bradley F.—author, World War II historian

SMITH, General Walter Bedell ("Beedle")—General Eisenhower's chief of staff whom General Patton detested

"SPRUCE," Sergeant Joe—real last name Scruce—driver of the Jeep carrying the hunting supplies and guns in the Patton caravan when Patton was injured December 9, 1945

SPURLING, Colonel Glen R.—General Patton's main neurosurgeon while in the 130th Station Hospital, Heidelberg

STALIN, Joseph—Dictator of Soviet Russia and one of the "Big Three" Allied leaders during World War II

STEPHENSON, William—British intelligence officer, code-named "Intrepid," who had close ties to President Roosevelt and OSS chief William Donovan

STONE, Major "Stoney"—OSS officer in Germany, not otherwise identified, who referred Stephen Skubik to OSS chief William Donovan, and later warned Skubik his (Skubik's) life was in danger

SUDOPLATOV, Pavel—head of the Soviet NKVD's "Special Tasks" department which included conducting kidnapping, sabotage, and assassination. He later authored a book about his activities

THOMPSON, Robert L.—driver of the truck that unexplainably turned in front of Patton's Cadillac resulting in General Patton's December 9, 1945 injury

TOOMBS, Technical Sergeant Harry B—one of two Counter Intelligence Corps (CIC) agents partnering with Stephen Skubik in the 970ᵗʰ Detachment field office

TRUMAN, Harry S.—new U.S. vice president who succeeded President Roosevelt following Roosevelt's death on April 12, 1945

TUCKER, Major Charles—officer along with Captain Ned Snyder who responded to the accident scene December 9, 1945 and transported General Patton to the Heidelberg hospital

ULBRICHT, Walter—German communist organizer and later head of Soviet Block East Germany whom Stephen Skubik arrested, angering the Soviets

VANLANDINGHAM, Lieutenant (no other information known)—mysterious visitor reported at the scene of the accident

WALLACE, Henry A.—U.S. vice president under Roosevelt supplanted by Harry Truman on the 1944 Democratic ticket because of his Far Left views

WEDEMEYER, General Albert C.—General Marshall aide and Patton supporter

WHITE, Harry Dexter—assistant secretary of the Treasury under Henry Morgenthau identified by Venona decrypts and former Soviet officials as an NKVD spy

WOODRING, Horace L. "Woody"—nineteen-year-old driver of the 1938 Cadillac limousine in which Patton was critically injured on December 9, 1945

ZHUKOV, Marshall Georgi K.—high-ranking Soviet general

CHAPTER ONE

★ ★ ★ ★

THE LAST RIDE

On a cold, dreary morning in December of 1945, a dark green Cadillac limousine with trumpet-like horns on the hood and large white stars on its doors pulled out from a narrow street in Bad Nauheim, Occupied Germany,* and began what was to be the fateful last ride for General George S. Patton, Jr. He was the highest ranking American officer in Europe and America's greatest fighting general. What exactly would happen on that car trip remains a mystery to this day. Key witnesses disappeared. Records are missing. Contradictions and questions abound. Not only did Patton have a dramatic impact on World War II, he is an American legend who might have shortened or even prevented the Cold War, America's longest and most damaging conflict[1]—had he survived.

But he did not.

Rumors persist that he was assassinated. Was he?

---

*An ancient town near the fabled Black Forest and headquarters of the U.S. Fifteenth Army.

Nicknamed "Blood and Guts" for his ruthless approach to warfighting, the tall, controversial 60-year-old general was, as the large limousine left Bad Nauheim and headed south on the Autobahn, already a legend. From his days in 1916 hunting Mexican guerrilla Pancho Villa to his brilliant leadership in the liberation of Western Europe, he had displayed "a genius for war"* unmatched by any of his contemporaries. He was a warrior, military scholar, disciplinarian, and tactician who achieved the rarest of military accolades: his battlefield enemies so feared him that their first question in strategy sessions was almost always "Where's Patton?"

He had done things militarily thought impossible. Just a year before, he had quickly turned the huge and unwieldy Third Army 90 degrees north from its easterly drive through France in snow and bitter cold to help save outnumbered and besieged U.S. paratroopers at Bastogne, Belgium. When he had proposed the rescue, his contemporaries said it could not be done. But he had been planning it for days. His drive across France and Germany was itself one of the most brilliant feats of the European War, and it broke the back of the Nazis' last major offensive—the Battle of the Bulge in the Ardennes Forest. It was rivaled only by D-Day, whose success he had ensured by acting as a decoy to convince the Germans he was readying a force to invade at Pas de Calais, far from Normandy. The ruse had worked spectacularly.

In the limousine with Patton on this fateful Sunday were Lieutenant General Hobart "Hap" Gay, long-time aide and former cavalry man, and nineteen-year-old Private First Class Horace "Woody" Woodring, his relatively new driver.[2] Patton and Gay were in the back of the Cadillac as they left Bad Nauheim, with

---

*As historian Carlo D'Este observed with the title of his 1995 biography.

enough space between them on the big car's rear seat for another passenger, and plenty of room in front of them. Behind and following the Cadillac in the cold was an open air half-ton jeep driven by a soldier always identified erroneously in later histories as Sergeant Joe Spruce. He was carrying rifles, a bird dog, and possibly other supplies. Patton was leaving Germany the next day. This trip—roughly a hundred miles south, past Frankfurt, to the woods beyond Mannheim—was to hunt pheasant. He loved hunting and had hunted many times while in Germany, so it was to be an enjoyable way to spend his final hours on the continent.

A voracious student of military history, Patton was by far the best tactician—and arguably strategist—of any of the Allied military leaders, including Supreme Allied Commander General Dwight D. Eisenhower, a long-time friend and contemporary whom he fought under in the recent war. But Patton, unflinchingly honest in public and infuriatingly impulsive, had repeatedly challenged his superiors' tactical and strategic decisions, as well as the post-war U.S. occupation policy, and thus courted trouble from his bosses and the press. Hell, as he often said in his profane way, the press was his enemy—except when he could use them. The press, largely threatened by his brash and strutting warrior persona—a persona he deliberately assumed for its effect, as he believed, of raising the morale of his men—often criticized him, especially towards the end of the war. Largely unrecognized by most of the news writers was the fact that he used his trademark swift, relentless, and crushing attacks—what they generally deemed brutal and uncaring—to save lives by enabling victory to be more quickly attained. Hesitation, he preached, was a soldier's worst enemy. A commander had to act swiftly and decisively in order to take advantage of fleeting, critical opportunities in battle. But his enemies, many of whom had never served and probably thanked

God for it, thought him devoid of compassion—as if that were a requisite for fighting—and a warmonger. He did love war but, as most warriors do, he loved it as a crucible, a test of his prowess and courage and, in his own peculiar religious way, a fulfillment of his destiny.[3] But he was fully mindful of war's horrors and pointed them out often.

His rivalry with British Field Marshall Bernard Montgomery, who outranked him but whom he regarded as timid and indecisive, was a volatile story that had gotten him public attention, good and bad. The two field commanders had clashed repeatedly, most publicly during the Sicilian Campaign in 1943 when Patton had beaten the cautious Viscount to Messina and had made sure the world knew it. The press relished the rivalry. Hell, Patton had, too! But it had been a headache for Eisenhower whose job it was to keep a united Allied front. And Eisenhower, whose reputation and political career had benefited from Patton's victories—which the politically astute Supreme Commander had not shied from—had certainly informed Patton of his displeasure.

Next, Patton had been pilloried for slapping a shell-shocked U.S. soldier in Sicily. He felt the soldier, being treated in a hospital, was a coward. He had done something similar earlier in the war without incident. But when the press started slamming him for it, Eisenhower took notice and forced him to make a public apology. While the incident deprived Patton of a coveted D-Day invasion command—a prize he deeply regretted not getting—he came back full force after he was let loose on the French mainland and began his Third Army smash east through France towards Germany. He had raged at his superiors' decisions to repeatedly halt his advances, most notably at Falaise where he could have killed thousands of Germans who escaped through a narrow pocket and returned to fight at the Battle of the Bulge; at the German border, where he could have crossed early and, he believed, shortened the war and saved American lives; and at the conclusion of the European conflict, just months before, when his pleas to go deeper into Eastern Europe and beat the Russians to crucial objectives, especially Berlin, had been sternly rejected. Fearing he might advance in spite of their orders not to, Eisenhower and General Omar Bradley, Patton's immediate superior, several times cut off his gas supply. Imagine that, he said to subordinates, subverting their own forces!

Gas, however, this Sunday morning on the Autobahn, was no longer a problem. As a conquering general with only peacetime needs he now had all he wanted. But by war's end, he had begun to resent Eisenhower and Bradley and others in higher places who, in return, had come to regard him as a kind of loose cannon, capable, alarmingly, of initiating controversial forays on his own without higher authorization. He had done exactly that at the end of the war in ordering a hasty, under-defensed raid on an out-of-the-way and dangerously situated German prisoner of war camp where his son-in-law was an inmate.[4] He admitted such apparent favoritism for a family member was probably the wrong thing to display. But as he was often at odds with his superiors' plans, he sometimes conveniently found ways to disregard their orders. For instance, on May 1, 1945, he went ahead and captured Trier, Germany, even though Eisenhower, thinking Patton did not have enough divisions to do so, had told him to stay put. Upon being called on the action, he signaled Ike, "What do you want me to do? Give it back?"[5]

He certainly could be impertinent to superiors. But he was not insubordinate as he was unfairly characterized. Commanders were usually given discretion in the field and most of his unauthorized actions had resulted in success—the ultimate measure of a

commander's worth. Nevertheless, the same commanders—
namely Eisenhower and Bradley—whose faulty orders he ignored
had no shame in reaping the credit. For the most part, Patton was
unfailingly loyal and professional and obeyed orders even when he
bitterly disagreed. A former jeep driver for him, Francis J. Sanza,
remembers Patton's eyes tearing up because he was so angry when
he was denied permission to go to Berlin.[6] But he obeyed, however
reluctantly.

They had not traveled very far on the autobahn when the Cadillac stopped at an ancient Roman ruin, near Bad Homburg in Saalburg, roughly twenty miles south and west of Bad Nauheim.
Patton's quest for historical knowledge was insatiable, and since
this was his final Sunday in Germany, it was probably his last
chance to see it. Woodring therefore detoured and they parked,
exited the limousine, and walked up a hill to inspect the ruin. It
was a cold, wet slog to the snow-covered higher ground and they
were glad, as Woodring later recalled, to get back to the limousine's warmth and continue on their way.

Once the war ended, animosities Patton had engendered—
mostly jealousy and competition from fellow generals, as well as
post-war politics—had combined to deny him medals and accolades he certainly deserved. While Eisenhower and Bradley had
been rapidly promoted, riding the victories he had mostly provided, his promotion was slow in coming. And he was relegated
to what, basically, was a bureaucratic purgatory.

While he had wanted to go to the Pacific and fight the Japanese, he instead had been made governor of occupied Bavaria, a curious post for a soldier of his reputation with the die-hard
Nipponese still to be conquered. He was a fighter, not a bureau-
crat. Nevertheless, he had done well in the position, getting the
vanquished Germans up off their knees. Germany was in sham-

bles. War wreckage was piled high along the road on both sides of their traveling Cadillac. The vanquished country was barely able to meet basic needs like food, shelter, and the security required to cope with the chaos of displaced millions, fleeing hardcore Nazis, and conquering nations vying boldly but surreptitiously—sometimes even violently—for whatever part of the victor's pie they could further wrench from each other.

Patton's attempt to do his post-war job well had been part of his undoing. With typical American goodwill, once the war had ended, he forgave his enemies—not the hardcore Nazis whom he disdained, but the rank and file whom he considered more victims of Hitler than proponents. Out of necessity, he installed some of them in crucial positions, such as mayor or sanitation manager, because they had experience. It made sense. The country had to get working again, and Patton did not want to create the same conditions in the defeated country that had given rise to Hitler after World War I. But in Washington, the policy, rigidly enforced, was that no ex-Nazi, however marginal, could be installed in any position of authority unless he or she was demonstrably against the Hitler regime—like the surviving communist partisans.

Communists? It offended his very being. They were enemies of democracy. At least Patton felt that way.

De facto punishment for all Germans was the official Washington goal. One particularly brutal plan eagerly put forth by Treasury Secretary Henry Morgenthau, a powerful member of President Franklin Delano Roosevelt's "New Deal" cabinet, was to reduce Germany to being solely an agrarian society so it never again would have the industry to make war. Patton vehemently criticized the Morgenthau Plan as unjust, publicly and privately,[7] but President Roosevelt supported it until other, chiefly military, advisors prevailed. But even after Roosevelt's death in April of

1945, the policy of wholesale German repression continued under President Harry Truman, Roosevelt's successor, and Patton, without apology, had continued to oppose it, further angering the administration and his military bosses.

Also damning in most of New Deal Washington's eyes was Patton's attitude toward the Soviet Union. Post-war Washington in 1945 was a lopsided political battleground. The stronger "Left," led by Democrats—the party of Roosevelt and Truman and thus the party in power—believed that communist Russia, led by Joseph Stalin, was sincere in its pronouncements of peace, justice, and a better world for all. It deserved, they believed, the "buffer" states of Poland, Bulgaria, Romania and other war-torn Eastern European countries which, as a result of the fighting and Allied agreements, it now occupied and was ruthlessly exploiting. President Roosevelt had been chief amongst those who believed that the Russians had borne the brunt of the fight against the Nazis, especially in terms of numbers of dead, and therefore were entitled to such a spoil. He admired "Uncle Joe," as he had affectionately called Stalin. He had looked favorably on the Russians throughout the war, even to the point of showing more respect for the Russian premier than he did for British Prime Minister Winston Churchill at the "Big Three" conference held at Tehran, Iran, in 1943.[8]

In addition, influential members of the American Left believed in at least some of the tenets of socialism,[9] if not full-blown communism itself—the great opponent of Western capitalism—which Soviet Russia and Stalin exemplified. They had emerged from the Great Depression of the 1930s, which had spawned the New Deal, believing that a utopia of sorts had been building in Soviet Russia under communism. Thus enamored, they naïvely viewed the Stalinist regime, on the whole, as benevolent, and wished understandably, now that the fighting was over, to continue the alliance created during the war—an alliance that was threatened by Patton's aggressive stance and inflammatory comments against Russia.

On the other side of the political battleground was the weaker Republican "Right," who saw the Soviets and communists as ruthless, exploitive, brutal enemies of personal and national freedom, and who could never be a true friend of the West. Patton had emerged as one of the Right's most vocal leaders—certainly one of its most famous—showing contempt for the Russians to their faces even before hostilities had ceased. A longtime anti-communist, he had been made aware anew, through his intelligence network and personal contacts, of the Stalin-sanctioned raping and pillaging conducted by the Russian troops and the loss of freedoms imposed on conquered populations as the communists fought their way victoriously west through Poland and into Germany and Berlin. A luncheon guest, Lieutenant General Bishop Gowlina of the Polish Army, had personally briefed Patton on how, in order to get a Polish prelate to incriminate two of his priests, Russian interrogators had tortured a young girl to death in front of the prelate, and made a recording of the girl's screams to use against others.[10] Though there were isolated instances of abuses by American troops, there had been nothing like the type and scale perpetrated by the Russians. Entire factories had been dismantled and shipped back to the Soviet Union. The ill-supplied Russian army was living off the conquered territories, confiscating everything, respecting nothing. Displaced persons (DPs), prisoners of war (POWs), even American soldiers caught in the Eastern Block countries at war's end had been sent to Russia *en masse* as slave labor or to be executed[11]—all with Washington's acquiescent blind eye to its Russian friends.

Though bound by Allied agreements, Patton hated to hand over displaced persons and prisoners of war to the Soviets, many of whom were worthy of American support and begged to not be returned. From anti-communists for whom "repatriation" was a certain death sentence, Soviet soldiers who knew that Stalin considered being taken a prisoner a treasonous act, to Germans on whom vengeance was certain, America had agreed to return all displaced persons and prisoners of war with no conclusive proof of reciprocal action from the Russians.

The Russians denied having Americans. But Patton had heard of unlucky American prisoners of war who were caught behind Russian lines and never heard from again. American POWs aside, repatriation of the others alone was merciless, even traitorous, in Patton's eyes. But since many of the displaced persons had fought for the Nazis[12] (considering the Russians worse), some on the Left thought it only just, given the horrors of the Nazi regime, (especially the persecution of Jews) for them to be returned to face whatever fate awaited them. The authorities were not going to let it become an issue that would undo the hard-won, fragile peace. Another war couldn't be tolerated. Washington and Patton's superiors stood firm against his protests.

After inspecting the liberated Nazi concentration camps Patton had become physically ill at the sights and smells of the piled-high, bulldozed bodies and the living skeletons huddled gaunt and dazed behind barbed wire. But he opposed the occupation policy of giving government-confiscated German homes exclusively to Jewish victims of the camps. "If for Jews, why not Catholics, Mormons, etc?" he had argued.[13] There had been millions of others besides Jews in the camps. He complained to higher-ups, some of whom told the press, and he had been branded anti-Semitic, a charge certainly suggested later in his diaries.*And as he increasingly made his contrary views known—on deNazification, repatriation, the evils of the Soviet Union, and how the Russians had to be stopped, preferably by war—those above him, like Eisenhower, who had warned him before, became angrier at him. They wanted him to shut up.

The situation had come to a head at a September 22 press conference, barely two and half months prior. Ignoring his staff's warnings that a reporter's question about why he was hiring Nazis in Bavaria was a trap, he offhandedly likened the controversy over such hirings to a typical "Democrat and Republican election fight." The remark had been fleeting and secondary to more serious and thoughtful answers he had given on the subject. But the press made it sound like it had been his main point and outrage ensued. Nazis were devils—not just to the Left, but to the world at large. To compare them to Democrats and Republicans was blasphemy. Every previous charge against him surfaced. Members of Congress joined in. He was branded pro-Nazi—and not without some reason. Behind the scenes, he proposed using U.S.-friendly German troops, whom he admired as fighters and disciplined soldiers, to help attack the Soviets whom he felt would not for years have the resources to sustain another large war. In his head and his heart, he believed war with the Soviet Union was inevitable, so why not get on with it soon—when America had the best chance of winning?

---

*Although there are good arguments against that characterization of him. See, for instance, "Patton & Preferences II: Competence is colorless" by Peter Kirsanow, *National Review Online*, February 11, 2004, in which Kirsanow argues that Patton's record shows that he did not care about race, creed or religion, only results. Victor David Hanson gives more evidence that Patton was not anti-Semitic in his review of Stanley P. Hirshson, *General Patton: A Soldier's Life* (Harper Perennial, 2003).

Under pressure, he had apologized for the press conference remark but Eisenhower had summoned him to occupation headquarters in Frankfurt and fired him. It had been a shock because he felt he had not really done anything wrong. A few words taken out of context? It was a setup, he believed. He was angry about it. But the arguments fell on deaf ears. He was deposed as commander of his beloved Third Army and reassigned by Eisenhower as head of the Fifteenth at Bad Nauheim. In reality it was a "paper" army consisting of little more than clerks, typists, and researchers charged with writing the history of the war in Europe. He was a general officer; a fighting commander of proven worth— the best. And he had been relegated to a backwater? It was like benching the star quarterback and putting him in charge of inflating footballs. As he had taken up his new job at Bad Nauheim in October 1945, he was resentful. Pro-Nazi? What were they thinking, he wondered.* He had probably been responsible for the death of more Nazis than any other American.

After a period of adjustment, he regained some of his optimism and decided on a new course of action for the near future. He knew his career as a warfighter was over—at least under the Truman administration. They were just more of the same. He was nearing retirement age. Obviously he was not being cheered by those in power. He told staff, like Gay, riding in the back with him now, that he was going to resign—not retire as was normal for an exiting officer in order to retain pensions and benefits—but resign so he would have no army restraints. He was independently wealthy and did not need the pension or benefits. He would then be free to speak his mind and give his version of the war and what had happened to him—the truth as he saw it. And his side would

---

*The Patton Papers, 790.

be a blockbuster. He knew secrets and had revelations, he said, he was sure would "make big headlines."[14]

What those headlines would have been can only now be guessed. Perhaps he meant to go public with the shocking cost of British Field Marshal Bernard Montgomery's poor decisions. Perhaps he meant to reveal explosive details about why his Third Army's race through France after D-Day had been repeatedly halted by his superiors, most notably at Falaise, where he could have killed thousands of Germans, delays which he and later historians, many of them military men, believed had lengthened the war—perhaps by a year—and cost untold American lives. Perhaps one of his revelations would have been how Eisenhower and Bradley, in Patton's mind, had subverted their own army. Perhaps he meant to defend his policies in Occupied Germany, denounce crooked dealings by the Allies, and condemn what he believed was Washington's complicity in the takeover of Eastern Europe and favoritism for the Soviet Union and communists.

Patton had been at the forefront at the most crucial times. He knew as much as any insider. Were there other dark secrets he could have revealed?

By this time, he regarded his old friend Eisenhower as purely an opportunist seeking the U.S. presidency.[15] Perhaps he meant to challenge him. Patton had returned home on leave in the summer of 1945 and been toasted and feted by throngs of cheering Americans, some of whom had urged him to run for office, even for the presidency, but he said, then, that he was not interested. Public office would have given him an entirely new and powerful voice, perhaps even a deciding hand in Washington policy. It was certainly a possibility in his future. At the least, he planned to write and lecture and develop a powerful public voice. He was looking forward to it.

And so, as the limousine slowed to enter the outskirts of Mannheim, a town situated on the banks of the Rhine River into which, just months previous, he had publicly urinated as a theatrical statement of his contempt for Adolf Hitler, Patton was a fearless and incorruptible four-star general with secrets to tell that some in high places, jealous of or angry with him, did not want told. Even after suffering through the world's most devastating war, he was willing to start an even worse conflict with the Russians. He was a hard-line conservative who had angered and threatened leaders of both the Left and the Right in the United States, Russia, and Great Britain. He was enjoying his last day in war-torn Germany—a hostile, unreliable environment filled with intrigue.

And in just a matter of moments he was to become the sole victim of an enigmatic car crash.

CHAPTER TWO

★ ★ ★ ★

A CURIOUS CRASH

More than fifty years after General Patton's death, I was jogging in the Santa Monica mountains near Patton's birthplace (San Gabriel, 1885) with my cousin, Tim Wilcox, when he startled me by saying the famous general had been assassinated. He knew a man who had been involved.

"Assassinated?" I said. "I thought Patton had died in an auto accident?"

"Not according to Douglas Bazata."

Tim is a private investigator—a gumshoe—and owner of Indianapolis-based International Investigators Inc., a respected detective agency which he built up after buying in 1970 from a group of former FBI agents.[1] One of the practices Tim had continued was using ex-intelligence operatives, or "spooks," as contracted investigators for major jobs. Bazata was one such contractor; a former World War II Office of Strategic Services (OSS—forerunner of the CIA) officer and post-war mercenary whom Tim had hired for several major cases.

Tim had been impressed with the former OSS operative. He "was a big guy, smart and tough, as credible as you can get. And in my job you learn to trust your intuition." Bazata had not told him a lot about the Patton case, but said he had passed a lie-detector test on the matter, "and I believe him. I use lie detectors. He knew things only someone familiar with them would." Bazata was extremely resourceful, he said, and had always gotten the job done, no matter how complex.

I was intrigued with the implications of Tim's claim. Patton assassinated? Could it be true? If so, it was a big story and would impact history. Patton was a vocal and determined anti-communist. He would have been the first major assassination victim of the long and disastrous Cold War. Patton was not only a great soldier but a man ahead of his time—strong, manly, and prescient. He was a throwback to the rugged individualists of America's earlier history. He had foreseen the Soviet threat long before others, especially our blind, appeasing, and often opportunistic leaders at the end of the war.

I wanted to meet Bazata.

In the weeks that followed, I researched Patton's death. He had not died in an auto accident as I had thought, but had been badly injured in one. He died several weeks later on December 21, 1945, in an army hospital in Heidelberg, Germany, where he had been taken with head lacerations and a broken neck following the accident. He was paralyzed from the shoulders down and had been in very serious condition for days. However, right before he died, he had actually made a substantial recovery for someone with such serious injuries. Preparations had been made to discharge him and fly him home to the states for Christmas. His belongings had even been readied. But approximately twenty-four hours before he was to leave, he had an unexpected downturn. He started having trouble breathing. Moving blood clots called embolisms appeared to interfere with his lungs, taxing his heart.

After incessant coughing trying to raise fluid from his lungs, Patton became unconscious and died—a hell of a way to go for a great warrior like him who had yearned, it was always said, for the last bullet in the last battle.

Notwithstanding his unexpected health improvements, Patton had a history of embolisms. They had struck him when he broke a leg and was hospitalized when he was younger. But that certainly could have been known and exploited by a would-be assassin.

There had been no autopsy.

One of Patton's doctors requested one but Mrs. Patton declined. After losing her husband in another country, she could hardly be blamed for not wanting to prolong the ordeal.

However, that did not mean something sinister had not happened. Patton was a controversial figure, hated and resented by some, a hero to millions of others. He was such an important person on the world stage at the time that the failure of the authorities to ensure nothing untoward had occurred seems incredible—if not intentional—in retrospect.

The lack of an autopsy becomes even more of an issue in light of the blatant anomalies surrounding the car accident that caused Patton's injuries.* Patton was traveling in a 1938 Cadillac Series 75 limousine, a U.S. touring car specially designed for European motoring. It was one of the larger ones of the time,

---

*Most of the details in this account are taken from the investigation done by Ladislas Farago, the first historian investigating the accident who both traveled to the site and conducted interviews with eyewitnesses. It is the next best source to an official accident report which appears to no longer exist.

boasting seating for seven passengers; it had space for two in the front seat, three in the backseat, and two stored chairs that were embedded in the floor but could be pulled up and used when needed. Presumably those hidden chairs were not deployed, so Patton and Gay had room in the back between themselves on the seat and a divider in front of them separating their larger compartment from the one containing the front seat and driver. The divider included a window that could be rolled down.

When they came into Kaeferthal, a war-torn and dilapidated industrial area on Mannheim's northern outskirts, they stopped at a railroad track crossing to wait for a train to pass. When the last boxcar had gone by, they continued on their way. They were traveling on a two-lane road that was practically devoid of traffic that Sunday morning. It stretched out straight in front of them for roughly half a mile with good visibility for the driver, Woodring. Recounting it later, Woodring said he saw a two-and-a-half-ton GMC army truck, a large vehicle with ten wheels, eight on two rear axles below a canvas-covered cargo bed—standard-issue at the time in Occupied Germany—slowly advancing in his direction in the opposite lane. It was nothing out of the ordinary, so he did not give it much thought.

Behind the vehicle, the soldier identified in later histories as Joe Spruce, who was carrying the hunting equipment, pulled out and around the limousine in his half-ton jeep to lead the way to the hunting area which Woodring had never visited. Earlier, at a stop at a check point, according to some accounts, the single hunting dog riding in the open-air jeep was switched to the warmer Cadillac because of the cold. The dog presumably would have been in the front with Woodring as the big army truck in front of them slowly advanced. Woodring, however, listening to Patton's backseat comments, was not paying much attention to the approaching vehicle.

The only book author, as far as I could tell, to ever go to Germany and try and retrace what happened in the accident was Ladislas Farago, a Hungarian-born former U.S. naval intelligence officer and author of the acclaimed *Patton: Ordeal and Triumph*,[2] the book from which the 1970 Academy Award-winning movie[3] starring George C. Scott had been made. He had conducted the personal investigation for his 1981 follow-up, *The Last Days of Patton*, which later had been made into a television movie,[4] also starring Scott.*According to Farago, who interviewed some who had been at the scene and had access to other close-to-the-accident data that has now disappeared, Patton was looking out the limousine's window, "his curious little eyes darting from left to right as he surveyed the countryside." The roadsides around them were piled with litter and war ruin, "forming an endless canyon of junk....Patton said, 'How awful war is....Look at all those derelict vehicles, Hap!' Then he said, 'And look at that heap of goddamn rubbish!'"[5]

At that moment, without warning or signaling, the driver of the two-and-a-half-ton truck heading toward the limousine in the opposite lane suddenly turned abruptly, almost 90 degrees, into the opposite oncoming lane. The bulk of the large truck was squarely in front of the advancing Patton car.

Woodring later said he had time enough only to stomp on the brake while trying to turn the car to the left (toward the middle of

---

*Farago's accounts of Patton's accident differ in the two Patton books he wrote. In the early *Ordeal and Triumph*, he apparently didn't research the accident well, and writes that Thompson signaled his turn and was legitimately aiming for a driveway leading to "his Quartermaster unit." But after an investigation himself for *Last Days*, he changed his account, writing the truck driver did not signal, was not aiming for any driveway, and was foolishly allowed to vanish. The first version, more widely read than *Last Days*, might account for why some think nothing awry happened.

the road). But he was largely unsuccessful and Patton's car hit the truck nearly head-on. The right front of the limousine hit the side of the truck just behind its elevated cab, damaging the right front fender and radiator.

Woodring was uninjured. But when he turned to see how the passengers in the back had fared, he saw a scene that made his heart skip.

Gay was not significantly injured. But Patton was lying across Gay on the backseat, cradled in Gay's right arm and pinning him with his weight. He was bleeding profusely from a gash that extended from the bridge of his nose to almost midway up his scalp. Patton complained that his neck hurt, and then said, "I'm having trouble breathing, Hap. Work my fingers for me." Gay did but Patton persisted, "Go ahead, Hap. Work my fingers."

Patton was paralyzed.

The accident occurred around 11:45 a.m. Military police quickly arrived on the scene. Lieutenant Peter K. Babalas and his partner, Lieutenant John Metz, had passed the general's convoy on the road heading in the opposite direction before the accident. They heard what they described as a muffled crash. Questioning Woodring and the driver of the truck, Technician 5th Class (T/5) Robert L. Thompson, Babalas "concluded that the truck had made a sudden sharp turn to the left just as the Cadillac was moving up," and the crash "had become unavoidable." Although Gay said he was looking out his side of the window at impact and had not seen what happened to General Patton, and Woodring had been looking forward and so also had not seen what had happened to Patton, they theorized that the general had been thrown forward from the backseat to the barrier dividing the car, injured his head on the car's roof or divider between the front and back compartments, and then bounced back at an angle into Gay's lap. There were no seatbelts in those days, so no one in the vehicle was restrained.

If the above were true, however, and the impact had been forceful enough to cause such substantial injuries to Patton, why were neither Gay nor Woodring likewise thrown forward or injured?

The truck driver's role in the accident also raises questions.

It seems that Robert L. Thompson, about whom information is scarce, had no reason to be on the road that Sunday morning. Farago wrote, "Thompson was 'in violation of the rules and his own routine. He had no orders to go anywhere . . . he had taken out the truck as a lark for a joyride with a couple of his buddies after a night of drinking. . . . The three of them were in the cabin, in another infraction of the rules. Only two persons were allowed . . . .'"[6]

And despite the fact that he seemed to be at fault in causing the crash, he disappeared after the accident, along with the two unidentified passengers in the truck. Unmentioned in any account of the accident was what happened to Joe Spruce—or the dog.

Did they too just disappear?

An unnamed woman who worked for the Red Cross at a nearby coffee and doughnut hut witnessed the crash, and ran about five blocks to the 290th Combat Engineer Battalion headquarters in Mannheim to summon help. The battalion's commanding officer, Major Charles Tucker and Captain Ned Snyder, the medical officer and physician, soon arrived with the unit's ambulance and attended to Patton, taking over from several others who had arrived earlier. Snyder decided to take him to the Seventh Army's new 130th Station Hospital, located some fifteen miles south in Heidelberg.

They left with the general at 12:20 p.m.[7]

★ ★ ★

My cousin Tim knew Douglas Bazata through Edgar "Nick" Longworth who had worked with the super-secret Counter Intelligence Corps (CIC) in post-WWII Japan. He later became a Republican campaign leader and Veterans Administration official in several presidential regimes. Longworth had met Bazata through John Lehman, the powerful secretary of the navy under President Reagan in the 1980s. Lehman had a reputation for being tough and demanding, which later secured his position as a member of the 9/11 Commission. He was not known to suffer fools. Bazata had worked as a close aide to both men.

Longworth was a savvy political veteran familiar with the intelligence world. He had become good friends with Bazata and was "in awe of all the things [Bazata had] done."[8] He knew the Patton story. But, as he told me, "Douglas talks around things. It's hard to pin him down. But I've never known him to lie."

Bazata had lived a fascinating life. Not only had he been a spy, saboteur, and intelligence agent, he had been a wine expert who had managed the famous Mumm Champagne works near the French-German border, and an artist so good that he had been touted by the so-called "Jet-set" of European high society and been given one-man shows by patrons such as Princess Grace of Monaco, and the Duke and Duchess of Windsor. And it had all been a cover for Bazata's secret work.[9]

Longworth, who had been urging Bazata to put his life story into a book, broached my interest to him and Bazata agreed to meet.

CHAPTER THREE

★ ★ ★ ★

THE JEDBURGH

The big, four-engine, B-24 "Liberator" winged low over the dark Channel waters, leaving nighttime England shrinking behind. World War II was raging and maintaining low altitude was a way for the plane to try to avoid German radar on the continent and night fighters prowling the moonlit skies above. Both threats were the chief menaces to the heavy U.S. bomber, which, in this case, was stripped of much of its armament, carried no bombs, and was internally reconfigured to accommodate parachutists and supply canisters.

It was late in the evening of August 27, 1944 or just after midnight the next day.* Moonlight was needed to illuminate landmarks, or those aboard would have preferred a moonless and starless sky to hide in. Occupied France, invaded at Normandy on D-Day nearly three months before, loomed menacingly ahead. General George Patton and his stampeding Third Army was

---

* Records of the mission are not more specific.

sweeping across Northern France—somewhere far in the darkness ahead—pushing the retreating Germans back toward their homeland. The parachutists inside the plane would be aiding Patton's push, but not in the main fighting. The Liberator would continue flying low and away from the main battlegrounds in one of many top secret Carpetbagger missions[1] to drop professional saboteurs, equipment, and supplies behind enemy lines to help the French resistance known as the Maquis. The Maquis was largely a civilian force, untrained militarily, which was now being urged to action by the invading Allies. It was hoped the Maquis would be another indigenous Allied army—more help for the invaders now attacking the Germans.

The specific mission on this night was to drop a three-man Office of Strategic Services (OSS) Jedburgh team, code-named "Cedric" into Haute-Saone, a largely rural, lake-and-forest-strewn region of northeastern France near the German and Swiss borders—an area behind enemy lines that Patton's forces were rapidly approaching. Flanked by mountains and named for the Saone River which winds its way through the region's western reaches, the picturesque area was prized in peaceful times for its hunting and fishing, as well as a special French cuisine featuring freshwater fish and forested game. Now, however, it was occupied by the Nazis; an angry place of police and military patrols, late night surprise searches, executions, reprisals, and rumblings of distant gunfire and troops—Allied and enemy—constantly on the move, advancing and retreating.

As the plane roared in above the French coast and over the mainland, evidence of sporadic firefights and bombings could be glimpsed in the darkness below along with scattered anti-aircraft bursts at night-sky intruders detected on searching German radars. The three Jedburghs waiting stoically in full gear in the Liberator's dimly lit innards were part of the OSS's first large-scale Special Operations. They were hand-picked fighters, trained in England for pre- and post-invasion missions.

Although largely controlled by British officers, the Jedburghs were U.S. pioneers. They were named, so it is said, by their British trainers for a small town on the Scottish border that was infamous for its ferocious guerrilla warriors who fought the English in the twelfth century. The men of Jedburgh, says a Scottish plaque in the region,[2] wielded "the Jedburgh ax and staff to such purpose that their war cry struck terror." U.S. "Jeds" were the forerunners of what would become America's vaunted green-bereted Special Forces who would hunt Islamic terrorist leaders years later. In fact, Aaron Banks, who would later become known as the "father" of U.S. Special Forces, was also, at this time, a Jedburgh.[3]

Leading team Cedric, which included young Sergeant William Floyd of Brooklyn, N.Y., a radio operator, and Captain F. Chapel, a Free French officer, was Douglas deWitt Bazata, thirty-four, a tall, muscled American infantry captain who had been an ace weapons instructor at Fort Benning. He was one of the first Jeds, handpicked by General William J. "Wild Bill" Donovan, creator and head of the OSS.[4] Bazata was older than most of the Jedburghs who primarily were young men in their twenties with fighting skills as well as language and technical abilities. The son of a noted Newark, New Jersey Presbyterian minister, the Reverend Charles F. Bazata—one of the greatest athletes ever to play sports for Southern California's Occidental College[5]—Douglas was also larger than the other two on his team at six-foot-one and weighing over two hundred pounds. He was lean, lanky, and red-haired, with a strong nose that had been broken many times and a patrician face that, despite its rough hewn toughness, made him appear almost aristocratic. And he had, when needed, charm and savior faire. An OSS evaluator, for instance, would later write that he had a "poised, articulate and almost suave personality... adroitly promoting social contacts for personal benefit."[6] In common terms, he had, on occasion, been called an operator, a promoter, and a smooth talker; in short, a guy with disarming sensibility or no-fear fury, whichever suited him best.

But right now he was devoid of emotion or pretense. Quiet and concentrated, the ex-Syracuse University football player just wanted to get on with the job—which was always his way at crunch time. Inwardly, it could be deduced from his writings and those who knew him, he was impatient, as he always was when the goal was in sight.

At fifteen, big for his age and looking older, Bazata talked his Princeton-ordained father into allowing him to join the Merchant Marines where he crewed steamers voyaging to the Caribbean and Latin America. It was during those summer cruises that he got, he said,[7] his first taste for what he liked to call "the clandestine" or "clandestiny"—secret intelligence work. Seeing his size and talent, he was asked by the U.S. Marine detachment on the boat to be a spy for them. The crews often included natives from the ports of call and the marines were interested in "scuttlebutt," or rumors, and whatever else he could pick up as they monitored revolts and insurrections in the tropics. He coolly agreed. But, in truth, he was excited. It was the kind of adventure he had been seeking.

He killed a man for the first time during one of those summer voyages.[8] He claimed self-defense. A crewmember was pimping girls and had beaten one of them. He got into an argument with the abuser and knocked him over the side of the ship. There was no rescue.

In addition to playing football, Bazata had run high hurdles at Syracuse but left the school during the Depression, lusting for adventure. He bummed his way on railroad cars out West where he became a cowboy in Colorado, a saloon bouncer and Friday-night, take-on-all-comers prizefighter in Wyoming, and a lumberjack in Washington State.[9] It was on this trek out West that he was forced to kill again when four hobos, seeing his relatively expensive clothes and leather briefcase, jumped him intending to rob him in a speeding, open boxcar.

"I did not intend to be killed," he wrote decades later in one of many diary-journals he secretly composed about his life.[10]

> The first two bums came at me with some suddenness—one from each side. I kept low—dashing for the open space, the two idiots turning to follow.... I caught the scruffy bastard on my right with the left hand—deep in his crotch—turning—twisting—squeezing his balls. This not only startled him but unbalanced him. Thus I continued past him—turning towards him and using both our momentums and the speeding freight train to heave him through the wide open space [of the boxcar door].
>
> I had time to back hand him across the back of the neck—to speed him out.... We all heard his last scream...his death scream...as he hit the siding or some merciful pole. This scream and my sudden action in leaping to [fight] so startled his cohort that he stopped short. One kick in the balls—then a knee to the forehead and he doubled. With both hands, I pulled him by the back of his jacket and number 2 went out.

What the other two waiting to take their turn didn't know, he said, was that he had hidden in his coat a fourteen-inch-long lead pipe.

He whipped it out.

"To be certain, and to violently impress [presumably other hobos in the speeding car]... I clobbered each unconscious... across their faces...where it showed the most....I pulled each 'cadaver' to the door and dumped each silently....I heard a few moans from...the remainders—all seated—one vomiting softly in his foul corner. Bums are weak; tough perhaps, in the clinging-to-life sense, but weak flee-ers [sic] from man."

According to his recollection, he was only eighteen at the time.

Even before he was a teenager, his father, an excellent pugilist, had taught him to box. The son, initially timid, grew to love the sport. "It enables you to conquer yourself, teaches you discipline and how to resist temptation, like throwing a roundhouse. You don't want to succumb to that. Use the jab. Punch straight in." He had a wicked jab and used to lie awake at night wondering why God had favored him so. Appropriately, he wrote in his diary, attack one spot. "That's what my father taught me. Think. Use your head. Don't get riled. Hit 'em enough times and they'll go down."[11]

In a letter he wrote to a friend much later, he recounted a fist fight he forced despite his fear. "You've got to courage it, stick to it without over-thot [sic]," or end up "sweating in the...night [like before a parachute] jump." Early in his military career, he was being bullied by a navy boxer and maintenance chief, bigger than himself "who hated me because I...was of Bohemian origin....He kept trying to pick a fight." Surprising the man with a cursing, 4:00 a.m. barracks wakeup, he maneuvered to get the angry adversary in front of him and facing a blinding spotlight. "This small ruse is/was ancient: but excited kids NEVER think" of such advantages. "I always wore 2 rings: one [for] each hand: but for this sweet PREPARED occasion...I placed both"—one with a ruby, the other his fraternity emblem—"on my left hand: 2 different fingers for a sweet broad spread.... Without warning I began...very rapid...straight left jabs....I felt his nose... smash...his cheek-bones cave...."[12]

It solved the problem.

In 1933, to the dismay of his father who probably wanted him to complete college, he enlisted in the Marine Corps, and after joining his regimental boxing team, became, by a succession of local and regional ring victories, the Corps's unofficial heavyweight boxing champion[13]—"the happiest four years of my life," he would later say of his overall four-year enlistment. "The marines were tough then but I loved it." As part of a marine contingent to the Chicago Century of Progress (World's Fair) exhibition in 1934, he said he had fought exhibitions against, among other notables, former champions Max Bear, Jack Sharkey, and Jack Johnson, the first Black heavyweight champion who was fifty-two years old at the time.[14] He lost all the exhibitions but considered each a privilege: "I loved those chaps."

He had a high tolerance for pain. "Nobody could make me talk," he wrote. "I practiced splinters up my nails...burned myself...filed my teeth." He had had a foot smashed in a bad accident in which a huge wall shelf holding vehicle engines collapsed and killed several marines. It had left his big toe permanently bent beneath the one next to it. The two looked like grotesquely crossed fingers.[15] Doctors said he would never walk again and certainly never box again. They had been wrong.

His eyesight and ability to shoot was so good, he had earlier been made a member of the Marine Corps champion rifle teams which had dominated the annual National Rifle and Pistol Competitions throughout the 1930s. By the time he went to Ft. Benning, where he would become an army weapons instructor after leaving the marines, he was known as one of the best shots in the military.[16] He would nearly lose an eye when a practice grenade had prematurely exploded as he was demonstrating it to a class at Ft. Benning.

Bazata had a rebel streak and an irreverence for authority that Bernie Knox, a fellow Jedburgh and later director emeritus of Harvard's Center for Hellenic Studies in Washington, D.C., would write was a "brazen audacity, both physical and verbal, that took people's breath away and enabled him to get away with actions and remarks that were, in a military milieu, outrageous."[17] He was known to address full colonels as "Sugar,"[18] and once reported for maneuvers straight-faced in bathrobe and slippers, his duffle bag militarily packed with pillows.[19] He sometimes had a cagey laugh and a wily manner that often signaled recipient beware. In 1934, he spent time in the steaming hot brig of the USS *Wyoming*, an aging battleship, for cold-cocking a marine captain. "He was snotty to me and I thumped him—not the thing," he would later admit, "for a [private first class] to do."

However, he could always be counted on in tough situations so the marines forgave him. "This officer has great initiative, energy, physical courage and daring," his immediate OSS superior would write in 1945.[20] At age nine, he had been up in a bi-plane when the door had suddenly flown open. "I'd found it scarily inviting.... I held [it] closed. I loved it. For me, the strength of courage was to do it alone—go it alone—into an unknown." He was a man of action, always preferring to enter the tempest, rules be damned, rather than cautiously wait for "legalities." As a result, he maintained that the Marine Corps had launched his career as a government hit man. In the choppy, personally coded, hard-to-understand style of many of his diaries—because, by that time, he had been so long in the secret world of intelligence that he seemed often to be trying to disguise what he was writing—he would pen this relatively decipherable passage: "Upon joining the marine corps March 1933—he [Bazata] fired expert with Springfield 30-06 Model 1911 [rifle]—This extremely rare on 1st cruise . . . and even more so first year. . . . For this reason and perhaps others—Baz was slowly—gradually sounded out—about possible willingness [to] join marine assassination team. Baz did not agree entirely, nor did he refuse . . . ."[21]

It had happened off Cuba, he would write in the diaries numerous times, while he was serving in a shipboard unit. He was given special orders. "My so-called pro-job there was to slay Herr Batista [Fulgencio Batista, at that time a Cuban army sergeant who had overthrown the government of Gerardo Machado in a coup September 4, 1933, and would himself be overthrown by Fidel Castro in 1959]." But after slipping over the ship's side with killing gear (atop his head) and swimming to shore, he was stopped on the dock by a mysterious friend on the island at the last minute. They knew he was coming, the friend, whom Bazata code-named "Peter/Paul" in his writings, and who would crop up later in Bazata's life, warned. Understandably—if this did happen—there is no record of it available to researchers, if there is, in fact, any record of it at all. An order to assassinate would have been highly sensitive and most probably verbal. But Bazata's CIA files do show that he received "a letter of commendation" from Rear Admiral C. S. Freeman, who was in charge of U.S. navy ships in the area at the time.[22] In the letter he is lauded "for services performed in connection with intelligence during Cuban situation dated 30 January 1934," roughly three months after Batista had grabbed power. Nine months later, according to the same record, Bazata was promoted to private 1st class.

★ ★ ★

The Liberator was nearing the drop zone and the three waiting Jedburghs were alerted. They took positions in the now-open "Joe hole," feet dangling in an approximate four-foot-wide opening, newly constructed of plywood and metal hitchings over the plane's rearward bomb bay. The noise of the outside air rushing by and the engine's roar was now deafening, rendering talking, restricted anyway to hide their identities from spies, almost impossible. So the parachutists fixed their eyes on the dispatcher near them who himself was watching specially rigged lights. The red bulb, already glowing, meant "action station." Green, soon to illuminate, meant "go."[23]

He would give the signal with his hand.

Up ahead, in the midst of the darkness beneath the plane, anxious Maquis, amidst local peasants, waited with a young, decorated British special forces agent, George Millar, whom the Jeds about to jump knew only by his code-name "Emile."* Those waiting on the fringes of a clearing in the midst of dense woods would pinpoint the drop zone with hastily lit bonfires and flashlights after they located the bomber in the night sky and received the proper code response through their radios. Eight miles away, German patrols on a main road were looking for just such activity.

This was the most dangerous part of the airborne delivery. The plane would be vulnerable flying slowly amidst mountains and the drops would be made at a very low altitude of approximately two hundred feet—or less.[24] Enemy night fighters were flying in the surrounding skies. The crew had been hit by cannon fire during an earlier drop mission. The twin-engine fighter—a Junkers 88—had attacked the Liberator, injuring the tail gunner and opening a hole

---

*Millar was decorated for action in North Africa, was a POW until his escape, and penned the acclaimed memoir *Maquis* in 1946.

through the fuselage the size of a washtub.[25] The attack had forced the plane into a nearby flak trap where two others of the crew were injured by bursting shells. The drop had been abandoned and the crew and Jeds had been lucky to return home on three engines—so they were understandably gun-shy on this August night.

The plan now was to first swoop in and drop supplies for the Maquis—ambush and sniping rifles, ammunition, and better radios with a longer range than they already had—items Millar had been constantly requesting. The first drop would give the planes' pilots a chance to orient to the drop zone, code named "Treasurer." It was thirteen kilometers north northeast of Besancon, an ancient town of churches and ruins dating back to the Romans, who, under Julius Caesar, had taken the settlement in 58 B.C. Since then the town, surrounded by a river and mountains, had been overrun by barbarians, absorbed into France in 1674, bombarded by the Austrians in 1814, and was now in the path of the mostly retreating Nazis.

The supply drop went without a hitch; those waiting below catching a glimpse of the big planes' illuminated belly as it swooped close over the field and then looped up and back around. Inside the fuselage, the green bulb lit as the plane neared for its second pass. The dispatcher, taking the cue, began dropping his hand at short, calculated intervals. First went Chapel, then Floyd, and finally Bazata. Chapel and Floyd got out easily. But something went wrong when Bazata, at the lowest altitude, dropped. Sources conflict[26] over where and why he encountered trouble—whether it was just as he jumped through the hole or on the way down, his parachute static line, a steel wire attached to the plane used to yank his parachute open, got caught near his groin and sliced upward through his jumpsuit and uniform, ripping into his inner thigh and opening a gash clear to the bone. The mishap forced him into the wrong position for landing and since he had jumped at somewhere between two hundred and one hundred feet altitude, he wrote, he did not have time to right himself and had landed badly—face first—adding further injury.

"I lay in agony, even in some alarm"—for the safety of his men and the success of the mission—he wrote decades later to Bill Colby, a friend and fellow Jedburgh who was (at the time of the writing) the director of the CIA.[27] But he got himself together when Millar, "aghast at his injury," found him and explained that they had to leave quickly because of the nearby Germans. Somehow, with the aid of others, he made it to a vehicle hidden in the surrounding woods and, dousing the bonfires, they all escaped. They had no doctor. "I was my doc...tied the damn viens [sic] into knots with my little fingers." His thigh "blew up like a black balloon...for nearly 3 weeks." But "trusting no one,"* and because his parents had taught him "never to complain of the physical,"[28] he had made no mention of the injury to his mostly British handlers back in London. His first communication sent back read, "Jedburgh CEDRIC reports 28 Aug the safe arrival of his party.... He is beginning to get organized right away...."[29]

The new arrivals were driven by back roads to a former French soldier's country home where arrangements had been made for them to stay—at least for the time being. Because of the heavy German presence in the area, it was decided that they should change into civilian clothes and destroy their uniforms. From then on, if caught, they could be considered spies by the Nazis and put to death rather than be granted prisoner of war status like uniformed soldiers. Millar, in the role of host to the Jeds, wrote that

---

*Probably a reference to the fact that he was leery of spies.

at first he worried about having to baby-sit them. But Bazata, despite his injury, quickly won him over. As "the big American" talked, "my reluctance faded," he wrote. He "was a blustering man with a heavy, Russian looking face...brilliant...a quick, eager talker.... [He] liked to sketch things in with broad sweeps of his imagination...and he picked out and hammered on the salient immediate supply necessities of the area as a good newspaper editor might have done. He was a get-things-done man."[30]

Millar, relatively isolated as he had been for months, realized quickly enough that Bazata's arrival meant the Allies were serious about aiding the fighters he had been organizing under strained conditions. He was eager to get more supplies from London. In a stroke of luck for Bazata, local Maquis chieftains hampered by the German presence around them could not meet for three days. He thus got that time to recuperate. Self-administering Sulfanilamide,*[31] which luckily he had pocketed just before leaving,[32] he had improved to the point of being able to function effectively despite his injury. He and Millar had decided, as they waited for more supplies to be dropped, to concentrate their efforts on harassing the flow of Germans on the Besancon-Belfort road and railway routes running north northeast from Besancon up to Belfort (another ancient town) around and through which most of the local German traffic was heading. The Nazis, retreating from Patton's Third Army, were being particularly brutal as they passed through the corridor seizing all available transport—cars, carts, bicycles, horses—and dealing severe reprisals for interference. As Bazata later wrote, "They burnt three villages adjacent to us two days after our arrival."[33]

---

*One of the first so-called "miracle" drugs, Sulfanilamide had been discovered in the 1930s and was commonly called "sulfa."

Bazata and his men were soon forced to go on the run. Because of poor security, they were continuously chased by Germans.[34] The Maquis they were organizing were scattered. They had to use a car to reach them. Millar acquired a shiny black Citroen he had stolen from the Germans in another area. He and Bazata, aided by false identification and brazen courage, posed as Gestapo agents* while reconnoitering, meeting with fighters, and making plans for sabotage. When and where they could, they cut telephone lines that might aid the enemy.

In another stroke of luck, they acquired a unit of approximately 650 Ukrainian soldiers forced to fight for the Germans, who had been talked into massacring their Nazi guards by the Maquis and joining the resistance. But the two leaders were still terribly short of weapons and ammunition. A drop of sixty supply containers from London backfired. In a breakdown of communication, the drop was not coordinated through them and the Nazis learned of it. All sixty containers were found by searching German soldiers. The botched drop angered Bazata who radioed London that in addition to the loss of valuable weapons, he and Millar's prestige with the Maquis had suffered. Why had their supposedly important Allied leaders, Bazata and Millar, not known of the drop, the local fighters wondered?

It was a kink that needed smoothing. But Bazata, charming and resourceful—not to mention courageous in the eyes of those around him for the way he handled his painful and debilitating injury—was "too sharp," wrote Millar. "He soon adopted the local habits with various enjoyable flourishes and exaggerations, for he was a born clown."[35] In spite of their reluctance, the vari-

---

*Nazi secret police.

ous local fighter chieftains warmed to the likeable American who let it be known he was impatient with their hesitation.

By September 1, he and Millar had the various resistance bands daily attacking retreating Germans with whatever weapons were available on secondary roads and railways, including the Besancon-Belfort line. Belfort, some sixty or so miles northeast of Besancon, was the gateway to the "Belfort Gap," an ancient and scenic passageway through the mountains into Germany near Switzerland. One day, Bazata and a driver went to Belfort, which was crawling with Nazis, including their secret police, the vengeful Gestapo. Leaving the driver, Bazata walked alone to the main railroad station in broad daylight and after reconnoitering which trains he wanted to hit, including asking locals for information, surreptitiously snuck into the engine yards and damaged several important escape trains bound for Germany and their tracks with dynamite as they were leaving. Details in documents are unclear as to the number of destroyed trains and loss of life. But in a write-up to award Bazata the Distinguished Service Cross, the army's second highest medal for bravery,* Colonel James R. Forgan— noting other praiseworthy train sabotages by the Bazata-Millar-led fighters—penned, "After this, the Germans no longer made any attempt to use rail transportation in this area."[36]

On September 4, Bazata wrote in his after-action report,[37] "the entire remnants of the German 19th Army" had passed through his area in a slow-moving "convoy of [mostly] camouflaged civilian cars." He could have blasted the vehicles already on the point of collapse he lamented, if only they had had the needed weapons. What he did not write until many years later when he attempted

---

*The Medal of Honor is the first.

to pen a book was the time he brazenly went down amongst the 19th Army soldiers and spoke to them in English, declaring he was a recent French graduate student of the language, which, tired and needing supplies from the locals, they bought. He thereby got on-the-spot intelligence. In response to his requests, London finally radioed that they were sending a special mission of ten officers with ample supplies and to get a secret field ready to accept the mission. The next day, however, reconnoitering, they discovered that the area they had selected, which had several towns and villages near it, had been overrun with German soldiers. The enemy was everywhere. Hastily, he and Millar had Floyd radio London to scratch the officers but go ahead and drop the supply containers—they needed arms badly enough to risk it.

As Millar would later write,[38] it would have been "madness" to light bonfires so they planned to use flashlights to signal and guide the drop. That night, they climbed in the Citroen and headed for the drop site which was in the vicinity of Vieilley, north northeast of Besancon. But in Loulans, a small town on the way, they ran into so many beaten Nazis trudging East that they had to pull off the road to let them through. Tanks were now beginning to rumble by as well. To find out more, they left the car in the care of the driver. When they returned, two Germans in Panzer uniforms were trying to requisition the vehicle. Luckily, the driver (who actually had the key) played dumb and managed to signal what was up to his returning leaders before they showed themselves. When the Germans left to get permission from their officers to take the car, the three jumped in and roared away. It was late and they had to drive fast to get to the drop site.

They took back roads, fearful that with the numbers of Germans they had seen, they might run into more, even a tank, and have more explaining to do than they could handle. As they approached the village of Cirey, one of the towns on the way, they were flagged down by a local who knew Millar. She warned them to go back. The Germans, in a foul mood, were in the village and coming their way. Bazata and Millar stepped out of the car. They could hear horses and commotion. They decided to heed the woman's warning. The driver tried hastily to turn the car around in the narrow road but it stalled. Just then, two Germans appeared on the road ahead of them, one with a sub-machinegun, the other with a rifle. According to Bazata, they were not more than fifty yards away. Bazata and Millar had little with which to fight.* Their rifles were in the car. The Germans started firing. "During this time our frantic chauffeur pushed every button in the dashboard eighty times," wrote Bazata.[39] "The car finally started and we jumped back into it." As they roared off, the last of perhaps seventy-five rounds was fired at them, but without inflicting any physical damage. "Bazata had been lying on the floor in the back," wrote Millar. "When he came up, we laughed heartily together. And thanked God that the Germans could not shoot."[40]

Their chauffeur drove like a demon until they could cut off into the woods where they hid the car in brush, erased its tracks, and continued escaping on foot. Meanwhile, others of their band had made it to the drop site and a fearless Maquis leader, Georges Molle, had, despite the presence of Germans in the immediate area, stepped out onto the darkened field and flashed the proper code with his "electric torch." The drop had been made with spectacular success—almost all containers hit a single field. The containers, forty-six of them, were hastily gathered and their contents—rifles, ammunition, grenades, anti-tank guns—were distributed among the local resistance groups.

---

*Bazata, in his after-action account, says they had pistols and presumably fired at the Germans. Millar indicates they did not shoot back.

Millar, Bazata, and the driver, unaware of this, spent the night fearfully hiding in the woods. As they climbed hills to get above the Germans on the nearby roads around them, they heard whiffs and saw the light of distant artillery fire indicating the advancing Allies (probably Patton's Third Army) were getting nearer. Finding what they thought was a relatively safe place high up, they tried to sleep. But throughout the night, they were kept awake by German voices which carried far in the woods. It was obvious they were surrounded, although the soldiers were not necessarily looking for them. Around midnight, it began to rain, making conditions, including the fact that they had missed the drop, more miserable. Only Bazata, writes Millar, was making jokes. But even he was depressed. Everything they had done so far had been predicated on getting to the drop site. And they had failed. By dawn, they decided they would have to make a move or be spotted. Taking different routes, and being as silent as they could, they crawled through the German-infested woods and, miraculously, made it out of the area safely. They were spectacularly buoyed when they heard the good news of the successful drop.

On 6 September, Millar and Bazata led a band of Maquis armed with the new weapons in an ambush of several convoys along the Besancon-Belfort route, killing seventy Germans and losing only one of their own—a rousing success.[41] Around the same time, they sent three young, newly trained Maquis into Besancon with a Welrod*and assassinated the Gestapo agent there who was second in command.[42] They next assassinated the Gestapo chief at Vesoul, a large town north and west of Besancon with road and rail links to Belfort that seved as a chief route for the retreating Germans.

---

*One of the first guns with a silencer, designed by the British just before the start of World War II.

After attempts to destroy a bridge spanning the Doubs River failed, they tried to have it taken out by Allied bombers. Though they were told it would be done, the air strike never occurred, reinforcing Bazata's opinion that what they needed, they would have to do themselves. All the while, despite his nagging injury, Bazata was a driven commando, setting up ambushes, reconnoitering, committing to memory military intelligence like artillery emplacements in his area, and demanding that despite odds against them, their small band of local and foreign resistors attempt any sabotage possible. Sometimes he and Millar disagreed. But "Bazata was a delightful companion," the British agent wrote in *Maquis*. "While the adventure merely made me feel dead inside . . . it stimulated him. . . . I began to take a real interest in what he said, to seek out his personality." He was a man of "tugging contrasts; an unhappy man and a gay one. A mixture of rapacity and generosity, of laziness and industry, at the same time sensitive and crude." But always determined. "I was afraid his determination would lead us into German torture cells. Walking with the tempestuous Bazata towards German lines was like riding a horse with a mouth of iron towards a precipice that the horse knew nothing about."[43]

Reconnoitering a village near Besancon, he and Bazata had been trapped in a German round up of all eligible men for what they guessed was some kind of forced work project. Six hundred soldiers and Gestapo surrounded the town and they knew their fake identifications would not hold up, especially since local French collaborated with the Germans and Bazata's limited French, spoken with a strong New Jersey accent, would not withstand such scrutiny. They ducked into a friendly house and Bazata, pondering their predicament, looked out a window and saw some older village residents gathering mushrooms that had sprouted from recent rains. He suddenly saw how to escape. He and Millar got blankets to use as shawls and peasant baskets and the two of them went out into the field to join the other oldsters, bending and picking. Soldiers all around gave them scant a look. But how to escape? They were in an open field with the woods beyond across a kind of no man's land with the soldiers largely in between. Bazata decided to cause a commotion. Bent over, crawling and picking, Bazata moved slowly toward "the largest Corporal" until the disinterested German was blocking his way. Suddenly, he stated loud and clearly "Boy, you are standing on my cloak and mushrooms!" pushed him and passed between his wide-spread legs while Millar "took total flight and the silly Krauts opened fire hitting naught." As all the soldiers concentrated on Millar, some running after him, Bazata "just stepped into the woods."[44]

They both escaped.

But almost as soon as they were safe, Bazata was proposing they go back in harm's way. They were getting increasing reports by this time that, as they had suspected, U.S. forces (likely Patton's Third Army and Alexander Patch's Seventh Army) coming from the south and the west were getting nearer. Bazata had precisely mapped locations of German defenses in their area that he wanted to get to the oncoming allies. Millar objected. The Germans, as they had just seen, were now streaming in larger numbers through their area. The dangers of detection and reprisals had mounted. They would have to go through as much as thirty miles of hostile, enemy-occupied territory, much of it on foot, to get to the Allies. "I doubted if his leg was strong enough," Millar later wrote in his book, *The Maquis*. "However, he was an expert at getting his own way, and I was half afraid that he might realize that I was not certain in my mind whether reason or cowardice made me resist the project."[45]

Bazata prevailed. But after two nights of ducking constant patrols, enduring freezing rain atop a mountain while watching Germans congregate unknowingly beneath them, and seeing burning villages in the distance, Bazata, furious at times at his comrade's "carefulness" and making jokes at other times to keep them going, relented. He agreed it would be suicide to try to continue on. However, when London advised that it had over 1,000 paratroopers poised to drop in their area who could help the advancing U.S. troops if requested by ground forces, even Millar's attitude changed. That was news that could prove crucial in closing the Belfort Gap, a vital strategic goal.

They were in the north near Vesoul west of Belfort when they heard from an informant that American troops were definitely in Rigney, a town southeast of them toward Besancon. But the Germans were blowing up bridges across the Ognon River which they would have to cross to get to Rigney. Only one bridge, it seemed, was left—the one at Cenans, the next town south of them—and enemy engineers were already beginning to place explosives on it. The informant had just come from there and seen them. "We can rush them, can't we?" Millar writes Bazata interjected.[46] They had recently acquired a big Terrot motorcycle, which only Millar had experience in driving. "If you can hold on behind me," he answered, "I dare say the bike will go fast enough to take us through."

They were on the "monster" as soon as they could get it up from a ditch it was in and running. They both had pistols, but Millar warned Bazata not to let go of him to shoot. He would need both hands to hold on since the roads were bad at Cenan. They took off in a bluster, Millar purposely going as fast as he could, about seventy miles per hour, over hills and potholes in order to get Bazata used to the speed. At some of the holes,

"Bazata nearly bounced over my head. The tears were pouring from my eyes," he wrote.[47]

The bridge was at the bottom of a steep hill, perhaps a hundred yards straight down to its entrance. Barreling over the crest, Millar gave the motorcycle full throttle and shot downward, steadfast in what he was about to do, seemingly oblivious to the consequences. "The bridge seemed to leap toward us, in a blur of speed." He was cognizant of "several figures" and two trucks on the side of the road, but in the intense concentration of the moment heard nothing but the roar of the motorcycle. They hit a bump and "the big machine seemed to buck clear of the ground and I was afraid she would twist in the air but somehow we kept going straight and Bazata was still there."[48] As they zoomed across the bridge, Bazata, who apparently was more cognizant of the dangers around, wrote that the startled Germans "fired at us with machine guns and blew the bridge."* But they were already on the other side and roared onward. Millar, he said, had "black and blue" imprints of his (Bazata's) hands on his lower chest "for a couple of days."[49]

Once across the river and heading for Rigney they were stopped by an American sentry who sent them, eventually—after much interrogation and handoffs to higher officers—to the headquarters of General Lucian Truscott, commander of VI Corps whose 3rd Infantry Division, Seventh U.S. Army, was moving up from Southern France into the Besancon-Belfort area after landing at St. Tropez. Truscott, according to Bazata in his report, was grateful for the intelligence, especially the news of the paratroopers, and

---

*Millar does not remember the soldiers shooting at them or the bridge being blown. He writes that he was told the bridge had been blown later. But Bazata's recommendation for the DSC repeats that it was blown just as they crossed.

after treating the two to dinner, asked them to relay his thoughts to London via their behind-the-lines, direct radio connection with instructions as soon as possible—a course of action Millar thought they could maybe delay at least a little bit in order to enjoy the safety and relative comfort they had reached. But, he later recalled, "I knew perfectly well that Bazata was crazy. Nothing would stop him from going back to Loulans (their base near Vesoul) that night, and I was not going to waste time arguing."[50]

Mounting the Terrot, they roared back through the German lines and aside from being "captured" by surprised Americans along the way, made it back to their base deep in occupied territory without major incident. As it turned out, London decided against dropping the paratroopers but for the next few days had Bazata and Millar overseeing the arrival of many smaller groups, some Jed, some U.S. Army drops. In the meantime, Truscott's forces continued northward until they were battling for Loulans. Caught in the middle of an artillery duel between German and American forces, Bazata, while on a sniping mission, was hit in the left hand by flying shrapnel and radioed somewhat facetiously that the Germans were "formidable...have lovely purple heart ready."[51] More serious, according to Bazata, was a bullet wound he suffered in the "gut."[52] The exact circumstances are unclear. But he said he had been dropped by his chauffer in the woods after sending a secret radio message from their car. A German had gotten a direct hit on him. He said it was superficial, but the trauma to his thigh probably compounded the issue. He "crawled into the woods and stayed there for two days" before his men came to get him. They took the bullet out. Like the injury to his thigh, he did not report it to London.

Back on his feet, he made continual trips across enemy lines to American headquarters and then back into enemy territory.

He was asked "to capture a German general and his one hundred guards."[53] He organized the mission. But when he arrived to lead the local Maquis in the general's area, he found they had been attacked by the Germans and fled. "So we lost our general." On September 11, he radioed London, "All is hectic. Doing liaison work for Americans in all directions. Delaying Boche...and cleaning up in rear"—meaning killing stragglers. As the American forces advanced, he gathered intelligence to aid them. And so it went. By September 21, U.S. troops had chased the Germans out of France and closed the Belfort Gap. London radioed, "You have all done a grand job and it is now time to come home." They would send a plane to retrieve him. Bazata radioed back there was still work to be done. Not until September 29, did he radio, "Everything settled now. Shall leave for Paris tomorrow. Should like to recommend Emile [Millar] for an American decoration."

It had been a very successful mission. In the time he had been there, according to his Distinguished Service Cross recommendation, "the number of Resistance personnel in his area had increased from a few to 6,000 Maquis with 1,000 additional Russian (Ukrainian) troops...." The actual awarded citation[54] said,

> Captain Bazata, after having been parachuted into [a part of France] heavily infested with Gestapo and enemy troops... and despite injuries...organized and armed Resistance Forces numbering 7,000; planned and executed...sabotage against rail and highway installations which interfered seriously with the movements of enemy troops and supplies; had highway markers changed in order to divert German convoys...leading them into well-prepared ambushes and causing them to lose many men and motor vehicles. With the

> arrival of American forces... Captain Bazata, at great per-
> sonal risk, made his way through enemy lines and supplied
> valuable intelligence... all... in civilian clothing.

He was lauded in a recommendation for promotion for his "courage and initiative" in organizing ambushes which had caused the Germans to greatly overestimate Maquis strength and have to commit forces against them that could have been better used elsewhere.[55]

But perhaps the most important compliment had come from a man Bazata would one day say he was at odds with over Patton— none other than his boss, the OSS chief himself, "Wild Bill" Donovan. When, in 1977, Colonel William H. Pietsch, Jr., also a Jedburgh, was asked by Bazata, who was then fighting the Veterans Administration to get full disability, to verify his injuries, Pietsch wrote to the VA: "I was present when Mr. Gerald E. Miller and Colonel Joseph Haskell (the two top-ranking Special Operations officers in OSS London Headquarters) discussed the qualifications of certain officers with Major General William Donovan, the director of the OSS." After listening to a description of Captain Bazata's wounds, General Donovan said simply, "There's no doubt about it. He's a hero."[56] Donovan certainly knew who Bazata was and, perhaps more importantly, of what he was capable.

★ ★ ★ ★

CHAPTER FOUR

A MEETING
WITH DONOVAN

Douglas Bazata's house was a modest one-story bungalow in a pleasant Chevy Chase, Maryland, neighborhood in the northern outskirts of Washington, D.C. The streets to it curved through forested hills hiding gentle ravines where, I imagined while driving there, shallow brooks trickled. A lot of former military and government workers retire near the capitol. In preparation for meeting Bazata I had done a little research.

Back in October 1979, Bazata had given an interview to the *Spotlight*,* a radical populist Washington, D.C. weekly, which had used the interview to produce two front-page articles saying Patton had been assassinated. The first, run in the October 15 issue, had concentrated on the motives to kill the general, of which, I knew, were many. He distrusted the Russians and wanted to go to

---

* The newspaper was published from 1975 to 2001. It had a controversial reputation while in publication, considered variously far right-wing and anti-Semitic by some opposed to its political views or populist and edgy by others.

war with them. He had damning secrets to tell about World War II; how badly it was run and how it could have ended earlier. Who knew what else? He did not agree with punishing all Germans, especially those who were not hardcore Nazis. The second article, which ran on October 22, bannered, "I Was Paid to Kill Patton: Exclusive interview with OSS 'Hit Man.'" In both articles, Bazata added a new element to the story. He claimed he had been asked by none other than OSS director-founder "Wild Bill" Donovan himself to assassinate the general. But he had not done it and had no intention of doing it since he knew Patton and liked him. The December 9, 1945 accident had been staged by an acquaintance whom he did not or would not name. Since the general had not died in the accident—as was intended—he said he was told a "refined form of cyanide that can cause embolisms, heart failure and things like that" had been used to kill him later in the hospital. It had been made in Czechoslovakia, and, in small amounts, could be "timed to kill" over a 'period such as 18 to 48 hours'"—an obvious allusion to the fact that Patton had suffered an unexpected relapse. Even though he had not done the job, Bazata told the *Spotlight*, Donovan mistakenly thought he had, and paid him $10,000, which Bazata had kept.

This was interesting new information to me. Bazata, it showed, had previously gone public. As if Patton being murdered was not controversial enough, he charged that Donovan had been part of the plot which elevated the claim considerably. "Wild Bill" Donovan was an icon, especially to most in the OSS. He was the creator and guiding light of the country's first large spy and intelligence network. It was the forerunner of no less a monumental agency than the CIA. Donovan had been commissioned by President Franklin Delano Roosevelt himself. He was a former U.S. Attorney for the Western District of New York where he had made a name for himself as a tough and honest prosecutor. He had been awarded the nation's highest military tribute, the Medal of Honor, for courageous action in the trenches of World War I. A noted biography about him was titled, *The Last Hero*[1]—an accolade then president Dwight D. Eisenhower gave him upon hearing of Donovan's death in 1959. Charging Donovan had been involved in Patton's death was like accusing the Pope—at least to most other OSSers.

But Bazata, disdainful of his former boss, had passed a lie-detector test on all he had told the *Spotlight*, according to its staff. They had had an unnamed "professional analyst" subject Bazata's interview to "the rigors of a content analysis survey using a Psychological Stress Evaluator (PSE)," the preamble to their articles stated. "The PSE is an advanced polygraph machine ('lie detector') in use by hundreds of police departments and intelligence agencies. His report: Bazata gives no evidence of lying." The *Spotlight*, it disclosed, had contacted Bazata after reading his charges in a *Washington Star* article a month earlier. Reporter Joy Billington had attended a "Veterans of the OSS" dinner at Washington's Hilton Hotel and "eaten," she emphasized "under a giant sepia photograph" of their deceased leader Donovan. At a table that included, among others, former CIA director William Colby, Bazata, she said, had responded to one of her questions by making his "controversial claim." She had quoted him, "Apparently quite a number of top-level people were jealous of Patton. I know the guy who killed him. But I was the one who got paid for it.... If you [Billington] get me killed, get someone to say a prayer over my grave."[2]

Bazata, I was to find out, was, among other things, a religious man.

I parked my car and was greeted by Nick Longworth, Bazata (now eighty-five), and his younger, French-born wife, Marie-Pierre.

The story was that they had met when she was to attend a lavish weekend engagement party in Southern France—but it just so happened to be *her* engagement party. Approximately twenty-eight at the time, she was a recent graduate, fluent in five languages, and betrothed to a prominent young French ophthalmologist. She was attending a medical conference with him in one of France's beautiful southern cities when, in the lobby of their hotel, "I saw this striking looking man. I could not stop looking at him." He saw her and she was embarrassed. "He knows what I'm thinking," she thought. But he came over. Did I believe in love at first sight, she asked me by way of explanation.

He was, at that time (the late 1960s), a free-lance mercenary, a continuing clandestine, working piecemeal for the CIA,[3] the French, probably the Germans and the British, and others who would hire him for tough missions their own could not, or would not do. These missions included sabotage, plucking hostage-held friendlies (military and non-military) from the confines of those who would do them harm, assassinations, and other extreme and dangerous intelligence jobs—and all the while hiding such activity under the cover of being the chief of staff for the vineyards of the famous Mumm Champagne estate located in Europe at Johannisberg, Germany, conveniently near the French and German border—an ideal location in Cold War Europe.

After WW II, following mysterious[4] Jedburgh missions to Denmark and Belgium, he had been assigned to the American Zone of Occupation in Southern Germany—Patton's territory—first spying on the French and then supervising captured German generals writing a history of their war efforts. He traveled frequently in the Bad Nauheim—Frankfurt—Munich axis putting him in close proximity to the fateful events involving Patton in December 1945. Within two years of Patton's death he had received from

Paris's Institute Agronomique a degree in Oenology, the science of wine and wine making, and had joined the House of Baron de Mumm, a player in Europe's economic and social scene. The baron was of German heritage and he and his wife were prominent in European society. In time, Bazata had launched a career as an artist and become a jet-set favorite, selling canvases throughout Europe and in America. It is easy to imagine what must have been a gregarious, swashbuckling Bazata, described by a CIA-connected agent then as "a native version of Zorba the Greek,"[5] the life-loving, exorbitant peasant, beguiling prospective patrons as much with his eccentric persona as with his paintings, which were modernist. The Duchess of Windsor and Princess Grace of Monaco[6] each gave him one-man shows. Museums in Europe and America displayed his canvases.[7] He hobnobbed with legendary artist Salvador Dali whom, he wrote, painted a portrait of him as Don Quixote which he later lost.[8] And although he considered himself a serious painter, as he would later write, the work with the brush, as with the wine, was still mainly a cover.*

This, then, was his situation in 1969 when he was asked by good friend and former Jedburgh, Phil Chadbourne, Jr., a U.S. Foreign Service officer in Monaco, to accompany him to what turned out to be the same weekend of parties and events Marie-Pierre was attending. They talked, at that first chance attraction, about the hotel's paintings, history, and other things two people attracted to each other discuss, and saw each other several more times that day, growing more charmed at each meeting. The next day was scheduled as a party for her and her fiancé. But that night she went back to the room she was sharing with the doctor, returned his ring, and left with Bazata the next morning. "Baz was

---

*Being an artist, he would say, gives one entry everywhere.

an extraordinary personality," Bazata's friend Chadbourne would later tell me.[9] "We were all in London one weekend drinking. We went outside and a baroness came by in her expensive car. Baz just opened the door and got in. We couldn't believe it. She couldn't believe it. He drove off and spent the weekend with her. She became his lover, fell madly in love with him and he grew tired of her"—this from a man, the suave Chadbourne, known as quite a lady-killer himself in his day. "After he met Marie-Pierre," said Chadbourne, returning to the matter at hand, "he informed me the next morning we were going to the hotel to get her bags and she was coming with us. I scoffed. I didn't believe it. But she came out smiling."

And now they were here in front of me, having been married for twenty-six years. He was an aged man, no question, bent somewhat, certainly the result, to some extent, of all his war wounds coming to roost. But he also had recently suffered a "terrible stroke," as he put it, and I was concerned about how that might affect our talks. But he was tall and strong-handed and showed no demonstrable effects of the illness for which he was being treated—at least not then. In fact, shortly after we had been introduced and in response to a question I posed, he fell to the lawn in a collapsing roll to show me how Jedburgh parachutists were taught to land.

Marie-Pierre was not what I had pictured. Her high voice and French accent on the phone had conjured in my mind a petite, almost pixie-like woman. But she was tall and dark-haired with a European freshness—as attractive as expected from what I had heard about Bazata. She and he were silently close. We all went to lunch. Bazata and I seemed to hit it off. In the middle, he suddenly announced to everyone, "I like him." I reciprocated. He was engaging, gracious, and a jokester—not at all the dark and brooding type I had envisioned for an assassin. With his white hair and trim mustache, strong looks and command of languages and history, he could have passed for a retired British colonel, or fading European film star—except for the Jersey accent. But there was also a hint of menace occasionally, a fleeting ferocity that flashed in his eyes when he touched on certain points. Then he would go silent, as if deciding he had said enough.

For the next several days I interviewed Bazata who was both forthcoming and reticent, sometimes claiming memory loss, other times lucid. I had purposely started out lightly by inquiring into his background, a good way to ease into the more controversial aspects. But it was not long before we were on topic. His grandparents had come to America from Czechoslovakia. His father, he said, before becoming a Presbyterian minister, ironically had caught the eye of George Patton when the two had been athletes in Southern California in the early 1900s. Charles Bazata, a multi-sport star at Occidental College, a major school in those days in the Los Angeles area, had actually halted an important football game in which he was a halfback and team captain over a miscall by a referee and had led his team off the field, threatening to end the game, until the error had been corrected, which, according to Bazata, it was. Patton, born in nearby San Gabriel and probably in his teens then, apparently had witnessed the highly unusual protest and never forgotten it. Bazata said Patton "had tremendous respect for my father." As a result, years later, when Bazata had been a weapons instructor at Ft. Benning, he said he had met the tank general who, after getting acquainted, had asked him to become an intelligence officer for him. Patton, independently wealthy, frequently had his own personal spies. But he had turned Patton down because he wanted to be a lone operative and his joining OSS, where he thought he would have the best chance, was already in the works. "For me, the strength of courage was to do it alone," he would later write.[10] He had "no intention" of being bossed by the "clown officers" he knew he would be under if working for Patton. But they parted agreeing on the codeword "Occidental," meaningful only to them, would be used if Bazata ever had information he thought Patton should know.

As we talked, it became clear that more had happened to him in France than Millar had recorded in his book, or had been put in official reports—and rightfully so. *Maquis* was Millar's story, not Bazata's. And, as any researcher learns, especially one re-searching spies, official reports are sometimes doctored. One such instance, said Bazata, was the omission of his abduction by French partisans as he was spying in Besancon.

"We've been watching you," Bazata said they told him. They took him to a hotel room. "What are you doing?" they demanded. He repeatedly told them he was on their side but his accent was bad and they did not believe him. He was tortured. They kept say-ing, "Prove it!" They removed his thumbnails with a "thin, sharp" screwdriver and then smashed the thumbs with a hammer. "I didn't shit my pants or yell . . . . I wasn't going to let them see me cry. . . . I believe you can attune yourself with God"—something he had learned from his father—"I didn't let it hurt me." After the initial damage, the pain was not that bad, he shrugged. "I thanked [God] for it." He figured he would have been killed but a Maquis friend, using an explosive, blew a hole in the wall, and he had es-caped in the commotion. As proof, he volunteered his thumbs as we talked. I had not noticed them before. They were large and dis-figured and minus nails.[11]

When he and Millar had made their daring motorcycle dash through German lines to get to American troops, Bazata said he had a secret mission about which Millar was unaware—which possibly explains the urgency Millar writes Bazata exhibited to make the dangerous dash.[12] The mission, he said, was to stop Patton's advance into Germany. It had been arranged, he said, by Donovan in a series of meetings he had with the OSS chief prior to his jump into France.[13] The brass were not happy with Patton, Bazata said he was told, and wanted to rein him in. How they were going to stop him is unknown. Bazata was vague about it. He told the *Spotlight*, they stopped Patton "militarily." But that is all he would say. In one of his diaries he wrote Patton's truckers were "encouraged to Black Market"; i.e., steal and sell his "gasoline... clothing and food" and "deliberately [send] wrong trucks... with drivers well known as Black-marketers, etc."[14] In fact, according to the record, Patton *had been* stopped as he was approaching the Belfort Gap, while Bazata had been in the area on the Cedric mission. However, most histories record that the halt occurred because Eisenhower had allocated scarce gas to General Montgomery, Patton's British rival, whose plan Eisenhower preferred, rather than to the Third Army. The lack of gas had incensed Patton, who was well ahead of Montgomery in a thrust toward the German border. But official plans were for Montgomery's "Market Garden" approach via the Netherlands to pave the way to the crossover. In 1979, Bazata had told *The Spotlight* he did not know who had told Donovan to stop Patton but "since Donovan was directly responsible to the president... I assumed... [Franklin Delano Roosevelt] knew and had authorized the action."[15] If he had not accepted the mission, Bazata said, he believed he would have been killed—"hit by a taxi in London," as he put it.* They thought Patton disobedient, disruptive, and

---

*Sources I've encountered say even refusing less extreme missions meant banishment for the one refusing. Donovan did not look kindly on the reticent.

uncontrollable and were going to stop him with or without "my help," he said. "We used a certain trick and it worked." He was stopped just north of Besancon and southwest of Belfort. But doing it was "disastrous . . . for me" because "we were in effect stopping Patton from going on and winning the war."[16] Patton, when he was halted, had the Germans on the run. Conversely, Montgomery's Eisenhower-backed Market Garden to cross the Lower Rhine at Arnhem had failed, thus giving the Germans time to regroup and recharge and, later, launch the Battle of the Bulge, the German offensive in which more Americans died than in probably any other U.S. fight with the Nazis. Bazata told me he had not realized the depth of antagonism toward Patton amongst some of the military elite until General Alexander Patch, commander of Seventh Army, to whom he had been directed after reaching U.S. lines with Millar, had "shocked" him by saying he did not want to help Patton,[17] and General Truscott had shocked even more by stating, "Somebody has to stop him [meaning Patton]." He went away thinking, "Good God, was he [Truscott] in on it too?"[18]

Interestingly, I was later to find some proof of what Bazata was claiming. Back in 1963, Austen Lake, a noted journalist and author of the time who had been a correspondent with the Third Army during Patton's dash across Europe, wrote in his regular newspaper column:

> I wonder if Bob Allen, a former G-2 leaf colonel who lost his arm in the pell-mell drive, will tell the . . . long hidden facts about the five distinct "Stop Patton" plots in World War II. For somewhere in the secret archives of the Pentagon there is a mess of controversial, never told data about the major occasions when the Supreme Headquarters Allied Expeditionary Force (SHAEF), immobilized Patton. . . . It was no

secret in American G-2 circles or the military press that certain Kudo-minded politicians such as Winston Churchill and generals, U.S. and British, did not want George S. Patton to add more laurels to his list of North Africa and Sicily. Indeed, there is a real unborn book still to be written on that subject...and I challenge either Dwight Eisenhower or Omar Bradley, who knew the truth, to add a postscript to their memoirs, revealing the fulsome details of...why, when and how the Third U.S. Army was halted.[19]

When Bazata had been hit by shrapnel in the hand in France, he had been on a sniping mission.[20] He was, after all, a world-class marksman lethal in a variety of ways.* In addition to Cedric, he said he had made "unofficial" jumps into France for which there would be no records. They were "special assignments," he indicated without elaborating, and by war's end, he said, he was a designated OSS assassin. There may have been more [OSS assassins]—he did not know.[21] And his job, he said, was not restricted to "eliminating" just the enemy. It included those supposedly on the Allied side believed to be spies. "If somebody knew something, or thought they did, and that would [hurt] us, we had to shut them up before he got to [the other] government. That was my job." He also, he said, eliminated those in the OSS who talked too much—"noisy guys within our own outfit." Killing then did not come easy to him, he said. What justified it was "you were doing it for your country." Often there were obstacles to overcome. Sometimes "you couldn't kill a guy in a railroad station with a pistol because the noise would bring the cops so you got them in a dark alley." He used a roll of coins or similar in his fist to deliver a blow to the back of the neck.

---

*A description I was to hear from many who knew him.

"It breaks the main bone there, knocks them out instantly. He doesn't make any noise.... If he's moving...give him a second.... I remember I hit a guy so hard that his feet came up and hit me in the balls. I was ashamed of myself."

One day in April of 1945, just before the war in Europe ended, he said he met with Donovan who asked what he wanted to do in the future. He said he told the director he wanted to continue in the clandestine service. Although this meeting was touched on only lightly in our interviews, Bazata's writings,[22] which I later would read, gave more detail: Donovan was pleased with his answer, saying "excellent," and continued that "they"—never defined—had a few "interesting" tasks for him "that should appeal to the adventurously patriotic qualities in you." The tasks would "concern [American] interests of certain complexity" and be "centered in Europe—mostly [Germany]—also [France] and a bit on the fringes." There would be "many diverse obstacles" but "an adroit chap like yourself can readily improvise as the target appears or moves or alters or magnifies." The targets would come from various fields—"[military]—political—industrial—criminal and from both Allied/Axis sources. If you agree, we'd like you to aid us...while continuing on as you are." Bazata asked if the job would be unofficial. "Yes," he wrote Donovan replied. "'That seems the most secure and safe manner.'" There would be no records. Why was he selected? Because of his loyalty and the fact that they knew he would "never denounce nor betray colleagues." What about expenses? "You'll have a chap to tap. This same chap will describe 'surprise' targets as they erupt." Other than that, he would be free to run his own show; arrange his own contacts, drops, safe areas, schedules. We "don't know what you do," he said Donovan said to begin the meeting. "No one seems to...but [we] do know you to be exceptionally capable—fearless—a totally devoted [American]."

"Baz very interested," he wrote in his typical terse, third person, often difficult-to-follow style. "In effect," he continues in the diary, "he [Bazata] was asked . . . to provide his own support [and] to do their dirty work. To be on [the] extreme end of [the] limb—with no support—no authority—no official backing/aid [and] would be thrown to wolves at any failure." If industry was to provide targets, then "Baz" he wrote, "was the peasant there solely to enrich those bastards." But the offer was exactly what he sought, a post-war job in the clandestine with both the danger and autonomy he coveted. He could not resist—so he agreed. "How stupid can we all be? Me to accept—they to ask [and] *believe* I accepted . . . . *Did* they believe me? Was I a patsy? Go carefully kid. But GO!" (italics mine).*[23]

Sometime after their earlier 1945 meeting—which he indicated to the *Spotlight* occurred in the fall of 1945 but was not time specific with me—he said he was again contacted by Donovan and, this time, offered $10,000—equivalent roughly to $100,000 today[24]—to kill Patton. "He said to me, 'We have a very important job for you Douglas. I got my orders from way up. Many people want this done.'" Donovan, he said, made a case that Patton "was evil. He had been doing things against America's interest and the situation could no longer be tolerated. American security was at stake. Bazata did not like Donovan, he said and wrote. He thought him a "phony" and derisively referred to him as "Mildew" or "Millie" because of what he felt was Donovan's humorless, dour personality and lack of real courage. But the director "was the number one guy. . . . I didn't doubt his orders."

---

*Bazata would jump pages to continue thoughts, write upside down and in large letters suddenly amidst a thought. He left out conjunctions, phrases, even verbs—all, I think, intentionally because he was leery of writing anything down.

Bizarrely, said Bazata, because they were friends, he had already, in the months before, secretly contacted Patton and told him, without revealing who or what, that enemies from his own side were out to "hurt" him. "He was a pretty gutsy guy and said well fuck 'em. They've got to run pretty fast to catch me. Things like that.... But what could he do? He wasn't going to stop or go away.... He had his destiny to fulfill.... Nobody could make him do that. He knew it all." So, he said, he listened to Donovan. He knew Patton "wasn't playing the game," and was "disregarding orders." Donovan said Patton was undermining all that had been achieved and was a threat to U.S. objectives. "It's difficult for me to talk about it.... All I can say is very slowly and unpleasantly I was convinced that they were right." Patton was a killer, Bazata said, as incongruous as that sounded considering his own exploits he had been sharing with me. "He should be eliminated."

He accepted.

It was now, obviously, the time to query him on the accident. But as we got into it, I realized that he was not taking the same stance he had with the *Spotlight*. That stance had been that he had only *known* the person who had caused the accident; that he had not participated in it and had worked to undermine the plot. But as we continued it became apparent that he was saying HE had caused the accident; that he had been there when it had happened and had, in effect, helped plan it. Although he was at first either confused or coy—I could not tell—saying things like, "I'm having a hard time remembering" and "I'm not sure but I think I was there." In fact, maybe the stroke he had had was legitimately interfering with his memory. Maybe I was too, since I was suggesting with my questions that he might have been there, a logical conclusion when one studied his *Spotlight* confession. Regardless, Bazata very quickly began telling me how the opportunity had arisen and how it was basically the "fulfillment of a plan."

In the *Spotlight* he had been precise in stating he did not want to execute the order and had only played along because he feared he would be killed if he did not. But now he was almost sinister in his recounting, chuckling quietly with a grin, "I operated. I operated." At least he said that in the beginning. Then he became remorseful. Mostly, he was matter-of-fact.

Over a period of days, as he related it to me piecemeal, the following scenario emerged:

Prior to the accident he met a man who became a co-conspirator with him. He claimed he never knew the man's name and identified him to me only as the "Pole," because, he said, he spoke with an Eastern European accent which sounded Polish. But he was not sure. He never asked, he said, as is the custom in his line of work. He said the Pole "shocked" him by indicating he, too, had been ordered to kill Patton. "Obviously somebody had talked," was his first guess. He could not understand it, he said, because he and Donovan had agreed no one else should ever know. But as they talked he began to think the man may have been sent as insurance by those who had ordered Donovan, or by others unknown to Donovan because, after Patton's death, Donovan had congratulated him for it. Donovan had assumed that he, Bazata, had been responsible. When I asked how the Pole had told him of his mutual assignment, he answered, "I don't remember the words exactly, but it was [just that] he was going to kill somebody. I don't think he said Patton. I think that came up later.... Whatever that guy said, I listened and I said ... he's one of the boys," meaning, I presumed, a professional assassin. He had also been paid, he told Bazata. The two of them decided to do the job together. The Pole, he said, basically planned it. Since Bazata was the best shot, "I would do the triggering and he would stand along side of me ... if I missed ... he'd back me up." Having an accomplice was best, he said he decided, because things can and will go wrong.

They had special-made weapons—two of them—fashioned in a foreign country and gotten from "private sources" whose identity he never knew. They were like rifles and could shoot any projectile—rock, metal, "even a coffee cup." At different times in the interviews he told me they had come from Switzerland, Czechoslovakia, and a "little country" he could not remember. The important thing was it was driven by "air" and a "spring" and thus silent, which was needed, and the damage it did to the victim would not appear to have come from a bullet. Additionally, what was shot, if found, would look like innocent debris—a rock from the road or metal from the car. "It was magnificent." Its limitation was that it was only accurate for short distances, "like across this room." He indicated the living room we occupied. He said he tested his with a rock "and unless you had a good rock, it would veer off.... For instance, if one part of the rock was large it would twirl." He was "almost positive" that the projectile they had used for the accident was a "square" piece of metal, but said his memory could be faulty and it might have been a rock.

He indicated that early the Sunday morning of the accident, he had gone to Bad Nauheim and had secretly trailed the Cadillac as it left. He had ways, he said, of knowing what was happening in Patton's headquarters. "When [General] Gay was in with Patton [deciding on the trip], I was in contact. They were going to go hunting." He said he had "people" (spies) in the Patton camp. He did not elaborate.

When, early in the trip, Patton had stopped to tour the Roman ruins at Saalburg, he said he had crept up to the vacated limousine and, on the side where Patton was sitting, inserted something small that jammed the window or windows—it was not clear[25]—so it (or they) would not close. The jamming created an opening about "four or so inches" through which he could shoot. Apparently after rigging the Patton car window (or windows), he had stopped trailing the limousine and gone ahead to the ambush area to await Patton's arrival. He said figuring out the route was not hard and implied they either had inside information or it was the logical route to the hunting grounds.

To set up the accident, they had positioned two trucks. The primary truck was a U.S. Army truck that would be moving up the two-lane road toward the approaching Patton car and then suddenly turn in front of it. The resultant crash and sudden halting of the limousine would give Bazata, hiding inside or beside[26] the shell of an abandoned vehicle amidst war debris on the roadside, an optimum shot. "But you had to be good to make that shot." The second truck was a local vehicle, not American, broken down and purposely positioned at a spot somewhat off the road and up from the turning lane on the right—which, from my earlier investigations I remembered as a path or entrance into something[27]—right in front of where they hoped the Patton car would be forced. It was there, he said, to block the limousine in case it veered to the right, around the turning truck. It would keep the limo within the shooting area: the killing zone.

They had gotten the stationary truck themselves, positioned it, and done something to it so it would be legitimately broken down where they placed it. But the army truck—the one that would do the turning—was to be waiting further down from them on the other side of the road and driven by an American who had some of his friends in the cab—"truck drivers or guys who drove the trucks just in the shop." He did not know them except to say he was sure "they are all dead now" and had been given money and liquor to participate. "I don't think they knew who was going to be hit but they knew there was going to be a problem." He and the Pole had signals set up to alert the driver waiting in the truck cab with his companions to the approach of the target vehicle. Those in the truck waited longer than they thought they had been told because of Patton's stop at the Roman ruin so he and the Pole had to give the truck occupants some "phony" explanations to ease their impatience.

As they waited, "I was watching from the vehicle...." "About how long a shot is that going to be?" I asked. "Let's say it is about maximum ten yards"; minimum, fifteen feet. He said he got "up and down many times" while waiting but was not worried about passersby seeing him. They were pretending to be attending their broken down truck. He drew a little diagram for me of the setup on the road showing the two trucks and where he was hiding. "And this guy [in the waiting truck]" does not move up here [to the site of the accident] until [he gets the] signal...that the [Patton] car is finally seen."

As to the actual accident, he did not give me a dramatic account. He just indicated everything went as planned except they did not kill Patton.

Basically they botched it—as happens more than not, he said, in such operations. There is always tomorrow.

I asked him, "You shot through the open window?"

"Yeah.... Side window. The windows were opened on the side, not on the back."

"Did you see where the thing hit?"

"I would have to say yes. Vaguely. He got hit in the face."

In 1979, the *Spotlight* had asked him, "And this weapon caused the total paralysis that Patton suffered?" He had answered, "That's correct... the force with which that projectile hit was the equivalent of a whiplash suffered at a speed of 80 or 100 miles an hour."

In the commotion that ensued, he said he was able to pose as a bystander and remove what he had placed in the window (or windows). "At a time like that you can do almost anything and it isn't really noticed," he had told the *Spotlight*.

He said he had gone to the hospital shortly after the accident with a poison "concoction" he and the Pole had made up but he could not get to Patton and had not been involved in Patton's subsequent death—therefore he could always say truthfully he had not killed him.

Rolling down the window and shooting Patton through it was the hardest part of Bazata's story to believe. He offered no proof, other than the fact that he was a world-class shooter. "What does it matter?" he said wearily, when I asked him whether there was anyone who could verify everything he had told me. "They're all dead now."

He shared with the *Spotlight* that the assassin had told him he killed Patton with cyanide—"a certain refined form...that can cause or appear to cause embolisms, heart failure and things like that." It had been made in Czechoslovakia and "was very effective in small amounts." In an obvious correlation to Patton's sudden hospital downturn, he added, "It can even be timed to kill in a given period such as eighteen to forty-eight hours."

CHAPTER FIVE

★ ★ ★ ★

VANISHED ARCHIVES, SECRET WRITINGS

The next day, Bazata was not feeling well but agreed to let me look through his private papers. Already, there were a few of them spread around, the result of earlier discussions. Marie-Pierre went down to the basement and brought up the boxes from which they had come—about six of them. In one vein, I think I was lucky to have come to him when I did—following his stroke when he was not as guarded or reluctant as he undoubtedly would have been in earlier, headier days. Now he seemed almost unconcerned, telling me to go through the papers and take what I wanted.

Among the boxes were many handwritten diary-journals he had penned about himself and his clandestine activities. He had been trying to analyze himself and write a book about his life. There were also many letters he had written to friends and others, and files about himself from the FBI and CIA. He had acquired them through the Privacy Act, sister to the Freedom of Information Act (FOIA). The Privacy Act allows an individual—but only that person, or kin, and not anyone else—access to what the government has about him in its files. In the case of a person like Bazata, there was a lot. I hoped I might find something in the FBI and CIA files about his Patton and Donovan claims, but Bazata told me there was no chance—there would not be any records about that unless Donovan had made some and they had agreed not to. At one point, he told me there was someone who could verify his involvement in the Patton accident. But the next day, he said I had misunderstood him.

I wondered.

In 1976, Bazata had met with *Washington Post* weekend magazine writer Gordon Chaplin, who was seeking spy secrets for an article. But Bazata, he wrote, after initial cooperation, turned silent when pressured by Chaplin. Chaplin had written, "Bazata's monologue in the [Georgetown restaurant where they met] gathered steam and soon he was using a kind of ribald referential shorthand that he proudly calls 'tripletalk'...his way of dealing with the doubters, the stuffed shirts, the friends who turn out in the end to be enemies."[1] Was Bazata giving me the same "tripletalk" he had given Chaplin in saying I had misunderstood him?

It was hard to tell. I had not pressured him but maybe he was getting leery of talking more. He had lived a life of secrecy and the habit of maintaining silence must have been a struggle to overcome. Regardless, I gathered as many of his papers as I could and that was promising. Soon I would be back home where I would have the time to go carefully through them. But first a trip to the National Archives would help verify his story. I wanted to dig up whatever I could about what Bazata had told me in order to see how much of it was the truth.

I was in for a shock concerning the Patton accident.

Almost everything Bazata told me about himself—other than the Patton/Donovan stories—was backed by documentation at the archives. I was lucky. By 1996, millions of records about the OSS, which had been kept secret by the CIA all the years since World War II, were finally released to the Archives and accessible. The acquired records contained much new information. I was able to find good records on Bazata's "Cedric" mission. They all jibed with what he had told me—with the exception of one thing he had not disclosed. When he had returned from Cedric, he had been the subject of an investigation to determine what had happened to 90,000 French Francs which he insisted had been lost in his chaotic initial jump. The suspicion that he had stolen the money had angered Bazata, and eventually the French had come to his rescue, attesting that they had found it at the jump site and neglected to inform him. The money had been used as it was intended, they testified—to help the resistance.[2]

His CIA file confirmed much he had told me about his early civilian life and his service in the marines and the army. Similarly, his FBI file showed he had served on merchant ships as a teenager, and confirmed some, but not all, of his train-hopping wanderings as a young man out West—where he said he had been a saloon bouncer, prize fighter, cowboy, and lumber jack. He was also perhaps the most decorated Jedburgh of all. He had a Distinguished Service Cross Bronze Star, three or four Purple Hearts, the Belgian Croix de Guerre, and campaign medals.[3] I was not able to confirm his claim that David Bruce, head of the OSS in London during the war and a U.S. ambassador after it, wanted to award him the Medal of Honor for his Cedric actions. Nevertheless, it became obvious—based on the records—that Bazata was a bona fide war hero and had been telling the truth about everything in his background. I still had questions about what he had told me, especially concerning several discrepancies in his Patton story during our interviews. But his memory problems could be a reasonable explanation. Ultimately, considering all the mysteries emerging in the Patton case, I concluded he deserved the benefit of the doubt—at least until other information proved him a liar.

What shocked me was the dearth of information at the Archives about the Patton accident. The National Archives is the repository for every shred of information available on the nation's meaningful history—people, events, and places. Along with acknowledged treasures like the first printing of the Declaration of Independence, even seemingly meaningless documents are kept according to the view that they may someday be found significant in their own right or supplemental to other key documents and therefore helpful to researchers. Yet nowhere in all the millions of papers stored in its huge, cavernous main complex in College Park, Maryland—or anywhere else available to researchers, as it turned out—was there an official report from the actual scene of the December 9, 1945 Patton accident. At least, that is what I would be told by countless officials I queried then and for many years—not only at the National Archives, but at the Patton Museum in Ft. Knox, Kentucky, and numerous libraries, military and civilian, around the nation and even in Europe where the accident occurred. Such a report would certainly be the starting point for any investigation of what led to General Patton's death. Yet it was—and is—nowhere to be found—at least according to archivists and my own digging.

And I knew such a report had existed.

In Seventh Army files, in whose U.S. occupation district in Germany the accident had occurred, I found a document dated 10 Dec '45—a day after the accident—written by a Seventh Army Public Relations Officer, Captain William R. Conklin, and addressed to "G-2," or army intelligence (apparently interested in the event), which mentioned the on-scene report. It read in part, "...This office obtained the official report of the accident from the 818 MP [Military Police] Battalion at Mannheim, and furnished the details of the accident to correspondents..."[4] (who, it added, were dissatisfied with not getting the report themselves). Another document by Captain Conklin, undated, said, "The official accident report compiled by members of the Eight Hundred Eighteenth [818] Military Police Company on the scene was made public today." It identified "First Lieutenant Peter Babalas" as the person who signed the report.[5] Babalas and his partner, John Metz, had been the two MPs mentioned as first on the scene by Ladislas Farago* so their inclusion rang true.

In several trips to the National Archives up to 2006, I must have looked through thousands of documents as possible sources for this report. But it was never there. Even archivist Will Mahoney, who kept his own personal file on Patton, told me he did not think any such record existed. Eventually, I was to get similar negative responses, verbally and written, from the National Personnel Records Center in St. Louis, which has one of the largest files on General Patton; from Bruce Siemon of the Historian's Group at the U.S. Army European Command in Heidelberg, Germany, the very city where Patton had died; from the U.S. Army Center of Military History, Ft. McNair, Washington, D.C., and many lesser archives. Typical of the responses was that from Daun van Ee, Historical Specialist in the Manuscript Division of the Library of Congress, a behemoth which may have more documents than even the National Archives: "Dear Mr. Wilcox, I was unable to locate a formal accident report in any of the files that we discussed over

---

*In both his books about Patton.

the telephone...." Underlining his opinion, he referred to the fact that Carlo D'Este's book *Patton: A Genius For War* states that "no accident report could be found"[6]—I was not the first researcher to notice its absence.

Long before D'Este, Ladislas Farago had lamented the disappearance. The missing report had been noted as early as 1953 when a reporter for the Gary, Indiana, *Post Tribune* newspaper, Allen T. Naive, had written the army for details about Patton's death.[7] Replying to Naive's request, Major General William E. Bergin, "Adjutant General," sent Naive a "Memo For Record." The memo, apparently a compilation of what General Bergin had found, stated, "Rept [sic] of investigation is not on file and details of accident are not shown in 201 file....Casualty Br [Branch] has no papers on file regarding accident.... There is no info re the accident in Gen. Gay's 201 file... Mr. Litsey, Safety Br., G-1... said they have an unofficial rept [sic] of the accident in their files. There is a signed statement by Horace L. Woodring taken in 1952 that he was the driver in which Gen. Patton was riding...."

Obviously, the Woodring statement—which, deepening the mystery, Woodring told Farago he had never made[8]—was not the on-scene accident report. It had been made (fake or not) seven years after the crash. In any case, a single missing report—if that, in fact, was the number made at the scene—does not constitute a bona fide mystery. The report, as I was often told by archivists, could have been lost or unintentionally destroyed over time, a speculation I would certainly agree with—except for one thing. The on-scene report was not the only report involving the Patton accident that was missing. At least three others concerning the accident that I found mentioned in my searches were also missing.

For example, no copy of the probe that Patton's friend and subordinate in charge of the Seventh Army, Lieutenant General

Geoffrey Keyes, conducted independently of the army, can be found. According to Ladislas Farago, who researched the accident while many of the witnesses were still living, Keyes heard rumors of foul play at the time and had his own suspicions. He had actually dined with Patton the night before the accident, stayed the night at Patton's Bad Nauheim residence, and left, like Patton, early Sunday morning, although for an appointment at his Mannheim headquarters, not the hunting grounds. Woodring and Thompson, driver of the truck, were questioned in the Keyes probe and Woodring was absolved. But Thompson, Farago writes, "was quite a bit equivocal. He actually sounded, as Lieutenant Babalas put it, too good to be true." Thompson told the probe he was delivering the truck to a depot and did not spot Patton's car— or see the stars on its license plate—until he had already turned and it was too late. "Thompson's testimony could have been challenged in every one of his separate statements," wrote Farago. "But it was not. And the case was left at that."[9]

Why Thompson was not grilled more, Farago does not explain. Certainly, if it was available, at least one copy would be somewhere amidst Patton's files at the National Archives, the Library of Congress, or the National Records Center in St. Louis. It might possibly be hidden in some dark archival corner, but I doubt it. The archivists, who are pretty good, would know about it, and none of them throughout the years I was looking ever mentioned it. Farago, who does not give a lot of sources in *The Last Days of Patton*, does not say how he heard about it, although my guess is from Babalas, whom he interviewed. But both Babalas and General Keyes are dead, so neither can be questioned or used to retrieve the probe. Thus, another key Patton accident document has disappeared.

Similarly, an investigation of the accident by the "Provost Marshal"—otherwise unidentified—is also missing. This is clear from a two-page "Headquarters Seventh Army" letter addressed to the "Provost" which I found in the National Archives.[10] Dated "18 December 1945" and signed by Seventh Army chief of staff, Brigadier General John M. Willems, the letter begins: "SUBJECT: Accident investigation.... The following information is furnished as a basis for your investigation of the automobile accident in which General George S. Patton was seriously injured...." Clearly the Provost Marshal, who apparently was in charge of military police, was, nearly ten days after the accident, looking into it. Yet his investigation appears unknown to custodians of our historical records since it was never once mentioned to me in all my queries. Interestingly, the letter concerning the Provost's investigation, which was accompanied by a "routing slip" to "G-2" (army intelligence), offered additional confirmation of the missing on-scene accident report, and new information about the accident itself and its aftermath.

For instance, on the evening following the crash—December 9—the letter said, a *Stars and Stripes* reporter "named Sontag" had telephoned the 818th Military Police Company (Babalas's unit) looking for details of the accident. He had spoken to a "Sgt. Jack Parrish.... As the conversation progressed, it became apparent that the sergeant was reading from some sort of record. When the reporter asked if he were reading the accident report, the sergeant said he was, and that he had the report right in front of him." Parrish, it said, had given certain details, like the names of the drivers, the road on which the accident had occurred—"N 38"—and that the truck had been making a left turn into the "Class II and IV Quartermaster Depot at Mannheim." However, it continued, "Sgt. Parrish did not tell the reporter that the cause of the accident was that the General's car was speeding in a 25-mile [per hour] zone. He did not give the exact position of the vehicles at the moment of impact; did not disclose that a German civilian employe [sic] was riding in the truck...."

Why these facts were withheld, the letter does not state. But the information about the German civilian employee was the first description of any of the possible passengers in Thompson's truck that I had discovered. A German civilian? Who was he? Why was he there? Obviously, those answers might be in the missing on-scene accident report, presumably being read by Sergeant Parrish, which was one of the reasons I was pursuing it. Or it might be in some of the other missing reports. Apparently the "Provost" letter had as one of its aims explaining why Sergeant Parrish had given out any information at all because its last paragraph discussed who was authorized to disclose information about the accident and ended, "Sgt. Parrish may be held at fault for failing to inform his company commander before he released the information."

Some sort of lid, cover-up—call it what you will—had been imposed on releasing information about the accident. Why? Was it just normal public-military bureaucratic secrecy, or did it stem from something more sinister?

Often in my search, I had been told, especially by archivists, that the dearth in records about the accident probably stemmed from the fact that it seemed little more than a "fender-bender"; that by this time—late 1945—the war was over and every serviceman wanted to come home and cared little about keeping records, or were keeping them badly. And finally, that Patton's accident, despite who he was, just was not of that much concern to authorities because it was peacetime and his usefulness was over.

The following, it seems to me, in addition to deepening the mystery about missing Patton accident reports, also belies those notions.

News of Patton's accident shot around the world quickly. Even before the next day's banner headlines about it appeared, reporters were scurrying for facts. An Associated Press correspondent, according to a War Department message I found,[11] called the Patton residence only hours after the accident seeking reaction and information. Surprised at the news, probably distraught, the family called the War Department.

On the same day—no less an authority than the sitting Supreme Commander, General Eisenhower, demanded that he be provided information on the accident ASAP. Accordingly, (December 9) the following order was sent to U.S. headquarters in Frankfurt, Germany: "General Handy has instructed that we [in his office, since they apparently had jurisdiction over Europe] notify General Eisenhower and General Surles of any new information coming in on General Patton." The matter was so important, wrote the author,[12] that he was to be awoken from bed by the night duty officer, should anything come in while he was away. And if he could not be reached, a "Colonel Westover" was to be contacted.

Certainly, the on-scene accident report would have been primary information to be sent to Eisenhower. But something went wrong. For some unknown reason, the order to Frankfurt never went out. In a "12 Dec 45" memo "for the record,"[13] Colonel Westover wrote that it had been discovered that the message had been marked by the "War Department Class Message Center with a notation 'not transmitted.' An attempt," he wrote, was in progress, "to determine who cancelled the message. No cancellation was ever given by European Section...." He continued to note that the message center was directed to prepare a memo "explaining reasons for [the message] not having been dispatched."

I could find nothing more on the investigation. Like looking for the on-scene report, as well as the other investigations, the trail went cold. Had the message been sabotaged? By whom? For what purpose? Was a lid put on the resultant investigation? I could only wonder. But I no longer thought the absence of the on-scene investigation was just a fluke. One, even two missing reports on the accident could be explained away by chance or accidental destruction. But four related reports or investigations which were given priority and mentioned in related documents?

I began to think that the odds that the records had been deliberately destroyed were mounting and that what I was finding were bits and pieces, hard to manage, that had somehow survived.

CHAPTER SIX

★ ★ ★ ★

CLANDESTINE

"**My full intention is to** tell the truth," wrote Bazata in a secret diary in 1979. "All espionage is 100% dirt—'played' mostly by dirty players—weaklings—liars—sneaks—cowards—thieves & especially betrayers. A specific that oft [sic] falls within the [espionage] area is murder-assassination."

Thus began one of Bazata's forty diary-journals[1] he composed in secret after his return to the U.S. for good in late 1971.

Would these yield any more information on the accident or Patton's death?

I hoped so.

First, they had to be mastered.

The compositions, mostly in letter size spiral notebooks, were Bazata's attempt to make sense out of a brutal, shadowy life that ended in deep dissatisfaction and to try to tell his story. They are not easy to decipher. Most are long, some as many as 350 pages. They were handwritten, difficult to read for that reason alone, and structured in a kind of code that included jumping pages to continue thoughts, inserting disjointed threads abruptly, and carrying thoughts from back pages to front rather than the normal front to back. They contained code words, pseudonyms, abbreviations, and different colored inks and letter sizes for different parts. Such obfuscation seemed a holdover from his life of secrets. But along with his personal letters and some other writings, the diaries, as the numbers I read mounted, filled in gaps, gave new details about his Patton claims, and further illuminated his clandestine life—all of which could be factored into the truth or falsity of his claims.

"Killing is...the most unpalatable area of this [the story he apparently was trying to write]. Killing was the life-time expertise of Baz—over 50 [years] of it in a multitude of forms and places and times, for a wide variety of reasons & for...certain... countries—organizations—causes...." Bazata's ledger continued.

The killing included not only what he had done in World War II, but before and after—as a freelance spy, secret agent for governments, a Cold War mercenary and soldier-of-fortune masquerading as an artist, and as the apparent leader of a secret group of clandestines like himself which he called variously the "Co-Op," for its bond of brotherhood, and "La Table," for the place where they periodically met in Marseilles, France. The group, comprised of far-flung members, did special jobs for governments and other employers, including body guarding and assassination, and carried on its own unlawful activities for profit and under what appeared (to them at least) to be a guiding philosophy that made war on whom and what they decided was bad for the world.

He often, in the writings, termed the killing "weeding." Those weeded included soldiers, spies, weapon and drug dealers, criminals, dictators, and political opponents of those who hired him or his group. They never, he wrote, conducted personal vendettas. That was against their creed. Their activities included kidnapping, robbery, and extortion, but in the latter case, only from people they determined were "evil." They would not extort those they deemed "innocents." But they would menace a bully, war profiteer, or vicious criminal. In Monaco, for example, they "tapped" an arms merchant who "sold to all sides" at "exorbitant prices." Bazata knew the man because he had painted a "Cezanne" and sold the fake as authentic to the unwitting gunrunner for $20,000, which was then given collectively—and it has to be said, generously—to the Co-Op.

The abduction had been "very simple." Disguised as local thugs, they had "picked him up at a bouillabaisse restaurant in an old port of Cannes." They drove him to a secluded place, "explaining first our intense loathing of [his] business...and him in particular." They removed his underwear, keeping it to mail to him later as a threat if need be, and "sliced his balls—the skin of the scrotum—seven times. He screamed...appeared to swoon, this tough hard, ruthless, vain, and self-adoring businessman, so I punched his nose to unswoon him....He whimpered and wept and pleaded—wife, good man, charity, etc....One more punch shut this shit up. It was explained he had been robbed by four dirty thieves—Italian or Corsican or Catalan....He didn't know which....We thus removed his watch, money, papers and a very vulgar diamond ring [inscribed to his wife] who had five prior husbands." He was to tell "the police that this was a normal, everyday take...or he and his wife would be executed within 3 days [and his] mansion burnt...He was to have $30,000—a pittance, but all we needed at the moment—the next day at his home in Monaco. A small delivery truck would appear to deliver a package of [lobsters]...a fish-kid—an innocent—would receive his sealed and unmarked envelope." If he continued to "work and thrive as before...he would hear from us again in a year or so...."

Weeding was Bazata's forte. He writes of killing "seven... Russian 'bully boys,' a very ticklish job." He was "alone on an open road" when he did it and "very uncomfortable. Took $1/_2$ bottle of Calvados[2] to even Baz's keel." He killed them with "two 45 cal. Colts. Got a peasant to pull the bodies into small wood and threatened him not to tell or [he would] join the bodies with his entire family." They got special weapons made in East Germany— a pistol that collected its own spent cartridges and one that sounded like a vehicle backfire. "You'd have a car nearby with a kerosene smoke device built in to draw attention." For the wartime and post-war French leader Charles DeGaulle, he rescued kidnapped French officers about to be executed by Algerian rebels and weeded leaders of the Charlemagne Division, a 3000-strong unit of French soldiers, many of whom had volunteered—treasonously so, in DeGaulle's eyes—to fight with the Waffen SS at the end of the war. "Baz was order-requested to do this," he wrote. "He said yes if his name not involved. DeGaulle agreed."

Anonymity and secrecy were paramount, both for Bazata and the Co-Op. His job as chief of staff at the Mumm Estate in Johannisberg, Germany, and reputation as a modernist European artist in the post-war continental culture were good covers and handy. One of his acquaintances told me he had a furnace there in which he could dispose of bodies. No one questioned his flamboyance, his travel, and unorthodox lifestyle. Those who knew were sworn to secrecy and well aware of the penalty for disclosure or even drawing attention. It was death.

So why was he now talking? The reasons, he wrote, were many. His parents, the only people he really feared knowing about his past, were now dead. The Co-Op was no more, several of its members having been assassinated in some kind of betrayal or ambush which resulted in him personally hunting down and killing those responsible—at least those are the indications in his writings. And the time was right. Many secrets he thought sacrosanct were—by the early 1970s when it appears he began talking—being disclosed in books he was seeing. America, he decided, needed to know what he knew—how it was betrayed by its leaders in World War II; how they had turned on their best, like Patton, and the war had been prolonged because of it. So many had died needlessly, he writes repeatedly. That war had been a dirty, vile business. It had enraged him.

But mostly, it appeared to me, he was talking because he felt personally betrayed. Over and over he writes that he had been promised rewards when he returned home, a good job and retirement in particular—most notably by Donovan when he agreed to be an OSS assassin and continue as such after the war. He had envisioned a job with the CIA. But instead he had been shunned. The new generation of intelligence bureaucrats did not know who he was or what he had done, and those who had some inkling had been standoffish and disowning. His records had been purged, undoubtedly to hide the involvement in dirty business of higher ups. All they now contained were slurs and innuendos that he said were lies. There were major omissions. He had to fight for years gathering signed statements from colleagues to eventually get his disability which, given the many wounds he suffered, finally ended at 100 percent—a fact verifiable by, for one, the Veterans Administration.

He was bitter and in need of money.

But the life he had led—still shrouded in mystery even in the diaries—troubled him deeply. "Lord, why have I done this," he wrote, omitting details. "Why am I so bad?" Why, he asked, was he given such skills and, yet, indecision about whether he was right or wrong in using them. "Man is vain, pompous, vulgar, mean.... And yet I am one of these men.... None know my terrible inner struggles, the restless nites [sic]—not even my wife.... I am plagued by doubts between so-called right and so-called wrong. And legality—man's convenient invention for himself—repels me.... I have no confidant save my God...." He was getting old and thinking of death. He coveted his father's Bible. Marie-Pierre said he prayed almost every night, lying prone in his bed, his lips moving silently. She knew not to disturb him. If, by mistake, she entered, he would open his eyes and his stare would say leave, which she would do.

He was not a "hit man," he insisted. Hit men enjoy their work, think it manly. He was a machine. He abhorred killings when the victim knew his fate:

> I've never seen [one] that wasn't slowed by pleas, stumbling, screaming, wild offers, betrayals, denunciations, farts, vomiting, fainting, pissing, threatening—usually a curse of [returned] vengeance.... If it's fast, it's the best. Get it over and disposed of. Successful weeding is devoid of emotion—no vengeance... brutality... or Hollywood flare.... 'Now mister, prepare to meet your maker.' It's silent, solemn... you, your God, and the target.... I even knew [a hit man] who had an orgasm at each hit—his sole orgasm.... Balls! You do it [only] when it's best.... I just shot a commie leader.... No ceremony.... No chest-pounding....Just...."Pop," the most convenient place in the body...."Pop".... Just good business and silence... on to the next weed.

Friends remark that while he was compassionate and devoid of ego, he also lacked a conscience. "Charming but deadly," is the way a former Jedburgh characterized him. He had a sixth sense. "Largely I fell back on ESP [extra sensory perception] and the strange will from a [mysterious] unconscious.... I believe in storing the very act of thinking. You gather, you decide," you program, "stopping activity in suspension to be reactivated unconsciously.... Ditto sight.... You feel-see a room or forest or person or situation as you do art or a painting...as some animals must by radiation...you feel police, spies, queers, nuts as you feel an immobile distant deer in a shaded forest." He used "self-hypnosis" to endure pain, preferred spur-of-the-moment to planning and welcomed obstacles as tests of his ability. "Everything is possible by daring, timing, skill and know how at the proper instant.... I can kill anyone in the world without capture or discovery."

Justifying the weeding, he wrote: "Civilization is advanced mostly through corruption by the eternal evils within man"—jealousy, pride, ambition, the lust for power and possessions. These were the causes of war, which was the worst of man's evils. World War II had been a folly of nations and leaders killing for power and possession. He recognized this first when he was asked by Donovan to "stop" Patton and then when the British refused to take the surrender of large numbers of Germans he captured during the Cedric mission. They wanted the war prolonged, he charged. He especially disliked phonies, power grabbers, and those who preyed on the innocent and he felt their transgressions justified retribution. "Thus Baz grants himself the authority to lie to liars...cheat cheats...deceive manipulators...brut [sic] the bullies.... Slay the dragons.... Killing is ending an animal...a mad dog [that] must be eliminated."

This philosophy had become almost like a religion, guiding and giving him purpose. It had grown, he wrote, from his relationship with a mysterious friend and mentor who had saved his life as he came ashore as a young marine to kill Batista, the revolutionary, in early 1930s Cuba.

He described his contemporary as suave, polite, and "always smiling," and he assumed he worked for Cuban intelligence. They never asked each other personal questions. Their ages were roughly the same and their relationship had flowered. "We were astonished to learn we slew none for vengeance or anger, none for satisfaction or orgasm. We both quietly aimed at eliminating evil." He admired this man more than anyone he had ever met, save his father. And vowing he would never disclose his identity—because of the harm that might cause—he used pseudonyms for him, sometimes "Peter," sometimes "Paul." This friend later became a founding member of the Co-Op.

In one of the diaries, Bazata elaborated on the terrible injury he received jumping into France for Cedric in August 1944: The safehouse Millar took them to that first night belonged to two granddaughters of an [unnamed] French general and hero of the 1870 Franco-Prussian War. After ordering the young and exhausted Floyd to take the lone bed in the room prepared for the two and "making a super human effort not to show my wound," he had joined in their parlor the two "delightful crones" who were "fully dressed and coiffed as befit proud granddaughters of a well-known French general." They showed him

photos of hero Grand-pa-pa and his medals. I spoke of [my] love of [France's history] and mother's ancient lineage of which, at the time, I knew next to nothing.... I was almost mindless with pain... but these "beautiful" octogenarians shamed me into... perfect behaviour [sic]. However, in a lax moment.... I felt the ooze [through] my trousers and saw with horror a large pool of syrupy blooded glob between my legs on their magnificent Louis XIV chair. They had given me the "throne" of honor, their absolute very best... [and] I had ruined this pearl....

Without recording their reaction, he excused himself and went back to his room. It "contained a long table with 2 wash basins, 2 pitchers of water and 4 towels. In total torture"—as an oblivious Floyd "snored... strongly and regularly," he removed his trousers and undershorts, "all massed with gelatinous blood and... flesh" and was "horrified" by what he saw. The wound "went absolutely to the inner hip bone, about an inch or so from my crotch and... higher up than my genitals. It was very jagged and wide. But the bleeding had stopped. I pulled away pieces of flesh with my fingers," tied "ends of what I thought were two small veins." Not wanting to "ruin the [granddaughters'] lovely towels," he swabbed the hideous gash "with two of my handkerchiefs soaked in water... filled the cut with... sulfamilimide from the brown paper bag in my jacket pocket," and bound the wound with four additional handkerchiefs he had. "I was to leave this tragic wound exactly like that for approximately 6 weeks without ever once even looking at it."

Cleaning up and disposing of the "mess" behind "a dense hedge... against the house," he put on fresh shorts and trousers and become "alarmed at the grotesque swelling" of the wound which "exaggerated [its] appearance at least 4 fold." Laboriously—for every movement was a knife stab in the gut—he eased himself to the hard floor. Once there and supine, he prayed, thanking God for "safe arrival" of his team. "It did not occur to me that I was not safe. It never did"—not before then or after. "From time to time, I would touch my stomach-abdomen startled to feel it swollen so fantastically high—a foot or so? Was this possible? Was I delirious?

Then I thought of [my] duty." It was to "take care of Floyd first, then to command our team—we 3, self included.[3] The 1st act..." (which would come in the morning) was to radio back to London, "to announce all well.... It never occurred to me to...say I was hurt. This was an agent's war and I had accepted it.... I must sound out Emile [Millar] very slowly, cautiously, carefully. I had special orders from both the British and the French. Emile...was felt to be strongly communistic. I must ascertain this and ascertain his influence-actions. The Americans knew nothing of this and must learn nothing. Thus I must code with infinite care, every word having been scrupulously pre-arranged."[4]

He must have dozed, he writes, for he was abruptly awakened by the sound of artillery fire. "I was stunned. Whose?...It couldn't be the Americans who were...far to the South.... But could it be Patton?...Are you beating me?" he asked as if addressing the general. "No, no. Even this semi-mad racehorse couldn't be that magic[al]. George was very far off. Well then, [could it be] the Germans? But why artillery at 04:30 hours, on a target of cob-webs"— apparently the little village he was in. "But it was drawing closer... I must alert Dick [snoring Floyd] and the 2 aristocrats. We must go down to the cellar. I tried to arise. Absolutely impossible. I was that stark stiff. Nothing bent save my arms and even [those] 2 power-houses ached. At length I rolled me over on my "front." It seemed a life-time of effort." Thinking his "insides [were] falling out," he "managed to get to my knees." Then, "pushed to super effort by this monster artillery" that continued to approach, "I staggered to my bare feet...panting...reeling." Because his legs "would not hold together inward," he was compelled to swing them in jerks like Frankenstein to the snoring Floyd "least I do a splitz and never recover. But when he reached the bed, Floyd was still snoring. "Why the hell wasn't he awake!" He called Floyd's name. The snores continued. "I shook him a few times, weakly, of course. He moved slightly but continued snoring." He was on the brink of shouting when "I heard it—an abrupt, violent downpour of rain." A thunder storm? Lightning lit the predawn darkness. "What the hell?" Suddenly he realized his mistake. In the graying morning, he stood "in total shame. Me, Bazata—Lebeau*—the great marine, hot shot, the most experienced Jed....I'd been conned by some lousy thunder...."

Bazata had returned to London from Cedric with an uncharacteristic unease. As he trained for more Jedburgh missions, his pelvic injury, he later told the Veterans Administration, continued to bother him, including leaving him impotent. There is evidence in his writings that he feared for his life and refused OSS treatment in a hospital bed because he felt he would be vulnerable to attack there. He successfully cured the impotence himself, he testified before the VA, by injecting himself with testosterone. The treatment had been suggested by a colonel friend at a London party who helped him get the hormone.[5] The suspicion of whether he had stolen money designated for the Maquis—quietly dropped when he was cleared by the French themselves—might also have factored in his unease. He felt he had done his job well and strongly resented what he perceived as an ungrateful, unloyal accusation. But a friend and fellow OSS member indicates, without knowing as much, that the "Patton problem"—then nearing its height—might have been the root of his post-Cedric trepidation.

"I first met Douglas deWitt Bazata in London...during the Spring of 1945," wrote Joseph W. La Gattuta, a retired army lieutenant colonel when he penned the statement for Bazata's VA

---

*Denny Lebeau, his individual Cedric codename which he would keep for other operations and use in coming years.

inquiry in 1978. La Gattuta, an OSS first lieutenant in 1945, had come to late-war Britain to, among other things, put some unnamed foreign nationals through parachute school. Bazata, whom he met in a bar there, had volunteered some "invaluable operational assistance." Despite this helpfulness and a friendship the two had forged carousing in London, "I was nevertheless impressed by the fact that he was laboring under considerable mental stress. I subsequently learned that Bazata had been seriously wounded during his parachute mission into then German-occupied France, and that additionally he was enduring some severe psychological reaction to some of the tasks he had [been asked] to carry out." Leaving London after several weeks, La Gattuta returned following VE-Day, May 8, 1945: "I saw Bazata again and was at once struck by his very nervous manner and apprehension over our imminent return to the United States." Aware of Bazata's clergyman father, he wrote that Bazata "feared" his family "would be horror stricken at his actions during the war." After the bombing of Hiroshima, August 6, Bazata had told him, "man's cruelty to man was almost beyond comprehension."[6]

Whatever the cause of his unease, this was towards the end of the period—from just prior to Cedric to the early post-war aftermath—that Bazata claims he was having meetings (8 in all) with Donovan that included the request to kill Patton. A "restricted" OSS order I obtained at the National Archives stipulates that Bazata, La Gattuta and a list of other OSS officers report "to the Director, OSS, Washington, D.C." upon their arrival in the capital, which was sometime in late June.[7] That, so far, is the only official record I have found of Donovan and Bazata meeting face to face. However, any meetings on such a sensitive and volatile subject as what to do with a troublesome Patton certainly would have been clandestine and not recorded in routine orders, even if, like this one, the order was classified. Early on, writes Bazata—in the summer of 1944 when he was preparing for Cedric and the meetings on stopping Patton had just begun—Donovan had wanted their meetings to be at his private apartment but "I said no Sir. I wished [to] be clear [of] listeners, traps....We met at small, quiet hotels...twice at 20:00 hours [8:00 p.m.]." The "conversations" were "unwitnessed [with] no notes" and sealed with only "our word." The "reason," he writes, was "survival"—his own.

At first, he writes, just after joining OSS in late 1943, he purposely flouted his qualifications as an assassin thinking he would get an assignment to kill important Nazis like Field Marshall Rommel, Nazi propaganda minister Goebbels, or even Hitler himself, an idea he said he seriously proposed not only to OSS but surreptitiously to several other allied countries, but without any takers.[8] "They must have thought I was insane or possibly a harmless crank.... It would have been quite easy.... One man, one bullet...." He, at that early stage, was looking for the most dangerous assignment he could attract; the highest adventure. He and his friend, fellow OSS Jedburgh, Rene Dussaq, a former Hollywood stuntman who would gain fame in wartime France as "Captain Bazooka" because of his skill and daring with the anti-tank weapon, would play tricks of exaggeration on what he writes were OSS "informers," persons apparently used by the hierarchy to keep watch on their own. "They [the informers] were so obvious it was laughable"—waiters where they drank, taxicab drivers who transported them. "Dussaq would say, 'Tell 'em about the time you killed those mobsters at sea.' I would say, 'Oh, they weren't mobsters.' It would build from there and they'd [the informants] go [back to their handlers and say], 'Boy, that guy's a killer.'"[9]

But the trick backfired. "I had no idea it would be an [important] American [he would eventually be asked to kill] and least of all a great general." Upon being identified as the type they were looking for, he wrote there was much "sparring" in the preliminary talks with Donovan, who probed him about his background, especially about the killings he had already done. "He [Donovan] was non-committal, very shifty, always 'OSS has no place for this type of brutality.'" But then he would ask for details. Bazata writes he told him about his exploits in Cuba, the bums on the train, others he "dispatched. I'd say, 'Of course, Sir. I ask only to aid our war effort in any small way'" and emphasized "my operating alone...never once caught, never once talked, even for survival. And I don't care about glory." Once accepted, however, he wrote, it was like a weight had been lifted from Donovan's shoulders. "He was afraid...relieved to throw it all on me...and maybe ashamed.... As soon as I said no problem...they [Donovan?] were instantly happy...had a magical belief in me...his [Donovan's] attitude and confidence in me [opened] up...he got bolder, using stronger language...."

For instance, in describing one of the undated meetings, he wrote, "[Donovan's] sycophant aids [sic] left the room. We were absolutely alone....He said, "Douglas, we have a most disagreeable, perplexing problem—a disobedient general. There is no time for dismissal, especially as he performs miracles. I have been ordered through proper channels to delay, detour and stop this general. He is George Patton. I want you to undertake this assignment." What specifically did he have in mind, asked Bazata? "Play it as it develops, dependant largely on Patton, the terrain, and the Germans. It must look like an accident of war."[10]

Throughout the discussions of "stopping Patton," Bazata writes he was shocked and confused, although he believed he hid it from Donovan. He did not know whether to accept or refuse. Sometimes he indicates he was just playing a game with Donovan and had no intention of doing anything rash. The idea of killing Patton—broached, he writes, in these meetings—

"repulsed" him. Other times he elaborates on how he was turned by Donovan into acceptance of what eventually became the killing order. He seems, in these post-Patton writings, to be end-lessly battling with himself about whether he had done right or wrong, whether he was justified or not, a patriot or a monster, battling with the truth of just how much involvement he had ac-tually had in any Patton plot—but always indicating that a plot to kill the general had existed. About that there is no confusion, no ambiguity.

In one such run, he writes, "What should I do?... Why did he [Donovan] do this to me?... He could have resigned—as I could have.... Should I try to counter? Warn Patton?"—something he claims elsewhere actually to have done. But here, relating what may have been a short moment in a long period of indecision, he writes, "Decided against any [counter] whatsoever. D [Donovan] had warned me [he] would deny me—as liar—madman—possibly admitting he had met me at "my insistence"... [but] never admit we discussed.... " He would have turned Bazata over to the army and "cashiering." And what else? Elimination? He had to be careful, he wrote. It was "a dirty, very dirty business."[11]

When Millar's book *Maquis* was rushed into publication in early 1945—an attempt by the British, according to Bazata, to get credit for the important Special Operations work in France—Donovan, "was green with fear," wrote Bazata. He thought "I'd collaborated with Millar to pop the Patton story." Bazata assured Donovan that he had not. "I told him I'd read the book & we had nothing to fear save betrayal by his [Donovan's] friends and spon-sors... the Brits." Thus challenged, "Donovan gulped." He asked if (Bazata) had any "specifics" regarding the charge he was work-ing for the Brits. Only when Bazata assured Donovan that he did not, he writes, did Donovan "relax."

Bazata is not the only knowledgeable person to believe that the unpredictable and secretive Donovan may have been a British agent. It is fairly well known that British agent-envoy, Sir William Stephenson, *A Man Called Intrepid*,[12] was intricately involved in getting Donovan selected as the head of the OSS. Donovan and Stephenson's friendship went back to World War I, according to Cave Brown in *Last Hero*, Donovan's biography. They both had served in the war, and Brown believes they had met at a French hospital, although that is in dispute amongst Donovan-Stephenson scholars.[13] Stephenson had been an infantryman and decorated fighter pilot in WWI, and Donovan, an officer in New York's famous "Fighting 69th," a unit about which a movie starring James Cagney was later made. It had been Donovan's later fact-finding mission to England for President Roosevelt in 1940 during the Battle of Britain that had helped FDR justify sending controversial war supplies to the besieged island nation. This was before Pearl Harbor brought America into the war and many Americans were not willing to commit to the European conflict. Isolationists, wanting to avoid any American involvement, felt Britain was on the verge of defeat and U.S. aid would be wasted. Roosevelt, wanting to help England, was facing reelection and needed a good reason and a lawful way to get involved. Donovan had returned with the report that Britain was indeed holding its own against the Germans and could prevail if supplied with American ships, planes, and other war items. He also helped fashion a lawful and politically acceptable way to do it: "Lend-Lease," a reciprocal arrangement where the supplies were exchanged for U.S. use of British bases.

While in Britain, Donovan forged close ties—almost too close. Reputable historians now believe Donovan was a British agent.[14] Stephenson had introduced Donovan to Prime Minister Churchill and members of the British military. And it was Stephenson—sent by Churchill to liaison with the U.S. government to help speed America's entry into the war—who suggested to Roosevelt that America form an overall intelligence-gathering agency and recommended that Donovan head it. Roosevelt agreed, and in the summer of 1941, he established the new position of Coordinator of Intelligence, which would soon morph into OSS, and made Donovan its head. Following that appointment, Stephenson cabled back to British intelligence chief, Stewart Menzies, "You can imagine how relieved I am after three months of battle and jockeying for position in Washington that our man [Donovan] is in a position of such importance to our efforts."[15] Stephenson was Donovan's "case" officer, writes former CIA staff officer, Thomas F. Troy, a historian who has looked into the matter.[16] He was given the codename "Q," adds Cave Brown.[17] Though there is no concrete evidence that Donovan was working for the British, he was certainly a sympathizer. And given the wartime animosity between Patton and Montgomery (still downplayed by the British) and the fact that the two nations, although close allies, had varying end goals in the war—America, to win and vanquish, and Britain, in addition to victory, to retain what it could of its far-flung empire— the possibility of British involvement with Patton's death is certainly plausible and is mentioned more than once in Bazata's writings. "I wondered," he speculates in one of the diaries, "was Mildew trying to prove himself to the Brits?"

Were they involved in any plot?

It's a legitimate question, but one, given Britain's stringent secrecy laws involving WWII, that's probably not answerable any time soon—if ever.

Throughout his writings, Bazata, although he has his own speculations on the matter,[18] claims no firsthand, personal knowledge about who was behind the wish to kill Patton, only that the request to do so came directly from Donovan. But one of the most intriguing aspects of his writings to validate his charges are the descriptions he gives of the meeting he had with Donovan in which he says the director made the assassination request. In a personal letter he wrote entitled "CO-OP!", dated "2 Aug. '75" addressed to a Dear Bill, whose identity is unknown, he wrote,[19] "Donovan called me to his office in Grosvesnor [sic] Street, London for a very PRIVATE [sic] chat....[20] We went over to the Claridge Hotel[21] to a Corner [sic] for lunch....[22] D seemed very reticent and embarrassed.... I put him easy at once with: 'General, Sir, you have an additional mission for me! You can trust me totally! I am the servant of the United States, of OSS and General D....'" To which he writes Donovan replied,

"Thank you, Douglas, I do indeed have a problem: that we all must settle. It is the extreme disobedience of Gen. Geo. P. and his very very serious disregard of orders for the common cause.... He grows more violent daily and surely must be ill.... This is in no way a reflection of my opinion: but that of the High Command and Higher (?)' [Bazatas' parenthesis and question mark].... We must stop this rebellious Gen.... I have my orders. I've selected you to execute them. But first I wish to remind you of your Oath....[23] I would like you to now swear yet again to silence: forever! Even if you do NOT volunteer for the mission undertaking...." I swore....[24] D then slowly spoke of stopping P "somehow".... He offered several possible solutions all of which amounted to an "accident"...i.e., food poisoning, or water, or command vehicle, or some such....I said a shot perhaps: accidentally in the nite [sic].... D squirmed.... that we didn't need to go that far.... Then he digressed...[25] for 5 minutes on how great and grand

P. was...what a magnificent contribution....[26] Ending with: this great Am. Servant is surely sick and not at all responsible: we must protect him from himself and suicidal irreparable damage to not only the U.S. and this War: but himself and his great reputation, , , , [Bazata's commas] etc. I waited and repeated "shot" saying: "but if I must, and 'tis the only way; shall I kill him Sir?" He waited. At last D. looked at me.... He bleated in a whisper: "Yes, Douglas, you do exactly what you must, it is now totally your 'creation': kill this man if you must.... " I felt like patting his arm and telling him it would be all-right.... I said instead, "Sir you have my word...."[27]

Donovan's saying Patton was sick reflects the view of General Marshall's War Department during the immediate post-war period. They thought he was insane and unreliable, which was not widely known at the time, so Bazata's knowledge of it certainly adds credibility to his account.

Bazata reiterates in his writings—just as he told the *Spotlight*—that the amount he was given was $10,000 plus $800 for expenses in "old 50 dollar bills."

Several times in the diaries Bazata stresses, "I did not kill Patton," the same as what he stressed in our interviews. He had only *injured* Patton. They had botched the assassination attempt at Mannheim and although he and the mysterious "Pole" had gone to the Heidelberg hospital to try and finish the job, they had not succeeded. However, just as many times in the writings he says, "We killed him." So he was conflicted on that point. And talking about Patton's accident and death to Nick Longworth, the deputy VA administrator, Bazata told his friend, "I did that.... I want you to know I did that."[28] Longworth believed him.

★ ★ ★ ★

CHAPTER SEVEN

HIT LIST

Counter Intelligence Corps (CIC) Special Agent Stephen J. Skubik was impatient.

He was frustrated, exhausted, verging on anger.

The Ohio State University graduate had been attached as an investigator to Patton's 89th Infantry Division until war's end when he was moved to the new post-war 970th CIC. Not only was he in the midst of trying to persuade higher-ups that he had uncovered a Russian-OSS plot to assassinate Patton, but on this late summer day in 1945,[1] the former Nazi SS corporal he had arrested was refusing to talk.

Almost every day in Germany since his arrival in February of 1945 had been chaotic for Skubik, both before the surrender and after. If it was not a scheming Nazi causing trouble, it was a Neanderthal Russian. He was tired of it, fed up. He had seen enough brutality to make any investigator sick. He was one of the first American intelligence agents—if not *the* first Allied soldier outright—to enter the Ohrdruf Concentration Camp near Czechoslovakia.

Decades later, he recalled the discovery.

"I came upon the gates of the concentration camp. It was deserted by the guards. I walked a short distance before being overwhelmed by an awful smell. Shortly I came upon bodies. Some were naked, others in striped uniforms." Beyond, he gasped at what unfolded: "thousands of emaciated bodies" everywhere—sprawled haphazard over the grounds, stacked like cordwood in eerie, vacant buildings. As he later recalled, "I became ill and retreated in horror. I must admit I ran away from that place as fast as I could. It was as if I was afraid the dead would rise to seize me."[2]

Ohrdruf was a grisly adjunct, they would later realize, to the nearby infamous Buchenwald, and one of the first Nazi death camps the Americans had liberated. Patton himself had thrown up after a visit to Ohrdruf.*

The CIC, secretive and powerful, was charged with thwarting spies and sabotage against U.S. Army forces and projects, investigating traitors, and, right after the war in Europe, primarily hunting and arresting fleeing Nazi war criminals who seemed to be everywhere in Germany. Its agents were trained military soldiers, linguists, and men with high IQs with special investigative skills and talents, physical and mental—"G-men in Khakis," the press would later call them.[3] They had powers of arrest, detention, and even execution, if they felt it warranted.

The job was always dangerous. Just months previous, Skubik had lost several men while attempting to arrest a Nazi bigwig who agreed to surrender at his house. But the house was booby-trapped. While the team went inside to wait, Skubik was out back,

---

*Patton, Eisenhower, and Bradley toured the camp on April 12, 1945.

pistol in hand, reconnoitering when he heard the awful explosion. Luck, God, and destiny had saved him, he would later tell his kids. They cornered the Nazi later and when they were about to arrest him, he tried to bribe them with diamonds to let him get away. Skubik had to pull his gun on a colleague to prevent him from accepting. It galled him that even CIC agents were susceptible.

Since entering Germany with Patton until the country's capitulation in early May, his 89th detachment had investigated seventy-one towns, interrogated 17,000 Germans and made seven hundred arrests.[4] He himself had made over thirty arrests, which included six spies and seventeen Gestapo agents. The work—even after the surrender and his transfer to the larger 970th Detachment—was always grim. Immediate post-war Germany was a hell of ruin and degradation. They worked amidst the threats of brutal war criminals; conflicting, often violent aims of the different occupying powers; millions of displaced persons needing almost everything; prostitution of all kinds—including children—and rampant, crime-breeding black marketeering, an out-of-control enterprise that corrupted many in Occupied Germany. Players could make a fortune. He had experienced tough times growing up in Canton, Ohio, but nothing like this—people digging holes in rubble to live in, eating garbage, selling their bodies for cigarettes which became almost the dominant currency. He had seen mothers whose cheeks were bitten off by raping, vengeful Russians. And they were the lucky ones. Often the Russians murdered their rape victims.[5] He had witnessed terrible suicides by desperate men who figured they would be hanged after arrest—like Hitler's brother-in-law, Martin Hammitzch, who put a bullet in his temple as Skubik and the arrest team arrived.[6] His sleep was still haunted by the screams of a horribly maimed American he had thought dead and accidentally stepped on as he ran fearfully through a house during a live battle.[7]

He hated the war.

He hated Germany.

And now this former SS corporal in front of him, stubborn and verbally stumbling—a pawn of the true local culprits, he suspected—was refusing to reveal who had given him the order to torch Schluechtern's only synagogue. Schluechtern was a centuries-old German village just inside the American Occupation Zone to which his three-man team[8] had retreated when the Russians had kicked them out of Zwickau on July 1. Zwickau, in eastern Germany flanking the Mulde River, was now part of the Russian Occupation Zone, a dangerous place his job sometimes took him secretly. Though Skubik was a Catholic, he grieved for the Jews of Schluechtern—a measly 400 of them who had been ravaged by the village's Nazi bullies, some beaten and murdered,[9] the rest shipped to the camps and probably now exterminated. Not a Jew had returned. Not one! The synagogue was still standing but gutted. He was not going to let this guy shield the ones responsible.

He was determined to get an answer.

The former SS corporal was "a small fellow...a vicious animal," said Skubik.[10] His name, it turns out, was Adam Nieman, confirmed Christa Krucker, a Schluechtern resident who investigated for me. He was a recognized dimwit and, in her opinion, Skubik was aware of that, which probably added to his frustration. Whatever the case, Nieman had confessed to torching the synagogue on "Kristallnacht," the infamous two nights in early November 1938 when Nazis all over Germany attacked Jews and destroyed their property. Kristallnacht meant "night of the broken glass" and is generally considered to have been the beginning of the Holocaust. Nieman had also confessed, according to Skubik, to raping two Jewish women and killing several Jewish men.

He felt big with the uniform on, he told Skubik, who spoke German, Ukrainian, Polish, and Russian. Skubik had interrogated over fifty locals himself and believed him. Nieman said he used gasoline to start the fire. "Just following orders," he said. But he would not reveal from whom.

"I kept telling him he would have to answer to God for his crimes and he said he didn't believe in God. But apparently the mention of God affected him. He showed fear in his face. He literally turned blue which upset me. So I sent him out into the lobby where he could compose himself."

What happened next was unexpected. The little ex-corporal asked to go to the toilet. Apparently he had a concealed penknife. Once the door closed, he started slitting his wrists. A guard in the hallway heard a sound—a "cry," says Skubik[11]—and opened the bathroom door. Nieman came running out, blood spewing. A former Schluechtern resident, Frank Theubert, who, as a little boy, was there that day, says Nieman was shouting, "I'll kill either you or myself." Skubik, in the midst of another interrogation down the hall, heard the commotion and gave chase along with others. Theubert, arriving to be with his mother who worked at the mansion the CIC had requisitioned, writes, "I saw a man sneaking out....Seconds later I saw office staff storming up the apple orchard hill [behind the mansion] in pursuit of their escapee." Neiman "continued to stab himself," said Skubik. "He finally collapsed in a geyser of blood...gave the final kick...and died." Theubert: "Today, more than sixty years later, the sight of this blood-covered man as I approached them is still vividly in my memory."[12]

The memory stayed with Skubik too, haunting him for years—part of a larger, nightmare mosaic of later death threats and experiences that at first, he wrote, he mostly blocked out of his mind, and then which returned in fragmented pieces causing extreme anxiety until he finally purged them with a series of acts including, it appears, returning to Eastern Europe in 1978 and writing a book about what must be considered the most important issue he dealt with in that chaotic time: General Patton's death. Prior to his death in 1996, he self-published *The Murder of General Patton*. The title describes how he believed General Patton died—by assassination—and is based on his own personal investigations made while an intelligence agent serving for and near Patton in Germany during and up to the time the legendary general died.

The book's forward begins: "It is my intention to explain the circumstances which lead me to believe: [1][13] that General George Smith Patton, Jr., was murdered; [2] that the [car] accident which took place on December 9, 1945 was set up by the Soviet NKVD (*Narodny Komissariat Vnutrennikh Del*) in collusion with the American OSS (Office of Strategic Services); [3] that Patton died at the Heidelberg Military Hospital on December 21 at the hands of an assassin." On page ninety-seven of the book, after taking issue with historians whom he believes have "bought the official line"—that Patton's death was an accident—he writes, "However historians do research, they are not trained investigators. As a trained Counter Intelligence Agent I have no doubt that General George S. Patton, Jr. was murdered."

Like OSS agent Bazata, CIC agent Skubik implicates not only OSS, but its chief, "Wild Bill" Donovan.

Stating that certain names may be changed—either by design or his faulty memory—Skubik's witness begins, ultimately, when he was an infant. The slightly built blond never knew his Austrian-born birth parents.[14] He was found in a basket left on the steps of a Ukrainian Catholic Church in Philadelphia in 1916[15] where he was raised by nuns until he was seven when he was adopted by a

Ukrainian family in Canton. As a child, he spoke only Ukrainian. While his adopted father, a steelworker, was respected, his mother, who ran the household, was mean, according to Skubik's children—adults today who supplied me with his book—and made him work long hours hawking newspapers. She imposed a daily money quota. He had a tough time because his English was bad. But wiry and nervy, he became a street tough with a reputation for having punishing fists. That toughness led to his eventually joining CIC as an intelligence agent. However, without his Ukrainian upbringing, he probably would not have been able to learn about the alleged Patton plot.

Because of his Slavic language background, he was given special duty by CIC to cultivate Ukrainian and other Eastern European sources. It was while doing that, he writes, that he first heard of the plot. He was meeting clandestinely with Stepan Bandera, a famous Ukrainian nationalist leader. They were in Munich, Germany, reputed to have been the birthplace of Nazism and one of the chief cities under American occupation. It was May 16, 1945, just days after the war in Europe had ended. Bandera, a controversial and enigmatic figure on the run at that time, was there with his many bodyguards. Eventually, Britain and America would use Bandera and his Ukrainians as infiltrators and saboteurs in the Cold War against Russia.[16] How exactly Skubik had contacted the revolutionary and arranged the meeting is not explained in Skubik's book, but, "he told me that the Soviet High Command had been ordered by Marshal Stalin to kill U.S. Army General George Patton."[17]

Bandera, who himself would be murdered by a Soviet assassin in Munich in 1958,[18] was being sought at that time by both the Russians and the U.S., who mostly wanted to help the Soviets catch him. Born in 1909, he had been brought up in a patriotic family. His father was an outspoken Ukrainian cleric, many of whom were political. Ukraine, in its Western reaches, was a vast and agriculturally rich area of European Russia bordering Poland, Czechoslovakia and Romania. Although it had long been part of Imperial Russia, and then the Soviet Union, most of its people did not consider themselves Russians. Their loyalty was to Ukraine, and, in fact, the area had been independent and a separate country not only in earlier centuries but briefly during World War I until swallowed up again by the communist revolution. Bandera, early in his life had been involved in nationalistic struggles against Poland and the USSR, both of which wanted to dominate Ukrainians. He became a guerilla leader and thinker, fighting for an independent Ukraine. And in the 1930s, after being sent to prison for the alleged assassination of a Polish leader, he had risen to head one of the main Ukrainian revolutionary groups—the Organization of Ukrainian Nationalists or "OUN"—fighting especially the Soviets.

As war clouds had grown over Europe in the late 1930s, he sought help against the Soviet Union from the Nazis who finally aided him once they broke their alliance with Moscow and attacked Russia in 1941. But when he demanded Ukrainian independence in return, the Nazis had thrown him in a succession of prisons, including Sachsenhausen Concentration Camp, and he was not freed until 1944 when the Germans became desperate for Ukrainian help. But by that time, the Germans were losing the war and could not enforce their demands. Once freed, Bandera, seeing his best chance ever for Ukrainian independence, attacked both the Nazis and the Soviets, both of whose armies were in the Ukraine fighting each other. There are allegations that Bandera, a small, unimposing man, was nonetheless a ruthless fighter and killed Jews as well as Nazis and Russians. While Ukrainians did serve with the Nazis, some as brutal guards in Nazi concentration camps, Bandera's part remains a puzzle, as does that of the OUN. Other Ukrainian groups may have been the culprits who sparked the allegations. First and foremost, Bandera was a nationalist fighting to free Ukraine from the communists. When the Allies won the war, Bandera had been branded a bandit by the Russians upon whom his guerillas had inflicted serious damage. Because the Soviets were among the Allied victors, the U.S. also was supposed to consider Bandera a fugitive.

But Soviet concerns were not Skubik's. He had already clashed enough with the Red Army to want to avoid them. Bandera, on the other hand, was the kind of high-level source the CIC agent's background and languages enabled him to exploit, which was his job, and he took advantage of the opportunity. Bandera, he writes, had spies in the Soviet Union and told him that Patton had incurred Stalin's "wrath"—and thus had been marked for assassination—when he indicated his intentions to fight the Russians, first in Berlin, where he wanted to confront them but was not allowed by General Eisenhower, and then in Czechoslovakia where his armies, rebuffed from taking Berlin, had been sent instead at the end of the war. "His incursion into Czechoslovakia infuriated Marshall Stalin," Skubik wrote Bandera told him. "How dare [Patton] interfere with the Soviet geopolitical plans for a greater Soviet Union"—which included making Czechoslovakia a puppet buffer. But Eisenhower, unaware of the Russian objection, had at first given Patton "permission to take all of Czechoslovakia," adds Skubik. It was a done deal and Patton was looking forward to it. "On May 4, 1945, Patton's Third Army along with the Fifth Corps under General [Courtney] Hodges rapidly advanced against the Germans and were at the approaches to Prague where they met the Soviet forces [coming from the East]." Patton, with the

largest army he had ever commanded—a virtual juggernaut—
"was fully prepared to push the Soviet troops out of Czechoslovakia. A few skirmishes ensued in which some Soviet troops were
killed or wounded." But then, writes Skubik, "Eisenhower received a phone call from the Soviet chief of staff, General Alexei
Antonov, telling [him] to stop Patton or else." Eisenhower "feared
the consequences" and halted Patton, who was "furious."[19]

The fact that a Russian general, ally or not, could stop Patton
is quizzical enough. But confirming Skubik's account, Ladislas
Farago writes[20] that General Antonov warned Eisenhower that
any move on Prague could result in a "possible confusion of
forces"—in other words, fighting between the two armies. Eisenhower, friendly to his Russian allies at that point—as was Washington in general—was loath to have such an occurrence.
Nevertheless, Bryan J. Dickerson, former editor of *Cold War
Times* and a World War II historian, confirms that, as Skubik
writes, end-of-war "clashes" between U.S. and Soviet troops did
occur.[21] "In the town of Rokycany [Czechoslovakia], Carmine
Caiazzo and other soldiers of the 9th Infantry Regiment had several hostile incidents with nearby Soviet troops." In fact, adds
Dickerson in his source notes, "Quite a few American veterans
told me of hostile confrontations with Soviet troops, particularly
in the first few days after the German surrender." So the two sides
had already come to blows, giving further credence to Skubik's intelligence that the Soviets, especially Stalin, were mad at Patton
and wanted to eliminate him. And if not for the intention and
clashes in Czechoslovakia, Stalin, at this time, had other reasons
to want Patton dead.

★ ★ ★

On May 7, 1945, still fuming over what he considered the sell-outs to the Russians of Berlin and Prague, Patton was hosting Robert Patterson, Undersecretary of War, soon to be elevated to Secretary of War, who had come to Germany from Washington. Newly installed President Harry Truman, and the administration he inherited at Roosevelt's death, envisioned good relations with the communists, who his administration—basically still Roosevelt's—naively believed had noble intentions. Patterson had brought the pro-Soviet attitude with him but Patton was not buying it. His inherent anti-communism and experience of the Russians in the war had caused him to regard them as little more than barbarians. ("Mongolians," was the phrase he liked to use.*) That night, according to Patton aide Major Alexander C. Stiller, who was present, he let his feelings be known to Patterson in the following conversation:[22]

> **Patton:** "Let's keep our boots polished, bayonets sharpened, and present a picture of force and strength to these people [the Russians]."

> **Patterson:** "Oh George, you have been so close to this thing so long, you have lost sight of the big picture."

> **Patton:** "Mr. Secretary, it is your privilege to say, 'Oh, George,' if you wish, but for God's sakes listen to what I am trying to tell you."

> **Patterson:** "What would you have us do, George?"

---

*Used often in his diary entries and his personal correspondence.

Patton: "I would have you keep [the American] armies intact...tell [the Russians] where their border is, and give them a limited time to get back across. Warn them that if they fail to do so, we will push them back across it."

Patterson: "You don't realize the strength of these people."

Patton: "Yes, I have seen them....Their supply system is inadequate to maintain them in a serious action such as I could put to them. They have chickens in their coops and cattle on the hoof—that's their supply system. They could probably maintain themselves in the type of fighting I could give them for five days. After that it would make no difference how many million men they have, and if you wanted Moscow, I could give it to you....Let's not give them time to build up their supplies. If we do, then...we have had a victory over the Germans [but] we have failed in the liberation of Europe; we have lost the war....We must either finish the job now— while we are here and ready—or later under less favorable circumstances."

Patton was flat-out calling for war with the Soviets.

Farago says the Harvard-educated Patterson, one of Roosevelt's wartime "Wise men"*advisors who would soon be promoted to Truman's secretary of war, was "embarrassed" by Patton's rant. It was definitely not the official Washington view, and was disturbingly threatening. Patton, at that moment, controlling a vast, victorious army, was as powerful a man as there was on the planet. His enemies might have wondered what would happen if he acted

---

*As they were dubbed by an adoring press.

on those views. It was known that Patton was sympathetic to Soviet displaced persons, mostly POWs at this stage, who resisted returning to Russia even though America had promised Stalin they would be sent back to their countries of origin. These included Ukrainians, Latvians, and Byelorussians who had fought the Red Army, either as Nazis or partisan nationalists, and knew repatriation meant certain death or slavery. Stalin was out for revenge, as well as to quell any resistance. There were even rumors that Patton was harboring German SS units that had surrendered to him for possible later use against the Soviets—rumors, as often rumors are, based in fact. Undoubtedly his inflammatory remarks to Patterson were relayed up the chain of command—to Eisenhower at Allied headquarters, and on up to the administrations in Washington and London, which basically would have had the same reaction as Patterson.

And from there, could his remarks have reached the ears of the Soviet Union?

Most likely. Not only were the Soviets favored allies and therefore privy to such information, especially since Washington was intent on proving its sincerity to them, but they also had the largest and best spy network in the world—one much more infiltrated into the British and American governments than was, and still today is, generally known. Stalin, because of his spies, often was informed of vital American secrets before even top level U.S. officials were— a fact that was just becoming evident at that time to very few.* But even if they were not advised of Patton's specific statements to Patterson, they and the world were already certainly aware of his

---

*America was beginning to break Soviet codes and was getting hints at just how extensive Soviet spying was. The super-secret code-breaking operation was named "Venona," with which I will be dealing later.

growing anti-Soviet sentiment—something that would have also angered Stalin, who tolerated no dissent.

In late April of 1944, for instance, Patton had been embroiled in yet another war-time controversy when American newspapers in sympathy with the pro-Soviet Left—which most at that time were—had falsely reported that he had failed in a public speech to mention "our brave Russian allies" as one of the countries, along with America and Britain, that would rule the post-war world. In fact, Patton *had* included Russia in the speech—the precise utterance, according to his diary, being "...it is the evident destiny of the British and Americans, and, of course, the Russians, to rule the world...."[23] But the supposed omission, in a short greeting to the ladies of Knutsford, England, opening a coffee house for American G.I.s, quickly resulted in editorialists and legislators calling for Patton's dismissal and Eisenhower, acutely attuned to their cries, warning Patton, his best fighting general, that one more public relations slip-up would cost him his job.[24]

And had there still been any doubt in Moscow about his ill feelings toward them, Patton had emphatically restated it on May 11, 1945, at a gathering of Allied hierarchy in Paris celebrating the German surrender which had occurred just three days before. As reported by Patton's nephew, Fred Ayer, Jr.,[25] the celebration was being held in a suite at the Hotel Majestic overlooking the Arc de Triomphe. Among the guests were Ayer, a special agent with the FBI in charge of European operations, his famous uncle, a group of other generals, their aides, diplomats, and high-level civilian guests, including "some sort of Presidential Assistant from the White House" whose "face and name, I am glad to say, have vanished from my memory."

Patton, however, was not celebrating.

Pointing a cigar "like a weapon" at his host—no less a partisan than Eisenhower deputy, Major General Everett Hughes—Patton burst out,

> It's all a God-damned shame.... Day after day, some poor bloody Czech, or Austrian, or Hungarian, even German officers come into my headquarters. I almost have to keep them from going down on their knees to me. With tears in their eyes they say, "In the name of God, general, come with your army the rest of the way into our country. Give us a chance to set up our own governments. Give us this last chance to live before it's too late, before the Russians make us slaves forever."
>
> That's what they tell me, and every damned one of them has offered to fight under my flag and bring their men with them. Hell, a German general offered his entire air force, the Third, to fight the Russians if necessary.... By God, I would like to take them up on it. I'll feel like a traitor if I don't.

At that point, writes Ayer, an "uneasy" feeling swept the room.

Patton disregarded it.

"These people are right. They won't have a chance. We've signed away their lives. By God, we ought to tear up those damned fool agreements [with the Soviets] and march right through to the eastern borders...."

Ayer, worried for his uncle, blurted out, "Uncle George, for God's sake, you can't talk that way here."

Patton shot back coldly,

> Yes I can. I'll talk any damned way I want. I know what we ought to do. We promised these people freedom. It would be

worse than dishonorable not to see that they have it. This might mean war with the Russians, of course; but what of it? They have no air force any more, their gas and munitions supplies are low. I've seen their miserable supply trains...I'll tell you this...the Third Army alone...could lick what's left of the Russians in six weeks....Mark my words....Some day we'll have to fight them....

If Patton's remarks to Patterson had been exploratory, this was a declaration.

Patton was prescient—and the spying Russians knew it.

But little, if any, of this was known to Skubik, although Bandera, he writes, did tell him that Patton was courting Soviet dissidents, like his Ukrainians, to possibly fight the Russians. "This contact [with the Ukrainian nationalists] was clear evidence to Stalin that Patton intended to start a war against the Soviets immediately rather than wait,"[26] wrote Skubik. But back then, what mainly was on his mind as he left Bandera that May 16, 1945 day was that he had gotten important intelligence concerning General Patton's safety, and it had come from a source, regardless of his past and politics, who should know—a renegade leader who had spies in the NKVD. Skubik, having served in the Third Army, had high regard for Patton. In order to get the information to higher-ups as quickly as possible, he decided to bypass the slower report or memo-writing route and go directly to CIC headquarters. His superior there, First Lieutenant William L. Gillespie, apparently sufficiently impressed, "suggested that I report this information to Colonel MacIntosh of the OSS."

But there the urgency stopped.

At OSS offices—location and date unspecified—he writes he was received by a "Major Stone" who referred him to General Donovan, who records confirm was in Germany at the time.*[27] Donovan, according to Skubik, was not impressed with the information or, apparently, with Skubik. In fact, he was perturbed—an odd reaction since Skubik was only doing his job, reporting what needed to be reported, and the two had never met before. "He told me that Bandera was on the list to be arrested. That [Bandera's intelligence] about Patton was a provocation." He wanted Skubik to arrest Bandera which "I couldn't do without killing twenty or more of his body guards."[28] This angered Donovan. Emerging from the meeting confused and angry himself, Skubik writes that Major Stone "thanked me and said, 'Stay away from Bandera. He's bad news.'... I was disappointed with my first visit to OSS."[29]

But several weeks later—towards the end of May, he writes—he got the same intelligence again—and again from a credible source—another of the Ukrainians he was detailed to interrogate.

The source was Professor Roman Smal-Stocki, a middle-aged Ukrainian scholar, diplomat and nationalist—very respected amongst academics for his ideas and writings. Skubik had him on an NKVD list of former Soviets the Russians wanted and was interviewing him at the Offenbach refugee center, near Frankfurt. A philologist who spoke more than a dozen languages and whose father had been a Ukrainian nationalist leader, Smal-Stocki, at a mere twenty-nine years of age, had been Ukraine's ambassador to England during the country's brief independence during WWI.

---

*As Cave-Brown writes in *The Last Hero*, (pages 728 and 735), "nobody could be more elusive than Donovan." However a search of Donovan's own files at Carlisle Barracks shows that he left for Germany around May 14, 1945 and returned around May 20.

Skubik was impressed with him. "He was a true intellectual who chose his words most carefully. He asked me what I wanted from him. I told him that the U.S. Army was under orders to cooperate with the Soviet request to return East European citizens back to their native lands." That seemed to frighten the professor, wrote Skubik, who nonetheless pressed him for why the NKVD wanted him. Smal-Stocki responded, "Perhaps because . . . of my involvement with the Promethean League."

Skubik had never heard of the League. "He [Smal-Stocki] explained that after the newly independent nations of the old Russian Empire were reconquered by the communists [at the close of World War I] certain political, academic, military and intellectual leaders formed a secret society with twelve captive nations involved [those put under Soviet domination]. He [Smal-Stocki] was made president. He told me, 'We had the very best intelligence organization in all of Europe. . . . The Soviet NKVD tried to destroy us, the Nazis also. Even the British tried to put us out of business. But we survived because we had many superior minds working with us.'" (The group's purpose was to foment revolution in the ethnic territories, like Ukraine, according to literature about it.) Then he told Skubik, "My best intelligence tells me that the NKVD will soon attempt to kill General George Patton. Stalin wants him dead."

Skubik told Smal-Stocki he had already heard this from Bandera but "American intelligence leaders just don't believe the Ukrainians. They think the . . . Ukrainians want to destroy the relationship between the Soviet Union and the U.S." Smal-Stocki, who is dead now, but who would later teach at Milwaukee's Marquette University, replied, writes Skubik, "God help America."[30]

At approximately the same time Skubik was receiving these warnings, Patton survived two mysterious near disastrous "accidents" which, in hindsight, look very suspicious. The first occurred on April 20, 1945. Patton was visiting unit headquarters dispersed within his vast Third Army in Germany. He was doing so in a light observation plane, identified by his aide, General Gay, as an "L-5,"[31] and a "Cub" by Lieutenant Colonel Charles Codman,[32] who was in another of the little, two-seat, single-engine planes flying right behind Patton. As the planes were low and only several miles from landing at III Corps headquarters, Reidfeld, near Munich, General Patton's Cub was attacked by a much larger and faster aircraft—a fighter.

In *War as I Knew It*,[33] his posthumously published memoir, Patton recalls:

> Just before we got there, I noticed some tracers [bullets] coming by the right side of our plane, which, at that instant dove for the ground, very nearly colliding with [the attacking] plane which looked like a Spitfire [the vaunted British-made fighter which did so well in the Battle of Britain]. This plane made a second pass, again firing and missing." Patton tried to get a photo of the attacking fighter "but was so nervous I forgot to take the cover off the lens.... On the third pass, our attacker came in so fast and we were so close to the ground that he was unable to pull out of his dive and crashed. While Codman and I were engaged in hedgehopping to avoid this belligerent gentleman, four other planes were circling over us, but did not engage in the attack.

Four planes circling above sounds like a classic ambush—send one guy in while the others provide lookout and cover. Only the skill of Patton's pilot, whoever he was, saved the general. Where had the planes come from? Who was the attacking pilot? Who were in the other planes and what were they doing circling like lookouts? Shortly after they landed, a search party was sent out to find the attackers' wreckage.[34] Patton, most probably with the results of that search in hand, later wrote in his diary that the Spitfires "were probably a Polish unit flying for the RAF. Why they were out of their area, I don't know?"[35] General Gay wrote: "The results and far-reaching repercussions of this event are not known at this time. In the first place, some explanation will have to be made as to why the RAF had a squadron in this area; in the second place, it will be hard for any aviator to claim that he does not—or did not—recognize an American L-5 plane."[36]

Historians do not say much about this incident. Farago does not even mention the attack in *Last Days of Patton*, although he gives it a few lines in *Ordeal and Triumph*.[37] The incident is certainly mysterious and suspicious. A Polish unit flying for the Brits? Though Polish pilots had escaped the Nazi invasion of their homeland in 1939 and formed separate squadrons under Polish command within the Royal Air Force, an aviation researcher I contacted in Poland wrote me that the only Polish pilots he could find flying in Germany at that time were in the "Polish Wing 131 (including Squadrons 302,308,317)" stationed at Nordhorn, on the north German coast, and so, because of the distance, it was "impossible that Polish Spitfire was trying to shoot down Patton." In addition, he wrote, official archives he searched showed that the Polish Air Force lost no planes or pilots on April 20, 1945.[38] On the other hand, the Russians by then had overrun Poland and the Poles under them were doing Soviet bidding. The Russians, too, had been given Spitfires by the British.[39] If the Spitfire that day *was* on an assassination mission, the Soviets certainly would not have sent a clearly identifiable Russian aircraft. Not only would that have been stupid, but their assassination style in countries outside their borders was to use locals under Russian direction.[40]

While there were no official reports about this attack that I could find in official U.S. archives—suggesting the incident had been buried—some of the scant mentioning of it I did find, like in Codman's *Drive*, indicate that a story went out that the Polish pilot was inexperienced and had made a mistake—a perfect cover for what really might have transpired. Even so, if, as Codman speculates, the pilot *had* made a mistake and had just wanted to shoot down a German plane, why had not he attacked Codman's plane as well?

Two weeks later, on May 3, Patton was riding shotgun in an open, traveling jeep somewhere in Occupied territory[41] when he was almost decapitated by a farmer's wagon with some sort of scythe-like implement dangerously protruding from it. "We were very nearly killed by a bull-cart, which came [at us] out of a side street so that the pole missed us only by about an inch," wrote Patton in his diary. But rather than condemn or question whoever was at fault, he concluded: "The American soldier is absolutely incapable of enforcing the rule that civilians stay off the roads during active operations. His goodness of heart is a credit to him, but I am sure it has cost us many casualties. In war, time is vital, and bull-carts cause waste of time and therefore death."[42]

Without elaborating, Skubik says that Patton was informed by CIC that he was on an NKVD hit list. "He didn't seem to worry about the threat. He enjoyed the fact that Stalin wanted to kill him." But "the two suspicious [near-death] events made a believer out of Patton."[43] I have not been able to find corroboration that he had been told of the threats by either Skubik or Bazata. But that does not mean he was not. He sought intelligence from many different sources. That was part of the reason he was so good on

the battlefield. He knew much about his enemies. And much of
the unofficial intelligence he got was verbal, not written. Skubik
indicates that gathering intelligence was one of the reasons Patton met with Eastern Europeans, several of whom are mentioned
in his diaries. Interestingly, although writers have only associated
it with Nazi assassination threats, most Patton biographers detail
how, at about this time, he became fatalistic, often talking about
his impending death. His bodyguard was upped and he began
sleeping with ready weapons at his side. Could the Skubik or
Bazata warnings have played a part in that? It has always been
puzzling that when Patton went home for the last time—for a
month in June of 1945—even though he received a hero's welcome from the American people and enjoyed himself immensely,
he told family members it would be the last time they would see
him. "My luck has all run out," he steadfastly maintained over
their protestations. "I don't know how it is going to happen. But
I'm going to die over there."[44]

This was *after* the war in Europe was over—not when he was
returning to face more combat.

How could he be so sure?

That summer, sometime after July 1 when Skubik, his two CIC
partners Ralph E. May and Harry B. Toombs, had been forced to
move their headquarters from Zwickau to Schluechtern by the occupying Russians, Skubik got a third warning—again from a
Ukrainian. General Pavlo Shandruk was a distinguished Ukrainian soldier. His memoir, *Arms of Valor*,[45] reads like a Russian epic,
full of the turmoil, fighting, and brutality that raged over Europe
in the first half of the twentieth century. An officer of the Imperial
Tsar's army in World War I, Shandruk, because of his abilities and
allegiances, was variously courted and then hunted by both sides
during the Bolshevik Revolution, eventually landing in Poland

where he joined the Polish army and fought against the invading Germans in 1939. Injured and captured by the Nazis, he managed, probably because of his stature, to get out of prison and live incognito until the Germans, desperate for help in 1944, changed their policies of oppression toward Slavs and began enticing them to fight against the encroaching Red Army—a policy nationalistic Ukrainians were quick to entertain. Several Ukrainian armies were raised. On March 17, 1945, Shandruk was given command of one of them, the First Division of the Ukrainian National Army. But he was not a Nazi, and with the Germans on the run by then, he had his soldiers swear allegiance to Ukraine and to fight communism, and after some brief, badly supplied actions for the Germans, surrendered to the Allies, hoping to fight the Russians for the victors. But at that point, it was not to be. Thus Shandruk, like Bandera and Smal-Stocki, was either in some kind of displaced persons capacity or POW status trying to avoid repatriation when Skubik interviewed him:

"He was very diplomatic and had a fine political sense....His knowledge of the history of Germany, of the United States and especially of the Russian Empire came through as we spoke. He told me that he was concerned about America becoming too much involved with the Soviet Union....He said that General Eisenhower should be wary of tricks played by Stalin through [Marshall] Zhukov [who had become friends with Eisenhower]. Then he said, 'Please tell General Patton to be on guard. He is at the top of the NKVD list to be killed.' I promised to try and warn General Patton."[46]

In *Arms of Valor*, Shandruk says he first met Skubik at the CIC office in Hoechst and that the meeting was amicable.[47] But that must have been earlier because Skubik writes that the interview he had with Shandruk involving the Patton warning was conducted at Regensburg, a German city closer to Munich than

Hoechst. Munich was where many exiled Ukrainians, like Bandera, were gathering in secrecy after the war. Regensburg appears to have been the site of a regional CIC headquarters—one of those nearest the Soviet Zone. As he left the building where he and the general had met, Skubik writes, "I noticed two men across the street looking at me. I figured they were the general's people." But as it turned out, they were not. He eventually decided they were Soviet agents tailing Shandruk. "I should have confronted them but I wasn't spoiling for a fight."[48] He had already had several run-ins with the Russians. Not only were such confrontations dangerous, they had become a source of trouble for him from his own side.

Back in May, while his team was still in Zwickau, he was told by two former SS minions about five notebooks containing the names, destinations, even codes to be used, of over 1,000 escaping Nazis. The minions, a man and a woman, had been at the secret meeting where the books were compiled and were willing to show Skubik where they were. They had been buried in a wooded area near Pilsen, Czechoslovakia, and would be a prize for Nazi hunters. Skubik had decided to take the two east with him into the Pilsen area, which the Russians occupied, and find the books. This was before the official occupation zones had been set up and he did not expect any problem.

Nevertheless, armed with two pistols, he loaded a jeep with some hand grenades, "a grease gun with five clips," and an M-1 rifle and started out. In a village near Pilsen, anticipating that he would need help, he got a Czech colonel to follow him with a truckload of German POWs to help with the labor. The two SS informers found the wooded site easily but were not sure precisely where the box containing the books was buried. But the POWS, systematically digging with their shovels, found the notebooks within three hours. Hoping to return to Zwickau before dark, he decided to take a different, shorter route back.

Mistake.

The further he drove the more Russians he saw. Soon he was passing manned checkpoints. At first the guards waved him on. But at the fourth barrier he was stopped, taken to a headquarters, and questioned by a Russian major who wanted to know what he was doing there. Concealing his real mission, he said his informers—now afraid they were going to be given to the Russians—were two Nazi prisoners he was transporting. The major was skeptical and made him go back to the jeep and wait with the two while he called Prague. When he returned, he said they would have to go to Prague. The commanding general there wanted to talk with them. "He assured me that I could keep my guns and take the prisoners with me. Not to worry. Well I was not worried. I was scared."

For the trip, the Russians sandwiched the jeep between two trucks. Each had soldiers in it armed with machine guns. "I wasn't a prisoner but I was not free to leave." He figured the worst was coming and as the convoy proceeded along winding mountain roads he thought hard how he could escape. He noticed that if he slowed down, the truck behind would slow enough to keep distance between them, but the truck ahead would continue at a steady pace. He also noticed that when they went around steep curves, the truck ahead would disappear. "I couldn't see [it], so they couldn't see me either." On very sharp curves, both trucks disappeared.

That would be his escape!

He began alternately slowing and then speeding up and tailgating, increasing the separation between both trucks. Eventually, he estimated, there was about 250 feet either way between the jeep and the trucks whose occupants did not seem to notice or care. At the next sharp curve, at precisely the instant the two larger vehicles left his view, he bolted. "I veered sharply to the left and jumped the jeep into the air onto the field and toward the woods. It wasn't fun. It was deadly serious." Behind him, the two SS informers saw soldiers from the rear truck leap out and start shooting. "But by that time I was in the woods and out of range. I sped hell bent toward the American territory."

On the way back they had to bust through at least one check point, his two passengers hugging the floorboards. "I gunned the jeep to its maximum speed and crashed through the wooden rail. The stunned Russian guards shouted at me....I'd expected the guards to fire...but they didn't"—probably because they had been surprised. He and his two passengers "laughed and cheered and even gave an Indian yell....It was touch and go but we made it."[49]

Back in Zwickau, he turned in the books to Lieutenant Gillespie and "slept well that night." The next day, however, he got a call from a "Colonel Leo Rodin," the superior to whom Gillespie had forwarded the notebooks. Rodin, presumably a CIC officer but never identified specifically as such, had an office in Bad Nauheim, where Patton would soon be headquartered. He wanted Skubik to come right over. Once Skubik was there, Rodin told him he was lucky to have escaped. "You better stay clear of the Russians. They know who you are and where to find you." It was as if he had done something wrong. And why did they know so much about him? He had lied to the Russian major. (Was it because of the intelligence he had been reporting about Patton? Had someone been giving the Russians information?) But then Rodin had indicated the value of what he had done by suggesting he kill the two informers. Rodin said "they might tell someone about our having the books which could alert the escaping Nazis and they could change names and locations."

Skubik balked. "I told him I wasn't going to murder anyone." He expressed an affinity for the two informers because they had risked their lives to help him find the notebooks. The colonel apparently changed the subject. He wanted to know "about my Polish connections. He knew that I had met Jan Karksi, a courier for the Polish underground who made frequent trips to London. He asked about my meeting with Mikolyczyk, the Minister of Poland. I told him that I had only spoken briefly with the man and had nothing to report." Rodin was also interested in his knowledge of a "Polish General Anders" and his soldiers. It was all very strange. Why the Poles? Why the worry about what the Russians thought? At one point, he writes, "Rodin was interrogating me for information which he might use in his work with OSS General Donovan."[50] At another, he wonders if Rodin was working for the Russians. If that were the case, he knew he was in trouble. Not only because of his Patton warnings, but because he had other run-ins with the Soviets as well.

Prior to the formal Soviet occupation, he had to confront a surly Russian colonel who, with a truck and squad of men, was trying to harass the non-communist German mayor of Zwickau that Skubik had appointed and loot the town's food supply. Arguing with the colonel, Skubik had charged that the Soviets were acting like Nazis. "You want to have your way by using threats and gun power against decent people." Furious, the Russians had exited but complained to American authorities.[51]

He had also, somewhat innocently, gotten involved in the very touchy subject of repatriation with the Soviets. Stalin wanted every displaced person and POW who had formerly lived in the Soviet Union sent back to the motherland, regardless of that person's wishes. In a chance meeting in Frankfurt, Skubik introduced a Ukrainian prelate, the Reverend Stephen Reshytylo, whom he was interviewing, to General Eisenhower who happened to be walking by and had spoken to him. Reshytylo, in Frankfurt to try to halt the deportation of his Ukrainian flock, had used the opportunity to speak to Eisenhower who became sympathetic—so much so that he sent the prelate to pertinent policy makers. As Skubik's obituary in the *Ukrainian Weekly* states, "That meeting led Gen. Eisenhower and the U.S. State Department to reverse U.S. policy on Soviet refugees, thus saving the lives of countless thousands facing death in Soviet labor camps."[52]

In addition, just before his team had left Zwickau, Skubik had arrested one of the Soviet's chief German operatives, the pro-Russian Walter Ulbricht. Ulbricht, who would later head communist East Germany and become noted for building the Berlin Wall in order to prevent escapes to the West, was an indicted murderer, Stalinist, and hard line communist organizer who had been rushed into Germany with the Red Army at the war's end to set up puppet governments throughout the occupied territories. A carpenter and militant socialist, he helped organize the German communist Party in 1919 and served as a communist delegate in the German parliament. In 1931, Ulbricht had ordered, under Soviet guidance, the murder by locals of two German policemen in Berlin.[53] When Hitler had come to power in 1933 and a warrant for Ulbricht's arrest in the murders was issued, he fled to Moscow where he stayed working as a henchman for Stalin, until being dispatched back to Germany with Russian troops in April 1945. Apparently, one of the early cities he entered was Zwickau because toward the end of their stay there, Skubik writes, he was confronted with Ulbricht trying to kick patients out of the Zwickau hospital so he could set up a headquarters there. He was also, with organizers, going to the

Zwikau prison, where CIC was housing its Nazi prisoners, and offering the Nazis freedom if they joined the communist party.

Skubik writes, "This made me furious. I went to the prison with GIs and kicked out the communist [organizers]." He then went to the hospital and arrested Ulbricht. But his actions were short lived. A few days later, the Yalta-agreed-upon Occupation Zones came into effect (July 1) and he and his team found themselves in a riot of chaos trying to get out of Zwickau before the Russians arrived. Many in the city who had helped CIC, and in other ways felt they would be persecuted by the arriving Soviets, begged to go with the team. They agreed and organized a mass exodus of trains and cars carrying all manner of goods and people to the newly created American Zone.

And they took Ulbricht with them.

"I suppose the worst thing I did to the Soviets, up to that time, was to take arrested communist leader Ulbricht with me." He and Harry Toombs had shackled the German and put him in their jeep. On the way, Toombs wanted to scare Ulbricht. Skubik writes he did not like the idea. For one thing, there was not enough time. They had to get to the American Zone. But Toombs persisted. "I want to show this son-of-a-bitchin' communist what fear means, I want to give him some of his own medicine," he quotes Toombs as arguing. Skubik reluctantly stopped and Toombs took Ulbricht into the woods where he played a kind of Russian Roulette with him. Feigning bullets in the pistol, he put the barrel to Ulbricht's head and pulled the trigger. After five pulls, Ulbricht collapsed. Satisfied, Toombs walked him back to the jeep and they continued.

But Skubik had been right. The time wasted had allowed two Russian trucks full of soldiers to catch up. They were led by a Russian colonel. "I spoke to him in Russian and told him that Ulbricht was our prisoner for violating our laws in Zwickau. He had his soldiers point their guns at us. He said 'Now he belongs to us.' I began a meek protest but a look at the guns convinced me to accept the Russian colonel's point."

They released their prisoner. He concludes, "I later found out that Ulbricht was the head of the Russian NKVD operating in Germany and was one of "Wild Bill" Donovan's recruits [apparently for spying on the Nazis]. No wonder my name was mud with the OSS General."[54]

And there were more reasons to fear trouble from U.S. and Soviet authorities.

Working counterintelligence, he had arrested two Russian spies with U.S. codes in their possession. It was a good catch in the undeclared "border wars" that were heightening between the Soviets and U.S. agents. But after turning the spies in, he learned that they had been released by "our intelligence officer" (not otherwise described). He went to Gillespie and complained. Exact reasons why are not given but Skubik and Gillespie ended up in the office of Colonel Rodin, who defiantly told them that actually it had been his orders that had caused the two spies to be released. Skubik was confused. Clearly, the two were enemies of the U.S. "I asked why? He said he had his reasons [and] I didn't need to know."

Skubik, if it is to be assumed that Rodin was CIC, was outranked. There was nothing he could do. But a short time later, he writes, he caught the same two again stealing secrets. Again they were released. "I got mad." He stormed into the office of his immediate superior, Gillespie, and underlined that "the information these spies had on them could be very useful to the Soviet military. It compromised our codes."

Gillespie's reaction, not explained further, was to send him back to the OSS.

At first it seemed he would get a better reception than he had before. He saw Major Stone who was "very appreciative" and sent him in again to talk to General Donovan. "That was a big mistake." Donovan again brought up the Patton warnings, saying they were just a provocation, and this time *ordered* Skubik to arrest Bandera. Skubik reiterated that there was no way he could do so with Bandera's twenty bodyguards. And anyway, because Skubik was a CIC agent, he was not subject to Donovan's orders. "The general understood...even he had no authority over me." And when he brought up the two Russian spies, he writes Donovan got madder. He said "it was my duty to do what Colonel Rodin said." This seemed proof to him that Rodin and Donovan were working together. Skubik countered that his duty was "to protect secret information." At that point, Donovan accused him of being a Ukrainian spy working for Bandera, a charge Skubik vigorously denied—and continued to deny his entire life. He spoke Ukrainian. That was why he was talking to Bandera. He was just doing his job. He decided, for whatever reason, Donovan was out to get him. "That incident with the Russian spies, the Patton rumor, and my involvement with the refugee business was building up a storm for me."[55]

CHAPTER EIGHT

★ ★ ★ ★

STRANGE BEDFELLOWS

Why would Bill Donovan be so hostile to Skubik and the Ukrainian nationalists, many of whom would eventually become operatives for the CIA?

Why would he simply dismiss reports of a possible assassination attempt on the highest ranking American general in Europe?

Such intelligence was the kind he and the OSS were supposed to uncover. Even if he thought it was a ruse, he should have interrogated Skubik and tried to find out all he could rather than being dismissive, hostile, and antagonistic which certainly complicated any attempts to get to the truth of the matter. Who, in those days, could be so sure that the reports from the Ukrainians, as connected as they were to the Soviets, were unquestionably bogus?

Donovan's and Rodin's actions are hard to understand; unless something else was going on—something hidden, as is often the case in the clandestine world.

It is little known today, except amongst scholars and surviving OSS agents, that midway in World War II Donovan had forged a top secret relationship with the communist NKVD, the OSS's Soviet counterpart. It was a logical and bold move by the risk-taking, determined-to-succeed-at-all-costs Donovan. The USSR, after its shocking alliance with Hitler had been shattered by an unexpected Nazi invasion in 1941, was suddenly, because of the invasion, an ally with the West in the fight against Germany and had a much better fix on the Nazis at that point than the fledgling OSS did. It was older and more experienced than the OSS, (with a lineage some traced back to the Tsars of previous centuries). Russia was also physically closer to Germany than the U.S. and thus its agents had an easier job penetrating enemy territory than the OSS.

The first World War II contact with the USSR by a U.S. leader regarding help in spying that I could find was made not by the OSS, which was just being formed, but by New Deal Secretary of the Treasury Henry Morgenthau, Jr., longtime friend, Hyde Park neighbor, and confidant of President Roosevelt. The Roosevelt administration had been the first U.S. administration to diplomatically recognize communist Russia as a legitimate government. The prior Republican Hoover administration had vigorously opposed such recognition. But the stock market crash and ensuing Great Depression of the 1930s had softened the anti-communist attitude of many Americans—especially amongst Democrats where socialism made gains. Roosevelt looked favorably on the communist nation, especially after the Nazis turned on their Soviet ally which, with Britain, left the two European nations leading the fight against Germany. Roosevelt felt rightly that the Soviet Union, in its fight against the Nazi invader, would be one of the keys in defeating the Germans.

In July 1941, as the U.S. became increasingly engaged in supplying the USSR with weapons and other lend-lease materials, Morganthau, playing on the Democrats' built-up goodwill, asked

Soviet Ambassador to the U.S. Konstantin Umansky if his government's spy agencies would provide Roosevelt and him with the identities of head German agents operating in America. The FBI was not doing the job, Allen Weinstein and Alexander Vassiliev quote Morganthau as telling the ambassador in *The Haunted Wood,* an acclaimed book on Soviet espionage in the wartime U.S. But the NKVD refused, one reason probably being, the two authors speculate, that the communists already had a strong spy apparatus in the U.S. and were working on infiltrating the new American intelligence organization which would soon become the OSS.[1] Presumably they did not want to draw undue attention to their covert activities.

Perhaps, then, it was from Morganthau that Donovan first got the idea of approaching the NKVD. Despite different political affiliations (Donovan was a Republican; Morganthau a staunch Democrat), the two men, both New Yorkers, had a working relationship that would grow throughout the war and beyond. In fact, as Donovan was negotiating with Roosevelt to take the job as the nation's first major intelligence chief, Morganthau was courting Donovan to run the New York state war bond drive, an administrative position, notes Joseph Persico in *Roosevelt's Secret War,* that certainly did not offer the prestige, adventure, or potential personal power that heading America's new intelligence agency would.[2] Persico reports that Donovan demanded of Roosevelt three basic requirements before accepting the more exciting post, which, of course, he preferred. First, he would report only to Roosevelt. Second, he would have access to Roosevelt's secret, off-the-books funds in order to pay for clandestine projects. Finally, all government agencies would be instructed to give him whatever support he requested—no questions asked. With Roosevelt's agreement in the summer of 1941, America's first major spy chief was crowned, and, by 1943, Donovan had agents and a far-flung network of secret missions established throughout the war-torn world.

Early on he realized that the Soviets, if inclined, could aid his intelligence operations. Positioned between Europe and Asia, the Soviets had good spy networks throughout Germany, Eastern Europe, and China. The Japan network was especially attractive. The U.S., surprised by the attack on Pearl Harbor, had few, if any, spies there. Russia's help could make a big difference. According to OSS files,[3] Armand Hammer, the American industrialist who traveled extensively in the Soviet Union (and who some say was a spy for the Soviets)[4] had sent Donovan his "book on my experiences in Russia" and offered his services as a consultant.[5] Donovan had private discussions with a Soviet naval attaché in Washington and actually contacted members of the communist Party, USA (CPUSA) to try to learn about Axis agents in the U.S.[6] U.S. civilians working in various occupations in the USSR were asked to become secret OSS operatives. But ultimately the idea of covert U.S. spies, military or civilian, operating on Soviet soil was discouraged. Not only was Roosevelt intent on showing good intentions to the USSR, and thus frowned on spying against them,[7] but "Russia has reputedly the best counter-espionage system in the world," says a January 23, 1943, OSS memo. "Any undercover representative would probably be disclosed upon arrival."[8] The U.S. did not want to get caught with its hand in the cookie jar.

By fall 1943, after considerable exploration of the matter, and despite warnings from some in OSS that the Soviets were just waiting for Allied victory to "let loose a communist revolution,"[9] Donovan, who is reported to have said, "I'd put Stalin on the OSS payroll if I thought it would help defeat Hitler,"[10] had decided the possible gains of collaboration with the NKVD outweighed the risk. And in late December, following the unfortunate loss of an envoy he was sending to Moscow who might have paved the way,* and with diplomatic channels widening with a new military liaison mission, headed by Major General John R. Deane, being established in Moscow, he decided to fly to Russia himself and plead his case in person. According to several sources, including an official memorandum[11] of the event published in John Mendelsohn's rare book, *The OSS-NKVD Relationship 1943-1945,* Donovan and U.S. Ambassador Averell Harriman were taken by Soviet Foreign Minister Vyacheslav Molotov to NKVD headquarters on Dzerzhinsky Street in Moscow right after Christmas, December 27, 1943. There, in a grim, forbidding, czarist-built structure housing the infamous Lubyanka prison, the two Americans, accompanied by Charles Bohlen of the U.S. embassy's staff, were met by NKVD chief, Lieutenant General Pavel Fitin, and a man Fitin introduced as "Colonel Aleksandr P. Ossipov," chief of the Soviets' "subversive activities in Enemy Countries." In actuality, the companion was Gaik Ovakimyan, a very productive NKVD spy of Armenian heritage who, according to researchers with access to NKVD files decades later, had been arrested and jailed as a Soviet spy in New York in early 1941. However, after Germany's surprise invasion of Russia that summer, he had been ordered released by President Roosevelt—apparently a gesture of goodwill—and deported back to the USSR where he had been rewarded for his trouble by being put in charge of all NKVD spying in North America, including the U.S.[12]

Thus the first meeting of Donovan and the NKVD he was courting began with a deception by the Soviets. But Donovan, all

---

*Sydney Weinberg was to have been an OSS representative in Moscow but was killed when a convoy on which he sailed was attacked off Norway and sunk.

accounts agree, was unaware. In fact, he was quite pleased with the relative ease with which matters appeared to him to be unfolding and began his pitch, according to the meeting memorandum, by telling the two Soviet spy masters all about the OSS. "General Donovan...outlined the organization, aims, scope of operations, etc...giving details of specific types of operations, means of communication, organization of groups within enemy countries...."[13] However, he need not have done so, for by this time the NKVD already had in place covert agents inside the OSS sending back all manner of U.S. secrets. The disguised Ovakimyan had been the Soviet agent overseeing the early OSS penetrations, which was probably the reason Fitin brought him to the meeting. The West now knows all this to be true largely because of a top secret U.S. code-breaking operation recently declassified (1995). During the war, the army's Signal Intelligence Agency, forerunner of today's National Security Agency, broke Russian codes under a project codenamed "Venona."[14] Because the project was so secret, few, even today, outside of World War II and Cold War historians are familiar with it. But decrypted Venona messages confirm the OSS penetration. Using the decrypts, and access to NKVD and recently released FBI files and Russian memoirs, researchers like *The Haunted Wood*'s Weinstein and Vassiliev have put together lists of OSS agents who spied for the Russians. *The Mitrokhin Archive*, co-authored with former KGB archivist Vasili Mitrokhin, who for years copied and secreted away Russian intelligence files, says the number of "Soviet agents at OSS headquarters [was] probably well into double figures,"[15] possibly as many as forty. Outside Washington, in various OSS installations throughout the world, the number was at least twelve.[16] The spies included secretaries, researchers, managers, economists, operatives in the field, even heads of major departments like Maurice Halperin who ran OSS's

Latin America Division, and Franz Neumann, head of the German section, especially crucial in a war against the Nazis. Halperin's NKVD codename was "Hare"; Neumann's was "Ruff." [17]

Perhaps most important among these NKVD spies within the OSS was Duncan Lee, a young former member of Donovan's New York law firm and one of the director's trusted personal aides. He had access to practically everything Donovan did. Lee was a descendant of the famous Confederate general, Robert E. Lee, as well as a graduate of Yale University and a Rhodes Scholar at Oxford, England. He was a favorite of Donovan's and joined OSS in 1942 at Donovan's behest. While at Oxford he met his wife, said Betty McIntosh, a former OSS agent who knew him well. "They went to Moscow as students and then came back," she said, explaining that Lee and his wife were good friends with her and her husband. "I think that's where he became a communist. He was a ladies' man. I know one girl who killed herself because of him. I never quite trusted the guy." Elizabeth Bentley, another American NKVD spy who went to the FBI shortly after the war and began telling them about numerous Soviet spies within the American government, said Lee, who was in her charge, was a nervous spy—he was always worried he would be caught—but a valuable one.[18] For instance, he forwarded to the Russians what amounted to advance word of the approximate date of the D-Day landings, perhaps the most important single tactical operation in the entire war. Had the information gotten into German hands, the invasion most probably would have been defeated.[19] As a result of some of Lee's forwards to the communists on secret OSS missions using behind-Soviet-lines anti-communists, those same anti-communists were later hunted down and killed by the NKVD.[20] Bentley also told the FBI that Lee informed the Russians that "something very secret was going on at Oak Ridge," Tennessee, where, it later became known, American efforts to make enriched uranium for the Pacific war-ending atomic bomb project were taking place.[21]

The NKVD therefore was already well versed about the OSS. But Fitin and Ovakimyan acted ignorant as Donovan laid out the reasons the two intelligence agencies should collaborate. They could exchange important information, keep each other informed about matters special to each, cut down on duplicate missions and research, and warn each other of intentions to operate in one another's territories, thereby minimizing duplication of effort and the possibility of clashes. Donovan went all out trying to persuade his audience. He told them things only known at the highest echelons of his own government. At one point, Fitin, dubious that Donovan could really be offering such important secrets, questioned whether the OSS director had an ulterior motive for coming to Moscow. Donovan assured him he did not. He was sincere. He wanted cooperation opened between U.S. and Soviet intelligence, something that had never happened before. Fitin then seemed to test him, asking how the OSS got covert agents into enemy countries, what kind of training and equipment they received? Ovakimyan, who is described as saying little during the meeting, inquired about American plastic explosives. Donovan answered both as completely and truthfully as possible. He wanted the cooperation badly.

From the Soviet standpoint, the Russians stood to get even more than they would have from their embedded spies. For instance, they were interested in intelligence from European countries where, because of the war, they had fewer agents, such as France or Italy, where the OSS was strong. They considered vital any intelligence about Nazi peace feelers that did not include them. Stalin was paranoid about possible end-of-war collaboration between the U.S., Britain, and Germany. He feared that Germany, seeing the inevitable and preferring the U.S. to Moscow as rulers and captors, might try to jump sides. They wanted to know what contacts America was having with anti-Soviets, like the Ukrainians, who were of special concern to Stalin. He knew such dissident nationalists were a potential spear in his side. He was always looking to crush them. And they were interested in scientific and technological secrets of which Donovan seemed to have many. For instance, Donovan told them about a suitcase radio, smaller than anything yet used, which was making communication much easier and safer for OSS operatives in the field.

By the end of the meeting, the two sides had agreed that exchanges should begin quickly and be sent only between the two agencies and their designated representatives, not through normal diplomatic channels already existing between the two countries. They would keep the relationship to themselves and their own higher authorities, which meant the White House and Stalin. Representatives from each organization would be stationed in Washington and Moscow in order to facilitate the cooperation; in effect, reciprocal spies would be admitted to each other's vital lair. Lee later reported to his handler, Bentley, "Donovan was very pleased that he and Moscow agreed to exchange missions and information.... The Soviet government made an enormous impression on Donovan, and he is fascinated by it. He considers Stalin the most intelligent person among all [those] heading today's governments...."[22]

Donovan, mindful of the USSR's increasing stock in Washington as the Red Army began halting and pushing back their German invaders, obviously thought he had scored a major coup. And possibly he would have, had his intentions been only to milk the

Soviets for what he could get, and had the Soviets not been in near control of the venture by already having their spies in the OSS— and elsewhere in the American government—who, in effect, could verify what Donovan was giving them. Stalin, according to Persico,[23] was briefed personally on the plan and immediately, if not gleefully, okayed the project. He knew his intelligence service had the upper hand. But American opposition quickly materialized. Roosevelt, it appears, always fascinated with the cloak and dagger, was, at first, receptive. But the FBI's J. Edgar Hoover, realizing communist agents would be given free reign in America, was livid.

Donovan and Hoover went way back. Hoover had served under him when Donovan had been a federal prosecutor in President Herbert Hoover's (no relation) administration. They had clashed. He had not liked Donovan then and he certainly did not like him now. Hoover regarded Donovan's OSS as an upstart intruder on FBI territory. Although separate bailiwicks had been set up for both organizations—the FBI was given all domestic spy and enforcement duties; the OSS was to operate only in foreign countries—Donovan, Hoover knew, had taken liberties with that restriction and ordered projects on domestic soil. A break-in by OSS agents of the Spanish embassy in Washington was but one example.[24] Now he was proposing to let Russian agents come into the country and operate at will? Hoover, a dedicated anti-communist dating back to the teens and twenties, was determined to stop the liaison and won over Roosevelt by making the president realize the political implications in the coming election (1944) of his willingly granting communist spies sanctioned access to operate on U.S. soil. They were already secretly here, he told FDR. He was battling them. Now they would be given a passport? It would be handing the Republicans a winning issue. Voters would retaliate.

Roosevelt agreed, especially when some of his military advisors did not like the idea either.* The army and navy's individual intelligence services felt encroached upon by what they regarded as the unproven, amateurish OSS and no one but the enemy wanted more foreign spies in the homeland. Roosevelt wrote Donovan that "an exchange of O.S.S. missions between Moscow and Washington is not appropriate at the present time...."[25] But Donovan was not going to be denied. Some in the joint chiefs liked the idea of cooperating with the NKVD. Above all, they wanted the Russians to declare war against Japan and this seemed a way of possibly influencing that, if only, perhaps, as part of a larger tit for tat? He dropped the mission idea but quietly, with FDR's acquiescence, went ahead with establishing a relationship of mutual cooperation on his own. Moscow, in view of the fact they already had their people covertly ensconced in Washington anyway, did not have a problem with the mission exchange falling through. Thus, a covert alliance began between the OSS and NKVD, two rival intelligence services that were inherently in conflict. The communists, as all those opposed to the liaison stressed, were on record as vowing to overthrow the U.S. government.

Nevertheless, for the next year and a half at least, the collaboration between the two services grew, although all sources agree that the Soviets, holding the better cards, got the best of it. "Throughout the Second World War the NKVD knew vastly more about OSS than OSS knew about the NKVD," write the authors of *The Mitrokhin Archive*.[26] An anonymous CIA analyst reviewing "OSS-NKVD Liaison" documents called the cooperation an "ill balanced" exchange, with the OSS heaping important secret

---

*Like Chief of Staff, Admiral William D. Leahy.

information on the Soviets, including fresh field reports, targeting data, and captured German papers, and the Soviets in return providing, among other meager offerings, a forty-three-page "less comprehensive" paper on Bulgaria, a seventy-six-page listing of German industrial targets compiled from "casual" POW interrogations "rather than a directed intelligence effort," and "unenlightening" answers regarding sabotage operations.[27] There were other exchanges but the disparity continued. Bradley F. Smith, in *Sharing Secrets with Stalin*, says simply, "The Soviets certainly had any advantage that did occur...."[28] Regardless, Donovan, fighting an uphill battle, was unfailingly enthusiastic and nurtured the venture. For instance, while advising Fitin that forwarded NKVD documents about German industry were incomplete and "production figures appear to us to be excessive," he thanked Fitin vociferously and asked in an August 23, 1944 communication if they could get even closer by exchanging technicians. "I am sure that [closer] cooperation would result in mutual benefit," Donovan wrote, "and would make more effective our common efforts to defeat the enemy."[29]

And so it went—even when, in September 1944, a major conflict arose.

As explained in *Shadow Warriors*,[30] OSS had been operating in the Balkans mainly to help downed American flyers escape. When the Red Army entered the Balkans, pushing the occupying Germans back toward their homeland, the rescue efforts were less needed. But a few OSS units stayed on primarily to collect whatever intelligence they could that had been left behind by the Nazis. Stalin got suspicious of the foreign activities in his newly acquired area and the Soviets ordered both the OSS and SOE (Special Operations Executive), the British spy agency also operating out of Bulgaria. Donovan, upset, contacted Fitin and got a reprieve for both intelligence services. But in return, Fitin demanded a heavy price—the names of all OSS personnel in Bulgaria and in any other territories occupied by the Soviets. Donovan surprisingly agreed, handing over lists of agents in not only Bulgaria, but Romania and Yugoslavia, and those planning to enter Czechoslovakia.

Identifying covert agents to anyone outside an organization is heresy in secret operations; treasonable in the eyes of most. It could lead to agents being neutralized or even worse, murdered. Yet Donovan did it, probably with the approval of his superiors, the Joint Chiefs and FDR. In addition, Fitin got Donovan to agree that future agents would be attached to the American sections of any Allied Control Commissions, the official bodies to be sent into conquered territories to administer them. In effect, those agents, officially listed, would be easily identifiable. OSS agents were also required, if operating in any Soviet occupied territory, to do so "in cooperation with the corresponding Soviet organizations."[31] In other words, they were to check in with the nearest Soviet office, certainly connected to the NKVD, and reveal basically what they were doing—an act not exactly conducive to secret operations. Clearly Donovan, either naively or recklessly, was treating the NKVD as a special and trusted partner. One could say he was solicitous in the highest degree. And if by chance he strayed, he was cuffed by FDR and other Soviet sympathizers in the administration for doing so.

Early in the fall of 1944, as the OSS-NKVD relationship grew, OSS in Finland got wind of a treasure trove of Russian documents including Soviet military and diplomatic decryption materials that would enable the breaking of Soviet codes. Most sources* state

---

* The episode is still mysterious with not all aspects revealed or agreed upon by scholars.

that the materials were captured and/or developed by the Finns who, afraid of Russian domination as a result of World War II, had joined with the Axis against the Soviets, with whom they share a common border. There are mentions of partially burned code books retrieved by the Finns after early battle victories over the Russians and also separate decryption documents, approximately 1,500, which a crack corps of Finnish code busters generated later. Exactly what was offered for sale is not clear. But towards the end of the war, after the Finns, realizing the Nazis had lost, left the Axis and were marketing the materials, Donovan offered to buy them. However, when he proposed doing so to Secretary of State Edward R. Stettinius he was told that since the USSR was an ally, the U.S. should do no such thing. Donovan, always aggressive and a risk-taker, went ahead anyway and bought the papers. Then FDR, whom Donovan himself advised of the purchase, protested and ordered all of it given back to the Russians "at once."

Was that the enigmatic Donovan's intention in the first place—returning the crucial papers to the Soviets as a way of engendering gratitude from them? The answer is currently not available in accessible documents—at least not those I have been able to find. While some accounts say he kept copies of the purchased material, Donovan, nevertheless, did as he was instructed. But in his letter concerning the return he made no mention of the controversy surrounding the purchase and sounded as if his first and only intention was to watch Russia's back. "I wish General Fitin to know at once," his classified letter states, "that we have obtained from enemy sources papers which we wish turned over...to a designated, highly trusted Russian at the earliest possible moment.... I am certain that these documents are of the utmost urgent importance to the Soviets. Please cable me at once [who in Washington] these papers should be turned over to."[32] Fitin, of course, was not only surprised and thankful, but probably amazed at the OSS director's seeming magnanimous gesture. Had the situation been reversed, he certainly would not have notified Donovan, let alone returned the material. (He was, at the very moment, receiving all kinds of stolen secret U.S. material from his spies in America.) After receiving it, he wrote Donovan, "I am very grateful to you for the information . . . relating to military codes . . . my sincere thanks for the aid given us . . . in this very essential business."[33]

Whatever Donovan's motivation, the give-back—which Smith in *Shadow Warriors*[34] says was akin "to giving an opponent the scientific formula for an important secret weapon"—did Donovan little perceptible good. Shortly after returning the code-breaking material in late February of 1945, Fitin, according to documents, denied Donovan's request to send an OSS team into Warsaw, Poland, where the Soviets were endeavoring to elevate a puppet regime—something they accomplished, in part, by keeping their allies uninformed.[35] Similarly, in April, Fitin declined to meet with Donovan in Paris[36] where the OSS head hoped to outline further cooperation, or give Donovan permission to visit Bucharest, Romania, another Eastern European capitol the Russians had occupied and were yoking.[37] In May, barely a week after the war in Europe ended, OSS was notified its four-month-old request to send a team into Soviet-occupied Hungary as well was denied. George F. Kennen, Charge d'Affairs at the American embassy in Moscow, who had been asked to handle the request, wrote resignedly that a silence lasting that long amounted to a "refusal," and they were withdrawing the request.[38]

Donovan was, by this time, hat-in-hand to Fitin. But the strangest episode involving the two occurred in the spring of 1945.

Shortly after the conclusion of the code-book matter, OSS entered into clandestine dealings with Major Wilhelm Hoettl, an enigmatic, high-placed German intelligence officer. Dr. Hoettl, who had earned advanced degrees in history and philosophy and held a professorship at the University of Vienna before the war[39] had been an aide to SS-commander Heinrich Himmler, a top Nazi. Hoettl supposedly had been the mastermind behind the daring German rescue of deposed Italian dictator Benito Mussolini, had been involved in a sweeping plot to counterfeit allied money at the end of the war, and was the Axis spymaster in the Balkans where the Russians, by this time, were banning OSS agents. He claimed to be a not-so-fanatical Nazi, a Catholic, who joined the party mainly because he was anti-communist. Through the OSS office in neutral Switzerland, headed by sophisticate-spy Allen Dulles, who would later helm the CIA, he offered the U.S. an intact network of operatives, some actually in Russia, who could spy on the Soviets throughout the Balkans and eastward.[40] In return, he asked for his freedom and volunteered his services to run the network for America. Apprised of this, Donovan had his men assume control of the spy ring in order to test it and see if, in fact, it was still in place and as good as Hoettl claimed. Making contact with the operatives, the probers judged Hoettl's spies indeed to be well situated and providing good intelligence. The Nazi operatives readily agreed to work with OSS. But rather than inform his bosses, FDR or the Joint Chiefs, of the intriguing possibilities, Donovan went instead to the European Theater G-2 (chief intelligence officer), General Edwin Sibert, who, according to Cave-Brown in *The Last Hero*,[41] advised that he double-cross both Hoettl and his operatives and inform the NKVD—one of the entities that would be the subject of the spying—about the offer.

Why Sibert would do this is not clear. However, Cave-Brown notes that Sibert was among those currently in talks with General Reinhardt Gehlen, Hitler's chief of intelligence on the entire Soviet

Union.[42] Gehlen, subject of a 1971 biography entitled *Spy of the Century*, was a bigger fish. He would become the CIA's main spymaster against the USSR once the Cold War was declared. But at this time—summer 1945—negotiations with Gehlen were only in the beginning stages. They could have fallen through. Perhaps, to be generous, Donovan's intention in accepting Sibert's plan was for Hoettl's ring to be sacrificed as a decoy in order to keep suspicions off Gehlen? Whatever Donovan may have been thinking, after consulting with Sibert, Donovan went directly to Fitin, told him of the unsuspecting network, and treacherously offered to help the NKVD "liquidate" it. Concluding that Hoettl was "evidently motivated by desire to stir trouble between Russians and ourselves," Donovan wrote his Moscow counterpart, "it seemed desirable that we (1) make such information available [to you] and (2) we discuss with the Soviet Union means of eliminating Hoettl's entire organization."[43]

In the meantime, the Joint Chiefs became aware of Donovan's offer to Fitin and got mad at him for revealing such a prize to the Russians and, doubly, offering it without consulting them. "The action by the Office of Strategic Services which led to the Russians being informed of the discovery of the Hoettl network was not coordinated with the War and Navy Departments and has not been confirmed by the Joint Chiefs of Staff *as required...*" they admonished in an "18 August 1945" memorandum to Donovan.[44] Cave-Brown speculates that in addition to being by-passed, one of the reasons for their displeasure may have been that Hoettl earlier "had provided Patton's G-2 with extremely important information about the Red Army in Austria—armies that Patton faced," and that Patton, hearing of the NKVD deal, "may well have protested." Also, if they double-crossed Hoettl, how could they hope to attract other ex-Nazis to spy for them?

But the deal had already been offered and could not now be rescinded without stirring Soviet suspicions and antipathy which the U.S. was trying to avoid. Stalin himself, according to *The Haunted Wood*, had already been briefed.[45] Interestingly, Fitin did not jump at the Donovan offer even though it amounted to a bonanza of counterintelligence dropped literally in his lap. He was cautious in his response. In an August 1, 1945, letter headed "Top Secret," he dutifully thanked Donovan but wanted answers to pointed questions before making up his mind.[46] Who were Hoettl's spies? What kind of documents did he offer to the U.S.? What proof was there that his agents were spying on the Soviets? Finally, had the U.S. "captured other network chiefs who have similarly worked against the Soviets?" The last question suggests he might already have gotten a whiff of the courting of Gehlen, which would not be surprising given the strong network of spies he had operating against the U.S. Fitin, of course, knew Gehlen's specialty and was hunting for him.

Whatever the case, in late August, Donovan apologized to the Joint Chiefs[47] and promised to consult with them on such matters in the future. Hands tied, they reluctantly gave approval to the deal and to "liquidation" of the network, which apparently meant killing the unsuspecting Balkan agents. But beyond that, the public documentary trail goes silent. Donovan and Hoettl, who lived the affair, are now dead, so they can not be consulted. Hoettl's *Secret Front*, an autobiography first published in 1953 and criticized as self-serving, does not mention the spy net. The wily Hoettl, however, who had dealt first with Patton, whose troops had captured him, and then Donovan through Dulles, was not "liquidated." In fact, by October, according to Cave-Brown, he had been freed from the Nuremberg prison where the European war's criminals were being kept and given a letter by U.S. officials allowing him free range within that city.[48] Somehow he had survived Donovan's attempt to help the Soviets.

Why was Donovan so pro-Soviet?

Not even a Soviet spy could have handled the Hoettl matter better for Russia than Donovan.

Was he simply following the administration's line of appeasing the Soviets in gratitude for their contribution toward winning the war and in hopes of maintaining their friendship in the post-war world? Did he really just not realize the Hoettl matter was that important to the U.S., as he implied in his apology to the Joint Chiefs?[49]

Or might he have had some secret agenda?

Donovan was the enigmatic leader of a secret spy organization. The truth, therefore, is not easy to discern. But as the war drew to a close, events began to back the OSS director into a corner from which he knew he would be hard pressed to successfully emerge. He began fighting what ultimately would be a losing battle. His great love, OSS, would be disbanded. In the midst of such mounting pressure, who knows what an ambitious, opportunistic, sometimes reckless risk-taker like Donovan might have done?

Since starting the OSS, Donovan had been under fire by a multitude of military and civilian intelligence chiefs, the FBI's Hoover being the most vocal among them. They resented or envied both him and his encroaching organization and wanted both toppled. On April 12, his sole, staunch supporter, President Roosevelt, died. It was not just a personal blow to Donovan, but a major professional one. Prior to his death, FDR had begun planning with Donovan a post-war super intelligence agency which, in fact, several years later, would become the CIA, and which Donovan, with good reason, expected to run. It would be simply an extension of OSS. As far back as August 1944, according to an item in the

OSS Society [50] newsletter, Donovan had begun working on creating the new post-war agency. It was, by all accounts, one of his most important future projects.

However, confidential plans Donovan had drawn up by February 1945 were surreptitiously leaked to some of his enemies (he never found out by whom but it was a source of great frustration for him) and consequently became the basis for sensational news stories: "NEW DEAL PLANS SUPER SPY SYSTEM; SLEUTHS WOULD SNOOP ON U.S.," blared one of the many headlines. "SUPER GESTAPO AGENCY IS UNDER CONSIDERATION,"[51] warned another. Most newspapers in this pre-TV era treated the news like an assault on personal privacy. Donovan was painted as an SS commander; his newly planned organization, a brutal secret police designed to prey indiscriminately on innocent Americans. The furor was loud and damning. The FBI's Hoover, Army and Navy leaders, and sincere and opportunistic legislators, led the attack. Compounding Donovan's problems was a secret study of the OSS done by army colonel Richard Park, Jr., an intelligence officer assigned to the White House. Just before his death, FDR mysteriously had commissioned the study. "Certain information had been brought to his attention which made such an investigation both timely and desirable," Thomas F. Troy, a CIA historian, quotes Colonel Park as saying in *Donovan and the CIA*, a formerly secret CIA history of the organization that has been declassified.[52] What that information was has never been disclosed. But Parks's report accused the OSS, according to Troy, of incompetence, bad security, and corruption. In addition, the fact that communists were working in and with the OSS was spotlighted by the report as were Donovan's "special secret funds," which were said to be almost unlimited and for which he had mostly no accountability. He could disperse the unvouchered funds at will for whatever he wanted. Hiring and working with communists and the specter of a blank check for anything he desired while most Americans tightened their belts for the war effort was not a winning image for the OSS director. The report damningly recommended that "General Donovan be replaced at the earliest possible moment."[53]

By Roosevelt's death, Donovan's plan to establish and head a post-war super spy agency seemed dead in the water—but not to the director. He took the plan underground, fully expecting to see the agency—and his hoped-for appointment of director at its head—resurrected. At his first chance, he took his plans personally to presidential successor Harry Truman. But Truman had been given a copy of the Park Report and unexpectedly—to Donovan, at least—rebuffed the director. The meeting, according to Richard Dunlop in *Donovan: America's Master Spy*, "could not have taken more than twenty minutes."[54] Truman, upon assuming office, had vowed to continue Roosevelt's policies, especially treating the Soviets with care in naive hopes of insuring a post-war peace and world tranquility. But the new U.S. leader was insulted by the idea of a super spy agency—at least in the early days after his sudden ascension. He would be damned if he allowed a "Gestapo" in his administration. Donovan, the ambitious head of a kingdom he had built from scratch, now realized he was going to lose it all. It had to be a desperate situation. What could he do to save it, or at least reconstruct it into the new super agency? He began lobbying fiercely within the government—but with little success. With FDR gone, he needed important allies; new friends whom he could help and who in turn could help him.

In June of 1945, as one of the lawyers involved with prosecuting war criminals at the upcoming Nuremburg Tribunal, he traveled to the Soviet Union. Did he only do work related to Nuremburg while there? I have not been able to find any more about the trip than the fact that he went.[55] Donovan was the most elusive American leader in the war. Shortly after the trip, the Hoettl matter came to a head. What had he done in Moscow? Who had he seen? What had they discussed?

As fall of 1945 began, Donovan was a man on the verge of his own professional demise, hoping and scheming to try to stay the execution, or, if it became inevitable—as it did—to take the reigns of whatever would follow. Undoubtedly, he made moves to help himself and his cause. He was in a good position as head of America's most secret clandestine agency, crumbling as it was, and willing and able—perhaps feeling duty-bound—to do the bidding of the leaders of the various factions, Right and Left, that were vying for control of U.S. policy direction at that very critical stage in the immediate post-war period. The intrigues must have been incredible.

This then was the hidden but pertinent background into which Skubik found himself immersed as he kept coming into conflict with Donovan and the OSS. Donovan, as part of OSS's dying machinations, was trying, for whatever reason, to placate the NKVD, which Skubik, unaware, considered an enemy. The OSS director was also presiding over a crumbling personal empire which he desperately hoped to revive and continue to dominate one way or another.

What secrets of that struggle, waged in the tumultuous period of time that gave birth to the Cold War and CIA, were buried in the OSS's demise?

Did some of them involve Patton?

CHAPTER NINE

★ ★ ★ ★

DANCING WITH THE DEVIL

I**t's not clear exactly when** Skubik had the second confrontation with Donovan. Probably it was sometime in the late summer or early fall 1945. In September, however, Skubik, Toombs, and May were charged by a fellow CIC agent with stealing and looting. An investigation was launched. According to formerly top secret documents I obtained from the National Archives, the charges stemmed from the mass exodus out of Zwickau when the Russians, per the Yalta agreements, were to be given that territory. In helping many to escape, the team had broken rules about transporting refugees, moved the refugees' possessions under their own names rather than the owners (which looked suspicious) and had strong-armed people to get them to do what they wanted. Some they had strong-armed were German officials.

The rival CIC accuser, in whose territory Skubik's team had sometimes surreptitiously worked—thus incurring his anger—brought in witnesses like Walter Ulbricht, the communist organizer

Skubik had arrested, to claim that he had seen them packing rail-road cars with loot and even carting off entire factories, a charge CIC investigating officer, Major Donovan Ault, found ludicrous. Testifying on behalf of the three were many Zwickau refugees who swore the so-called "stolen loot" was what was being transported for them. Not only did they have no other way to get their own posessions out, but everything had been given back to them after they reached their destination. While Major Ault wrote that the three acted as "big shots" and "displayed poor judgment," he con-cluded that there was no evidence to substantiate the charges and declared them innocent. Skubik was exonerated, and in fact he was promoted on November 3 to sergeant.[1]

November 3 was a little more than a month before Patton's fateful accident. What Skubik had been doing in regard to the warnings about Patton is unclear. He does not address it per se in his book. Presumably he had to spend considerable time defend-ing himself from the looting charges. He also had a full plate con-tinuing his daily job of hunting Nazis and countering Russian espionage, which was on the increase. The Russians were now in firm control of Eastern Europe and stepping up espionage in the Western sectors. In the meantime, Patton had been fired by Eisen-hower and exiled to Bad Nauheim, which made him more vul-nerable. As the governor of Bavaria, he had been bowed to, pampered, and attended by many who could protect him. But the clerical 15th Army had few such amenities. "Patton's bodyguards were removed," wrote Skubik. "I have spoken to Bert Goldstein, one of Patton's bodyguards at that time. Bert told me that...had the bodyguards not been removed Patton would not have been murdered."*[2]

---

*I have had no success confirming a Bert Goldstein in connection with Patton.

The stage, in Skubik's opinion, had been set. But before anything happened to Patton, Skubik would have a final row involving Donovan after accusing a Russian general of planning Patton's assassination.

A few weeks before Patton's accident, Skubik was ordered to arrest his own driver, Alfred Schoenstein, a Yugoslav refugee. Schoenstein was one of several "camp followers" Skubik's CIC team had acquired. The camp followers were "happy to share our billets . . . food . . . and were generally useful," including as sources of local information. Skubik had commandeered a large Horch automobile which he believed had belonged to [Nazi Air Force chief] General Herman Goering. "It was a real beauty, grey with red upholstery . . . bullet proofed."* The internet indicates it might have ended up in Russia, which is pertinent here, or in the hands of a private U.S. or other collector. When Schoenstein, hoping to catch on with the CIC, had presented his papers, Skubik writes he realized they were "tainted, thus I learned Schoenstein was a Russian spy" and, since he would be working with American intelligence, "a double agent." But it did not bother Skubik. "I used him and he used me." For instance, it had been through some crafty manipulation of their relationship that Skubik caught the two Russian spies who had the U.S. codebooks. Skubik thus had made Schoenstein his Horch "chauffeur." Eventually, his superiors, who either knew of the game or found out about it, wanted the relationship ended. But when he went to Schoenstein's room to arrest him, he found that someone had tipped off the double agent and he had taken flight in the Horch, which Skubik prized.

---

*An extremely rare, pre-war luxury car, Goering's Horch is hard to track. The Horch Museum, Zwickau, confirmed that Goering owned a Horch 853 "with special roadster coachwork" but could not provide any other particulars or its whereabouts today.

Schoenstein was Jewish. Back in April, prior to Germany's surrender, Skubik had saved two Jewish teens from the SS who, though resistant, released the imperiled teens in a bargain with Skubik.[3] Audi and Lilli Weil were now grateful camp followers. He went to them. "I explained that [Schoenstein] was a Russian spy and that he must have gone over to them for safety. Audi promised to go to the Jewish underground to get their help."[4]

Three days later, the teen reported that Schoenstein had been spotted at the headquarters of a Russian colonel in Regensburg. "The Horch was parked in the back." He and Audi sped there in a jeep. But while Skubik was talking with the colonel, Schoenstein escaped again. Audi had seen him driving "out at full speed in the Horch...heading for the autobahn." They gave chase but the Horch could do 120 mph.

Their jeep could not.

They lost him.

Audi felt it was his fault. "He said he should have let the air out of the [Horch's] tires. I told him that he did right to stay with the jeep. We might have had to walk home if the jeep had been stolen. He promised to find Schoenstein." Several days later, the teen reported the car and Schoenstein at the Supreme Headquarters Allied Expeditionary Force (SHAEF) complex in Frankfurt. It was housed in and around the I. G. Farben building, one of the few in Frankfurt untouched by bombing. Schoenstein was in the Russian section.

"I hurried to Frankfurt, parked my jeep and knocked on the huge doors of the castle headquarters and residence of General Davidov, Chief of the Russian Compound." Waiting, "I realized how stupid I was going alone into the den of the Russian bear. Only Audi and the Jewish underground knew where I was."

The door opened. A major checked his credentials, admitted him to a foyer, and asked him to wait. After ten minutes, he was led up a spiral staircase to a large dining room with a huge mahogany table in its center. "Across the table already seated was General Davidov," and next to him, a young woman translator (although Skubik, who spoke Russian, did not need one). "Standing behind the general were 24 Russian officers with various rank. All had bald shaven heads, no eyebrows and tan uniforms. Apparently they were NKVD officers who disguised themselves with wigs, etc., when in the field."

The general had a "half smile on his plastic face." Skubik returned the smile. They small-talked until Skubik finally said he was there to arrest "a criminal, Alfred Schoenstein." Davidov said he did not know Schoenstein. Skubik said he had good information the general did. Davidov wanted to know his sources. "You don't really expect me to tell you," said Skubik. Then he brought up Patton.

"I asked him to tell me if he had heard of the rumor that his NKVD was ordered to kill [General Patton]. He stared at me. How dare I ask such a question? His answer was that the question was ridiculous. 'Why should our government be involved in murdering a fellow comrade in arms?' I knew instinctively that I had scored well with that question. His answer was evasive but it told me that he knew of the NKVD plot because he and his dogs were all NKVD. I looked squarely at the general. He blinked. His men didn't. Their stone faced stares were intimidating. I decided to get back to the matter of Schoenstein."

Apparently Audi had told him Davidov wanted the Horch. "Schoenstein is a criminal, a black market thief, wanted by [my government]. I know for a fact that you are negotiating with [Schoenstein] to buy Goering's Horch." Davidov again denied knowing Schoenstein. Skubik persisted. "I am sure that your superiors in Moscow would not take kindly to your negotiating to buy a car stolen from the United States Government.... Give me Schoenstein and I will give you the Horch with official papers."

At first, writes Skubik, Davidov glared at him. Skubik did not flinch. "Is it a deal?" Davidov suddenly smiled and signaled with his hand. One of the officers behind him abruptly left and went downstairs. Shortly, he returned with a surprised and sullen Schoenstein. "Thank you General," said Skubik. He told Davidov the Horch was his and he would receive the official transfer papers in a few days. "I was glad to get out alive." As they drove back, "I gave Schoenstein hell," Skubik wrote, telling Schoenstein he would kill him if he tried to escape. When they returned, he turned him in to Lieutenant Gillespie with a report of his discussions with Davidov, including what had transpired about the Patton threat.[5]

CHAPTER TEN

★ ★ ★ ★

NKVD

Just who was General Davidov and why did Skubik confront him about Patton?

Skubik does not say much more about it than what I have written. He may have had more information than he discloses. His book sometimes gives that impression. It is not well organized, often omitting connections and explanations that an inquisitive reader instantly wants to know. But Skubik was not a professional writer. He was an old-school investigator, divining often by the gut. The facts, in this case, were on his side. Davidov, it turns out, was the head Soviet in the American Zone at the time. As such, he likely would have known about, if not been in charge of, any Soviet plot regarding Patton.

Not much is known about Davidov. As Skubik notes, he basically disappears not long after Patton's accident and death.[1] Russian researchers I hired found no mention of the general in Soviet and Russian reference works (although, interestingly, a Horch said to have been Goering's is reportedly now in Russia).[2] But he is

positively identified in formerly classified documents from immediate post-war Germany.

At the time Skubik met him, Major General Alexander M.
Davidov (sometimes written as "Davidoff" or "Davidow"), was
the chief Soviet liaison officer for repatriation, meaning he headed
Stalin's effort to return all Soviets and Soviet-dominated displaced
persons (DPs) to territory under his control. But in an equally, if
not more important post, he was, as Skubik wrote, also head of
NKVD operations in U.S.-occupied Germany. In effect, he was the
top communist there. A formerly top secret document I found at
the National Archives labels him a spymaster.[3] Prior to coming to
Frankfurt, it says, he participated in "cleaning action...against
the White Russians in 1936." Undoubtedly these were assassinations. The White Russians were anti-communist Tsarist loyalists
whom Stalin tirelessly sought to annihilate. After early intelligence
work, it continues, he joined the Soviet military in June 1944 as a
colonel, and, according to an article by a Samford (Alabama) University scholar,[4] arrived in Frankfurt as repatriation chief in August 1945.

Davidov, according to written sources, ruled with an iron hand.
A top secret report on "Operation Bingo," a U.S. intelligence surveillance of Davidov and his men, says an informer was so intimidated by him, he skipped a meeting Davidov ordered him by
phone to attend for fear he had been found out and Davidov
would kill him.[5] One of his top aides and operatives, a "Colonel
Gavriloff," according to a CIC report,[6] got drunk at a U.S.-Soviet
gathering November 30—roughly two weeks before Patton's fatal
accident—and began threatening that the USSR was soon to defeat
the U.S. in war. "What do you think I am over here for?" the report quotes him as saying, "Just the repatriation of Russian DPs?
No. I have a much more important and bigger job than that...I

am a Secret Intelligence Investigator." To prove it, he ripped open his shirt to show a Russian Eagle tattooed on his chest—"the insignia of the Russian Intelligence Corps." Grabbing a Seventh Army cavalry captain (one of two signing the report), he said, "in a rather venomous way," that should the captain "work against Russia, or be in his way, he would eliminate him."

At this particular time, it was not the captain who was threatening Russia, but General Patton.

Interestingly—or suspiciously—according to two Soviet officer surveillance reports, the same Gavriloff and his boss, General Davidov, received authorization—and thus vital traveling papers—from USFET (United States Forces European Theater) to be in the Mannheim-Heidelberg area for unspecified purposes "between 9 and 19 December 1945." Patton was injured on December 9 in Mannheim and died in Heidelberg on December 21. The report says, "Gen. Davidow [apparently a mistake in the U.S. agent's spelling of Davidov] visited Col. Gavriloff 12 December 1945 at Heidelberg. On the same date both . . . departed for an unknown destination."[7] Mannheim and Heidelberg, according to the reports, were "centers or cells of [Soviet] political and Secret Service activities."

Coincidence?

Were they involved in Patton's accident or death? Was Gavriloff, or even Davidov, Bazata's "Pole"?

It is, of course, impossible to tell from such circumstantial evidence. But in concert with other apparent coincidences and enigmas surrounding Patton's death, it is suspicious enough to warrant further investigation. Unfortunately, given the buried, if not hidden, status of documents which might shed further light, especially their probable dispersion in largely inaccessible Russian archives, such investigation led to a dead end.

On February 22, 1946, according to more documents[8]—two months after Patton's death—a group of Davidov's spies was arrested in the American Zone disguised as U.S. Army soldiers. They had fake identification and a stolen U.S. jeep. One of the arrested was, as Bazata calls his nefarious associate, a Pole. Shortly thereafter, a second such group was also arrested. The group contained two Polish spies—the point being that Poles—such as the one Bazata says was with him at Patton's accident and the pilot who attacked Patton—were definitely working with and for the Russians who now had complete control of Poland. Davidov complained vigorously about the detentions of these agents, a brazen move on his part given the fact that they had been caught red-handed and were compounding the problem with lies and at least one escape attempt, according to the records. But Davidov persisted, eventually enlarging the dispute to include his anger over refusals by American officials to repatriate disputed displaced persons—one of the charges against Patton—and "dissemination of rumors about the inevitability of the Western Power-USSR war," another of the things Patton, while he was alive, had been saying. The Russians pretended to be shocked but Davidov's own Colonel Gavriloff had spouted the same thing—to the horror of his comrades—when drunk.

The dispute, according to the documents, went all the way to Washington. Officials there, incredible as it seems, sided not with their own men in the field, but with Davidov. The documents given to me were missing redacted pages and were sent badly copied with words and lines cut off so there may be more to the story than I have been able to extract. But what they indicate is that rulings unfavorable to Davidov by local officers were overturned at the highest levels, and U.S. occupation officials were given a stern warning to stop the rumors—at least from the American side. "The dissemination of rumors as to the inevitability of the Western Powers [word or words missing] war are of deep concern," the document states. "Such actions are prejudicial to the good relations [word or words missing] between our two countries. Steps will be undertaken to take countermeasures [word or words missing]."[9] Davidov, it appears, was being catered to by a servile Washington that, in the interests of keeping peace with the Soviets at all costs, did not want him riled.

However, the most interesting information about Davidov was in a declassified file bearing Skubik's name recently sent over to the archives from Ft. Meade, Maryland, one of the main CIC repositories.[10] Ft. Meade had repeatedly responded to my Freedom of Information Act (FOIA) requests for any documents regarding Skubik by saying they had conducted a thorough search and could find nothing. Now, in their handovers to the archives, a Skubik document suddenly appears? So much for public access, as FOIA supposedly guarantees. And what a quizzical document the file is—some twelve pages designated "NW26959" by the archives but with only five pages of any substance. The rest of the pages had been replaced with what was labeled a "Top Secret Document Replacement Sheet." The sheet contained long numbers and dates and other indecipherable (at least to me) information presumably with which those authorized could maybe find what had been removed—if it still existed.

The few pages with any substance were meager. But one, dated 29 Dec. 1945, discusses Davidov's interest in acquiring a Horch— this one ironically in Bad Nauheim, Patton's last residence. It confirms at least Davidov's interest in rare cars.* Another page is an undated CIC letter discussing Stepan Bandera, the Ukrainian

---

*And perhaps explains why Goering's Horch may be in Russia.

nationalist who was the first to tell Skubik about the Patton plot. It says while most think Bandera is working for the Soviets, this should not be believed. But the most intriguing aspect of this newly declassified file is the fact that several of the removed top secret pages clearly involve Skubik, who is named in the retrieval information. And at least one of the lifted pages includes Davidov's name with Skubik's. The two are linked. Nowhere have I been able to find reports Skubik claims to have made, both verbally and in writing, on what Bandera, Smal-Stocki, and General Shandruk told him, let alone his confrontation with Davidov. Like the reports on Patton's accident, Skubik's reports about Patton have disappeared. Could these removed pages be those reports? Could they be pages even more explosive?

The day following his confrontation with Davidov, wrote Skubik, "all hell broke loose." He was ordered to report to CIC subregional headquarters at Hoechst, near Frankfurt, where he had first encounted Ukrainian General Shandruk. "NKVD General Davidov had complained to OSS General Donovan. He wanted the papers to the car and he wanted my hide. Col. Rodin tore into me. He said my report is a bunch of crap. He told me that I'd had no authority to contact General Davidov. 'Damn it!' I said. 'I risked my life to get Schoenstein. My orders didn't say where or how I should catch Schoenstein.' Rodin called Skubik 'a damned fool' and said 'he had no choice but put me under house arrest.'" Donovan had ordered it.

Skubik was restricted to quarters. "I was fuming. I did one helluva job. I arrested a mighty slick spy. But my reward was being arrested." For six days he was restricted to his room, given no explanation beyond having overstepped his authority. On one occasion, he said, they tried to entrap him, sending to his room "a guy... with a bottle of whiskey and a pack of cigarettes, compliments of Colonel Rodin." The visitor had a hidden tape recorder and made a sexual advance. Skubik threatened to "knock" his "head off" and the visitor "ran out... Rodin had tried to discredit me as a [homosexual]."

At last a "captain," presumably CIC but not otherwise described, came and told Skubik he was free to go. Davidov had told Donovan that he, Skubik, was an agent for the UPA, one of the Ukrainian forces fighting the USSR. Donovan knew he had been meeting with Bandera, the UPA leader. That was why he had been held, said the captain. Skubik blew his top. "Bull!" he protested. He was not an agent! He was just doing his job. The captain was skeptical but sent him out to arrest a Nazi, which he did, and then back to Lieutenant Gillespie, who appears to have been on Skubik's side.[11]

A few days later, Patton was injured in the December 9 crash.

Skubik learned about it around 3:00 p.m. that Sunday and became convinced the intelligence he had gathered had become reality. He asked to be sent to the scene to investigate. But Colonel Rodin telephoned back in reply to Gillespie's request with "strict orders" that Skubik "stay the hell out." Others, said Rodin, "were assigned to the case."[12] Subsequently, wrote Skubik—probably years later—he "learned that there is no record of a CIC investigation of the accident or of the death of Patton." He believed the CIC investigation, if it was made, "was removed by the same people who stole the other files"—presumably the missing accident reports.[13]

He was stymied.

CHAPTER ELEVEN

★ ★ ★ ★

MYSTERY
AT MANNHEIM

While official records of Patton's accident have vanished, the opposite is true of his subsequent hospitalization. One of the largest single sections of files I have on Patton is crammed with hospital reports, news accounts, and personal recollections of the general's December 1945 ordeal, beginning with his admittance to Heidelberg's newly established 130th Station Hospital.

The hospital, understaffed and still under construction, was not the biggest or best equipped in the area.[1] That honor belonged to Frankfurt's 97th General which was also an army hospital. The 130th had only been established in the former barracks of a German cavalry unit for about four months[2] so, fledgling as it was, there is reason to ponder why Patton, with a broken neck and in need of the best available treatment, was taken there. But Frankfurt was almost fifty miles away, while Heidelberg was less than half that—perhaps fifteen miles distant. The doctor credited with being the first physician to arrive at the accident and transport

Patton to Heidelberg, Captain Ned Snyder, of Brownwood, Texas, additionally decided to bypass hospitals in Mannheim. He and his commanding officer, Major Charles Tucker, had been summoned to the crash by a female Red Cross worker who had witnessed it and run to their headquarters for help.[3] Dr. Snyder had examined Patton at the scene and then helped load him onto a stretcher and into the battalion's ambulance. The strange thing was that he had written in his article that Patton, when he, Snyder, had arrived, "had no head or facial wounds that I remember," although he recognized the paralysis. Before they moved him from the Cadillac, Snyder wrote that Patton told him, " 'I am paralyzed from the neck down,' Later as I tried to straighten his neck into an approved position for transporting neck injuries, [Patton] cautioned, 'If you move my head I will die, go easy.' Again, I remember no scalp wound to be repaired."

This contradicts most other witnesses at the scene, and all those who mention seeing Patton's bloodied face and scalp, including the two other occupants of the Cadillac, Woodring and General Gay, as well as hospital records and news accounts. It seems most probable that Snyder's memory is faulty on this point, but his recollection might possibly be the source of a rumor that Patton was bludgeoned to death on the way to the hospital. You see the rumor on the Internet with no verifiable evidence substantiating it. However, someone reading Snyder's account might theorize, given the doctor's witness, that Patton's bloody head wound was inflicted en route. If this was true, Captain Snyder, who died in 2001, would had to have been party to the attack since he drove with Patton to the hospital, presumably with others. "I remember practically no other conversation in the ambulance on the way," he writes.[4] Snyder's memory also appears to fail him in declaring that the car he helped Patton from was a "black Mercedes," and not the olive drab Cadillac every other source mentions.

Other strange stories at odds with the accepted accounts of Patton's accident have also surfaced. Are they true? It seems unlikely. But given the mysteries surrounding the accepted account, who really knows? One thing they ultimately prove is the suspicious level of murkiness surrounding an event that should have been extensively investigated.

Earl Staats of Sturgeon Bay, Wisconsin, claimed that Patton was not in a Cadillac when injured. It was a "1941 or 1942 Plymouth staff car," he is quoted as saying in another *Military* magazine article.[5] He knew, he said, because the accident occurred in Heidelberg where he was stationed—not on the outskirts of Mannheim as all other witnesses attest. Staats claimed to have been at the scene. He said Patton, on that December 9 morning, had stopped by in Heidelberg "on the way to Mannheim"* to see his boss, Colonel Sitzinger, a Patton friend whom Staats identified as commander of the 14th Field Observation Battalion of the Fifteenth Army.** Patton told them he was going home to resign and "straighten this mess out."*** The accident had occurred moments after Patton left their office. They heard the crash and ran several blocks to see the car and truck "smashed" and Patton incapacitated. He claimed an ambulance took Patton not to the 130th but to the 115th Station Hospital where he expired not two weeks later, but *that very day*. In addition, claimed Staats, General Gay, contrary to reports he had seen, was not in the car when Patton stopped to visit their headquarters, nor was he at the scene of the accident.

---

*This makes no sense because Mannheim was between Bad Nauhiem and Heidelberg, not the other way around.
**This also seems bogus since Heidelberg was in Seventh Army jurisdiction, not Fifteenth.
***Presumably the U.S. policies in Germany to which he objected and which got him fired.

A Niagara Falls, N.Y. policeman, Kazmir L. Sawicki, claimed that as an MP serving in Germany when Patton died, he had been the first person to the accident scene and had cradled the general until he was basically ordered to leave by higher-ups who arrived and stated they would take over. Patton, he said, was not injured inside his car, as all other witnesses claim, but was hit by a passing truck while he was urinating outside and beside his vehicle.[6]

Lester Gingold, a Memphis, Tennessee, newspaper publisher who claims to have taken the only photo of truck driver Robert S. Thompson at the crash scene, says contrary to the charge that Thompson and his passengers were drinking prior to the accident, he only saw empty bottles of whiskey in *Patton's* car.*[7]

Dr. Gerald T. Kent, one of the physicians who later attended Patton at the 130th hospital, wrote that General Gay told him the reason Patton had been injured was that they were doing seventy-five miles per hour on the autobahn had swerved to avoid the truck, and ended up in an ditch.**[8]

Finally, Farago writes that in the early 1950s, the *Post-Tribune* of Gary, Indiana, was contacted by an "A.D.C. Atchison" who claimed *he*—not Woodring—was driving the Cadillac on December 9.[9]

As dubious as these alternative stories might appear, without the missing reports and investigations, who can really be sure of the truth? In addition, certain aspects of the accepted story also raise questions.

---

*Gingold, whose pictures show a "goofy" and "scared" Thompson, as he described it, made the charge to me in an interview. He said he saw the bottles.
**He also writes in the book, contrary to all available evidence, that Patton arrived at the 130th hospital not in Snyder's ambulance, but in the wrecked Cadillac limousine. He says he looked outside and observed it.

Horace Woodring, driver of the Patton Cadillac, has probably been the most vocal witness to the crash—and not because he necessarily wanted to be. Accessible like others involved were not, questioners continually sought him. Generally, he told the same basic story, although sometimes details differed: he accelerated from a stop at a railroad track crossing and was listening and reacting as Patton, from the backseat, pointed out war debris piled along the roadside. Then a truck he noticed ahead advancing toward them in the opposite lane had suddenly, without warning, turned across their path. Although it does not appear in all his retellings, in several, most notably the one in Martin Blumenson's, *The Patton Papers 1940-1945,* one of the earliest of Woodring's published accounts, he is quoted as saying there were *two* trucks ahead, not just one.[10] This coincides with what Bazata said, although it is not clear on which roadside each truck seen by Woodring was, or if they were separate or together.[11]

More ominously, most of Woodring's retellings, including the long quote in Blumenson, say the truck that turned into them was stationary and parked on the roadside until the train had passed and they started up again. Only then had it moved out onto the road and started slowly toward them. Woodring's statement in Blumenson reads in part, ".... When the train got by, we passed the Quartermaster Depot which the General was looking at and commenting on. About six hundred yards beyond the railroad track, I noticed two 6 x 6 trucks ahead. When I first started up, one of these also pulled away from the curb and approached in our direction...."

That sounds like the truck was *waiting* for them.

In most of the public interviews Woodring gave during his lifetime he indicated that while he never totally dismissed the possibility that the accident was part of an assassination plot, he himself did not believe it was. Brian M. Sobel, author of *The Fighting Pattons*, who interviewed Woodring for his book in the 1990s, shows this conflict in Woodring's thinking by quoting him as saying: "To this day I don't know where the truck was going. The only entrance they could have been pointing towards was a large German [barracks] with a big stone wall around it and an iron gate which was probably fifteen feet from the pavement. The accident happened so quickly I didn't even hit the brake pedal."[12]

Several who have studied the accident believe Thompson, the truck driver, was turning into the driveway of an outlying quartermaster installation. But his actual destination is still a matter of debate.[13] In any case, turning at that precise location, which apparently had some kind of entrance, would probably have been part of any sinister plan, had one existed. The entrance would have provided justification for the sudden swerve into Patton's path and also for why the truck was going slowly—to enable it to time its turn at a precise moment and location.

In May 2005, I contacted Woodring's son John, who told me his deceased father always had suspicions about the accident but did not feel it was his place to air them in public. "There was a 6x6...sitting up front a quarter of a mile down the road on the other side," he said.

Sitting there?

"Yes, sitting there on the shoulder. And as they left the railroad tracks, he [the truck driver] pulled out as well. So they were heading towards each other. My dad had gotten up to about twenty-five miles per hour[14]...and as soon as he [the truck driver] got to him he veered right into the car—three drunk [truck occupants] who pretty much disappeared....With all the general's flags and what not, [they] accidentally turn into that? I don't think so. Not even if they were drunk."

Did John's father think it was a set up?

"No, he never really....Well, you know, he always had his thoughts possibly that it could have been. But he was just a kid at that time....He never really brought it to the public....He always felt it wasn't his place to suspect."[15]

In 1986, Woodring gave an interview to Suzy Shelton, believed to be a relative.[16] In that interview, while omitting the second truck from his recollection, Woodring reiterated the truck driver's suspicious behavior. He told Shelton, "When the train passes, the only vehicle in sight either way was an army truck which is facing me a half mile down the road, pulled off the shoulder of the road, and starts moving in my direction. Approximately a quarter mile from the railroad crossing, he makes a vicious turn into the front of the car. I had no opportunity to avoid him whatsoever."

General Gay, who died in 1983, never did much public talking about the accident. (He was strangely silent about it considering it was probably his greatest claim to fame.) But after it, date unknown, he authored, probably at the behest of higher authorities, a four-page statement describing what he recalled happening. As they left the railroad tracks, approximately "600 yards" into their acceleration, he wrote,

> The general remarked: "Look at all the derelict vehicles" which were in parks along both the right and left sides of the road. He further remarked, "How awful war is. Think of the waste." The Cadillac slowed to allow Sergeant Scruce [sic], who had been following us...to pass....Almost immediately after Sgt. Scruce [sic]* had passed us and while I was still

---

*Gay spells Sergeant Joe Spruce's name "Scruce" three times in the statement so the spelling appears intentional. Could it be that Spruce—one of those who seems to have disappeared since the accident—is really "Scruce"?

> looking to the left at the derelict vehicles, the General ex-
> claimed, "Look!"[17] I looked up and saw a 2 $\frac{1}{2}$ ton truck turn-
> ing at a 90-degree angle across the road in front of us. I had
> time to say "sit tight"; to think that one should relax like
> when falling from a horse; then we crashed.[18]

What had Patton seen? Possibly it was the truck turning into their path. But Farago, who interviewed Gay years later, quotes Gay as saying Patton's exclamation referred to seeing a "heap of god-damn rubbish!" Whatever it was, neither Gay nor Woodring could know for sure. At the moment he spoke, Patton, according to their accounts, was looking to his right out one of the back windows, Gay, sitting on the same backseat in the other corner, was looking left out a window in the opposite direction. Woodring, in the front seat, was also looking elsewhere. They could only assume they knew what he saw—just as they assumed they knew how his face and scalp had been cut. Might then, the general, instead of seeing just rubbish or the oncoming truck, have seen something equally worthy of exclamation like a figure or a weapon, or both, peek-ing out from the debris? Maybe he did not recognize what he was seeing, if he did see something. Perhaps it was something unusual that caught his eye and made him exclaim.

In confidential Seventh Army documents[19] discussing how the press was being handled during Patton's hospital stay, Gay, in probably his earliest statement, is quoted as saying Patton's exact words at that crucial moment were, "Look at that!"—a somewhat curious phrase if the intention was "Look out!" (in warning against an oncoming truck) but quite in line with something less dangerous but possibly more curious to his perception. And if Pat-ton had been suddenly thrown any distance in the car, as is pre-sumed by Gay and Woodring at the collision, would not he have extended his arms out to shield himself? Accident investigators say that is the natural reaction in such a situation. No one, however, including physicians who examined Patton shortly after the accident, reported any injury to his hands, arms or elsewhere, only to his neck and head.

But if he had seen something suspicious or just out of the ordinary, would not he have remarked about it later? Had his trauma erased or blocked what he saw from his memory? It is hard to imagine a warrior like Patton, old Blood and Guts, fearless survivor of so many close calls in war, being so spooked. But then nothing he had encountered before had ended in such traumatic injury. And with the reports missing, who can know what they might contain about what he said or saw?

The scene immediately following the accident begs more questions.

According to several accounts, the collision occurred on a wreck-strewn stretch of a flat, two-lane straightaway running through the northern Mannheim suburb of Kaeferthal, a sparsely populated industrial section on the city's marshy outskirts. Not many Germans were permitted to drive in Occupied Germany and there were few American installations in that area so traffic was irregular. Nevertheless, a procession of military people quickly arrived. Initially, these officers included, variously, Brigadier General Nicholas B. Cobb, Major Curran,[20] an army "ambulance" with a "med" sergeant,[21] and Sergeant Leory Ogden[22]—all in the first few minutes. A Sergeant Armando DeCrescenzo,[23] said in a newspaper article from the time to have "rushed to the scene" with "three other soldiers" and administered "treatment" to Patton, was probably the medical sergeant. Ogden, most likely, was one of the soldiers with him. Apparently, DeCrescenzo put a makeshift bandage on Patton's head where he was said to be bleeding profusely. Later—as many as twenty minutes after the accident, according to Gay—Captain Snyder and his commander, Major Tucker, arrived with the 290th Engineer ambulance which would take Patton to the hospital. None of these arrivals, with the exception of Snyder, were ever heard from again publicly. Gay wrote that Brigadier Cobb drove him to the hospital in Heidelberg, but then he too disappeared—at least in the retrievable record.

Who were these first responders? How and why, in a seemingly lightly traveled and sparsely populated area, did most of them arrive so quickly at the scene of an unexpected accident? Why, if they participated in what clearly has to be called a momentous event for those times,* have we heard so little from or about them? Relying on available accounts yields few answers. The accounts in circulation of those on the scene are meager and conflicting—a veritable "maze of contradictions," according to historian Denver Fugate.[24]

According to Farago,** the first military policemen (MPs) to arrive did so fairly quickly.[25] Lieutenants Babalas and Metz, motoring to their 818th Military Police Company headquarters in Mannheim,[26] had passed the Patton limousine going the opposite way on the Kaeferthal road. They had noticed the four stars on the Cadillac and were speculating that it was Patton, since he was "the only four-star left in Europe," when they heard the crash behind them. They turned around and drove to the accident, which certainly—if within hearing distance—would have put them there as

---

*Patton was famous in those days. His death generated big headlines and multiple-page special sections in newspapers across the country—not to mention his subsequent place in 20th Century military history.
**Who had access to reports now missing.

soon as any of the others. Yet, Woodring has repeatedly said Babalas was not at the scene, or at least not there when he was.[27]

Curiously, Babalas's military separation papers,[28] which should contain a record of all his assignments, do not list his MP billet. They show him arriving in Europe in May 1944, participating in the battles of Normandy (D-Day invasion of Northern France), the Ardennes (Battle of the Bulge), and the Rhineland (Germany), and being part of the 423rd Infantry's "Anti-Tank Company" until discharge in June 1946. He was later called up in early 1950 for the Korean War and ended up serving for two years as a lawyer in the army's Judge Advocate Corps.

However, a Seventh Army memo confirms that Babalas *was* there. It says that information obtained on the accident by authorities and later given out to the press came from a report made by Babalas at the scene.[29] Ladislas Farago, who interviewed Babalas in 1971 for *Last Days*, writes that the young MP, a law school graduate of Greek heritage, was suspicious enough of Patton's major injuries—given that Gay and Woodring were barely scratched—that he decided to make an on-the-spot investigation.[30] "Blood [was] smeared on the cushions," and in a "four-inch pool" on the limousine floor, said one press report.[31] "The backseat... was covered with blood," said another.[32] Babalas told Farago that he tried to get a copy of the report he had made but had been informed by military authorities no such report existed. Either through "misfiling or misplacing... or by some higher intervention that removed these records.... General Patton's accident has acquired sinister connotations," wrote Farago, who, in *Last Days*, both dismisses and incites suspicion.

But Babalas's integrity, it turns out, *is* in question. Although he seemed beyond reproach when Farago interviewed him in the 1970s, his subsequent career as a Virginia state legislator ended in controversy. Following service in Korea, the Boston-born, Harvard-educated first lieutenant, an eventual graduate of the University of Virginia Law School, became, in 1967, a state representative from districts including Norfolk and Virginia Beach. In the ensuing years, his power grew, and he became a broker in the state's budget, port, and real estate affairs. In 1986, however, he was accused of "casting votes that benefited one of his private firm's clients."[33] The client was a large mortgage company seeking to keep buried loan charges high. Babalas, it was alleged, received bribe money for a vote to kill legislation lowering the hidden charges. He was later acquitted in court of criminal charges but "became the first member of the Virginia General Assembly to be censured by his colleagues for unethical conduct."[34] In 2002, a book, *Friend of the Family: An Undercover Agent in the Mafia*,[35] charged that Babalas, who died of cancer in 1987, was involved with the mob.

If Babalas consorted with outlaws in Virginia, might he have done the same in Germany?

Another mystery of the accident scene is the presence of a Lieutenant Vanlandingham. Neither Farago's interviews with people at the scene nor Gay's account mention him. But Woodring, in several interviews,[36] insists he was the main investigating officer.

I learned of Vanlandingham in the following way:

One of the first persons to publicly raise the question of Patton possibly having been assassinated was Frederick Nolan, a British-born writer and historian whose novel about the alleged assassination, *The Algonquin Project*,[37] became a 1978 film titled *Brass Target*.* First published in England in 1974, the book and movie

---

*Starring George Kennedy as Patton, Sophia Loren as his love interest, and Max von Sydow as the assassin.

both show the killer using a specially constructed rifle very similar to the description of the one Bazata claims he used. It shot a non-penetrating rubber bullet, not identifiable as such at a crash scene. Did Bazata get the idea for his claim from reading the book or seeing the movie? If so, that would impugn his claims. Or, conversely, had Nolan heard the story and used it? That would bolster Bazata.

At least three people—two of his colleagues and a professional journalist—say Bazata told them about causing Patton's accident prior to 1974, which means his story was hatched before Nolan's. Two fellow former Jedburghs, Phil Chadborne, who roomed with Bazata in France in the 1960s, and Bernard Knox, a renowned classics professor in Washington, D.C., told me[38] Bazata had disclosed his claim to them of somehow being involved in Patton's demise prior to 1972, although neither could be absolutely sure of the date or recall exact details of what Bazata told them. Both, at the time, said they were skeptical and so largely dismissed the claim. But Joy Billington, a British-born writer working for the old *Washington Star-News* then, distinctly remembers that Bazata disclosed his involvement to her when she interviewed him for a story about his art which appeared in the *Star-News* September 17, 1972.[39] "He said he'd done it," she told me. "I could hardly believe my ears. I, of course, knew of Patton from my school days in Cheshire (England). He was a hero."

It had been Billington's public disclosure in 1979 of what she first learned in 1972 that had led to the *Spotlight* articles. When Bazata disclosed the secret he had asked her not to write about it, and she had honored his request.* But by 1979, he was ready to

---

*I later found evidence of this in Bazata's diaries. Talking about the 1979 dinner, he writes that she had asked to report the story eight years prior.

go public. He arranged to have her at the OSS veteran's dinner in September that year and ask him about it in front of OSS colleagues, including William Colby, who said he knew nothing about it. Bazata countered, according to his diaries, by saying of course Colby and others were ignorant. "We didn't discuss such things." *Spotlight* editors saw Billington's subsequent story in the *Star-News* and called Bazata.

It turned out, Bazata *had* read *Algonquin*. I found mention of the book in his diaries. It had been brought to him, he writes, by an acquaintance who had read the *Spotlight* articles in October 1979. His comments were basically that the book was accurate in some parts and fantasy in others. Novelist Nolan, having written *Algonquin* before Bazata went public, had never met the former OSS operative. He emailed me that he "made up" most of the book, including the gun, although "I cannot be entirely sure.... It's been so long ago now." He remembered that he checked the "mechanics" of the gun with a "gunsmith friend" who told him, "it would work" but "be damned clumsy....I'd overheard some Pentagon brass talking about Patton at a reception and one of them said something along the lines of, 'Everyone knows they killed the old bastard.'" He thought to himself, "now there's a story that needs telling." Researching, he said he found "a lot of loose strands" supporting assassination. Interviewing Woodring, which he wrote he did at "endless length," two things stuck in his mind. One was truck driver Thompson who had disappeared "even though...he had absolutely no reason or right to be where he was...had taken a joyride after a night of boozing," and had "two other GIs in the cabin although regulations permitted only driver and one passenger." The other was "an officer at the scene...whose involvement," Woodring had lamented, "was never mentioned again." That officer was Vanlandingham.

Woodring had given Nolan a photo of himself standing next to the wrecked Cadillac. On its back, he had scribbled "Lt. Vanlandingham" and "7340" beneath it, indicating it was Vanlandingham's service number.[40] Nolan emailed a copy to me.

After considerable searching, I located a veteran I thought might just be the mysterious Vanlandingham. It was not a common name. His first name was Arlis Vanlandingham. He fought in Germany at the end of the war. A photo of him as a company platoon leader in the 90th Infantry Division,[41] whose commander was pictured with Patton, led me to his son, Glen Vanlandingham of Round Rock, Texas. Glen was a Baptist choir director and said his father had died ten years earlier but he remembered watching a movie about Patton showing the accident and his usually quiet dad saying, "I was there." But little else. Apparently he never talked about the war. Glen said he had papers tucked away that showed his Dad had won some medals. He would go through them and send what he could.

Arlis turned out to be an authentic hero. Like Babalas, he had been at Normandy, and gone through France and into the Rhineland with Patton's Third Army. He had won four Bronze Stars and a Purple Heart, which is pretty impressive. One of the medals was awarded for leading his men against Nazi night attacks after being separated from his main unit. Despite his being wounded, they captured two hundred enemy prisoners.

This was the type of bold courage sought by intelligence groups like the OSS for special operations, which may or may not have been in a soldier's records. When I got to the end of the papers, however, it said that he departed Europe 11 Sept. '45, which was roughly three months before Patton's accident. Further notations, however raised more questions. While they implied he was in the U.S. and "unassigned" through 1946, one notation said, "officer promoted to captain 19 December 45"—not even two weeks after Patton's accident. Was he still in the service? Why was he promoted after coming home? The military is notorious for discharging soldiers as quickly as possible in order to minimize future government benefits. A promotion guaranteed more benefits— and for an idle soldier? Were the dates and places authentic? Or were they fake like others I have seen which cover clandestine assignments? That was the way organizations like the OSS—and the CIA today—hid secret missions. Whatever the truth, Arlis, his son insisted, had told him, "I was there."

Still another MP said to have been at the accident was Lieutenant Joseph Shanahan, identified by Farago as "a former deputy Provost Marshal in Patton's Third Army." The provost was said to have conducted its own investigation into the crash. The results of that investigation remain a mystery as they are nowhere to be found. In 1979, Shanahan, of Lambertville, New Jersey, told his hometown newspaper that the reason no on-scene report of the accident was made was that the accident was "trivial"—the limousine's windows were not even broken—and Patton was unhurt.[42] But the medical record, plus references to the on-scene accident report and later accident investigations unearthed in formerly secret documents belie that witness. Patton *was* hurt. Reports *were* made. Shanahan has not been heard from since—at least as far as I know. I could not find him. He joins the other mystery men, silent and unable to be found, as part of the chaotic, contradictory, shadowy accident scene.

And I have not yet addressed Technician Fifth Class (T/5) Robert L. Thompson, driver of the truck which turned in front of Patton's limousine. As if stalking the Cadillac—as Woodring's description of the truck "waiting" implies—as well as abruptly turning in front of Patton's car in clear daylight on an untraveled road was not suspicious enough, the veteran driver who had safely piloted vehicles through dangerous war zones for nearly two years prior[43] was allowed to vanish from the scene and, for the most part, disappear. The same goes for his two unlawful passengers— if that was the number in his cab—one of whom was identified in a confidential Seventh Army Public Relations Officer (PRO) document[44] as "Frank Krummer, a civilian employe [sic] of the signal company." Both Thompson and Krummer, according to the document, worked at the 141st Signal Company of the 1st Armored Division at Gmund, some fifty miles south of Mannheim, near Stuttgart. What were they doing that far north on a shutdown Sunday? According to Farago, Thompson was "in violation of the rules" in having two passengers in the cab and "out of his own routine. He had no orders to go anywhere this Sunday morning."[45]

Apparently another officer at the scene—also not heard from again—took a sworn statement from Thompson. Second Lieutenant Hugh O. Layton of Babalas's 818 MP Company in Mannheim is listed in a further Seventh Army PRO document[46] as having arrived after Babalas and interviewed Thompson under oath: "At approximately 1200 hours [I] was traveling north on Highway N38," the document says Thompson told Layton. "I was approaching the Class II and IV QM [quartermaster] depot. In making my left turn from the highway I noticed a general's car approaching me. As I had already started my turn I could not avoid the car hitting the rear of the . . . truck. I did not notice the car until I had started to turn."

Was he blind?

At least one reporter claims to have talked to Thompson after the crash: In a story datelined "Frankfurt, Dec. 13," which appeared in U.S. papers a day later,[47] journalist Kingsbury Smith, who would later become widely known as ABC television reporter and anchor Howard K. Smith, would write that "in discussing the tragic event for the first time," Thompson told him, "The general's car was speeding... or he wouldn't have hit me so hard." He was making the turn "into a side street," Thompson told Smith, and didn't see the collision coming until "it was too late.... If I had tried to straighten out, I would have hit Patton's car head on. Patton's driver slammed on the brakes and slid about forty feet before he smacked me, knocking my... truck about five feet...." The limousine was speeding? Woodring, wrote Smith, denied the charge. He was not speeding. However, in a deviation from future recollections about the pre-crash moments, Woodring, according to Smith, told him that contrary to actually halting at the railroad tracks, he had just slowed "to five miles an hour" to cross them. "We were then about 300 yards from the scene of the accident. I could not have picked up much speed by the time I reached the truck,"[48] he said. Gay's memoir also says they slowed rather than stopped.

In addition to being different from what Woodring would later say, it was a weak denial.

Following the collision, Thompson told Smith, "I got out of the truck and I was pretty mad....I was going to tell them off. Then I saw the stars on General Gay's shoulder and then on Patton's. I nearly fainted. And I decided I'd better not argue." Again, Woodring's version differs. He has always maintained that Thompson and his passengers had been drinking. They "were drunk and feeling no pain," he told Brian Sobel in *The Fighting Pattons*. "It seemed they were having a big time....I asked him, 'Do you realize who you hit? This is General Patton and he is critically injured. What the hell were you doing?... The driver said, 'Oh, my God, General Patton,' and made kind of clown-like gestures and turned around to his buddies and said, 'General Patton, do you believe it?' It was stupid behavior and I was angry.'"[49] Lester Gingold, who took the only photograph that has ever surfaced of Thompson purportedly at the scene, says he did not think the truck driver was drunk, just scared. But his photograph seems to support Woodring. Thompson's hat is askew, his lowered hands appear to be flapping like birds, and he grins open-mouthed as if giggling.

What was the truth?

Neither driver was ever charged although documents and newspaper stories say both were driving recklessly.[50] But, as Ladislas Farago wrote, "Thompson's testimony could have been challenged in every one of his separate statements. But it was not. And the case was left at that. Although it was still nominally open and pending on December 21 [when Patton died] it was never pursued after that. The investigation of this historic accident was far less thorough than even that of a minor traffic incident that claimed no life and involved no figure even remotely as important as General Patton."

One final puzzle involves Woodring's account.

There apparently existed at one time a dubious report about the accident in government files. As already briefly mentioned earlier, Farago writes that in an early attempt to get information on the crash, the army wrote back to a questioner—who is not identified by Farago but which he implies is the *Post-Tribune* newspaper of Gary, Indiana—that it had on file an "unofficial report of the accident" consisting of a statement made and signed by Woodring in 1952. What is on the statement is not discussed. But when Farago says he asked Woodring about it in 1979, Woodring told him he had no recollection of "ever having made a statement" in 1952 or "having signed one" in that year.[51]

In other words, as far as Woodring was concerned, it was a forgery.

A forgery?

Why, if Farago's report is true, would there be a forged note about the accident in government files?[52]

★ ★ ★ ★

CHAPTER TWELVE

THE LAST BULLET

The ambulance transporting Snyder, Patton, and whoever else was inside arrived at the gates to the 130th hospital's main three-story building at approximately 12:30 p.m., according to the hospital's commanding officer, Colonel Lawrence C. Ball, M.D.[1] Hospital records state Patton was officially admitted at 12:45 p.m.[2] The head physician attending him in the hospital's first floor emergency room was Lieutenant Colonel Paul S. Hill, Jr., the 39-year-old chief of surgery. Assisting was Dr. Kent of Cleveland, Ohio, who would later erroneously write that Patton had arrived in the Cadillac.* The two were at, or just concluding, lunch, according to their memoirs, when summoned to the emergency room by a corpsman.[3] "The general lay on a litter which had been placed on an operating table," wrote Hill. With him was

---

*Kent's recollections further complicate what happened at the accident scene. He says Gay told him they were on the autobahn when the truck that caused the accident suddenly appeared from a side street; that Patton was injured when Woodring swerved and hit a ditch.

General Gay and "a medical officer summoned to the scene of the accident," probably Snyder. "He had lost quite a bit of blood," was "very pale" and in "shock," but "conscious and oriented." Attendants carefully cut away his clothes but were reluctant to remove what remained beneath him for fear of jostling his injury. Patton managed to joke, "Relax, gentlemen, I am obviously in no condition to be a terror."[4] His neck, because of his injury, was "flexed forward," causing some pain, especially to the touch, but "it was obvious he had neither sensory nor motor function below the neck"—an initial observation, slightly modified later by tests, that established the bottom of his collar bone as the point below which he was paralyzed and without feeling. It was also later determined that he had some faint reflexes, shoulder tip sensation, could manage "a flicker" of movement in one leg and some toes, and, while one lung was not working, he could breathe with the other, which, of course, was crucial.[5]

On his head was a "dressing" loosely "held down with adhesive tape." Hill removed it and described the "severe laceration" to Patton's "nose, forehead and scalp" as "a long, deep Y-shaped" wound extending "from the bridge of his nose running backward across the forehead" and onto the top of the head. It was "a ragged deep laceration with jagged ramifications, lifting a circular flap of [skin] and leaving bare the bone in its entire length.... A good view of the forward part of the skull was obtained thru [sic] the flap-like laceration."[6]

No bones below his neck appeared broken.

Speculation was that Patton had been hurled forward and hit his head on the top of the rear compartment or possibly somewhere on the dividing partition between the front and rear compartments. The partition contained a window that could be rolled down, which may or may not have been open. It also contained a

casing that protruded slightly around the window and, supposedly, a clock. Any of these, it was assumed, could have caused the
"ghastly" wound, as Farago labeled it. Farago, who interviewed
Hill, writes, "Patton himself told Colonel Hill that he thought he
had fallen against a clock in the partition and was scalped by its
sharp edges."[7] But he did not know for sure. "He does not know
if he became unconscious" at the time of the injury, wrote Hill.
"But witnesses state that he was unconscious for about a
minute."[8]

In fact, no one knew for sure how he had been so injured.

It was *all* conjecture.

Patton was speculated to have been sitting up on the edge of
the seat and that was why he had been thrown forward. But
Woodring later told author D. A. Lande, "he rarely *ever* sat on
the edge of his seat."[9] The idea that he was hurtled around violently in the limousine's roomy passenger compartment yet had
not broken any bones in his hands, arms, or legs is unusual. And
his wound was quite nasty to have been caused by a small car
clock, or a smooth and lined roof, or a slightly protruded window
casing. It could have been caused if the window between the two
sections of the car had been open and he had vaulted through it,
scraping himself on its edge, depending on the sharpness of the
edge and the casing. But surely his head would have been caught
or at least further impacted in his return momentum from the collision which would have put additional wounds on his face.

Was this large and ugly wound that had prompted Lieutenent Babalas—if Babalas can be trusted—to decide to look further at what
happened and make a report—the report Lieutenant Shanahan
insisted was unnecessary?

An examination of the car would have likely ended such
speculation—had there been any real urgency to make such a

determination, which there does not appear to have been. It could have shown where flesh and blood had been left, or a dent had been made, and thereby help pinpoint, if not definitively establish, where and what Patton might—or might not—have hit. But the doctors accepted the explanations sight unseen. They seemed logical. Their job was not to investigate what had happened at the accident but to try to fix the resulting damage, however it was caused. And by early afternoon, the car seems to have been towed from the accident scene, which, according to available evidence, was done rather quickly. Within hours of the accident, it was already on its way to an unknown[10] military junkyard where precisely what happened to it would become yet another mystery.

The exact nature and direction of Patton's face wound is in question. According to an unsigned "Case summary," dated 12 December 1945, Patton's "scalp peeled forward *down* to the bridge of the nose." This appears to contrast with Dr. Hill's December 9 admittance-day description that the wound began at the nose and traveled *upward*. Dr. Kent supports Hill, writing that it "ascended" to the scalp, but differs in that he says it began at "mid-forehead" and traversed the scalp all the way "to the rear."[11] Just like accounts from the accident, there are contradictions. What is the truth? Memories are frequently faulty. Did it begin on his face or his scalp? At his nose or his mid-forehead? Was the unsigned description, terse as it is, just a phraseology that did not really mean to imply initial direction? In the absence of definitive proof, such details are important in order to determine exactly how and by what Patton was cut.[12]

For his shock, a potentially deadly condition on its own, Patton was warmed with blankets and given a series of blood transfusions. Before the day ended, he would receive 300 cc of blood and 1500 cc of plasma.[13] The little hospital had to recruit donors on the spot but the infusions did the trick. Dissipation of symptoms began almost immediately. Patton's color returned. His blood pressure rose eventually to acceptable numbers. He was started on regular injections of penicillin and other antibiotics, new in medicine in those days, and eventually an indwelling catheter was inserted into his urinary tract.[14] Under medical questioning, he disclosed he had last urinated up at the Roman ruins around 10:00 a.m.[15] Such information, along with the time of the accident, variously given as around 11:45 a.m., helps establish a time line for the trip with its reported stops from Bad Nauheim.

As soon as Dr. Hill started working on Patton, General Gay, accompanied by a "Brigadier General,"[16] according to the hospital's administrator, Colonel Lawrence C. Ball, went directly to Ball's office and "made some telephone calls."[17] Presumably, as a result, at 2:30 p.m., having rushed to the hospital by plane, medical brass from Frankfurt arrived. They included Major General Albert W. Kenner, chief army surgeon in Europe, and Colonel Earl E. Lowery, head consulting surgeon in Frankfurt and Hill's immediate medical superior up the chain of command. After consultation, a portable X-ray machine was brought into the emergency room rather than moving Patton and chance worsening his injuries. Eventually it confirmed much of what was suspected. Patton's neck was dislocated at the junction of the third and fourth vertebrae in the neck. There was "approximately 4 mm displacement," accounting for his distention. A small piece of the bone on the underside of the third vertebrae had fractured and broken away. The doctors felt the spinal cord had been cut but probably not completely because of the feeble movements observed and his ability to breathe. Not even the X-rays could tell them if the cord had been completely severed. They decided to supplant a temporary traction apparatus they applied to his neck with "Crutchfield tongs." These were rather brutal-looking clamps with sharp, pointed ends, similar to old-fashioned ice tongs. The tongs curled into the skull from a helmet-like apparatus with a lever holding five pounds of weight. It was placed on Patton's head. Under local anesthetic, small holes were drilled into his skull where the tong tips were inserted. The tongs, lifting his head toward their helmet base, were designed to reduce compaction of the neck bones due to the injury and hopefully realign them to their proper place. Only time would tell if the treatment would be successful. It was uncomfortable, to say the least, but Patton did not complain. In fact, he made a joke, according to Dr. Kent, about it feeling "drafty" in his head where they were drilling.[18] Patton was described as a "model patient."

Patton's head lacerations were also cleaned and then stitched under local anesthesia, an operation Patton seemed to take some pride in, remarking that the first stitch by Dr. Lowry was his seventy-second lifetime stitch and that he would like them to keep count.[19]

At 6:45 p.m., the doctors finished their initial work. Patton had a temperature of 102 degrees but was "stable." He was given morphine for pain[20] and was moved to a small first floor room across the hall from the operating theater, his condition listed as "critical" and "guarded."

Long before that, as early as 2:00 p.m., according to Farago, "the calm" of the 130th had been "shattered." In addition to "a dozen generals...every correspondent, reporter, stringer, freelance rubberneck and photographer" in the theater had descended on the hospital.[21] The atmosphere outside the emergency room turned tense. After delivering Patton, Captain Snyder, outside the main hospital building, said he was "accosted" by "a diminutive brigadier" who cautioned him to "keep my mouth shut about the accident...and later to go along with the Army release of information."[22]

What did that mean? Was it just typical military precaution or was something else afoot?

Had they told other doctors to go along with army releases, too?

Why such a shutdown of information?

The next day, according to one of the first newspaper stories to appear about the crash, the United Press, a news agency comparable in power and audience to any of today's major television networks, reported that Patton was "under a twenty-four-hour daily guard by white-helmeted soldiers. The guard was set up," said the story, "after Patton, who was conscious and still at least partially like his old self heard someone talking about him in the hall and said he did not like it."[23]

What had he heard?

Were the guards just to keep the press out? Or were there greater fears?

Regardless, the guards were not able to stop the onslaught. Farago wrote that reporters posed as patients, donned hospital gowns to try to look like medical personnel, and attempted to bribe the designated hospital cook—privileged to serve Patton by himself—with cartons of Lucky Strikes, nylon stockings, and Hershey bars in order to be able to take a meal to the general, all in pursuit of exclusive stories and hopefully, the prize—access to Patton's room and the general himself. At least one, according to Farago, got through the cordon. He wrote that an Associated Press reporter, "Richard H. O'Regan by name," obtained an "exclusive by posing as a patient." A nurse, just wanting to ease concerns about Patton's well-being amongst patients and not realizing O'Regan's ruse, apparently disclosed to him that the general was sipping whisky in his room, which, left out of the story, had been prescribed by doctors in minute amounts, and thus was, not to worry, his crusty old self. The resultant story caused an uproar. "Flat on His Back, Skull Clamped, Patton Calls for Shot of Whisky" said one of the headlines. The story showed his mood swinging from jokes and being "cute" with his nurse, to saying, "I probably will be dead by morning."[24]

By Monday—the day after Patton was admitted—the number of press people assaulting the hospital had swelled to thirty,[25] "straining [the] meager facilities beyond the breaking point." The reporters were loud, demanding, and were "stepping on each other's toes" to get access. "No precautionary measures could keep all of them out all of the time"[26]—this in a country where nylons could buy love, and a little more could buy even murder. In such an atmosphere—had there been a plot—anyone could have been an imposter, especially those trained and equipped for it. Press cards, forged and real, were easily obtainable on the German Black Market. Posing as a nurse, medical technician, or even doctor, would have been relatively easy, especially for a professional with skill and nerve. It had been—and would be—done often, even by amateurs. Guards or no guards, Patton, paralyzed and continually medicated, was vulnerable as he lay in that first floor hospital room.

One of the first outsiders to learn of the accident was Patton's wife, Beatrice, back in Boston, where the Pattons had their permanent home. According to formerly confidential War Department documents,[27] Mrs. Patton was informed by an Associated Press reporter "on the morning of 9 December"—an amazing feat since the accident had only occurred that morning. But it was made possible by the time differences between the U.S. and Germany. The reporter was looking for details which, of course,

Patton's daughter, Ruth Ellen Totten, who had answered the phone and relayed the inquiry to her mother, did not have. The daughter immediately called authorities in Washington. They gave her the few details available—broken neck, "unknown if the spinal cord was cut"—and offered to fly her mother to Heidelberg, a courtesy Mrs. Patton quickly accepted. A noted U.S. neurosurgeon, Dr. R. Glen Spurling, who had earlier returned from army medical service in Europe, was located on a train where he was en route to Washington D.C. to be separated from the service. He was literally plucked off the train so he could fly with Mrs. Patton who was leaving immediately. Colonel Spurling, a pioneer in spinal and nerve disease, was renowned in his field. In the meantime, another top neurosurgeon, British Brigadier Hugh Cairns, a professor at Oxford, had been flown in by the army from London. He had observed that the Crutchfield tongs were slipping because of the shape of Patton's head, and recommended instead that zygomatic hooks be applied for better traction. These were clasps resembling ordinary fish hooks that were inserted into Patton's cheekbones on the sides of the face for a better hold. Dangling from another head apparatus were ten pounds of weight, double the amount on the Crutchfield tongs. The apparatus, in addition to being more painful than the "ice hooks," was also more cumbersome. But Patton is said to have endured its application under local anesthetic without complaint.

Patton's first nights were rough. He dozed intermittently, getting little real sleep. His neck was painful, his temperature ranged from 100 to 102 degrees, and most of the time an intravenous setup (IV) dripped fluids often times unknown to him into his veins. At 5:00 a.m. the first night, according to his "Nurse's Notes," he was "apprehensive—feels a 'choking' sensation when falling asleep." His breathing with only half a diaphragm working was labored.

The other half was paralyzed. He was given the sedative Luminal and finally dozed for about an hour around 6:00 a.m. With short periods of improvement, treatment continued throughout the day. The next night, December 11, at approximately 1:00 a.m., the nurse noted, "Patient resting well but is unable to sleep—appears apprehensive over IV bottle dripping which he is able to see. Asking questions concerning IV fluids—'When will it be finished?—I don't think it's going through—I can't feel it.'" She disconnected the IV and it calmed him. He went to sleep "ten minutes later." The danger of an IV to a vulnerable patient—should he be targeted for malevolence—is that anything can be injected into the needle port without the patient feeling it, or, if the IV is out of view, even knowing it until the effects begin. Then it can be too late to counter. In the case of Patton, paralyzed as he was, he could be stuck with a needle almost anywhere below his shoulders and not know it.

Farago tells of Patton's depression and concern about death during this time and then, in the afternoon of December 11, his wife and Dr. Spurling arrived. The doctors had hoped his wife's arrival would buoy Patton and they were not disappointed. By Patton's request, the first thing his wife did upon coming to the hospital was spend a half hour alone with him. What was discussed will probably never be known by the public. It was private. But she emerged from his room confident and, according to Farago, with a list of books her husband requested. Farago quotes her as optimistically saying, "I've seen Georgie in these scrapes before. He always comes out all right." She added that he requested his visitors be curtailed. "The strain is getting too much for him." In other words, visitors had previously been allowed. Certainly, it is assumed, they would have been frisked before entry. But who knows? Nor was it explained why Patton wanted them stopped, although it is indicated that he did not want others, especially acquaintances, seeing him incapacitated. Writes Farago, Mrs. Patton's "voice hardened.... Under no circumstances does he want to be visited by General Bedell Smith,"[28] Eisenhower's powerful chief of staff whom Patton disliked intensely. He considered the soon-to-be ambassador to Russia (1946-1949) and director of the early CIA (1950 to 1953) a personal enemy. When Eisenhower had fired Patton from the Third Army just months before, at the end of September, it had been Ike's "hatchet man" Smith who had phoned Patton with the bad news. "I did not trust Beedle [sic] Smith," Patton had written in his diary October 2, 1945. And nearly two weeks later, he told Eisenhower, "I could not hereafter eat at the same table with Beedle [sic] Smith."[29]

Dr. Spurling, who would basically preside medically over Patton from that point on, examined his new and important patient. He found what the others had. Patton's condition was "precarious," mainly because of the "restriction on breathing." The part of his diaphragm that was working was doing double duty, the strain of which was worrisome. An operation was "out of the question" simply because there was no operation to "restore" a damaged spinal cord. And even if there was, it "would have been almost an impossible task because the patient was barely able to breathe under normal conditions, much less under anesthesia." Whether or not he pulled through, he would never ride horses again, Spurling told Patton in response to the general's private questioning when they were alone. Of Patton's reaction, Spurling said, "he thought a moment and he said 'Thank you, Colonel, for being honest.' Then in a flash he returned to his old jovial mood."

The following day, wrote Spurling, "there seemed to be a distinct improvement in the General's condition. He regained a little more power in one arm and a very minute amount of power in one leg.

Also the muscles of respiration began to function feebly. This gave us high hopes that the cord was not as seriously damaged as we had every reason to believe in the beginning. In addition to these favorable neurological signs, his general condition remained remarkably good. He was cheerful and took a well balanced diet freely. His temperature and pulse remained normal...."[30] Improvement, wrote Spurling, continued for several more days until it "ceased and he showed no further return of his spinal cord function. Yet, in spite of this grim outlook, his general condition held up remarkably well."

On December 17, with the hooks in his cheekbones "each day" becoming "more unbearable," it was decided to try removing them and substituting a "light plaster cast" to support his neck. Tests showed that the tongs had done their work. "The flow of spinal fluid was free and there was not the slightest indication of pressure" at the injury. The bone alignment was "perfect." The hooks were removed and the cast was molded to his shoulders and neck in his room "without disturbing him in the least." Patton "was much happier."[31]

By December 18, he was doing so well that it was decided, at the urgings of Mrs. Patton, that he would best be served at a major hospital near his Massachusetts home. His nurse wrote on his chart that day that he was "cheerful, very alert."[32] Farago says he told her, "I am feeling really well, Ann. For the first time."[33] Usually not hungry, she noted he ate, "soup, mashed potatoes and gravy." A comprehensive physical spurred by the turnaround showed that despite the problems caused by his paralysis, he was otherwise generally in "excellent" health. He might never ride horses again, but his blood pressure was normal. His heart tones were good. There were even some new movements detected in his thigh and biceps.[34] Dr. Spurling, the most optimistic of his doctors, cabled the surgeon general's office in Washington: "Arrangements being made air evacuation General Patton, 30 December," he wrote.[35] It was set. Patton would be home a week after Christmas. Sergeant Meeks, his black orderly and friend who had attended him throughout the war, began a crash course on how to function as Patton's nurse during the return. Farago likened Patton's improvement to the time almost exactly a year before when, during the Battle of the Bulge, he had ordered his chaplain to write a prayer for clear weather so Allied planes could fly in support and the prayer had been answered. It was "mysterious," an "enchanting miracle," he ventured.[36] Patton had done it again.

Then he had a sudden downturn.

Since she arrived, wrote Spurling, Mrs. Patton "had been concerned about the possibility of an embolism"—the obstruction of blood flow in an artery, usually by a piece of clotted blood that breaks free in one place in the circulatory system and travels to another. It is a problem particularly for older patients who are bedridden. Air, fat globules, pieces of errant tissue, or even hardened pus can cause obstruction. In 1937, while riding with his wife, Patton had been kicked by her horse when it suddenly bolted. The kick had broken bones in his right leg. Bedridden with a cast for nearly four months, he had developed "thrombophlebitis," a blood clot condition which had sent two emboli to his pelvic region.[37] But he had recovered and been formally certified by army doctors as free of "any illness of a chronic nature," a requirement for him to be put back on active duty.[38] The medical examination then specifically noted that all his vitals, including heart, blood, and respiratory systems, were "normal." Nevertheless, wrote Spurling, Mrs. Patton "kept saying to me every night, 'If he just doesn't get an embolism I think he may pull through.'"

But according to Spurling and at least some of Patton's other doctors, an embolism—or multiple emboli—suddenly attacked him late in the night of December 19. Copies of Patton's medical records from those hours, sent by the Army Reserve Personnel Center in St. Louis, are so faint that they can not be deciphered. But Farago writes—and a hospital summary[39] appears to agree—that shortly after 10:00 p.m. Patton "was jolted awake by a violent coughing spell." Farago's is the only account that describes the attack. He portrays it this way: "No crisis was expected and the tension had eased in [Patton's room. His nurse], whose shift was ending, was standing at the door, talking with another nurse. When she heard the patient's sudden discomfort, she rushed to his bed...."[40]

In other words, Patton was alone in the room when the attack began.

Dr. Hill, in a letter, called the attack a "shower emboli," which presumably meant more than one embolism. With his paralysis impairing his ability to cough and breathe, Patton had trouble raising fluid from his lungs. "For minutes afterward," continued Farago, "he remained in desperate straits" until doctors arrived and he was given codeine and other medications that eventually steadied him. His diminished breathing during and after the attack combined with blood traces in his sputum made doctors suspect embolism (or emboli) had hit his one working lung and caused the crisis. The problem causes tissue around the obstruction to die and thus deprives the lungs of more oxygen-supplying cells. By morning, Dr. Spurling wrote in his memoir, "he was feeling fine again." But Farago cautions, "the improvement was superficial and deceptive."[41]

The dying process was beginning its final stages.

At 10:00 a.m., Patton's neck and chest were x-rayed. Eventually, according to hospital notes,[42] the films "showed evidence of an acute pulmonary complication...of embolic nature." In other

★ ★ ★ ★

Patton poses with one of his Cadillac staff cars.

 ★ ★ ★ ★

(LEFT) Patton loved hunting and was on his way to hunt when seriously injured December 9, 1945.

(BELOW) Patton was a student of history.

(ABOVE) Patton triumphant.

(BELOW) He inspired his troops.

(LEFT) At a parade,
the picture-perfect general.

(LOWER LEFT) In battle.

(LOWER RIGHT) Patton with
his rival, British General
Bernard Montgomery.

* * * *

(ABOVE) The damaged Cadillac, probably wherever
it was hauled following the December 9, 1945 crash.

all these buildings
were built since 1945

Thompson

PATTON

* * * *

(LOWER LEFT) Contemporary picture of the road outside Mannheim where
the accident happened. Taken from where the railroad tracks that the Cadillac crossed
used to be. The accident occurred a short distance later up the road. *Credit: Denver Fugate*

(LOWER RIGHT) The remote street in 1945 is now bristling with buildings.
It was approximately in front of the big building in the center that the truck
suddenly turned in front of Patton's limousine, causing the accident. *Credit: Peter Hendrikx*

★ ★ ★ ★

The Cadillac probably right after the accident, and probably being
hooked up to be towed. Note the ground—it is the same as in the pictures
of Robert L. Thompson and his truck at the scene.

★ ★ ★ ★

Nineteen-year-old driver of the Cadillac, Horace Woodring,
looks at the damaged Cadillac. He said the splotches
on his jacket were from Patton's blood.

(ABOVE LEFT) Robert L. Thompson at the scene of the December 9, 1945 crash, moments after he turned his truck (in the background) without signaling in front of Patton's limousine.

(ABOVE RIGHT) The two-and-a-half-ton army truck Robert L. Thompson was driving when Patton's limousine hit it. This and the photo to the left were taken right after the accident by Lester Gingold.

(LOWER RIGHT) A mysterious picture of Robert L. Thompson at what looks like a blackboard, describing something. Efforts to identify it have been fruitless but one report suggests he was in London right after the crash.

(ABOVE) The damaged Cadillac presumably at a place it was taken after the accident. Note the chains hanging from its front which were probably used to haul it there.

(LEFT) Newspapers like this bannered the news of Patton's injury.

Credit: Courtesy of The Bancroft Library, University of California, Berkeley

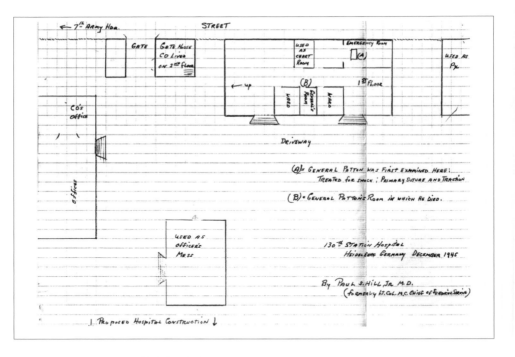

Diagram handwritten notes:

← 7th Army Hdqr. STREET

GATE

GATE HOUSE
CO LIVED
ON 2nd FLOOR

USED AS
CHART
ROOM

EMERGENCY ROOM
(A)

USED AS
PX

← UP

(B)

WARD

General's Room

WARD

1st FLOOR

CO'S
OFFICE

OFFICE

DRIVEWAY

(A) = GENERAL PATTON WAS FIRST EXAMINED HERE;
TREATED FOR SHOCK; PRIMARY SUTURE AND TRACTION

(B) = GENERAL PATTON'S ROOM IN WHICH HE DIED.

USED AS
OFFICER'S
MESS

130th STATION HOSPITAL
HEIDELBERG GERMANY DECEMBER 1945

By PAUL S. HILL, Jr. M.D.
(FORMERLY LT. COL. M.C. CHIEF OF SURGICAL SERVICE)

↓ PROPOSED HOSPITAL CONSTRUCTION ↓

★ ★ ★ ★

(ABOVE) Diagram of the grounds of the 130th Station Hospital, Heidelberg, Germany, where General Patton was taken after the accident. He was put in a room in the largest building, fronting the outside street.

(LOWER LEFT) Douglas Bazata, OSS agent and post-World War II operative, as a young man traveling the West.

(LOWER RIGHT) Bazata as a member of the world champion Marine rifle team in 1933. He was also unofficial heavyweight boxing champion of the corps.

BAZATA, Douglas D.
Enl 10MAR33
Photo Taken 13MAR33

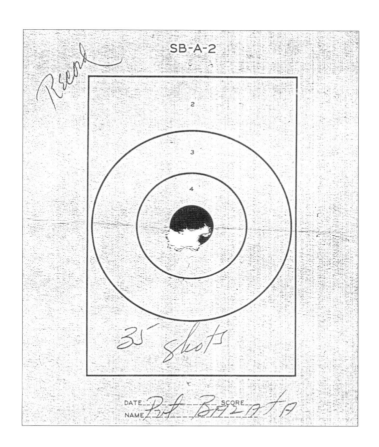

SB-A-2

Record

2

3

4

35´ shots

DATE _____ SCORE _____
NAME _Pvt. BAZATA_

★ ★ ★ ★

(ABOVE) Bazata's record-breaking 35 bull's-eyes as an officer candidate at Ft. Benning.

(LEFT) Captain Bazata right around the time he joined the OSS in 1943.

ONS

ausgestellt für Herrn Douglas Bazata
anerkanntes Pseudonym
geboren am 17. Febr. 1911
zu Wrightsville/USA
wohnhaft zu Johannisburg/Rhein.

Frankfurt/Main, den 25. Febr. 1954

Der Inhaber:

Der Präsident
der ONS

Nicht gültig
für internationale
Veranstaltungen

Dieser Ausweis berechtigt zum Start bei allen
genehmigungspflichtigen nationalen Veranstaltungen
in Deutschland und zu solchen Rennen, die aus-
drücklich für die Inhaber des nationalen Ausweises
ausgeschrieben sind.

★ ★ ★ ★

(ABOVE) One of many foreign driver's licenses acquired by
Bazata as an intelligence operative in post-war Europe.

(BELOW) Bazata, an acclaimed painter, explains one of his creations
to Princess Grace of Monaco, who hosted a showing of his work.

★ ★ ★ ★

(ABOVE LEFT) Bazata and his wife Marie-Pierre after returning from Europe and working in the Reagan administration.

(ABOVE RIGHT) Stephen J. Skubik as a young CIC agent in immediate post-war Germany. He is seated on the left.

(RIGHT) Returning to America in fear of his life, Skubik eventually went to work for Republican administrations and is seen here with President Ronald Reagan.

(LOWER RIGHT): Joe Scruce with young relatives.

★ ★ ★ ★

(ABOVE) The Cadillac exhibited at the Patton Museum, Ft. Knox, Kentucky, as the same that General Patton was injured in. But new evidence indicates it is not in fact the original, but actually a very good replica.

(BELOW) The backseat of the Cadillac at Ft. Knox—a good replica of what General Patton and General Gay were sitting on when the accident occurred.

★ ★ ★ ★

(ABOVE) Hard-to-find area of the Cadillac chassis at Ft. Knox showing crude scrapings intended to obliterate the identification number, indicating foul play. *Credit: Frank Jardim*

(BELOW) Honor guard carrying General Patton's casket during funeral ceremonies.

★ ★ ★ ★

"I have known the call to Battle."
—"Through a Glass, Darkly," General George S. Patton, Jr.

words, it confirmed that an embolus (or multiple emboli) had caused the crises in Patton's working lung. They logically suspected it had originated at the site of his neck injury. But tests showed Patton's "spinal condition to be stable."[43] Spurling said, "We had accomplished a perfect reduction of the fractured vertebrae...as far as the spinal cord injury is concerned he was making very good progress."[44]

So what was the origin of the embolism?

Still thinking it was the neck injury, they could not be sure.

Exasperated, Spurling wrote in his memoir, "There was no predicting where the embolism might have formed. There was certainly no external evidence of phlebitis [inflammation of a vein] in any part of the body."[45]

The situation did not change substantially the rest of the day except that around 3:30 p.m., Patton, according to his chart, had another coughing spell.[46] While records do not indicate it was as violent as the earlier one, his condition continued to deteriorate. Each cough taxed his heart. The vital organ had to work harder pumping blood in order for him to expel mounting fluid from his lungs so he could breathe better. His lungs got wetter. His blood pressure got weaker. He was given medicines through the mouth and IV but they did not stop the deterioration. At 9:00 p.m. his nurse wrote, "No coughing. Restless & tired." Copies of his released hospital records for the rest of the night are too faint to read but Farago says sometime during those hours he told his nurse, "Why don't they just let me die?"[47]

At 7:00 a.m., December 21, obviously not doing well, his charts say he "refused breakfast." The doctors continued testing and treating him. By 10:30 a.m., his nurse noted, "Patient sleeping or resting quietly." At noon, he drank some eggnog and seemed to feel better. Nevertheless, according to hospital notes, he "told nurse several times that he was going to die."[48] Around 2:00 p.m., according to Farago, he fell asleep again and his wife left the room, probably to get some sleep herself since she had been in an almost round-the-clock vigil since the coughing had started. She had a room down the hall.

Just after 3:00 p.m., according to his chart, he started coughing again. By 4:00, he was "very drowsy" and "unable to take fluid." Soon he was sleeping and "breathing irregularly," his pulse fading. Alarmed, the nurse summoned Dr. Duane, who, seeing the gravity, according to Farago, "ran down the corridor to summon" Mrs. Patton, "who came immediately, followed by Colonel Spurling."

Too late.

Patton was dead when they arrived.

CHAPTER THIRTEEN

★ ★ ★ ★

MURDER
BY TRUCK

Patton's War Department death certificate lists "Pulmonary Edema & Congestive heart failure" as the cause of death,[1] meaning his heart failed trying to clear his lungs.

It sounds like he died from complications caused by the car accident.

But we do not really know.

There was no autopsy.

Dr. Spurling, apparently not certain about the exact cause of the embolisms, requested one, but Mrs. Patton refused.[2] She did so, Spurling later wrote, "for two reasons: First, there wasn't a fully qualified pathologist available...and, second, Mrs. Patton felt that under the circumstances she would prefer not to have one performed. I am sure, though, had there been adequate facilities for careful study of the remains, she would have granted permission."[3]

In such circumstances, Mrs. Patton's wishes would have to be respected. But not having a "fully" qualified pathologist or "adequate" facilities seems a weak excuse, as Spurling gives it, and something the authorities could have remedied easily. They certainly had spared no expense or effort in locating Dr. Spurling thousands of miles away on a train in Ohio and immediately flying him and Mrs. Patton back across the Atlantic. They found other medical specialists throughout Europe and flew them in too. Upon Patton's death, authorities "rounded up" two registered morticians, according to Spurling, and immediately started planning a major funeral and burial procession by train to Luxemburg, a distance traversing two countries. The costs and effort for the procession alone easily would have exceeded any to find a qualified pathologist. And would not one of the hospital's surgical rooms or labs have done for the facilities?

Farago notes that "within hours of his death," rumors that Patton had been assassinated spread "throughout Germany."[4] And not only amongst Germans. Rank and file U.S. soldiers who had served in Patton's Third Army, most by then home and returning to civilian life, believed he had been murdered.[5] These were honored and hardened troops, not prone to exaggeration or naiveté. General James M. Gavin, leader of the 82nd Airborne Division, which had jumped into Normandy, later wrote, "It seemed incredible when we learned . . . he had died . . . . We followed what we assumed was his recovery . . . and expected at any time that he would be out of the hospital."[6] Patton's nephew and friend, Fred Ayer, Jr., an FBI official stationed in France, wrote that upon initially hearing of the accident, his immediate response was, "Accident hell. It was murder. Those communist sons of bitches killed him." Intelligence operatives thought the same.[7] In view of such speculation, wouldn't officials have wanted to quell the rumors? Patton had been front page news since landing in France after

D-Day, and his being fired in September had been widely covered. His controversies with ranking Allied generals, the Russians, the Democratic administration and its punitive deNazification, and general anti-German policies were well known and had become one of the big stories of the immediate post-war months. Those believing the rumors pointed publicly to his detractors—respected Allies all—as possible perpetrators.

Most curiously, it appears that Mrs. Patton herself had questions. In spring 2006, FOX News *War Stories* with host Oliver North broadcast an episode entitled, "Remarkable Life and Mysterious Death of General Patton." In the show, Patton's grandson, James Patton Totten, an adult now and spokesman for the Patton family, is quoted on camera as saying, "My grandmother hired several private detectives to investigate [the death]. They didn't find anything to substantiate the rumor." He gives no details but his statement shows she, at least, wondered. Why? When? What prompted her to pursue such an investigation?

My attempts to question the Patton family, now several generations removed from their famous World War II general and patriarch, have been rebuffed. Early on, when I had gathered only the broad outlines of evidence, mainly Bazata's claims and Skubik's book, which I felt warranted re-examining Patton's death, I was told through an intermediary that "this is a subject that is not new to the family and I perceive they assign it no credibility." The inference was clear: I was resurrecting something they had already dismissed and would not appreciate visiting again.

I can understand their concern.

In one of Bazata's diaries there is an exasperatingly short and somewhat confusing entry that he and Patton's son, George S. Patton (IV), an army general himself, now deceased, had sparred face to face. The meeting, at a Washington restaurant, apparently was arranged by a mutual friend, Lou Conein,[8] a former Jedburgh and notorious CIA agent, following the publication of the *Spotlight* articles in 1979. Since the articles claimed Bazata only *knew* who had set up the accident (rather than revealing he had participated himself), Patton's son was not aware of Bazata's claims to me— unless he told the son too, and I doubt that. Bazata wrote that the meeting had degenerated into insults, which probably left the family with a bad taste.* I know they had not seen Bazata's journals, and I doubt they have researched, as I have, Skubik's experiences, whose 1993 book, as tantalizingly full of leads as it is, nevertheless was so badly organized that it would not be surprising if they had tossed it after the first few pages. In any case, my contact informed me that the family was not interested in talking to me. Therefore, questions like who Mrs. Patton's detectives were and what they had found are unanswered—at least publicly.

Patton's adult granddaughter, Helen Patton-Plusczyk, was also in the *War Stories* episode. Clearly skeptical, she revealed that while abroad she was approached by a "mysterious colonel who had been a spy for the Russians." He told her he had some information for her, "A nurse or a medical aide had been instructed to open the windows of Grandpa's room so he would contract pneumonia." Even though she did not give it much credibility—nor tell what happened next—it would be productive to know more. I have a file of names, Russian and others—mostly agents— involved in various ways in Patton's demise.[9] Leads deemed dismissible earlier could be important in light of new information.

---

*Bazata's limited and confusing entry says Patton's son challenged him on a point concerning the railroad tracks near his father's accident and on why his father's intelligence people had no knowledge of Bazata's claimed meetings with his father.

For instance, diagrams of Patton's first floor hospital room—a small one at that, according to Farago, who says it was a former horse stall—show one wall facing a street.[10] If it had a window as the mysterious Russian spy implied, it would have been relatively easy for a harmful substance to be introduced from the outside at an opportune moment.

Such a scenario is not far fetched in the clandestine world following World War II. Exploding cigars, poison needle umbrellas, even radioactive coffee have been publicly shown to have been weapons in the Cold War arsenals of the CIA and KGB.[11] World War II was an incubator for such grisly exotica, including bio-chemical assassination weapons. They were used surreptitiously by both sides. By the start of the Cold War, the Russians operated a "Special Bureau" with a lab for "undetectable means of exterminating human beings."[12] For instance, Soviet agents used an "atomizer" containing a bio-poison "which leaves no wound or other evidence of the cause of death."[13] "Natural killers" were created that could induce heart attack, "cerebral apoplexy," and other medical maladies leaving little or no trace.[14] For assassination, according to a formerly classified CIA study, "the contrived accident is the most effective technique. When successfully executed, it causes little excitement and is only casually investigated."[15] In a hospital, "drugs can be very effective," the study continues, "if the assassin is trained as a doctor or nurse and the subject is under medical care. [It] is an easy and rare method. An overdose of morphine administered as a sedative will cause death without disturbance and is difficult to detect." Bazata told the *Spotlight* that a form of "refined cyanide" can "cause or appear to cause" embolism.*

---

*However, he told me that he thought Patton had died "before others could get to him."

Most pertinent, assassinations using traffic accidents and hospitals—or both—were known methods of NKVD murder at the time Patton died. "As an intelligence officer [and WWII veteran]," Colonel John H. Roush, Jr., (Ret.), wrote to me, "I often wondered if the auto accident was a "staged" event, for the Soviets often used such an incident to eliminate someone they hated, and they did hate Gen. Patton."[16] Soviets used trucks for assassinations according to Dr. Mark R. Elliot of Samford University. During a Soviet purge of mostly Russian Orthodox priests shortly after the war, writes Elliot, Eastern Rite Catholic Bishop Theodore Romzha was "struck [and murdered] by a Red Army truck while traveling in a horse drawn carriage." Another death, he writes, resulted from a priest being "pushed from a sidewalk into the path of a truck." From 1986 through February 1991, KGB-caused "suspicious" traffic accidents to "Christian activists" alone numbered fourteen, wrote Elliot, director of Samford's Beeson Divinity School when he made the charges.

Looking deeper at the Romzha assassination, it turns out to be remarkably similar to the circumstances surrounding Patton's demise. No less an authority than Pavel Sudoplatov, head of the NKVD's "Special Tasks" department—its murder, kidnapping, and sabotage bureau—discloses that the bishop actually did not die in the 1947 accident. Rather, the accident "was badly handled." Romzha "was only injured and sent to the hospital"—as Patton was—where he was then murdered with a surreptitious injection. Sudoplatov, who managed assassinations for Stalin throughout WWII and after, makes the disclosure in his 1994 book, *Special Tasks: The Memoirs of an Unwanted Witness— A Soviet Spymaster*, which historian Robert Conquest[17] calls "the most sensational...devastating...autobiography ever to emerge from the Stalinist milieu."

According to Sudoplatov, who organized the murder of Stalin's arch rival, Leon Trotsky, the Romzha assassination was ordered by Stalin because Nikita Kruschev, who was then in charge of suppressing Ukrainian nationalism, said the prelate was aiding rebels. Sudoplatov, a Ukrainian himself who had caught Stalin's eye with his assassination of an earlier Ukrainian nationalist, Yevhen Konovalets, had dispatched a kill team with "an ampule of curare," a paralyzing, plant-derived muscle relaxer normally used in surgery with the patient safely on a breathing machine. But without the machine—as Romzha was in his room—the victim, unable to raise even an eyelid, suffocates in what appears to be lung failure. The poison, writes Sudoplatov, was given to a "local...agent who worked as a nurse in [Romzha's] hospital and she delivered the fatal injection."[18]

In a similar assassination, A. Shumsky, another Ukrainian nationalist, ill and in exile, had written a "disrespectful" letter to Stalin and threatened to organize other exiles against him. Stalin ordered that he be "liquidated," writes Sudoplatov. "It was my job to prevent his supporters from knowing that he had been murdered." Shumsky was in a hospital but was recovering and hoping to be out soon—as was Patton—when he could carry out his threat. "Gregori M. Maironovsky, head of [NKVD] toxicological research, was called in as a consultant to the hospital...where Shumsky lay ill and did the job with poison from his laboratory. The execution was made to look like a natural death from heart failure."[19] Throughout World War II until 1947, Maironovsky and similar henchmen carried out "death sentences and secret liquidations with their poisons."[20] Sudoplatov, who spoke German, is said by Skubik in his book to have been in Germany when Patton died.[21]

Stalin himself, according to intimates, favored traffic "accident" as a surreptitious killing method. In 1996, I met the late Valentin

M. Berezhkov who served as both Stalin and Soviet Foreign Minister V. Molotov's personal interpreter during World War II. He had translated for Molotov when the foreign minister had met with Hitler to sign Russia's shocking pact with the Nazis in 1939, and for Stalin at the historic Allied summit at Teheran in 1943. He gave me his memoir, *At Stalin's Side*, an account of his life in Russia and years at the Kremlin. In it, he discloses that when Stalin wanted to get rid of Soviet Consul Apresyan, who had served Moscow in China but whom Stalin decided "knew too much," the consul was killed in a pre-arranged car accident on a mountain road. Saying Apresyan knew too much was "the signal, and the esteemed consul fell into disgrace," writes Berezhkov. "His fate was already sealed. But the boss didn't want to make too much noise about it. He decided to remove Apresyan quietly. Events soon followed an establish pattern." He waited to have the auto accident staged until Apresyan had returned to Russia on his regular leave and gone on vacation. "None of the people around the Great Leader had any doubts that Stalin had arranged the accident. They had heard the sentence: 'He knows too much!'"[22]

A truck, as in the Patton accident, was used in another Stalin-ordered murder, writes Berezhkov—but of a much higher-level official. The official was Maxim Litvinov, who served in the important post of Soviet ambassador to the U.S. in Washington during the early years of World War II. Litvinov had a good relationship with President Roosevelt and other American officials and was involved in securing lend-lease help for the USSR. The country was in desperate need while fighting the Nazis who had attacked their former Soviet ally in June 1941. But Molotov was jealous of Litvinov, according to Berezhkov, and when the danger to Russia subsided, the foreign minister "began weaving a web of intrigue around Litvinov." The ambassador was eventually recalled. Stalin, who then bugged Litvinov's subsequent meetings with Americans who came to Russia and conferred with their old friend, became convinced he was a traitor. The dictator "hatched" a plan for Litvinov to die in a car crash. Berezhkov wrote that Anastas Mykoyan, chairman of the Presidium of the Supreme Soviet, told him, "I know the place where it happened very well, not far from Litvinov's dacha. There is a sharp turn there, and when Litvinov's car came barreling around it, a truck was parked across the road. It had all been prearranged. Stalin was an unsurpassed master at things like that. He would call in the NKVD people and instruct them personally, one-on-one, and then a car crash just happened, and the person Stalin wanted to get rid of was killed. There were a number of cases like that."[23]

However, if the intended victim was put in the hospital, it made him or her more vulnerable. A noted case among Soviet watchers is that of Lev Sedov, son of Leon Trotsky, Stalin's arch rival. Trotsky and Stalin had vied for power in the early days of the communist revolution. After winning, Stalin became obsessed with liquidating the exiled Trotsky, which he eventually succeeded in doing.[24] Similarly, he was after Sedov, who was headquartered in Paris. But because Sedov, whose organization was penetrated by NKVD agents, was a good source of anti-Stalinist, Trotskyite information, he held off until early 1938 when Sedov had finally outlived his usefulness. After several failed attempts to assassinate him, the plotters were handed their best chance.[25] Sedov suffered acute appendicitis and needed an emergency operation. Rather than enter a French hospital, one of the plotters, thought by Sedov to be a trusted aide but who was really an NKVD agent, persuaded him to use "a small private clinic run by Russian emigres." What happened next was very similar to what happened to Patton. "Sedov's operation was successful and for [five] days he seemed to be making a normal recovery," write Christopher Andrew and Vasili Mitrokhin. "Then he had a sudden relapse which baffled doctors. Despite repeated blood transfusions, he died in great pain." While there was no smoking-gun proof that the NKVD had done the killing, the authors note, its "medical section...was capable of poisoning Sedov" without leaving traces, and "it is certain" they "intended to assassinate" him.[26]

OSS was familiar with death by truck, too. According to an article accompanying the first of the two about Bazata in the *Spotlight*, other OSS veterans told "of the widespread belief among intelligence insiders that Lieutenant Colonel Anthony "Tall Tony" LoScalzo, a regular army finance officer attached to OSS in Italy, was assassinated when he threatened to wreck a scheme" thought up by renegade OSS conspirators. The scheme was to exchange devalued European banknotes for inflated official rates which OSS had access to. But LoScalzo balked. "Shortly afterwards, he was reported to have died of injuries received in a collision involving a huge Army truck." The death triggered a criminal investigation but there were no indictments.

The article, by George Nicholas, also quotes Colonel Paul Lyon, "an experienced military intelligence officer who saw duty with the OSS," and who was one of those who believed Patton was murdered. "The vicious conspiracy against 'Old Blood-and-Guts' was by no means an isolated incident," Lyon told Nicholas, who wrote other articles for the *Spotlight*. "Other officers who were stubbornly patriotic or who clung to their anti-communist convictions met quick, violent, unexplained deaths, especially when a chance assignment landed them at the fulcrum of a critical situation. Take the case of Major Francis Holohan." An OSS officer, Holohan was murdered in northern Italy in 1944 by members of his OSS team after he refused to yield to communist partisan demands. Motives were never crystal clear, but Lieutenant Aldo Icardi, second in command, and Sergeant Carl LoDolce, according to *The Last Hero*, later confessed to the crime. Most OSS officers served courageously and honorably, Nicholas attests, but some were "wild and ruthless," he quotes a third unnamed intelligence veteran, as saying. "But they were not stupid. They knew how to make a hit and get away...."[27]

By the time Stephen Skubik learned of Patton's death, he was so frustrated over his thwarted attempts to prevent harm to the general that he decided to submit a request to go home, an option he had under occupation rules because of service points accrued. He had already had a third confrontation with Donovan, he writes, which, in view of his previous run-ins, he had tried hard to avoid:

Pavel Shandruk, the Ukrainian general he befriended while interrogating him, had asked him as an American agent sympathetic to Ukrainians to give Donovan dossiers on communist spies he had accumulated. Shandruk showed Skubik "hundreds" of notebooks and envelopes crammed with intelligence. Skubik balked. He was not on good terms with Donovan and Donovan did not like Ukrainians, he told the general. But Shandruk persisted. Reluctantly, Skubik took the intelligence and turned it over to Major Stone, seemingly his only OSS friend, and, as he expected, Donovan had erupted.

"There I was once again with that angry S.O.B. who believed all Ukrainians were Nazi collaborators, anti-Semitic and trying to cause a war with Russia. He believed I was [a Ukrainian] agent. 'Soldier, what kind of crap is this you're bringing me?'" he quotes Donovan as demanding. "'Why did General Shandruk ask you to deliver this to me?' I said this is not crap. It's reliable." Donovan braced him. " 'Stand at attention, Private,' he shouted. I said, 'Sir, I'm a Special Agent, C.I.C., not a Private.' He said, 'Take this stuff to the British. They're dumb enough to believe the Ukrainians.'" With that, he "stood up, threw me a salute and walked out," later threatening to bust him to private and court martial him for "improper and insubordinate" remarks.[28]

In addition, his Ukrainian sources, Skubik writes, were telling him that "Patton was killed by Davidov and his NKVD dogs." One of their spies had "infiltrated" Davidov's NKVD unit at Frankfurt and had seen Soviet assassin chief Pavel Sudoplatov at the Russian compound. The same spy had seen truck driver Robert L. Thompson there too, they claimed. "I was certain that Thompson was an OSS/NKVD agent who had known exactly where General Patton would be on the morning of December 9." He had been tipped off by spies at Patton's camp, had stolen the truck, and disappeared, leaving Skubik with only questions. Who was Thompson? Why was he not cited? Why was he, Skubik, prevented from investigating Patton's accident?[29]

"There were too many unanswered questions," he writes, too many "strange coincidences"—the accident taking place just a day before Patton was to leave, Patton dying after rallying and being readied for the trip home to Boston. No autopsy. "These strange coincidences and happenings are just the kind of events to lead any investigator to be suspicious." He would have interviewed certain Ukrainian agents—especially Ivan Malij, a mysterious figure he discusses briefly*—"people on the scene...bystanders" at the accident."Captain Snyder, the ambulance driver, would have

---

*Malij is a mystery. He's mentioned in the foreword as having been executed by the NKVD for what Skubik suspects was involvement in the Patton killing but he mentions him nowhere else and I have not been able to find anything further on him.

to explain why there was the delay of more than thirty minutes be-fore leaving" the accident.[30] "I would have talked with the medics who accompanied Patton in the ambulance." He would have "checked with the Signal Corps to find out who permitted Robert Thompson to drive away with the GMC truck," interviewed "all of the radio operators at the Signal Corps and at Patton's HQ."

At the hospital, he wrote, he would have inquired "if Patton's broken neck was in any way unusual" and checked the back-grounds and especially activities during the crucial hospitalization period of all who doctored, nursed, or in any other way attended Patton.

> My prime suspects would have been the news reporters and photographers.... I had known a very distinguished Ameri-can journalist who served as a spy for the NKVD. I knew that the NKVD and the OSS used the press as a cover for their agents. I would have been especially interested in talking to any reporter who had bribed any of the German attendants at the hospital.... It would have been important to read the reports of the military police, the security officers at the hos-pital and the intelligence officers in Patton's HQ. I would have secured all reports.[31]

In view of what he had learned himself, he would have interviewed Davidov, Donovan, and others in the NKVD and OSS. But, of course, that was not going to happen. He was convinced Patton was murdered. But he was helpless, a restricted and watched CIC agent becoming gun-shy of inquiring further.

He had been warned.

Then a series of quick events convinced him he had better leave Germany as soon as possible.

Word came that Donovan, possibly after conferring with Davidov, who was still angry at him, had prevailed in disciplining him and he had been busted to private. The demotion did not matter. "I never cared too much about military rank anyhow.... I was going home. I was being honorably discharged."[32] His commanding officer, Gillespie, was putting him in for a medal.[33] "He [Gillespie] had tears in his eyes when he read the citation to me. He was a damned good friend. He said, 'Steve, I'm sorry for all the trouble you've had. I want you to know that I consider you a real fine C.I.C. agent.... I'm glad you nailed Davidov.'"[34]

But returning home after a farewell party given him by Ukrainian leaders, including Shandruk and Professor Smal-Stocki, both of whom had earlier warned him Patton was in danger, he was arrested by a "captain"—not otherwise identified—and accused of "fraternizing with Germans," a charge which made little sense. Fraternization laws were loosening by then and Skubik's military records say nothing about any such infraction. Nevertheless, he writes, he was jailed for two days until Gillespie, raising hell, sprung him. Gillespie, he writes, suspected the arresting captain was "fishy"—possibly even some kind of OSS imposter—but had to threaten a court martial to free him. "Gee Steve, why can't you stay out of trouble?" the weary lieutenant inquired. "'Gillie,' I said, 'The buggers are out to get me.'"[35]

He was a marked man.

He could not get to the ship home fast enough.

He arrived in Brooklyn, N.Y., on February 19, 1946, hoping to put everything behind him. A trip to Canton, Ohio to see his foster parents did not help. There had never been much love exhibited by them toward him, especially, say Skubik's children, by his foster mother, who had treated him basically as slave labor. The wartime separation had not helped the relationship. A girl he had met before going to Germany, Ann McCarroll Davis, a trusted U.S. Army cryptographer working at what became the National Security Agency, was in Washington, D.C. They had corresponded while he was in Germany. He went there and she helped him find a place to live. She would soon become his wife. He took a job selling food products and was doing better "except I had problems with shell shock and amoebic dysentery." His "nerves were shot," says his son, Mark, who remembers that waking his father in the 1960s was "tricky as he would jump to his feet in a fighting position." He was worse in 1946. But Ann, a Phi Beta Kappa at Duke, recruited by the code-busters even before she had graduated because of her language skills, aided greatly in his readjustment. They were quite the couple. "I once sat down and tried to figure out how many languages my parents spoke," said Mark. "Including the ones where only limited knowledge could be assumed, I came up with eighteen."

As time passed and things got better, "I decided to try and get my rank reinstated. I knew that my reduction in rank was not properly handled." He probably wanted the post-war benefits the higher rank entitled. To his chagrin, however, in the process, he was directed back to the same Colonel MacIntosh he had been at odds with at OSS Germany. It looked like trouble again. But MacIntosh "greeted me like an old friend...asked me to call him 'Mac.'" He addressed Skubik as "Steve." He told Skubik that General Davidov was "in some kind of trouble." He invited Skubik to lunch at the Mayflower Hotel where Washington luminaries like FBI director J. Edgar Hoover had permanent tables. MacIntosh greeted Hoover as they passed by. On the way home, he asked Skubik if he would like to go back to Germany as a liaison officer. OSS had been dissolved and they were now SSU— the Strategic Services Unit.* Things were different now, he said.

They would make him a first lieutenant. He would have more pay and benefits. They could use his language skills. Skubik said he would think about it if they would make him a captain. To his astonishment, MacIntosh agreed.[36]

It was enticing. But while he was contemplating the offer, he ran into Major Stone,[37] the OSS officer he had befriended in Germany. "He was in Washington on assignment. He asked me what I was doing?" When Skubik told him about the MacIntosh offer, Stone looked troubled. "Don't do it," he warned. "They want you back in uniform in order to kill you . . . . You're political dynamite. You've got the Russians mad as hell" for accusing "General Davidov and the NKVD of murdering Patton." The fear rushed back. "What am I supposed to do . . . can't they kill me here?" They can, acknowledged Stone, "only it would be neater if you were in uniform." Go underground for a few years, Stone advised. Skubik's wife-to-be got access to his file—a file, like most others involved with Patton's demise, impossible to find today—and "understood why I was so nervous." Apparently she saw something which led her to believe his Patton story. He contemplated going to the authorities but Ann cautioned he could not prove anything.[38]

He dropped out, or "sort of did," as he puts it, traveling from Boston to Miami with his food brokerage, keeping a low profile. "I always was on the alert and I never stayed near the area from which I made telephone calls." His son says he would not stay in the same hotel room twice. In 1947, he and Ann married and set up a home in the D.C. suburb of Arlington, Virginia. But he con-

---

*OSS was formally disbanded by President Truman, October 1, 1945. While it took longer for it to go into effect, many agents stayed on under the newly formed War Department SSU, which had firmly supplanted OSS by the summer of 1946 and was eventually absorbed by the CIA when it was established September 18, 1947.

tinued with the same cautions until two things happened. One, Ann had their first child, a daughter, while he was away and had to be taken to the hospital by a stranger. She vowed it would not happen again. She wanted him to stop traveling and work nearby. Second, conservative Republican senator Robert A. Taft of Ohio, learning of Skubik's background, recruited him to work at the Republican National Committee in 1951. "He was going to run for president. Since I was from Ohio and I was a Democrat...he had me checked out after one of his staff secretaries recommended me."[39] General Donovan's collaboration with communists and Russians in fighting fascism, says his son, was one of the reasons Skubik decided to change party affiliations. The Taft connection finally made him come out of the shadows. "I felt free to roam the streets," he wrote. His support for the Ukrainian struggle was still strong and Republicans, especially conservatives, were interested in fighting Soviet tyranny in Eastern Europe. "Skubik authored the Liberation Policy platform that was debated during the 1952 Republican National Convention," wrote a Ukrainian-American journal.[40] Taft, he writes, promised him that when he became president, he would investigate Patton's charges that German POWs were being mistreated in the occupation and also Patton's "murder." But Eisenhower defeated Taft at the convention and Skubik eventually was dropped from the Eisenhower campaign team but not before, he writes, he helped convince Eisenhower's soon-to-be secretary of state, John Foster Dulles, to adopt the liberation policy.

About this time, he joined the Prudential Insurance Company as a licensed broker. With determination and an optimistic persistence, according to acquaintances, he began a rise with both the company and the Republican Party which would see him eventually become head of Prudential's District of Columbia office and serve Republican campaigns as an advisor on Eastern European affairs and public relations into the 1980s. "He worked with the Dulles brothers on writing the policy to " 'free the captive nations' of Eastern Europe," his daughter Harriet wrote me in 2004. "He helped to develop the Heritage Counsel comprised of leaders from various nations who were dedicated to democracy and fighting communism and its spread."[41] While not wealthy or famous, he and Ann, whose father had been a newspaper editor and Washington correspondent, socialized with nationally known political figures including President Nixon, Evangelist Billy Graham, and Chinese-born Anna Chennault, widow of "Flying Tiger" creator, General Claire Chennault. Harriet's godfather was the late Vice Admiral William L. Rees, a World War II intelligence officer and commander of the Atlantic Fleet in the late 1950s. "It puzzles me now that I work in a senior government position[42] as a graduate of Harvard, why my parents had such consistent access to senior politicians," writes Harriet. Regularly meeting with Ukrainian groups, he may have been involved in post-war clandestine matters, she concedes.

In the early 1960s, he was suddenly, and somewhat jarringly, reminded of Patton's demise. A defected Soviet assassin, Bogdan Stashinsky, revealed in interrogation that he had murdered Stephan Bandera, the Ukrainian nationalist from whom Skubik had first learned of the threats to Patton's life. Bandera had been found dying outside the entrance to his apartment in Munich, Germany, in 1959. After autopsy, the death had been officially ruled the result of a natural heart attack. Little publicity was given to the death. But in a well-publicized trial in 1961, Stashinsky had testified he had been ordered by the KGB* to assassinate Bandera,

---

*The KGB was the successor to the NKVD.

proof of Soviet assassination aims and methods that the outside world could not ignore. Stashinsky had killed Bandera with a specially designed gun that sprayed gaseous hydrogen cyanide in Bandera's face. The cyanide, a massive artery and vein constrictor, had induced heart failure. Its vapors dissipated, leaving the poison undetectable. He had used the same "spray" gun two years earlier, Stashinsky confessed, to assassinate another Ukrainian leader, Lev Rebet—also thought to have been a natural death—and been told then that the weapon had been used successfully many times prior.

On Patton?

Skubik could not help but wonder. And, in addition to knowing that the Soviets certainly had reason enough to kill Bandera for his anti-Soviet activities alone, he became convinced they had also murdered him because of his Patton knowledge. "The fact that UPA General Stepan Bandera was himself assassinated, and UPA/NKVD agent Ivan Malij was executed by the NKVD, lead me to believe that they were killed to silence them about the Patton assassination," he wrote.[43] He wondered if the Soviets had *him* on a hit list. "I think Dad took Bandera's assassination personally," says Mark. What exactly he did about the concern is unclear. He continued working his job and helping the Republican Party. Among other things, he co-edited a book for the party entitled *Republican Humor*[44] and gave political speeches. But in 1976, his wife Ann died unexpectedly of a stroke. "My Dad went into a deep inward depression and in working his way out of it, did some very unusual things," recalls Harriet.[45] Among them was traveling to Eastern Europe. He had a lifelong interest in icons, possibly because of his Ukrainian background. "He started taking uncharacteristic risks," writes Harriet, traveling to communist-dominated countries and returning with iconographic art. A Florida church museum exhibited some of it, she says. He had a helper-interpreter in Czechoslovakia named Helena Copova. In 1978, Harriet and Mark visited Copova while their father traveled through the communist block.

The trip had an aura of mystery, writes Mark, because prior to their leaving, his father, he says, was contacted by Israeli intelligence "who offered him an emergency phone number to use while in Prague," presumably if he got in trouble. "We talked about this a little bit at the time. It seems somebody had noticed that he'd applied for visas to Russia and Czechoslovakia . . . . My guess is that his name was on a list of Americans friendly to their [the Israeli's] cause, and that his record of working with the Jewish Underground to capture Nazi war criminals in Germany is documented."[46]

While the three were in Eastern Europe, things got stranger. Harriet's passport was pick-pocketed from her at a Czech nightclub—a misfortune, she was informed by the American embassy, that could have kept her a virtual prisoner in the communist country which would not have made exception for missing papers for up to six months. But then the documents were returned by a hotel employee who cautioned her to be more careful. A mysterious phone call followed in which she was told the theft was just a warning. "Get out of the country and never come back." She never discovered the meaning.

Meanwhile, as they visited Eastern Europe, their house in D.C. was broken into and Skubik's important historical papers, including the reports he had made about the Patton threats, appear to have been stolen. In truth, he had not looked at the Patton reports since returning from Germany so he could not know for sure exactly when they were taken. In 1994, with the publication of his book about Patton's murder, he told *New Hampshire Sunday News* writer Pat Hammond, "All the papers relating to Gen. Patton's murder were stolen from my files. Whether they were taken in transit from Europe . . . or in the United States, I have no idea."

But they were stolen—either in 1976 or earlier.

Finally, returning to Czechoslovakia from his sojourns, where his children were staying with his aide, Mrs. Copova, Skubik was strip-searched, detained, and almost arrested. He had only been hunting icons, he insisted, and was eventually able to talk his way out. But a year or so later, Mrs. Copova mysteriously died in what was said to have been a fall in which she had broken her skull on a Czech street. "I was never really sure that was as much of an accident as we were told," writes Mark. "She seemed a little too healthy for the kind of accident described to us by her husband."

Was any of this related to Patton's death?

One can only speculate.

CHAPTER FOURTEEN

★ ★ ★ ★

A SOLDIER, NOT A DIPLOMAT

Why would someone murder Patton?

In considering such a question, a good place to start is North Africa, 1942, three years before his mysterious accident and death. That, it appears, is when his fall from grace began in earnest.

Recognized by General George C. Marshall, head of the army, as one of the country's top pre-war combat officers, Patton had, by late 1942, successfully led American troops ashore in French Morocco as commander of the main U.S. contingent in the joint British-American "Torch" operation, the Allies' first big offensive aimed at taking Europe back from the Nazis. The Vichy French, rather than their stronger German allies, defended the North African beaches so the landing and resultant victory was comparatively easy. Then, months later, plucked from where he had been reassigned to help plan the upcoming invasion of Sicily, Patton had been rushed by a worried Eisenhower, overall theater commander, back to the North African battlefields to help regroup green and demoralized U.S. troops routed by General Erwin Rommel's experienced Afrika Korps at Tunisia's Kasserine Pass. The Germans had mounted a successful counter-offensive and inflicted heavy loses on the relatively inexperienced Americans. In record time, Patton, principally, had reshaped the battered U.S. troops into an improved fighting force and saved Eisenhower further losses which, had he not done so, probably would have cost Eisenhower his job. Combined with the British, Patton had gone on to help drive the Germans out of North Africa and become, for a short while, military administrator of some of the conquered territory.

But he was a soldier, not a diplomat. And French North Africa, secured as a staging area for the Sicily invasion, was a precarious political minefield. The Vichy government had been formed as the new authority over the portions of France (mostly in the south) not occupied by the Germans after her defeat in 1940. Vichy France was in limited collaboration with the Nazis in return for partial freedoms. Many French citizens opposed it. Britain, which fought Vichy, had broken off relations. The U.S. had not. Feelings were high on all sides. Patton needed cooperation from the North African locals who, for all practical purposes, were controlled by Vichy officials. The conquered cities—Casablanca, Oran, and Algiers—still had to function. With the Germans his primary concern, he did not want to have to worry about Vichy subversion or Arab revolt as they planned the Sicilian invasion. So he decided to make friends with the collaborators, in particular the right-wing commander of Vichy Forces in Africa, General Auguste Nogues, whom he regarded as somewhat of a scoundrel but a good soldier.[1] In addition, heady with confidence from his victory, and believing he had a better grasp of the situation than his distant bosses, Patton disregarded War Department requirements that

Vichy representatives sign a formal surrender. Instead, at the public surrender ceremony, he deliberately ripped the surrender documents sent from Washington into pieces. It was a presumptuous act on his part calculated to show respect to the prideful losers and thus gain their favor. All he required was Nogues's sworn word as a soldier that he would cooperate.

Nogues and his Vichy officers were impressed. From then on, the two collaborated, Nogues basically doing Patton's bidding. And, according to Robert Murphy, Eisenhower's personal representative (and watchdog) in the area, Patton, who spoke French, was wise to have done what he did because the War Department documents "ignored the special conditions prevailing in Morocco" and "would have virtually abolished the [French] protectorate [giving native Moroccans independence], thus infuriating all patriotic Frenchmen and creating chaotic administrative conditions." Patton, whose "action certainly was irregular and probably illegal," in the opinion of Murphy, had nevertheless advanced the Allied cause.[2] As a result, the more important job of planning and preparing for the Sicilian invasion continued unhampered.

But back in the U.S., the political Left, particularly prominent New Dealers, cried foul. They objected to any Vichy collaboration—just as they would Nazi collaboration. And to them, it looked like Patton was flaunting it. Influential liberals like Supreme Court Justice Felix Frankfurter, top presidential advisor Harry Hopkins, and syndicated radio and newspaper journalist Drew Pearson criticized the administration and Patton in particular for fraternizing with fascists.[3] The criticism began to reflect badly on Eisenhower who had already come under fire for a similar deal earlier with Vichy Admiral Jean Darlan, the top military man in the North African Vichy government. In exchange for help with Torch, Eisenhower agreed to honor Darlan as the political head of North Africa. America was in bed with Nazi collaborators and anti-Semites, howled the critics. It got so bad after Patton favored Nogues, writes Murphy, that General Eisenhower's brother, Milton, associate director of the Office of War Information in Washington, came to North Africa and demanded, "Heads must roll." At the very least he wanted Nogues fired. His brother was getting creamed. Leading newspapers and radio commentators were "even calling [*Eisenhower*] a 'Fascist.'"[4]

President Roosevelt was uncomfortably in the middle of all this and hoping to duck the criticism. The dominant philosophy amongst war-runners in Washington was to do anything necessary to aid the Allied effort. Extreme measures were needed. So the president, as best he could, was trying to turn a blind eye to the Vichy-courting. FDR received flak for it not only from the press but privately from aides like Treasury Secretary Henry Morganthau, who broke ranks with his colleagues in being angry over any deals with anti-Jewish collaborators.[5] FDR did not particularly care for the French and, to boot, was an anti-colonialist which sometimes put him at odds even with close ally Britain who had a substantial colonial empire—and wanted to keep it. More important to the president in North Africa was the well-being of native Moroccans and those oppressed by Vichy, which included North African Jews. The U.S. had a longstanding relationship with Morocco's sultans, and the president was maneuvering to end France's grip on North Africa. In that spirit, Roosevelt had penned a letter to the reigning sultan sending his greetings and asking help for U.S. war aims in the region. But he was perplexed when he heard nothing back.

As it turned out, the reason for the silence involved more of Patton's brashness.

According to Robert Murphy, Patton's protege Nogues, somehow intercepting Roosevelt's letter and fearing it "might encourage the sultan to feel more independent in his relations with France," had "pigeonholed" it. Brought to Patton's attention, he read the letter himself and, surprisingly, *agreed* with Nogues. "Not enough mention of the French in it," Murphy quotes him as saying. Patton then set about rewriting the letter, ignoring incredulous protests from U.S. authorities "that nobody should change a Presidential message without the President's consent." Not until a perturbed Eisenhower's office officially intervened was the original letter finally delivered.[6]

When FDR learned of this, as he certainly did, he must have been angered. Patton worked for Roosevelt—not the other way around. Eisenhower, feeling the brunt of the anti-Vichy protest, certainly was not happy either. He and Patton had an unusual relationship. Patton was older and had been Eisenhower's superior right up until America entered the war. But a favorite of Marshall, for whom he had worked in obscurity in Washington in the prewar years, Eisenhower had suddenly been elevated above Patton and others higher in rank, to what, in effect, was Supreme Allied Commander in Europe, a title he later officially was given. The relationship between the two amounted to a rookie ruling a veteran. Patton had taken part in the Mexican border wars and had been decorated in World War I. Eisenhower had never been in combat. Patton felt professionally superior to Eisenhower, although he was dutifully and sincerely respectful.* For his part, Eisenhower acknowledged Patton's combat prowess but now had

---

*The two had always been friends, and, indeed, Eisenhower, seeking a combat role, had come hat in hand to Patton earlier asking for a tank assignment.

the responsibility and added power of a commander's job. He was Patton's boss. The situation was touchy and Patton, flaunting Nogues, was bringing attention to what Eisenhower had hoped to keep quiet—his and Patton's dealings with the enemy. He withheld personal condemnation, but as Murphy, Eisenhower's eyes and ears on the scene, wrote, "This was the first time, but by no means the last, when Patton created a problem in public relations for General Eisenhower"—and by extension, for Marshall and FDR too.

In the meantime, Darlan, more powerful in the Vichy hierarchy and therefore harder to silence than Nogues, was mysteriously (and conveniently) assassinated in a clandestine act that appears to have been a forerunner to future Allied political assassinations during the war and after. Facts in the murky murder are, even after all these years, still in debate. A French gunman, F. Bonnier, was arrested and quickly shot for the crime. But it was never certain that he had acted alone. Who had put him up to it, and aided him with weapons and information, were unanswered questions. Among the chief suspects were the OSS and its British counterpart, the Special Operations Executive (SOE), one of the West's oldest clandestine organizations. British Prime Minister Winston Churchill in particular loathed Vichy and its collaborator officials. Donovan biographer Anthony Cave Brown writes that Donovan actually had fore-knowledge of the assassination and had warned his Algiers station that "the murder was contemplated."[7]

Did this mean he was in on it? Former diplomat and Yale professor Robin Winks believes that is probably the case. He notes that OSS agent Carlton Coon, the renowned Harvard anthropologist, was linked to the Darlan murder through Bonnier membership in an anti-Vichy commando unit Coon was training. Additionally, Coon had owned the particular type of Colt pistol Bonnier used on Darlan.[8] According to Cave Brown, Winks, and others, Coon "was an advocate of political assassination as an instrument of the state." In a later report to Donovan, he proposed "an elite corps of [OSS] assassins," just as Bazata claims existed.[9] The world was now "too small" to continue on its course by "trial and error," Coon wrote. A secret group of capable decision makers should be authorized to eliminate problems as soon as they appear. "If such a body existed in 1933," he wrote, "its members could have recognized the potential danger of Hitler and his immediate disciples and have killed [them]. . . . A body of this nature must exist undercover. It must either be a power unto itself, or be given the broadest discretionary powers by the highest human authorities."[10] Popular historian Stephen E. Ambrose asked,

> Was Darlan's murder the first assassination for the American secret service [OSS-CIA]? Was Ike himself in on the plot? . . . At the time, in 1942, few Americans would have believed it possible for their government to be involved in such dastardly work; a generation later, however, millions of Americans would take it for granted that if there was foul play and the predecessor of the CIA was in the area, and if the Americans benefited from the foul play, then the OSS must have been involved.[11]

Whatever the truth, getting rid of Darlan eradicated a major political problem for the Allies; Roosevelt, and Eisenhower in particular. Nogues was eventually removed, and, combined with Darlan's assassination, the protests at home quieted.

But Patton's administrative actions, such as those with Nogues, were not the only irritants to his superiors.

Supremely confident—at least in public—Patton was always outspoken. He was no different in North Africa. Given command of the Seventh Army, the U.S. part of the upcoming Sicilian campaign, Patton consistently disagreed with Eisenhower about planning and tactics and was openly hostile about Eisenhower's perceived deference to the British. At lunch in Tunisia with deputy theater commander Everett S. Hughes, writes David Irving in *The War Between the Generals*, Patton "described Eisenhower as crazy and too British in the combat zone."[12] Hughes went back to his headquarters and confidentially wrote, "How [Patton] hates the British."[13] In fact, for whatever reasons—wanting to keep the Allied coalition together, believing the British were more experienced, or that he simply was intimidated—Eisenhower and his staff did show preference for the British, allowing them to dominate the planning. Irving, himself a Brit, writes that the Sicilian campaign "was a textbook example of how alliances should *not* operate. The Americans were treated as greenhorns who could not be trusted with a lead role in a campaign. The British laughingly assigned the Seventh Army to guard the rear—as Patton put it—of Montgomery's Eighth Army as it advanced victoriously around the island."[14] Patton was livid. Aware of the resentment which permeated his American commanders, Eisenhower, according to Patton's diary, gathered his generals at Algiers and then singled out Patton, declaring, "George, you are my oldest friend, but if you or anyone else criticizes the British, by God I will reduce him to his permanent grade and send him home." Later, according to Patton biographer Martin Blumenson, Eisenhower thought twice and sent a tactful letter to Patton stressing that while he was a prized and needed fighting general, he had "a ready and facile tongue," and seemed to act on impulse rather than on "study and reflection"[15]—a charge that belied Patton's lifelong study of battles and history and almost encyclopedic knowledge of same. Patton responded in his diary, "He [Eisenhower] means well and I certainly have thus far failed to sell myself in a big way to my seniors."[16]

Finally, he challenged superiors, even national leaders, to their faces.

In mid-January 1943 the first summit meeting of Allied leaders since their seizing of the initiative in the European War was held at Casablanca, Patton's territory. Patton acted as one of the guides and hosts, conducting tours and dining with Roosevelt and Churchill, two of the "Big Three" leaders there to plan the war's future conduct. Stalin was the third of the Big Three. He had been invited but could not come, he said, because of the fighting at Stalingrad which, after much struggle in the previous months, was finally culminating in a Soviet victory. One of the major announcements from the week-plus summit was the declaration at an ending press conference that the Allies would only accept "Unconditional Surrender" from Germany. This was an important concept to Roosevelt—and controversial. He was convinced, having had to deal with ingrained German militarism as an assistant secretary of the navy in World War I and now fierce Nazi aggression in World War II, that it was a perpetually warlike nation and that only its total destruction would end the German threat to world peace. In this view he was supported and prompted by aides such as Secretary Morganthau who had made the persecution of Jews under the Nazi regime one of his primary wartime concerns. As Michael Beschloss in his recent book *The Conquerors* details, eventually Roosevelt, egged on by Stalin, would call for the castration of German males and execution of fifty thousand of their leaders. Roosevelt, like Morganthau, hated the Germans and wanted to see them punished.

However, not everyone agreed on the unconditional surrender. Churchill and Marshall, for instance, rightly feared that the declaration would end all hopes of an early peace through secret negotiation with anti-Hitler Germans and cause many more Allied deaths because it would force Germans to fight "to the bitter end." But their disagreement was in private, not even shared with FDR at the time. In fact, writes Thomas Fleming, in *The New Dealer's War*, although privately "dumbfounded by FDR's [public] announcement," Churchill, in "what may well have been his finest hour as a political performer...chimed in [at the press conference] with a hearty endorsement" of the policy.[17] Not so Patton. To those who would listen, he argued, "Look at this fool unconditional surrender announcement. If the Hun ever needed anything to put a burr under his saddle, that's it. He'll now fight like the devil because he'll be ordered to do so. They'll do that, the Germans—hold out when there isn't even the ghost of a chance.... [Victory] will take much longer, cost us more lives, and let the Russians take more territory. Sometimes, we're such God-damned fools, it makes me weep."[18]

But it was his attitude toward the Soviets that drew the greatest concern.

Roosevelt was absolutely steadfast in his belief that the Soviet Union's government was, at its heart, benign and should be dealt with as a friend and partner needed after the war to bring peace to the world. How much of this stemmed simply from his Left leanings and how much on intelligence he was getting—or not getting—is not clear. But Stalin, he said, was basically a good person, just rough around the edges, and one whom he could "handle" with his own personal charm.[19]

He had always had a soft spot for the Soviets.

When Roosevelt and the New Deal swept into power after the election of 1932, one of the main foreign policy changes made by FDR's administration was granting diplomatic recognition to the fledgling communist nation. Until then, because of the USSR's vow of world revolution and its vehement denunciation of capitalism, few Western countries had been willing to give them such powerful status. But the economic ills of the Depression had, by 1933, when the New Dealers took office, made communism more palatable, even fashionable in certain circles, especially amongst intellectual elites like those in the universities. Over a million Americans voted for either the communist or socialist candidates in 1932[20]—this at a time when the country's population was less than half of what it is today.* Roosevelt, somewhere in that Leftist spectrum, saw the Soviet Union at least as a deserving market which would be opened to the U.S. by the new recognition. Enhanced relations of any kind never materialized, however, for a variety of reasons, chief among them the fact that the Soviets used their new status to infiltrate spies and foment unrest in the U.S., especially within labor, which led to public criticism, most vocally from the Right. But FDR, perhaps influenced** by powerful cover-ups of the true situation in Russia,[21] continued dogmatically in his favorable view of the communist dictatorship. For instance, in 1939, when his internal security advisor, Adolf Berle, assistant secretary of state, handed him a well-sourced report stating that Morganthau aide, Harry Dexter White, and Lauchlin Currie, his (FDR's) own personal advisor, were both Soviet spies, he exhibited

---

*A little over 125 million in 1933, according to the U.S. Census Bureau, as opposed to 300 million today.

**U.S. ambassador to Moscow, Joseph E. Davies, was shameless in his adulation of Stalin and refusal to report the devastating famine and horrible atrocities occurring in the USSR in the 1930s. Similarly, the *New York Times's* Pulitzer prize winning Moscow correspondent, Walter Duranty, another Stalin lover but one with tremendous influence, continually omitted the Soviet Union's failed and devastating economic policies and Stalin's brutal purges and gulags from his reporting about Russia.

no interest, and even got mad and forbade mention of the problem. "He seem[ed] to have dismissed the whole idea of espionage rings within his administration as absurd," write Andrew and Mitrokhin in *The Sword and the Shield*. "Equally remarkable, Berle [who wasn't a fan of the Soviets] simply pigeon-holed his own report. He did not even send a copy to the FBI until the Bureau requested it in 1943."*[22] When Hitler turned on his Soviet ally and invaded the USSR in 1941, Roosevelt promptly sent Harry Hopkins, his close aide of like mind, to Moscow to work out a lend-lease deal in order to help the besieged country as quickly and strongly as possible.

Once the U.S. and USSR were allies, Roosevelt's benevolence towards the Soviets knew few bounds. They were bearing the brunt of the fighting against the Germans, he emphasized. The Allies should be grateful. Russia was the "key to defeat of Germany."[23] The U.S. must do everything it can to aid and cooperate with the Soviets. To Donovan, he said "Bill, you must treat the Russians with the same trust you do the British. They're killing Germans every day, you know." When Navy Secretary Frank Knox balked at hiring communists as radio operators, FDR admonished that the communism that toppled the Tsar "had practically ceased to exist in Russia. At the present time their system is much more like a form of the older socialism...."[24]

The Torch operation in North Africa had been a fulfillment of an FDR promise to Stalin that the Allies would provide a second major battle front in the war as soon as possible in order to divert German resources from their Russian campaign. The Soviets must

---

*The source of the report was Whittaker Chambers, a *Time* magazine editor and former member of the U.S. Communist Party who would become nationally known in the later trial of Alger Hiss, Harry Dexter White, and other Soviet agents accused of espionage by Chambers who had been their courier.

be placated as much as possible, he and the War Department further argued, because the Allies needed them to enter the war against Japan. This was something Stalin had so far declined to do because, he said, he did not also want to be fighting on two fronts—the West and the Pacific.

Roosevelt was like a passionate schoolboy in his courting of Stalin. *Sword and Shield* authors Andrew and Mitrokhin quote how FDR, in order to win favor with the inscrutable dictator, had no pangs ridiculing his friend Churchill at the upcoming Tehran summit in November 1943. "Winston got red and scowled, and the more he did so, the more Stalin smiled. Finally, Stalin broke out into a deep, hearty guffaw.... I saw the light. I kept it up until Stalin was laughing with me.... I called him 'Uncle Joe.' He would have thought me fresh the day before...but he came over and shook my hand. From that time on our relations were personal.... We talked like men and brothers."[25]

Patton, of course, disapproved. Did he make his feelings about the Soviets known in North Africa? I have not been able to find any public record of his doing so, but it does not mean it did not happen. He had plenty of chances to give his anti-Soviet views, not only with his own staff, who certainly were aware of his opinions, but with the high-ranking officers in the Allied commands in North Africa with whom he had daily contact, and even with Roosevelt, Hopkins (whom Patton called "pilot fish"* and FDR's "boyfriend" because of his attachment to the president), and General Marshall, each of whom he spent ample time alone with during the Casablanca talks. At least twice, according to his diaries, he was alone with Roosevelt, talking "for about thirty minutes" in one

---

*Pilot fish stick close to sharks and enjoy a symbiotic relationship wherein they consume parasites in exchange for protection from predators.

instance (January 19, 1943 entry) and then for "two hours" (an October 17, 1945 entry in which he recalled the earlier trip) as he drove the president back from a seaside lunch. "We talked history and armor....Then he got on to politics...."[26] Did Patton hold his tongue? Not likely. That was not his style. And since he was praised by conferees, his confidence to speak out must have been high. The trip was a chance to influence the highest decision maker. But even if he just listened, Roosevelt, who relished the clandestine and always had a silent agenda and private sources of information—as most in his position would—certainly knew Patton's opinions. It was his job, and his advisors' jobs, to know. That was one of the reasons he had established the OSS, which basically was his own private intelligence service, as opposed to using the military intelligence services which were parochially beholden to the admirals and generals. Donovan reported only to FDR, and occasionally, the War Department. So it may not have been coincidence that it was just several weeks after the Casablanca meeting, in early February 1943, that Eisenhower had summoned his generals to Algiers to order them not to talk badly about the British. Also prohibited in the gag order was any criticism of the Soviets.[27]

It was Patton who was doing the most vocal Soviet bad-mouthing.

President Roosevelt, one sadly has to believe, had no idea how infiltrated Soviet spies were in his administration. (If he did know, that would be even worse.) What he believed to be a noble and time-has-come society—one needed to insure world peace—was actually a place of repression, assassination, and lies as bad as Wisconsin senator Joe McCarthy, however objectionable his methods might have been, portrayed in his denunciations.[28] Even Mc-

Carthy, who frequently charged communists were rife in American society, did not know how bad things really were. He was not privy to the deepest secrets that are only now coming to light. The numbers of Communist agents reporting to Moscow and sympathizers aiding them in America at that time is staggering, probably reaching into the thousands. It included the American communist Party, now known to have been supplying the USSR with recruits.[29] The result was a clandestine army, and not just in low, inconsequential jobs. There were Soviet spies in virtually every part of the U.S. government during the war, stealing secrets and influencing policy—all to aid Stalin and the USSR.

Americans spying for the Soviets were operating at the highest tiers; at State, Treasury, Justice, in the Congress, in the military, in the intelligence agencies, defense industries, the media, even in the White House with influence over the president. They were working in the country's most secret science projects, such as Manhattan which was creating the atomic bomb. In fact, had it not been for a lucky change in the Democrat ticket for president in 1944, America would have emerged from the war with two Soviet spies heading major cabinet positions and a president, Henry Wallace, who believed, as they did, that communist Russia was the light of the world.

One of the reasons historians now know much of this is because of the Venona project, the secret wartime U.S. endeavor to read coded Russian diplomatic messages. The project was not declassified and made public until 1995, more than fifty years after it had been initiated. A lot of history has been written without it but the media, generally still locked into portraying the era as one of "McCarthyism" and "The Red Scare," has done almost nothing to publicize Venona, which gives the lie to their shallow portrayal. As a result, the general public is still largely unaware of what the code-breaking operation shows.

Begun on a small scale in 1943 in response to fear that the Russians might be negotiating a secret peace with the Nazis, Venona continued under the National Security Agency until 1980 when it was finally halted but remained classified. From the beginning, the project, born under NSA forerunner, the army's Signal Intelligence Service, was a hard, exasperating task conducted by a few dedicated individuals. The smallness probably reflected the pro-Soviet attitude in Washington at the time. Suspect the Soviets and you were suspected yourself. But such favoritism did not deter the Soviets. They were so pervasive in their U.S. spying that they were actually alerted by a spy *within* Venona shortly after the war and changed their codes thereafter. But thousands of messages in the earlier code that had been cracked had already been sent. Codebreakers had material from roughly 1940 through 1948. So they continued their painstaking work secretly for decades. What has emerged so far, supported by the testimony of Soviet defectors and rare Kremlin files that have surfaced in the interim, shows the great power Stalin wielded in Washington at the time Patton died. What has been deduced from Venona so far is rewriting history.

The alternative scenarios to the actual guilt of accused communists in America—propagated by the Left in response to the "Red Scare" in the late 1940s and early 1950s and based on hope and naiveté rather than facts—have been shown largely to be myths. Julius and Ethel Rosenberg, a seemingly benign New York couple executed as Soviet spies amidst great controversy that claimed they were innocent of McCarthy's witch-hunt charges were indeed, Venona shows, on the NKVD payroll. They were sending classified secrets back to Moscow such as stolen U.S. atomic data that helped the Soviets build nuclear bombs—which threatened America for decades after. Julius Rosenberg's code names in the Venona traffic were "Antenna" and "Liberal." The spy ring he and his wife worked in was one of several receiving nuclear secrets from, among other U.S. scientists, J. Robert Oppenheimer, *head* physicist of the Manhattan Project and another portrayed by the Left as an innocent victim of communist "witch hunts."* But Soviet assassination chief Sudoplatov, in his post-Cold War memoir, *Special Tasks*, describes Oppenheimer's espionage. He was a secret member of the Communist Party in the United States, according to several sources including Sudoplatov, and helped get spies like Klaus Fuchs into the Manhattan project.

Penetration of the U.S. atomic bomb project and the abandonment of Eastern Europe to the Soviets are considered among the most important espionage-related coups in U.S. history. Russia was the next nation to build an atomic bomb and thus check America's monopoly, and its U.S.-aided takeover of post-war Eastern Europe precipitated a half century of expensive and violent conflict in the Cold War. The Korean War and the Vietnam War must be counted in the death toll. Most prominently, State Department officials Alger Hiss and Laurence Duggan, Morganthau advisor Harry Dexter White in Treasury, and trusted White House economic aid Lauchlin Currie, a close Roosevelt confidant, are all shown to have been Soviet agents by Venona or Soviet files and memoirs (like Sudoplatov's) that have surfaced since the breakup of the Soviet Union. Each was accused under the Roosevelt administration and protested his innocence. Some still have Old Left and family connected defenders. But the evidence is overwhelming. For whatever reason, they betrayed their country.

While acknowledging he did not know whether Hiss, one of the first to be arrested for espionage-related crime, was a paid

---

*Oppenheimer's security clearance was revoked during the Eisenhower administration.

agent or not—a distinction that in terms of the outcome of the espionage makes little difference—Sudoplatov wrote that Hiss "disclosed...official U.S. attitudes and plans" to Russian intelligence. Hiss's codename in Venona is believed to be "ALES" and Sudoplatov and others give buttressing details of his spying. At Yalta in February 1945, Hiss was the "source," according to Sudoplatov, "who told us the Americans were prepared to make a deal [on] Europe"—that is, basically concede Eastern Europe to Russian domination in the post-war.[30] Hiss met daily with a top Soviet intelligence officer at Yalta, briefing him on American positions, wrote Jerrold and Leona Schecter, authors of *Sacred Secrets*, another of the myth-busting books based chiefly on Russian sources. One outcome of Hiss's help, according to KGB archives cited in *Sword and Shield*, was to give Stalin "detailed knowledge of the cards" in his opponents' hands in negotiation over whether Poland would remain free in the post-war, which it did not.[31] "By giving away the American and British positions in advance of the negotiations," conclude the Schecters, "Hiss abetted the lowering of the Iron Curtain"—and, by extension, the Soviet enslavement of Eastern Europe.[32]

Patton saw this coming and wanted to head it off by going on to Berlin, as he had been briefed was the Allied plan, and capturing it before the Russians did. But he was stopped by Eisenhower for reasons that are still controversial today.* Earlier, Eisenhower had told his generals Berlin was the objective. As *National Review*'s Jonah Goldberg recently wrote, "the concessions at Yalta were possible because America [Roosevelt] chose to let Stalin occupy Eastern Europe. If, for example, General Patton had had his

---

*Some say Eisenhower made the decision; others that it came from higher up. Why the decision was made is in dispute too—to save American lives or facilitate the Soviet Union's taking of Eastern Europe?

way much of the occupation wouldn't have been a fait accompli."[33] In other words, the Cold War might have been averted if we had taken Berlin, which was the key to controlling Eastern Europe after the war. It was shortly after he had been reined in from advancing on Berlin and liberating Prague, another capitol given over to the Soviets, that Patton, in anger and disgust, told Undersecretary of War Robert P. Patterson that "we have had a victory over the Germans" but "failed in the liberation of Europe." If he wanted Moscow, Patton ventured, "I could give it to you." But the undersecretary, part of the pro-Soviet administration in Washington, was only shocked at Patton's anti-Soviet sentiments—sentiments he certainly told his bosses.

It is pertinent to note—because the purpose here is to show Soviet influence in Washington that could have been mustered against Patton—that Patterson, who would be promoted to Secretary of War under FDR-successor Harry Truman, was as blind (or uncaring) for whatever reasons to the infiltration as other New Dealers. When Nathan Silvermaster, an agriculture official and Near East specialist who worked in several mid-level administration jobs, was accused of being a Soviet spy, which, in fact, it was later proven he was, Patterson, on the advice of Lauchlin Currie and Harry Dexter White, both Soviet spies themselves, backed Silvermaster. "I am fully satisfied that the facts do not show anything derogatory to Mr. Silvermaster's character or loyalty to the United States, and that the charges [brought secretly by the FBI and the War Department] are unfounded," Patterson wrote to the government Board of Economic Warfare, where, among other sensitive jobs, Silvermaster had access to classified information.[34] Yet he saw Patton as a threat.

Silvermaster, a naturalized citizen born in Russia whose Soviet code-names, according to Venona, were "Pal" and "Robert," was the spymaster liaisoning Hiss, as well as Currie, to Moscow.

A third member of his ring was Treasury's White who historian Harvey Klehr, co-author with John Earl Haynes, of *Venona: Decoding Soviet Espionage in America*, argues was more hurtful to the American government than Hiss. "As assistant secretary of the treasury, he was Henry Morgenthau's closest aide....One message shows White briefing Soviet intelligence about American negotiating strategy at the first United Nations conference."*[35] According to *Sacred Secrets*, White directly influenced U.S. policy in several areas. One involved Japan prior to America's entry into World War II. The Russians did not want Japan attacking them from the Pacific. They feared having to fight on two fronts. Accordingly they asked White to help raise tensions between the U.S. and Japan, hopefully to get Japan to go to war with America— not Russia. To this end, wrote the Schecters, White proposed that the U.S. demand Japan get out of Manchuria, a demand he knew the Japanese, who had been there since the early 1930s, would not accept. Such demands eventually led to Pearl Harbor and America's entry into World War II.

White was also instrumental in a Treasury decision to give the Soviets monetary plates which they used to flood post-war Germany with marks and thereby cost the U.S. "hundreds of millions of dollars."[36] White was the architect of the "Morganthau Plan," the blueprint championed by the secretary to de-industrialize Germany and turn it into a toothless agrarian society. Patton actively opposed the plan on several grounds, including the fact that, like the punitive World War I surrender measures giving rise to Hitler, such drastic measures would cause unrest, probably revolution,

---

*The United Nations was a Roosevelt dream and one of the reasons he wanted Russia handled with kid gloves. Roosevelt believed that Russia's participation in the United Nations was vital and he therefore did not want to antagonize them for fear they would shun it.

and open the country to communism. Following FDR's death, Truman, despite warnings from the FBI, kept White in his successor administration (although White voluntarily left in June of 1945). On a recent C-Span broadcast, R. Bruce Craig, who champions White as a misunderstood and overzealous New Dealer in his *Treasonable Doubt: The Harry Dexter White Spy Case*, said that following White's seeming natural death of heart failure in 1948, rumors persisted that he had been murdered by the NKVD as a way of silencing him.*[37]

Similarly, Currie and Harry Hopkins—perhaps Roosevelt's closest advisor—are now known to have been Soviet spies, although there is still debate about Hopkins' exact role—whether he was an actual paid spy or simply a deeply committed sympathizer. Both, as presidential advisors, were at the heart of American government during World War II. They had enormous influence, especially Hopkins. In addition to successfully going to bat for Silvermaster, Currie—White House economic advisor to Roosevelt—was the Democrat administration's man in China before its fall to communism. After the war, Currie was blamed for America's role in that fall. While Currie's code name in the Venona traffic was "PAGE"; no code name for Hopkins has emerged but he was considered by the Soviets to be one of their most important spies.

According to Andrew and Mitrohkin, when Donovan acquired the fire-damaged Soviet code materials from Finland, an "out of breath" Currie reported to Moscow, "the Americans were on the verge of breaking the Soviet code."[38] But Currie's alarm to his Soviet handlers turned out to be unnecessary because Roosevelt,

---

*Like Patton, White had a history of the ailment that killed him—in White's case, it was heart trouble.

unlike his treacherous Russian ally who showed no similar concern for their partner, incredibly ordered Donovan to return the material to the Soviets post haste.

With his own privileged position and so many spies in the OSS and other government agencies, Currie had a variety of ways of learning about the Russian code books—including from Donovan himself. Currie and Donovan had a relationship that grew during the war if for no other reason than their mutual access to the president and having worked together on priority war missions. In one, initiated by Secretary of State Cordell Hull and forwarded to Donovan by Currie, German supply lines through Turkey and Greece were to be attacked.[39] An FBI report on Donovan in the early 1950s, prompted by his appointment by President Eisenhower to be Ambassador to Thailand, lists as a detriment Donovans' law firm representing "a public relations firm, Allied Syndicate, whose clients [include] Lauchlin Currie." The information was based on confidential but probable former OSS sources who told the agents that Donovan was an "anti-anti-communist" who had "always been 'soft and mushy' in his treatment of communists in the government," as well as elsewhere, especially the OSS.[40]

Harry Hopkins was probably the highest placed government insider revealed to have been working for the Soviets—that because of his closeness and influence over the president. An architect of the New Deal and prominent New York City socialist who caught Roosevelt's eye, he was picked early by the new president for his administration when it first came to Washington in 1933. After World War II began in Europe, he was appointed by the president to run the vital Lend-Lease war supply program to Britain and the USSR. Because Hopkins was insistent upon the Soviets receiving uranium through Lend-Lease, General Leslie

Groves, head of the Manhattan Project, began to suspect him, according to Romerstein and Breindel. Others did, too, but could never prove anything because his power and prestige kept them at bay. Now the authors write unequivocally "Hopkins was a Soviet spy."[41] They and others who have studied the new sources say Hopkins, among further pro-USSR moves, removed anti-Soviet officials from crucial U.S. government positions thereby helping the Soviets gain influence. He also tipped Soviet Ambassador Litvinov that the FBI was bugging his Washington phones. He advised Soviet Minister Molotov on how to persuade Roosevelt to open a second European front—something the Russians desperately wanted from the Allies but the War Department wanted stalled. They did not want to invade until America was ready. And he tried to have an important Russian defector, Victor Kravchenko, sent back to the Soviet Union and certain death.[42] Kravchenko, a Soviet officer, knew too much about Soviet misdeeds. He published in 1946 *I Chose Freedom*, one of the first books to expose Stalin's use of starvation, slave labor, and execution, especially in subduing the Ukraine, Kravchenko's homeland. The defector who married here and took up life under an assumed name died from a supposed gun-inflicted suicide. But his son Andrew believes he might have been the victim of a KGB execution, according to the documentary film *The Defector* that the son produced about his father.

Another probable NKVD execution—this one by exit from a skyscraper window—but "officially" listed as suicide,* was the death of Laurence Duggan in 1948. Duggan was one of the most ideologically-motivated of the war-time American traitors. Head of State's South American desk, he had worked for the Soviets

---

*His family and others who looked into the story dispute the official ruling.

since the mid-1930s and provided Moscow mostly with classified diplomatic cables, including those about Argentina, which supported the Axis. But he experienced an ideological crisis over Stalin's terror purges and signing of the non-aggression pact with Hitler. He could not understand why either occurred. He quit spying for awhile but resumed after being soothed by his Soviet handlers. Code-named "Frank," "Prince," and "19," he and Hiss worked together, although it is not clear either knew about the other being a communist spy. As a close adviser to Secretary of State Cordell Hull, Duggan had top-level influence. Overall, according to *The Haunted Wood*, he passed hundreds of classified documents, including secret transmissions sent to Washington from the U.S. embassy in Moscow.[43]

There were many more: Michael Straight, a personal friend of the Roosevelt's whose parents founded the liberal *New Republic* magazine. He became a communist at Oxford in England in the 1930s. British universities were an incubator for Soviet spies in that period. Mrs. Roosevelt got him a job at State. He provided the NKVD with armaments reports and potential spy recruits.[44] Samuel Dickstein was a New York congressman, code-named "Crook." The Soviets knew his bottom line. He demanded increasing amounts of money for his treason while the quality of his product correspondingly dropped. Still, it included providing Moscow with information on American fascist groups unearthed by his Congressional un-American activities committee. At the same time he steered Congress away from investigating communists.[45] More appreciated by the Soviets was Harold Glasser, another of Morganthau's Treasury staff. His code-name was "Ruble," as in money—which he was to the Soviets. The son of Lithuanian immigrants, he joined the communist party in 1933. With the help of Harry Dexter White in Treasury he survived an

FBI background probe that could have ousted him. He provided intelligence from the War Department and the White House which was deemed so important by the NKVD that seventy-four reports generated from the material went directly to Stalin.[46] General Fitin, Donovan's counterpart and close associate in the OSS-NKVD cooperation—to whom all the U.S. espionage was funneled—was so pleased with Glasser that he recommended the Treasury officer be awarded the "Order of the Red Star," a Soviet medal given usually to soldiers for "exceptional service in the cause of the defense of the Soviet Union."

These spies, plus the hundreds in other U.S. agencies at the time, including the military and OSS,[47] permeated the administration in Washington, and, ultimately, the White House, surrounding FDR. He was basically in the Soviet's pocket. He admired Stalin, sought his favor. Right or wrong, he thought the Soviet Union indispensable in the war, crucial to bringing world peace after it, and he wanted the Soviets handled with kid gloves. FDR was star struck. The Russians hardly could have done better if *he* was a Soviet spy.

According to one of the few comprehensive books about the secretive Counter Intelligence Corps—the same organization Patton-plot investigator Stephen Skubik belonged to—Roosevelt ordered in 1943 that the CIC "cease any investigations of known or suspected communists and destroy all files on such persons immediately."[48] The order, according to the books' authors, was the result of an investigation of a "leftist" friend of the Roosevelt's that went wrong and made the president angry.*And the order was not confined only to the CIC. Patton's nephew, FBI agent Fred Ayer, Jr., wrote, "intelligence personnel in Europe [where he was

---

*The investigation involved possibly uncovering a sexual relationship between Mrs. Roosevelt and the friend, an army sergeant, according to the *Secret Army* authors.

stationed] were officially forbidden to report, much less investigate, anything that our Red Allies were up to," making their jobs, he added, "frustrating and ulcer-causing."[49]

Similarly, General Albert C. Wedemeyer, aid to War Department head Gen. Marshall and among the planners of several major Allied campaigns, including D-Day, wrote that he learned early in the war it was "taboo for any American in an official position to expose, denounce, or openly oppose Stalin's aggressive action and sinister aims." It was "positively unpatriotic...to voice dislike and distrust of our 'gallant ally,' the Union of Soviet Socialist Republics, or to denounce the tyranny of 'good old Uncle Joe'.... Naturally, the press [generally supporting Russia and Stalin] affected Washington's political judgments." From higher-ups like Marshall and Hopkins, writes Wedemeyer, he constantly experienced "admonitions not to refer to the Russians in a critical sense or to the dangerous implications of communism."[50]

Just how insidiously powerful Moscow had become in war-time Washington is illustrated by the facts concerning Henry Wallace, Roosevelt's vice president and icon of the Left who ran for president as a socialist in 1948.* As Roosevelt's early secretary of agriculture, the farm-born Wallace instituted the then-radical idea of farm subsidies as a way of raising prices for American farmers. It was one of the beginnings of public-trough welfare still existing today. Elevated to vice president in 1940, Wallace became a vocal champion of the Soviet Union, an example, he believed, of what society should be in the modern world. In 1944, he visited Russia and returned with glowing accounts—not realizing he had been duped with lies, phony statistics and shows, and a brutal gulag dressed up to look like a summer camp.[51] Privately, in late Octo-

---

*He was the candidate of the Progressive Party.

ber 1945, as Truman's secretary of commerce (and only a little more than a month before Patton died), he met with Anatoly Gorsky, the NKVD station chief in Washington, to urge that Stalin help him combat U.S. "fascists," one of whom, he said, was his own country's new secretary of state, James F. Byrnes.[52]

Luckily, Roosevelt, feeling pressure from Democrats who believed Wallace's far-left pronouncements might cost the party the 1944 election, decided to replace him with the less radical Democrat Sen. Harry Truman. Wallace was then given the commerce position as a consolation prize. But had Wallace been kept on the ticket, the White House, upon FDR's death only months later, literally, would have been all but run from Moscow. Wallace is said to have stated that had he succeeded FDR, he intended to make Laurence Duggan and Harry Dexter White his Secretary of State and Secretary of the Treasury respectively.[53]

This was the administration Patton, a severe Soviet critic, was subject to as he continued his bumpy rise and outspokenness.

The Allied Sicilian campaign of July 1943 was a hard-fought victory, highlighting Patton's bold, aggressive generaling but also revealing traits which would further alarm his superiors. The British, because of the defeat at Kasserine, regarded U.S. troops as unreliable. They therefore commandeered the planning, with Patton's British counterpart Montgomery taking the lead. To Patton's chagrin, it was with Eisenhower's blessing. Patton, heading U.S. forces, was relegated to a support role. It angered him. "Ike is more British than the British and is putty in their hands," he wrote in his diary.[54] Once the battle started, and without informing Eisenhower, he jumped in a B-25 and flew to General Sir Harold Alexander, theater invasion commander, to argue that Americans, without whom there would be no invasion, should be given a larger role. It was unfair and tactically unsound for Montgomery to get all the glory. He pointed out that Washington, upon whom the British counted so much for aid and support, would not take kindly to learning that its army was being relegated to such a minor role. Patton knew his stuff. Alexander had no rebuttal and granted Patton permission to do more than had originally been planned. Without informing Eisenhower again, Patton took advantage of the opportunity to break out from solely supporting Montgomery's flank, performed a tough, quick movement of his troops northwest and then east over rough and heavily defended terrain and, after taking Palermo, beat Montgomery, who was bogged down with German resistance, to the coastal city of Messina where the bulk of the Germans had been pushed. Messina was supposed to have been Montgomery's prize. Tainting the victory somewhat was the fact that most of the enemy, rather than surrender, escaped across the narrow straits to nearby Italy, meaning they would be able to fight again. Regardless, American morale "soared," as did Patton's image. He "had effectively exorcised the Kasserine Pass demons," wrote Eric Ethier in *American History* magazine. The press, as it had in North Africa, made him a hero.[55]

But the celebration was short-lived. General Omar Bradley, serving under Patton at the time, had not liked the dash to Messina. He thought it unnecessary and basically ego-driven. The move distanced him from Patton. Similarly, Eisenhower, who had not been happy with Patton's independence in Morroco, had now seen it in battle. Patton had gone against plan and should have informed him. Basically, in Eisenhower's eyes, he was deemed untrustworthy.

Then came the slapping incidents.

In a fit of temper, Patton cursed and struck two soldiers at different times while visiting Sicilian hospitals. He viewed the two soldiers, suffering from shell-shock, as cowards, not worthy of being amongst wounded heroes. Because one of the soldiers was rumored to be Jewish, there were also whispers of anti-Semitism. Patton, historians point out, may have been suffering shell-shock himself.[56] But when Eisenhower first learned of the incidents he was incensed. "No letter that I have been called upon to write in my military career has caused me the mental anguish of this one," he wrote in reprimand. "I assure you that conduct such as described in the accompanying report will not be tolerated."[57] He demanded Patton apologize to the two soldiers, show contrition to him personally, and cease such "brutality" forever. But knowing he would need Patton for future fighting, he stopped short of any official action for fear of ending Patton's career and thus losing his service. Nevertheless, on August 24, he wrote General Marshall in Washington, "George Patton continues to exhibit some of those unfortunate personal traits of which you and I have always known and which during this campaign caused me some most uncomfortable days.... I have had to take the most drastic steps; and if he is not cured now, there is no hope for him."[58]

Obviously, they had talked derisively about Patton before. Marshall himself had witnessed a Patton outburst at his men while the troops had practiced the Sicilian invasion in North Africa. Farago describes the scene thusly: "Patton went out of control" as "Marshall...Eisenhower and a bunch of generals nearby observed... in embarrassed silence."[59] But Eisenhower's private action regarding the slappings should have been the end of it. However, rumors eventually reached correspondents covering the war. At least one of them, John Charles Daly, a CBS radio reporter who would later become an early television star, believed Patton had temporarily gone crazy at the hospital.[60] The implication was not lost on Eisenhower but he talked the correspondents out of reporting the story. They agreed on the need for Patton in future fighting. The situation again seemed solved—at least from Eisenhower's perspective. Then, three months later, Drew Pearson, a Leftist, pro-Soviet broadcaster and "muckraker," (as Carlo D'Este calls him), learned of the incident while touring Sicily and reported it with great sensation on his syndicated radio show. A public uproar ensued. The hero of only a few months prior was now characterized by most of the press as an out-of-control Nazi preying on the sick.[61] Congressmen demanded Patton's resignation. As in Casablanca, the controversy quickly entwined Eisenhower. He was accused of a cover-up. Why did he not fire Patton? How could he tolerate such fascist behavior? Eisenhower was straightforward in his answers. He had dealt with the matter in the strongest terms but he needed Patton, who was a great battle commander. A surprising number in the country came to Patton's defense. War was not pretty. They understood the need for discipline and that sometimes the lines of appropriate action were blurred. Secretary of War Henry L. Stimson was forced to defend both Patton and Eisenhower in a letter to the Senate. While Patton's action was "indefensible," he wrote, winning the war was top priority. "Off the record," wrote D'Este, the secretary "rebuked Patton, writing of 'his disappointment that so brilliant an officer should so far have offended against his own traditions.'"[62]

The controversy subsided. But Patton was deep in his superiors' doghouse and, as a consequence, on their punitive radar, his career hanging on by a thread only because he was desperately needed. And that is key. Any other general would have been long gone. But he was basically, at that point, irreplaceable. One has to think that if Douglas Bazata is telling the truth, this was probably the time—late 1943—when the "Stop Patton" plot which he says arose and could have eventually evolved into an assassination order was born. They knew they had to use him later. How would they control him? It was a problem that needed answers. For his part, Patton was contrite in letters to Eisenhower and Stimson,[63] and in his apologies to the two slapped soldiers and his troops in general, the latter which he decided to do on his own. But privately he was resentful. He wrote in his diary, "Ike and Beedle [General Walter Bedell Smith, Eisenhower's chief of staff] are not at all interested in me but simply in saving their own faces...."[64]

He still believed his prowess would prevail.

Then things got even worse for him.

As plans for the invasion of Europe unfolded, Bradley, his underling, was awarded command of American forces in the upcoming invasion of Europe, the biggest show of the war. The job should have been his, Patton believed. He had earned it on the battle field. But Eisenhower said Bradley, quiet and unassertive, was more stable, more dependable—an observation that had to mean in following orders as well. Patton was put in limbo for a possible assignment on the continent once the landings succeeded—but only if he behaved. He was warned to keep his mouth shut or, needed or not, he would be gone. It was a blow. Patton was angry. But he adjusted. He knew acceptance was his only chance of staying in the game. In the meantime, his name, now known to put fear in the hearts of the German high command, was attached to a fictitious paper army made to seem like the one being readied for the cross-channel invasion. Its location, paperwork, and radio traffic indicated a landing at Calais, the closest and most logical place for invasion in the minds of the Nazis trying to decipher the Allies' plans. He was to be part of one of the great deceptions of the war. All he had to do was be quiet and play the ruse, and he might get a real part later.

Then he was blindsided.

Patton did not really want to attend the opening of a new "Welcome Club" for American troops in Knutsford, England as he waited to do his part. But the women of the club persisted and it was for the troops, so he consented. He even arrived late, so as to keep a low profile.[65] Still, news photographers were waiting for him and he made them promise not to publish the pictures or report he was there. It was April 1944, two months before the invasion, and he was still part of the ruse. Then, unexpectedly, the hostess announced he was going to say a few words and the audience was already clapping before he could decline. So he went to the podium and spoke briefly. Basically, it was a short welcoming, and as he himself, Blumenson and others describe it, it included, "I feel that such clubs as this are a very real value, because I believe with Mr. Bernard Shaw, I think it was he, that the British and Americans are two people separated by a common language, and since it is the evident destiny of the British and Americans, and, of course, the Russians, to rule the world, the better we know each other, the better job we will do."[66]

He left.

The next day, to his surprise, he awoke to another controversy. There are no tapes of the speech and Patton himself spoke without notes so his exact words can never be positively known. But most British newspapers included the reference to the Russians as sharing rule of the post-war world, while American papers generally did not—which was why the controversy was loudest in the U.S. Despite assurances to the contrary, the press at Knutsford had broken their word and reported Patton's "off the record" remarks.

The press in America, still angry over the slappings and knowing his anti-Soviet sentiments, compounded the problem by distorting the reportage to make it seem like Patton had slighted "our great ally" Russia. The distortion was all they needed to vilify him again. The *Washington Post* editorialized that Patton had "progressed from simple assault on individuals to collective assault on entire nationalities . . . ."[67]

Congressmen joined in. A Republican, Karl Mundt of South Dakota, declared Patton "has succeeded in slapping the face of every one of the United Nations except Great Britain."[68] War Secretary Stimson was "horrified," writes Patton biographer Stanley Hirshson. Stimson had to deal with Congress daily and saw the criticism as one more wrench thrown in his task. He leaned on Marshall, who leaned on Eisenhower, who, already having a tough time dealing with Soviet Union in his coalition, had enough. While acknowledging there may have been extenuating circumstances, he wrote back to Marshall that Patton was "mentally unbalanced" and he, Eisenhower, was ready, if Marshall agreed, to send Patton home."[69] Marshall, however, taking note of the attacks on Patton's sanity, nevertheless threw the problem back to Eisenhower. The coming need for Patton was too great. "Do not consider War Department position in the matter," he cabled. "Consider only Overlord [the coming invasion of Europe] and your own heavy burden of responsibility for its success. Everything else is of minor importance."[70] It was a sobering reply. Could he take back Europe without Patton? Who was better? He decided to reconsider. After summoning a confused and rightly peeved Patton and berating him, then making him wait in dread for days to find out what his decision would be, Eisenhower wrote Patton, "I am once more taking the responsibility of retaining you in command in spite of damaging repercussions resulting from a personal indiscretion. I do this solely because of my faith in you as a battle leader...."[71]

Patton took the reprieve as a sign from God. "Divine Destiny came through in a big way," he wrote his wife on May 3, 1944.[72] In his diary, he penned, "My final thought on the matter is that I am destined to achieve some great thing—what, I don't know, but this last incident was so trivial in its nature, but so terrible in its effect, that it is not the result of an accident but the work of God. His Will be done."[73]

Perhaps Patton meant that God was helping him get his relationships straight because, from that time on, his and Eisenhower's longtime friendship was basically over. He still had a soft spot for Ike. But he resented the fact that the supreme commander did not go to bat for him, especially in light of the conflicting evidence. Additionally, he had begun to think Eisenhower had his eye on future political office once the war was won and therefore, more often than not, would do what was politically correct or expedient in accordance with what those above him wanted, rather than what was militarily or ethically right. Patton did not like that. Even his critics agree he was a man who spoke his mind and acted on his beliefs no matter what—to a fault, as Eisenhower admonished, saying, "You talk too much." He became leery of Eisenhower. And as he was soon to lead the actual fighting in Europe, he would find himself increasingly at odds with not only the Soviets, but his superiors who, despite needing and using him for conquest, ultimately had come to regard him as a wildcard psychotic who, after using him, had to be stopped.

CHAPTER FIFTEEN

★ ★ ★ ★

A TALE OF
TWO DRIVERS

What happened to Robert L. Thompson and his passengers?

This is one of the major unsolved mysteries of Patton's death.

Thompson and his reported passengers appear to have been waiting on the roadside for the Patton Cadillac. When it appeared in the distance, Thompson started the truck out onto the road and then, suddenly, without signaling, had turned across the oncoming limousine's path, causing the accident which ultimately led to Patton's death.

Yet only Thompson had been interviewed, cursorily at that, and then all three—if that reported number was accurate—had disappeared, never, at least publicly, to be heard from again.

It made no sense. They should have been detained and interrogated.

There was talk that Thompson was logically turning into some kind of depot or truck spot. But it was a quiet Sunday morning. The depot, if that is what it was, appears to have been closed, if not deserted and abandoned. It was in an area strewn with wreckage and discard with little noticeable activity. So why turn into it? In any case, Thompson, according to Farago, was not authorized to have the truck, which meant it probably was stolen. And if there *were* two passengers, that in itself, according to Farago, was against army regulation and therefore another reason the truck's occupants should have been detained.

To get answers, I was going to have to find Thompson or people who knew him. How? He had such a common name. He had disappeared more than half a century ago. He was basically unknown, an obscure young soldier like so many others in the war, and obviously had kept a low profile. It was not even clear where he was from. Initial reports said he lived in Illinois, a mistake which might have deterred previous searchers and hidden him further. However, as I probed deeper, it became apparent he was from the Camden, New Jersey area. Camden was right across the river from Philadelphia. It was a hugely populated area on the eastern seaboard that had changed mightily since 1945. Since Thompson was identified as in his early twenties at the time of the accident, he would be around eighty when I started searching. If he was still alive, would he still live in the same place he had as a youth? Patton's nephew, Fred Ayer, Jr., had written back in 1964, "I was told that the driver of the truck in question felt such deep remorse that he later attempted to commit suicide."[1] If Thompson had killed himself, the best I could hope for was to find relatives or friends.

That hunch proved right—not the suicide, but that all I would find were relatives and friends. Denver Fugate, a former associate professor of history at Elizabethtown Community College, Kentucky, had tracked down Thompson's whereabouts for an article he wrote in 1995. Entitled "End of the Ride," it was published in *Armor*, the professional journal of the U.S. Army's tank corps, headquartered at Ft. Knox, Kentucky, reportedly where the Cadillac limousine in which Patton was injured was kept. Thompson had indeed come home from the war, lived in obscurity, and died June 5, 1994—just months before Fugate called Thompson's home in Bellmawr, N. J., a Camden suburb. Thompson's widow, Alice, who answered the phone, told Fugate that her husband had always "felt like a murderer,"[2] which was intriguing. And when he asked her if the rumors that Thompson had committed suicide were true, she puzzlingly replied she "wouldn't doubt it because he was the nervous type."[3] The answer implied she did not know how he died. But when he called back to inquire further, she had clammed up. Had somebody gotten to her? Fugate was not too concerned. His article mainly reinforced the idea that Patton's death had been the result of a "freak" accident.

Fugate, now retired, freely gave me Alice's telephone number, a long shot, to be sure, since it was over ten years old. Not surprisingly, it was no longer in service. But I now knew where he had ended his days. New Jersey would only release his death certificate to relatives. But eventually a search of Belmawr-area burial records revealed his funeral home. Although representatives there also would not release information, they contacted Gloria Pagliaro, who had been married to Alice's son, Thompson's stepson. Apparently they had her listed as the next of kin. Luckily, Gloria called me. "No way" Thompson died of a suicide, she said. She and her husband were there at the hospital when he expired. "It was a short illness. For some reason, the doctors could not determine what was wrong with him. He had a lot of pain in his stomach. They were running tests and such. The day he died he suffered terribly. I remember it vividly because it was very upsetting."

Alice, Gloria's mother-in-law—the same that Fugate had talked to—was Thompson's second wife. His first wife, Joan, had been murdered in a 1982 robbery. It had been a big story at the time. The Thompsons had owned a travel agency in a declining Camden neighborhood. It had been Polish-Italian when first started but was changing to Black-Hispanic. Crime rose. According to the *Philadelphia Inquirer*,[4] the killer and his brother, locals, entered Thompson's agency around mid-morning. Thompson, recuperating from a heart attack, was not there. One pointed a .38-caliber pistol at Joan and demanded money. The agency had been held-up before and Joan, just a day or two prior, had told friends she would resist the next intrusion. She pulled out the .32 they kept hidden in a drawer and pointed. The robber said he would shoot. She said, "Go ahead. So will I."* Shots followed. Joan was hit in the arm, hand and abdomen and bled to death at the hospital. Her assailant took a bullet in the chest, collapsed outside and also died at the hospital. His brother, who fled, was later arrested trying to retrieve their gun and sent to prison, probably for murder. Gloria did not know Thompson then and never really got to know him even after marrying Alice's son. "He was a very private person," she said, and rarely talked about anything, much less the Patton accident. Most people did not know he had been involved. Once Alice brought it up in her presence, she said, but Thompson "blew it off." Alice was a "controller," said Gloria, and ran things in the

---

*Or something similar, according to Gloria Pagliaro.

household. Alice thought Thompson was a "liar." A second marriage for both, they did not get along, said Gloria.

When Alice died, Gloria went to her house and gathered what was left. She found only two things of Thompson's in the house: a large *Colliers Photographic History of World War II* and a scrapbook about him and the war. The two items had been in a closet, practically forgotten since she had found them. At my request, she sent the scrapbook to me. It had pictures of Thompson as a young man, maps of Patton's progression through France and Germany, and news articles about Patton's accident and death, including those naming Thompson as the truck driver. Apparently, Thompson had been with Patton's Third Army. There were magazine pictures of a "tank destroyer," a truck-like vehicle with a tank's tread and a mounted gun, which Thompson might have driven. I figured his mother had clipped most of the items from newspapers and magazines while he was in Europe. They were pasted into the scrapbook in rough chronological order. Most interestingly, loosely inserted into the very front—not pasted in like the other items—was one of the two multi-page *Spotlight* articles about Douglas Bazata, headlined, "I Was Paid to Kill Patton."

There he was—Bazata, in various pictures, text, and quotations, making his 1979 claims. The assassin "had arranged for several trucks to be on hand that day.... Patton was supposed to die in the auto accident. He didn't, however, die, so there was even more...." On and on it went. And Thompson, the articles in his scrapbook showed, knew all about it. He had obviously seen it because the last item pasted into the scrapbook was right after the war—thirty years before. This was more recent. Without naming Thompson, Bazata charged in the article that the truck driver, although innocent of the true nature of the plot—killing Patton—was nevertheless involved. It was a damning indictment. Why, since the *Spotlight* articles went public, had not he challenged Bazata for incriminating him? They had appeared fifteen years before Thompson died. That was a long time to keep quiet. Was he still just too ashamed and leery of any more publicity? Or was he fearful of dredging up something that might lead to more sinister revelations?

Was Bazata right?

Gloria got me Thompson's death certificate. He appeared to have died of natural causes. Similar to Patton, no autopsy had been performed. I visited the house where Thompson spent his final days. Howard Beck, a retiree who lived across the street, remembered him fondly. "I'm not surprised," he said when I told him Thompson might have been involved in a plot to kill Patton. Thompson mostly kept his Patton background to himself, said Beck. The only reason he knew about it was that once, when the matter came up between their wives, Thompson loaned him a book[5] on the crash that said it was an accident, which Thompson wanted him to see. But they would go out and Thompson would tell him how he had been involved in the Black Market in Germany. He was a "dealer, procuring things for his unit, a 'scrounger,' I think he said." He was tall and "homely" and wore glasses, said Beck—"but women liked him. When we'd go out, he talked a lot. He'd tell jokes. They liked the jokes." Beck said his son was still in touch with one of Thompson's two sons, the eldest. And he had a daughter too.

He gave me a number.

"My father had a lot of mysteries about him," Jim Thompson, Robert's oldest son, told me. Jim owned a New Jersey satellite TV sales and service company. His father, he said, "had his own little things going on. I never got a chance to know him well." By the time his father died, they were estranged. Among other things, his father was a "philanderer. He tried to hook me up with the daughters of some of the women he was dating.... He was a dog." He thought his father was seeing Alice, the second wife, before his mother was murdered, and that was one of the reasons father and son became estranged. After he married Alice, Jim said, "he'd always have an excuse why I couldn't come over and see him. After awhile you say, Jeez, how many times do I have to be blown off before I say forget it." He stopped calling. "I always thought it was because of her [Alice]. She felt guilty and didn't want us around." He did not know for sure, though.

So, in effect, Thompson cut his ties with his first family when he remarried. His father was passive "on the surface" but "paddling like a duck underneath," Jim said. His mother Joan was more family oriented, the one who organized trips. She would take the kids, skiing, scuba and skydiving, which she enjoyed herself. "She was tough," her son said fondly, which may have explained the shootout. His father would stay home when they all left, "maybe to see his sweeties," he joked.

Joan and Thompson had married after he returned from Germany, and Jim was born soon after. But he only remembered Thompson talking about Patton once. "My mother didn't like it. I guess she was embarrassed," he said. He was ten or twelve. "We found a bunch of articles cut out and put them into a scrapbook. It's disappeared now. But he [his father] told me he was driving a truck, out looking for booze for the guys—basically doing something he wasn't supposed to be doing. That was my dad for you."

I told him I knew where the scrapbook was. He was surprised to hear about it, asked how he could get in touch with Gloria, and continued.

His father, he said, told him, "basically he was coming up an incline or whatever and he turned left and this limousine came over the hill and hit him broadside." Patton happened to be in the back and "hit his head or whatever.... We hadn't really heard anything about it until then.... I remember my dad getting a call when the Patton movie came out.... They wanted to interview him and talk to him about it but he refused. He didn't want any part of it.... I don't know whether it was because my mom said no or maybe because he had something to hide. But he told us he didn't want to be bothered."

An "incline" or a "hill"? That's why he had not seen the Patton car? That was the first time I had heard that. Mannheim was near the Rhine River. It was on a flood plain. Flat. Travel books attest to it. No witness describes any hills. Fugate, who had traveled there, had sent me pictures. One was taken from the point where the railroad tracks used to be. They are gone now, he said. But the pictures showed the road stretching flat and level far up ahead. The accident spot, which he marked, was roughly in the middle of that straightaway. There were no hills or inclines. Not even a bump.

Jim said his older sister June might know more. He gave me her number. June, like Jim, had been estranged from her father. She had done some research into Patton's death. "I don't know if I believe in a conspiracy or not" but "he had a very weak personality.... He was not the smartest bulb on the planet. He would have sold his soul to the devil. Anything for a buck."

She remembers her mother cautioning her about Patton. "We were not supposed to talk about it and in those days you did what your parents said or you were up against the wall." She remembered her brother assembling the scrapbook and that her father "was supposed to be dishonorably discharged" because of the accident, "but then it became honorable." She knew, she said, that when he was readying to come back to the U.S. after the war "he had a suitcase full of money but couldn't bring it back. The Duetch mark wasn't worth much here so he just turned it over, the whole suitcase, to an old lady there."

Where did he get the money?

She did not know. "I do remember him saying he was grabbing pieces off Patton's car and selling them. He was a shyster. I also remember contraband. He was really into the Black Market." When I asked her about the hill which her father told Jim had prevented him from seeing the Patton car, she said, "My father was a really good liar—I do not know about the 'good,' but I do about the liar." Married, herself, to a German, she said she had been to Mannheim partly because she knew that was where the accident had taken place. "It's flat. It's a flood plain," she confirmed. There were no hills, as far as she had seen.

June gave me the number of her other brother, Ed, Thompson's youngest, now a car dealer. He echoed his siblings and gave the intriguing news that Thompson's friend, Robert Delsordo, a New Jersey lawyer, had recently surprised him by saying, "you should see what's in your father's will." Nobody in the family knew what he was talking about, nor had they yet found out.

I called Delsordo, a former municipal judge, who acknowledged there was a secret he knew regarding Thompson and the Patton accident. It was not in Thompson's will. It was a "confidence" Thompson had given to him and he was not going to divulge it, even to the family. "His family doesn't know about this," said Delsordo. "He didn't trust his family. . . . It's something he disclosed to me in confidence. . . . I will not disclose it during my lifetime. He asked me not to and I'm going to honor that." The secret information, he said, exonerates Thompson—at least in his (Delsordo's) opinion. Thompson gave it to him, he said, in case accusations were ever made against him after he was dead and it was needed to prove his innocence. I was at least inquiring, I pointed out, but he said, no, he was not going to divulge it—not until someone states flat out that Thompson deliberately caused the accident. Then he would defend Thompson with it. Otherwise, he said, it is in his personal safe deposit box and will remain there until his death when he plans to will it to a nephew who is attending West Point. The nephew, whom he did not name, can then do with it what he wants.

Delsordo had never heard of Bazata, he said, and did not know Thompson had articles about the OSS officer's charges. But when Thompson had seen *Brass Target*, the 1978 movie about the accident staged so an assassin could shoot Patton, he had wanted Delsordo to sue, an action Delsordo discouraged, he said, because the movie was fiction. Nobody was saying it was true. Then he told me what Thompson had revealed to him about the accident—in effect, Thompson's attorney giving me his client's version. Such a version was not exactly unbiased but the closest to Thompson's version I would probably be able to get.

He said he did not know why Thompson was in Mannheim. Thompson had not told him—or he (Delsordo) had forgotten. But Thompson was alone in the truck. Delsordo emphasized this. No passengers. Thompson was low on gas. He saw a fuel dump and decided to turn in to it. There was not any traffic at the time. He turned uneventfully—which is contrary to what Woodring and General Gay said. But before he could proceed across the entrance, he saw a little ravine ahead with water in it. The big truck was in two-wheel drive and he did not think it could make it across. He stopped, and with most of the truck still extending out into the highway, exited the cab and changed to four-wheel drive. "If you remember the deuce-and-a-half, you had to go out and lock the hubs." He got back in the truck and was beginning to slowly pull forward through the rivulet when he said "over the hill this car came flying at him. He [Thompson] said, 'I never could understand why he [Patton's driver Woodring] didn't go around me. I was in low gear. I couldn't move out of the way fast enough.'" The Patton car slammed into the truck broadside. It hit in back of the cab where the outside gas tank was. Thompson expected a fire or explosion. Then he saw the general's flag on the car and said, "Oh shit!"

Those were all the details he had.

I reacted by saying there was no hill—at least according to all available evidence. Delsordo said Thompson said there was, and he believed him. It was not part of the standard story, he speculated, because, in Thompson's opinion, the standard story was a "saving story" for Woodring. "Bob seemed to lay the blame on Woodring," said Delsordo. "He told me, 'For God sakes, why didn't he [Woodring] go around me?'" The answer, he ventured, was that Woodring was "Patton's buddy." The witness by Gay and Woodring that Thompson had made the sudden left turn in front of them was a "fiction"—in other words, a lie—made up to save Woodring. That was what he now believed based on what Thompson told him.

Then he told me some new information about Thompson's whereabouts following the accident. "I don't know if you know it or not but the army CID [Criminal Investigation Division] got him out of Germany that night. They flew him to England." He thought they had taken him to Sheffield, but was not sure. "He was incommunicado for a couple of days. What happened was that after the accident, General Gay got out of the car and said, 'Get the MPs. Get an ambulance.' He [Thompson] didn't know what was going on. They kind of kept him away. Then the CID picked him up and took him right to England. He was scared to death. He said, 'You know, I figured I'm going to get a firing squad for this.' Bob was always a little bit of a hyper guy and I could picture him scared to death. But it turned out they were taking him there for his safety. Patton was so well loved by his troops they figured they couldn't protect him in Germany."

If what Delsordo says is true, it explains why Thompson "disappeared"—at least initially. Howard K. Smith interviewed Thompson for a story datelined "Frankfurt, Dec. 13," four days after the accident. So he was back in Germany at least by then. But that seems hardly enough time to believe he was out of danger from any revenge takers—if that, in fact, was the reason for his disappearance. Patton was not dead yet. He was, by then, recovering. So the danger of retaliation early seems minimal. In addition, the idea that CID, or even just regular uniformed MPs, would have been concerned for Thompson's safety seems like a stretch. Why would they be? Thompson was just a lowly GI truck driver. He was not a celebrity or somebody of high import. And if they were concerned about his safety, why not Woodring's, too? Initial public reports about the crash said both drivers were responsible.[6] Why did they take him all the way to England when other safe havens were nearby? Frankfurt was much closer and was an American fortress, as was Nuremburg, near Berlin, which was heavily guarded and contained the notorious Nazi war criminals. Why not take him there? Furthermore, no reports have ever put CID at the accident scene—unless someone like the mysterious Lieutenant Vanlandingham was CID. But Vanlandingham's records give no indication of his being CID. They were the military's professional investigators, elite detective-like specialists who were only summoned if a major crime was suspected. But all reports, especially by those who argue against any plot, like Joseph F. Shanahan, insist the collision was just a "routine" traffic accident. That is why, they argue, there are no reports.

So the questions mount. Delsordo's new information only enlarges the mystery. If CID *was* there, then a crime *was* suspected. What information brought them to the scene? And how did they get there so fast? Did they have it prior to the accident? Surely Thompson would have been interrogated in England. Where are the reports? Nothing has surfaced. Another Patton researcher, Peter J.K. Hendrikx of the Netherlands, whose article, "An Ironical Thing," explored the accident, sent me a picture showing Thompson in a somewhat disheveled uniform standing before what looks like a blackboard. He is grinningly pointing with a pencil at something indistinguishable.* Hendrikx had gotten the photo, he said, from *Stars & Stripes*. But our efforts to track down their source had been fruitless.[7] Did it show Thompson in England? If not, where was he? What was he doing in the picture? Why had it been taken?

Possibly the most mysterious story of all, however, is the strange tale of Joe Spruce—or more accurately, Joe *Scruce*—for that, it turns out, was his real last name—a fact that has escaped all Patton biographers and researchers.

Scruce was the sergeant driving the jeep behind the Patton car carrying the dog and hunting rifles for the generals. Just before the accident, according to most accounts, he had passed the Cadillac and pulled ahead of it on the fatal road in order to show the way to the hunting area. That meant he passed the Thompson truck ahead and presumably had seen or heard the crash close behind him. Babalas appears to have been even farther away than

---

*Even in blowups I cannot make it out.

Scruce, having passed the two Patton vehicles while traveling in the opposite direction, and *he* heard it.

Yet Scruce is never seen or publicly heard from again.

Apart from the basic instinct to help others in trouble, this sergeant, charged with leading two generals, one of whom is the most important on the continent, does not return to help?

He just drives on and disappears?

It made no sense.

To this day, Scruce is identified by everyone purporting to have researched the accident as *Spruce*. That includes the Patton family members who have written about Scruce and the major Patton biographers who go deep enough into the story to mention Scruce's part. But anyone seriously reading General Gay's memoir, the earliest known and single largest written recollection about the crash, should have had a question about that name. Gay in the memoir identifies the sergeant as Scruce—not once, but three times—which made me think it was not a typo and wonder if perhaps Scruce—not Spruce—might be the last name of the person to seek if I hoped to learn more.

I shared this with Christine Samples, one of my cousin Tim's investigators, and after a lengthy search she located probably his only living offspring, a dark-haired, fifty-six-year-old daughter who was surprised to be contacted. She did not know her father had been involved in the Patton accident. But she knew he had been a career soldier and had died in what she considered a mysterious way in 1952. And the more she learned about it, because of certain other things she knew about him, she said she became worried that her father may indeed have been involved in a plot to kill Patton, if only peripherally. That new worry added to a personal crisis she had on and off all her life over who her father was and why she was deprived of him so early in her life. She had been just an infant when he had died. Although I have never felt there is reason to be fearful of Patton plotters—too many years have passed—she requested her name not be used. I'll call her "Angela."

The following is the story she helps tell:

Born in Italy in 1901, Joseph Leo Scruce came to the U.S. as an immigrant in 1919.[8] His Italian name was pronounced "Screwsee." He came to America with his brother, but his father and mother, and possibly other siblings, remained in Italy. Described as five foot seven, 147 pounds with brown hair and brown eyes on a 1951 military ID Angela has, he spoke English with an accent until he died in 1952. According to personnel documents from the National Records Center, he had enlisted in the Marine Corps from which he was discharged in 1928. In 1933, he joined the army and listed his occupation as "cook." By 1936, he was a private first class at Fort Davis in the Canal Zone, Panama, and listed his primary occupation as "soldier." He was in the infantry. He left the service briefly in 1938 and rejoined in early 1941. What happened to him in the gap is not in the records or known to Angela.

From 1943 through 1945, he served with the 29th Infantry Division—the "Blue and Grey"—which had been in the vanguard of U.S. troops landing on Omaha Beach on D-Day in Normandy, France, June 6, 1944. According to a *Stars & Stripes* booklet entitled "29 Let's Go,"[9] which is about the unit, the division "hammered through hedgerows at St. Lo," helped capture Brest on the French coast south of Normandy, and then fought valiantly north through France and into Germany and met the Soviets near the Elbe River, where Germany was divided into East and West. He was awarded a Bronze Service Star "for meritorious service" from "6 June 1944 to 8 May 1945." Division commander, Major General C. H. Gerhardt, wrote in Scruce's hardback copy of the

"Let's Go" booklet: "To Sgt. Scruce, who as division mess sergeant did so much to help."

That dedication was part of what worried Angela. Why would a general write such praise to a cook? She wondered if he had done more than just prepare and oversee meals. The 29th Division was back in the U.S. by January 1946. But Scruce, a master sergeant, had been assigned to Patton's last command at Bad Nauheim after Patton had been fired by Eisenhower in the September, 1945 controversy. In addition to being qualified an "expert" in a number of weapons, including the M-1 rifle, he was trained as a driver of various vehicles, including the "jeep," or quarter-ton truck, which he had been driving the day of the accident. Brian M. Sobel, author of *The Fighting Pattons*, identifies "Spruce" as "Patton's aide,"[10] apparently based on what Woodring told him. If he was that close to the general, it is even more interesting. He was not assigned there, according to the records, until Patton was. His records say nothing about Patton's accident or death. But on December 31, 1945, right after it, Scruce is accepted into the "regular" army, a distinction of sorts. Not only does one have to meet certain criteria to be so honored, but most were saying good riddance to service—and the service was only keeping its best. He was a master sergeant at his death and was buried in Arlington National Cemetery.

Angela was only eleven months old when her father died—a time about which she says she has no memories of her own. Her mother, Glenice, who died in 2002, had married Scruce, who was almost twice her age, in 1950. She was barely out of her teens. But it was a good marriage which lasted two years, until his death. By Angela's account, gleaned largely from her mother over the years and an aunt who is also now dead but had introduced the two, the couple was deeply in love. Both were appreciative of what their age differences offered the other—a budding young bride and stable home for him; a caring, worldly husband and the same stability for her. He wrote her numerous love letters, some of which Angela let me read. No question he loved her and considered himself lucky to have found her.

But her father never talked about the war or past, she said, which was fine with her mother. A professional soldier when she met him at a service dance, his military life seemed too mysterious anyway. He lived in a remote retreat in the woods at Camp Picket, Virginia, a huge forested training base near Washington, D.C. where he catered weekend getaways for high-ranking officers with whom he seemed to be close.* Bazata did the same kind of thing shortly after he returned to America from Europe after decades away in the early 1970s running what was, in effect, a clandestine's retreat. With help from CIA friends and others, Bazata managed a remote farm in Maryland where he raised birds and staged hunts for friends and brass, many of whom had connections with the spy business at the CIA, whose headquarters in Langley, Virginia was nearby.

There was more than a modicum of security where her father worked, says Angela. Most bases allow visitors to enter as long as they are registered at the gate.[11] But that was not the case at Picket in those days. Her mother told her that her father, presumably before they were married, would have to put her in the trunk of his Buick to sneak her onto the base so they could be together overnight. And in addition to being a cook and driver, he was also a revered marksman—just like Bazata. "My mom said his reputation on the base was as a shooter, a hunter—that's what soldiers

---

*In one letter he wrote that he consulted a general about the feasibility of getting married to Angela's mother. The general said he thought it would be "ok."

she talked to told her." "He was a great shot." He hunted all the food he served at the cabin, she said. He could shoot "five pheasants before you can blink an eye." He also shot wild turkey and other edible game for his guests. He had his own garden, guns, a jeep, and hunting dogs, which he loved and trained. Her mother once objected to the dogs sleeping in their bed. "He hunted for all the colonels and generals who came out to party on the weekend."

Her father, it seemed, was involved in more than just cooking, said Angela. "It was such a cushy job." How could just a cook get that? He would go off for periods of time and had mysterious routes to get to the cabin. And she could not understand his silence about World War II. "He never talked about the war, said my mother. Never. Why? Everything I know about him is he was such a down-to-earth, caring man. He'd bring food to our relatives when they were having a hard time." He was gregarious, she said. "He just wasn't the silent type. For him not to talk, I just don't understand. He was Italian. I know men don't talk about the war but it wasn't like him. He was warm and open."

I wondered if she was not letting the new and controversial information about Patton I had brought overwhelm her. She was only recalling what her mother had told her and I emphasized I had nothing concrete. But she persisted. "I'm a spiritual person," not religious in the traditional sense, "I just have a premonition." She meant that probably believing he was doing his duty, he may have been involved in a plot. She was convinced her father would have returned to the Patton accident scene, not only to aid the injured, but because of the dog that, according to Farago, had been switched to the limousine from her father's care in the open air jeep. "He'd already put the dog in with the generals. He was in the lead. He would have looked in his rearview mirror. I know he would have come back. He would have been desperate to help."

And if by some chance, he had not been aware of the accident, he would have found out later and then appeared, at least to have been interviewed.

What also worries her is the way he died. It was on his birthday, March 11, 1952. He and Glenice had a little house by then. It was in Blackstone, Virginia, a small town—at least in those days—near the base. Two weeks before the birthday, Glenice wanted to plan a celebration. "She says, 'Joe, I'd like to have a nice party for your birthday. You have the day off, don't you?'" He seemed troubled. "He looked at her and said, 'No Glenice. No party. I won't live to see it.'" She could tell he wasn't joking. "She was horrified. 'Why do you say such a mean thing? You know it will hurt me.'" He tried to gloss it over. "He said, 'I'm sorry. Calm down. I just don't want a party. I want to wake up on my birthday, make love to my beautiful wife. I want you to feed me cake and coffee for breakfast and then play with our child, the love of my life.'"

Was he ill?

According to Angela, "He could run miles without even panting. My mother said he never complained of anything more than an occasional headache—and nothing big. He'd take an aspirin and that would be it."

On the day of his birthday, she did just what he wanted. "What happened was she said they woke up. They started making love. And all of a sudden he stopped and said, 'Glenice, I can't feel anything in my left body. I'm going numb. I'm paralyzed. Call the doctor.'" She jumped from bed and began dialing. Then he told her to forget the doctor and call an ambulance. She redialed for an operator begging for help. By the time she turned around, he was hemorrhaging. "Blood was everywhere. She was screaming and crying and hugging him and blood was all over both of them and she said I was in the other room crying hysterically. She didn't know what to do. She just kept screaming."

It took the ambulance half an hour to forty-five minutes to get there—probably the result, she says, of their Blackstone house being in the country and help being relatively far away from where the ambulance was dispatched. But she wonders, was the delay on purpose? By then he was dead. Army doctors later told her mother he had suffered a brain aneurysm—a burst blood vessel. Symptoms include a sudden, severe headache, which he did not have, but sometimes paralysis on one side of the body, which he did. Such gushing of blood, however, I could not find in any description of the illness. As in Patton's death, there was no autopsy.[12]

Could he have been seeing a doctor without telling Glenice?

"Then there should be some reference to it," she said, and showed me some army medical checkups he had had in the past. There was only one dismissal from duty for one day in all the records.

Months later, with the help of information from his official records,[13] she got in touch with and met what was left of Scruce's family—mostly elderly cousins of hers descended from the brother who had originally come to America with him. They revered her father, whom most of them remembered vividly, and it was an emotional time for her. "My cousins are great, though not much help as far as [the Patton story]" she wrote me. "I just don't think Joe ever told *anyone* of that fateful day."[14]

Why would he keep it a secret?

And what about Frank Krummer, the German civilian reported in the Seventh Army documents to have been in Thompson's truck? Seventh Army had jurisdiction over the accident. The papers discuss an investigation of the crash that has never been found.

Are we just to dismiss the documents?

I have not been able to locate Krummer or any of his family, which is not surprising given the meager information I have and the fact that Krummer is a fairly common German name. It is also possible that whatever effort I did expend was for naught because, like "Spruce," the name might have been mistakenly or purposely misspelled.

And what about the possible third passenger others have written was in Thompson's truck?

Despite attorney Delsordo's insistence that Thompson had no passengers, Delsordo, like the rest of us, was not there, as he concedes. He only knows what Thompson told him, some of which he refuses to reveal so it can not be addressed. And the story he does relate on Thompson's behalf is inconsistent in several respects from what correspondent Howard K. Smith reported Thompson told him only four days after the accident. In that exclusive interview, Thompson made no mention of any hill or of his truck being stalled on the road. In fact, the closest document to an official report about the accident yet discovered—the Seventh Army memo,[15] which purports to be based on the official report (now missing)—states flatly that "the smash occurred as the truck was making a left turn," not after it had already completed the left turn (as Delsordo argues). Considering Scruce's strange disappearance from the accident scene and later aftermath, and his—and even Thompson's—mysterious deaths, something seems not right about all of it.

CHAPTER SIXTEEN

★ ★ ★ ★

STOP PATTON!

When Patton returned to war on July 6, 1944—touching down on a Normandy airfield exactly one month after D-Day—he was determined to avoid trouble lest his chance at fulfilling what he believed was his destiny—to become a revered military hero—be removed.

Eisenhower had warned that one more controversy and he would send Patton home.

He was on his best behavior.

Forget that he been passed over as commander of American troops at D-Day despite having successfully led the U.S. contingents of the North African and Sicilian campaigns and had more military experience, especially in combat, than Omar Bradley, a subordinate, whom Eisenhower had chosen over him.

Forget that Bradley, once ashore after D-Day and bogged down in stalemate, had used Patton's ideas to formulate a plan, codenamed "Cobra," to break out of the stalemate and then had taken sole credit for the plan.[1]

Patton did not care. He was back in the fight. While he had been the idle decoy in England—a role he found humiliating but had dutifully accepted—he had read *The Norman Conquest* by Freeman, "paying particular attention to the roads William the Conqueror used in his operations in Normandy and Brittany."[2] He had served in France in World War I and earlier, as a military student in France, had actually reconnoitered many of the areas he expected to be fighting in. These factors combined with his fluency in French meant he was seriously prepared on the eve of his dash across Northern France which would ultimately spearhead that country's liberation and send the Germans fleeing for home.

But that same drive and success would again put him in conflict with his superiors, beginning with what has come to be known as the "Falaise Gap."

After the newly reorganized Third Army had been given the official go-ahead, on August 1, nearly two months after D-Day and following the tough breakout at St. Lo, France, Patton and his tanks hit the road roaring. In the next fourteen days, the Third Army, "advanced farther and faster than any army in all history," wrote Colonel Robert S. Allen, Patton's combat intelligence officer and celebrated Washington journalist.[3] Patton's forces, along with General Courtney Hodges's First Army, first turned west and cut off and neutralized Brittany, the huge French land mass jutting into the western Atlantic below the Cherbourg Peninsula. The Germans had concentrations of infantry, armor, and vital submarine pens in Brittany. But with their supply lines cut by Patton and Hodges, they were toothless. Hitler did not stand by. In a risky move, German Panzers and infantry, not yet under attack in eastern France, were ordered to thrust west towards Patton and Hodges with little regard to their flanks, and counterattack. Their mission was to split Allied forces which would be a major threat to the Allied advance.

But the Allies, aided by "Ultra," their breaking of German codes, learned of the Nazi offensive. Both Patton and Hodges's forces met the thrust at Avranches and Mortain, two towns at the base of the Cherbourg Peninsula which governed the area. Fighting raged for days. In a brilliant subsequent move, Patton, in consultation with Bradley, saw a chance to entrap all the Germans engaged. He would send Third Army elements deeper south and east to Le-Mans, gateway to Paris and headquarters of the German Seventh Army, most of which was in the fighting, and encircle the thrusting enemy. The elements went swooping down and around the counterattacking Germans, beginning the encirclement.

Encirclement is every battle commander's dream. Once an enemy is surrounded—cut off from its supply lines with no route of escape—the surrounding force can dispose of it almost at will, tightening the noose with every kill. In modern warfare, much of the slaughter of a target so captured comes from planes. It is merciless—like throwing grenades at schools of fish in a pond. This was Patton's intention: annihilate the enemy and his weapons in the pocket that was forming. Once LeMans was taken, he had only to swing sharply back up north towards the sea to link with Montgomery's troops, who were supposed to be advancing due south from Caen, the British general's first objective after D-Day. Falaise, a small town on the imaginary north-south line connecting Caen with LeMans, was projected as the meeting point. It would be there that the trap would be closed. However, Montgomery, who had been meeting stiff resistance and was having other problems advancing, many of his own making, was bogged down and way behind schedule. The invasion plan had called for him to retake Caen the first day. This was now two months later. When Patton's troops reached Argentan, a village about twenty miles south of Falaise, Bradley, prior to linkup, had abruptly halted Patton's forces, leaving an opening—the twenty-mile wide "Falaise Gap"—through which Germans, being beaten at Avranches and Mortain and already sensing the trap, were started to retreat.

Why Bradley did so has long been controversial. Boundaries of operation for American and British troops had been preset by Montgomery, who was Eisenhower's deputy for the invasion and thus the highest ground commander on Normandy at the time. Bradley, under Montgomery, at first said he was adhering to those boundaries.*Patton frantically protested. They were losing time! They had a chance to crush an entire German army! It might win the war. Let him close the gap, he begged. "Nothing doing," Brigadier General Albin F. Irzyk, a Patton tank commander, records Bradley retorted, "You're not to go beyond Argentan," which was Montgomery's cutoff point for the American advance in that sector.[4] As strange as they might have been—especially coming from Bradley who had sanctioned the encirclement and who was not a Montgomery fan—those were the orders.

Twice more Patton sought permission to close the gap. The second time, Bradley was with Eisenhower, who, by that time, had come over from England and was at Bradley's headquarters prior to establishing his own in France. Irzyk records that Patton, his troops still poised at Argentan, probing units already on the outskirts of Falaise, could not get Bradley on the phone so he asked Bradley's chief of staff, General Allen, to get Bradley to go to Montgomery directly and seek permission. But Bradley, in front of Eisenhower, "urged that the...boundary continue to be ob-

---

*After the war, he and others came up with further excuses—there was fear the joining Brits and Americans might fire on each other, the Brits had seeded the area with time bombs (roundly challenged), and the Germans, determined to get out, might destroy the tanks closing the gap (called ridiculous by most).

served." Eisenhower, supreme commander, who should have been cognizant of the opportunity on his battlefield and closed the gap—said nothing. He missed ordering a decisive blow. "Once again, as in North Africa and Sicily," writes Irzyk, "Ike appeared more like a bystander than a commander. He rubber-stamped Bradley"—and, by default, Montgomery.

In a third try, according to Irzyk, members of Bradley's staff, seeing the urgency and apparently siding with Patton, had phoned directly to Montgomery's headquarters for permission. But members of Montgomery's staff had rebuffed them[5]—not surprising since Patton scholars such as Charles M. Province feel Montgomery was the real culprit. Montgomery, as big a prima donna as Patton ever was, "insisted, or rather, demanded, that he be allowed to close the gap," writes Province. "Monty wanted the glory and the credit for the 'ripe plum' situation which had been created by Patton's brilliant leadership and Third Army's speed and daring execution."[6]

There was nothing more Patton could do, although his urge was probably to simply disregard the refusals and close the gap anyway. But he restrained himself. He was in the doghouse and knew it. Any transgression and he would be gone—and this one would have been a huge transgression.

Eisenhower *himself* had said no.

In the near week it took Montgomery to finally close the gap as many as 250,000 Germans—including important battle commanders—along with their equipment could have escaped through the Falaise Gap.* There's no way of knowing the exact figure.

---

*Various figures are given by scholars of the battle. Rohmer in *Patton's Gap* says 250,000. Breuer in *Death of a Nazi Army* indicates fewer than 40,000. The consensus seems to be 100,000, given, for instance, by such authors as Allen in *Lucky Forward* and Axelrod in *Patton*.

Allied airpower found the Germans in the pocket as they streamed out the gap and beyond and blasted them, causing considerable damage and carnage. The Germans, gap or no gap, suffered a huge defeat—primarily because of Patton's near encirclement. But the numbers killed and the war weapons destroyed pale in the face of the consequences of the blunder of not closing the gap. Not only would many of the German soldiers, commanders, and Panzer tanks that escaped return in December to batter U.S. troops in the devastating and surprise, last-ditch counterattack known as the "Battle of the Bulge," but the very war itself might have been ended had Patton been allowed to close at Falaise, which most historians agree he could have done. "If closed," wrote Major General Richard Rohmer, a fighter pilot at the time in the skies above the pocket and one who has written extensively about it, the gap "could have brought the surrender of the Third Reich, whose senior generals were now desperately concerned about the ominous shadow of the great Russian Bear rising on the eastern horizon of the Fatherland."[7] They knew it was only a matter of time before they were done—and better to surrender to the Americans. Bradley's own historian, Colonel Ralph Ingersoll, wrote, "The failure to close the Argentan-Falaise gap was the loss of the greatest single opportunity of the war."[8]

American correspondents, censored as they were, reported little, if any part of what happened at Falaise. It was really only known in totality at headquarters and by the troops, tankers, and pilots who lived it. The reading public at the time was only told of the great victory won at the "Battle of Normandy" and the subsequent slaughter. Even the fact that Patton was leading the charge was not yet known. When he had first arrived in Normandy, the Germans were still guessing where he was, holding back crucial reinforcements, thinking they would need them when he eventually landed at the Pas de Calais. It was good strategy to keep his presence quiet and the Germans guessing. But by the battle for Mortain, they were well aware of who they were facing. Still, his name was not released, a fact that galled him. It was Eisenhower who was quoted as to the extent of the slaughter in the victory and was therefore generally credited for the overall success—which was ironic in view of his part in not closing the gap. Even today, what happened at Falaise is generally not well known except amongst military historians and enthusiasts. It is certainly not part of the popular D-Day invasion aftermath lore or even the general story of World War II in Europe. I suspect the reason for its obscurity is how badly it would have reflected on those who disingenuously emerged as heroes of that battle, most pointedly Bradley and Eisenhower, who had vested interest in keeping the true facts about Falaise quiet.

But Patton and his troops who were there knew. He wrote in his diary, "This halt [was] a great mistake. [Bradley's] motto seems to be, 'In case of doubt, halt.'" And in an obvious dig at Eisenhower, he wrote, "I wish I were supreme commander."[9] But he was not. And, after Falaise, as he continued his historic chase of the fleeing Germans east through Northern France, stung as he was by the obvious lack of combat leadership in his superiors, his attitude of compliance began to change. His nephew, Fred Ayer Jr., wrote that instead of continuing to adhere strictly to the rules as he had earlier resolved, "He told me that...he did in fact stop sending back any position reports, because otherwise, "some directive-reading S.O.B. would tell me, 'Patton, you've already reached your designated objective, so stop there and await further orders.' Why hell, the only thing for an army to do when it has the enemy on the run is to keep going until it runs out of gas, and then continue on foot, to keep killing until it runs out of ammunition and then go on killing with bayonets and rifle butts."[10]

Little did he know that he soon actually *would* be out of gas, and not for any reason of his own—or any good reason at all, for that matter. For as he and his Third Army, its tanks blazing the way, had raced across France in an unprecedented display of military brilliance, enabling, among other feats, the liberation of Paris, and had entered areas near the German border where Douglas Bazata was operating, Montgomery, north of Patton and considerably behind him in terms of advancement, was hatching a plan to penetrate Germany that would siphon Patton's gas, ammunition and even troops, and do what the Germans so far had been unable to do—stop Patton. The plan, code-named "Market Garden" and supported by Eisenhower over a similar thrust into Germany proposed by Patton—even though Montgomery had not done anything remotely as impressive as Patton (in fact, had done the opposite) would fail. And with the failure, Eisenhower would lose yet another chance to end the war before 1945, thus dooming U.S. troops to more fighting and dying and adding to a legacy of blunders like Falaise which he hoped would be kept secret.

By August 31, Patton, putting Falaise behind because he believed he would destroy the escaping Germans when he overtook them, had advanced his tanks to the east bank of the Meuse River, the next to last physical barrier before the German border, sixty-three miles to the east. This was only 140 miles from the Rhine River, the fording of which was believed to be the key to conquering all of Germany. One hundred and forty miles was less than half the distance they had traveled in the previous twelve days, according to Irzyk. That was more than twenty-five miles per day, an astounding pace for tanks.

Now euphoria gripped us tightly. The roads were clear ahead and the Moselle River [the last natural obstacle before Germany] would be undefended. From there the avenues to Germany were wide open. The American forces had by now destroyed the bulk of the enemy needed to man the empty fortifications of the Siegfried Line. The [fleeing Germans] just could not retire fast enough to reach, much less organize, man, and defend those defensive barriers which had been constructed just inside their homeland. And not too far behind that was the Rhine with, realistically, undefended bridges. The possibility was high that the Germans would collapse when the Rhine River was reached.[11]

Patton was poised to roar into Germany as unstoppable as he had been in France.

Then, on August 31—as his tanks prepared to ford the Meuse—his gasoline allotment was suddenly cut by 140,000 gallons. And that was just the beginning. In quick order, he did not have enough to continue. The Third Army was guzzling gas at the rate of 350,000 to 400,000 gallons per day.[12] The cut was a huge chunk. Suspicious, he wrote in his diary, "This may be an attempt to stop me in a backhanded manner," but then tabled the thought.[13] Curiously, according to Fred Ayer, Jr., Patton was warned by Marlene Dietrich, the singer and film star who was entertaining troops that "someone or some group of persons was 'out to get him'. . . . I did not then press [Patton] for details and can add none today," wrote Ayer, although he guessed she meant reporters, who had been after Patton since the slaps in Sicily, or other powerful persons at home with whom he was unpopular.[14] But it shows, as Bazata said, that Patton already knew he was being threatened by forces on his own side.

The next morning, rather than radio Bradley about the shortage (for fear the enemy might be listening and learn his predicament), Patton went personally to see his younger boss, who, following Falaise, was now sympathetic to his pleas. However, Bradley informed him, Eisenhower was not. The Supreme Commander had decided to give Montgomery Patton's gas and a portion of his supplies, as well as all of Bradley's entire First Army. Bradley did not like it either. Montgomery, as far as they knew, had talked Eisenhower into supporting an ambitious plan in which he would first capture the needed Belgian port of Antwerp off the North Sea—needed because of the problem of supplying such rapidly advancing armies—and then air drop the largest force of paratroopers in history to help his tanks and infantry cross the Rhine at Arnhem, relatively close and north from Antwerp. Once in Germany, he would "dash" to Berlin and end the war, he promised. It was enticing. Eisenhower had given him what he wanted. In fact, according to Irzyk, "once given the priority for [Patton's] gasoline and supplies, Montgomery had demanded 'all,' everything, and in order to have it, wanted Patton stopped 'cold.'"[15]

Montgomery's demand, interestingly, is reminiscent of what Bazata had claimed was going on—that there was a separate underlying clandestine plot beyond immediate military need to "stop" Patton. If that was so, were the British involved? Was this the origin? Did a plot stem or grow from Montgomery and Patton's antagonistic relationship? Montgomery and Patton were, at least, rivals. There is a good case to be made that they hated each other. Bazata was in the area and had hinted he was working for the British who, operationally, were practically running the Jedburgh program. Was Montgomery's demand, if not Dietrich's warning, alluding to something darker—a plot, the momentum of which would eventually grow and morph into assassination?

British World War II records are not as accessible as are those in the U.S., which themselves are not easily gotten. Much of what is in England is still classified and will remain so by law for many years—a veritable treasure trove of secrets. My own mailed questions to British archivists remain unanswered. However, I did manage to find a Donovan memorandum to President Roosevelt stating that at this exact time—"August 1944"—"General Patton through the O.S.S. detachment asked the FFI [otherwise known as the Maquis] to protect the flank of his armored divisions."[16] This indicates that Patton had an OSS contingent that was helping him, and he was probably involved with the Maquis in the area, both of which mean Bazata, as he indicated, could have had access to Patton and may have been involved in some way then in stopping Patton's advance—as he had cagily, but obscurely, put it, "We did some things." James M. Gavin, one of the U.S. paratroop commanders dealt to Montgomery for Market-Garden, says without equivocation that there was a plot. "It is ironic," he wrote, "that at about the same time [as Patton's gas was diverted], the Germans, too, were deeply preoccupied with Patton. They considered him their most dangerous opponent and pitted their best troops against him. So both sides were doing their damnedest to stop Patton."[17] Apparently, the "Stop Patton" plan was known by more than Bazata.

Whatever the case, Patton was told by Bradley he would just have to bide his time—at least until they came up with solutions for more gas. His advance was halted even though the way ahead—clearly the shortest route into Germany, and probably to Berlin—was open and, more importantly, undefended by the German army in retreat. This was mainly because the German army he was chasing was spread thin and disorganized and was generally being decimated at this time all along the front. On the day he was stopped, the Germans in the West were in total disarray. A top German general involved at the time, Siegfried Westphal, General von Rundstedt's chief of staff, later said, "The overall situation in the West [for the Germans] was serious in the extreme. The Allies could have punched through at any point with ease." Moreover, Patton had fewer obstacles to overcome than Montgomery, who, north of him, was closer to the sea and had numerous canals and waterways blocking his—and Market Garden's—advance. As his gas dwindled to fumes, Patton wrote, "The British have put it over again. We got no gas because, to suit Monty, the First Army [already requisitioned and preparing for the mid-September operation] must get most of it, and we are also feeding the Parisians [who, freshly liberated, were being aided by the Allies]....It is terrible to halt....We should cross the Rhine...and the faster we do it, the less lives and munitions it will take." Time was running out, he knew. Good tank weather—absence of rain and halting muck—would soon be gone. "This was the momentous error of the war....No one realizes the terrible value of the 'unforgiving minute' except me. Some way I will get on yet."[18]

Meanwhile, Market-Garden failed. "Overall, the Allies took heavier casualties in Market-Garden than they did on D-Day"— 7,579 killed or wounded, wrote historian and Eisenhower biographer Stephen E. Ambrose. The British 1st Airborne Division suffered the worst losses of any Allied division in the war.[19] Patton historian Martin Blumenson puts the casualties at a higher 12,000.[20] As gallant as the Allied attackers were, they were thrown back. Why? *A Bridge Too Far*, the 1974 Cornelius Ryan bestseller about the huge operation, gives a succinct answer in its title. The paratroopers were dropped too far from their main objective, the bridge over the Rhine at Arnhem, had too much to overcome as a result, and were beaten back by fresher, stronger German defenders who had been mustered while Patton was stopped. Many of those defenders had actually escaped from around Antwerp because Montgomery, in his haste to get to the Rhine bridge, had failed to subdue them after taking the city. Eisenhower, as the Supreme Commander, was ultimately culpable, according to General Gavin among other generals in a position to know, not only for the mistakes in the operation itself, which, as overseer, he should have recognized and corrected, but for choosing Montgomery over Patton in the first place.[21] "Monty at the expense of Patton?" writes an incredulous General Irzyk. Monty had not won a battle since El Alamein in 1942. In fact, he had botched everything else.

> Someone up there must have had clouded vision ... where was the awareness, reason, logic? During the periods when I attended service schools, we were told repeatedly that you reinforce success, you do not reinforce failure .... In our society we have long believed that you should go with a winner, be it sports, politics, academia, industry, the military. It appeared that such a belief was being disregarded, for this time we were not throwing in our lot with the winner. I just could not believe that this was a purely military decision—politics, surely, had to be involved.[22]

It seems so. Patton, in the vernacular of the time, was "behind the eight-ball," persona non grata. Eisenhower and Marshall did not trust him; obviously did not want him leading the final, crucial drive. Could it be, as they got closer to the Soviets, they were afraid they could not control him? The question is as good an answer as any yet provided. The need for a closer supply base is often given as the reason Eisenhower went with Montgomery—that, and the promise of a quick end to the war. But that reasoning is challenged by the fact that Patton, by hook and crook, was, despite the supply problems, maintaining an extraordinary pace— a pace putting Montgomery to shame. Air drops and intermediate supply bases were aiding Patton. Montgomery did not secure Antwerp as a supply base quickly anyway, which is one of the reasons Market-Garden failed.* A Patton offensive also offered a quick end to the war. Patton, more than Montgomery, had proven he could win—and win fast. At best, going with Montgomery over Patton was just a bad decision by Eisenhower—another, like Falaise, that would hold up the winning of the war, result in months more fighting and lives lost, and give the fleeing Germans time to regroup and come back hard in the Battle of the Bulge as they did three months later.

Patton himself took it personally, dropping whatever pretense left that he had toward conciliatory cooperation and reverting to the Patton of old. "To hell with Monty," he wrote in his diary September 17. He would not be halted. He determined to go forward with whatever he could muster. "I must get so involved [in operations] that they can't stop me."[23] To his men, he openly began referring to Eisenhower as "the best general the British had," a knock that General Gavin wrote soon got back to the Supreme Commander and his staff, further alienating Patton from them.[24] He did not care. They would need him and he knew it. In his diary he wrote, "Monty does what he pleases and Ike says 'yes, sir.'"[25] It angered him. To his wife, Beatrice, he penned, "I have to battle for every yard but it is not the enemy who is trying to stop me, it

*The Germans there whom he should have subdued snuck away and helped repel him at Arnhem.

is 'They'.... Look at the map! If I could only steal some gas, I could win this war."[26]

And steal he did—or at least he intimates he did. "There was a rumor," he wrote, "which, officially," he added, tongue-in-cheek, "I hoped was not true, that some of our Ordnance people passed themselves off as members of the First Army [detached to Montgomery] and secured quite a bit of gasoline from one of the dumps of that unit."[27] In addition, troops of his had captured large stores of enemy gas and supplies and Bradley had been able to scrounge up more and had given him permission to cross the Moselle, thirty miles ahead, and go for the German border—all unknown to Eisenhower. Patton, in effect, would launch his own offensive. Eventually, he even told Bradley not to call him during certain periods in order to shut down the possibility of receiving countermanding orders. But the stop-Patton move by that time had already done its damage. In war, sometimes hours, even seconds, make the difference. Taking advantage of Patton's halt, Hitler had rushed a new commander, Field Marshall Walter Model, hero of the Russian fighting, to the crumbling Western front. Model had already begun reorganizing and invigorating the retreating Germans, as well as bringing in new troops, green but eager. Hitler was especially afraid of Patton. While Patton's troops had crossed the Moselle in certain places on September 6, their hold was tenuous as they met increasingly stiffer resistance as a result of reinforcements and found themselves bogged down in fierce fighting all along the river. Worst, the autumn rains began, adding mud—a great hindrance to tanks—and eventually an epidemic of debilitating trench foot* to the shortages of gas, ammunition,

---

*Trench foot is an infection caused by long bouts of standing in wet conditions.

replacement troops, and other crucial supplies already bedeviling the Third Army. The Germans, repositioned and revitalized, were dug in, and now, with the knowledge that they were defending their home soil, found new purpose for fighting—which they did, as Blumenson writes, with increasing "skill and tenacity." They were not just waging a war. They were defending their nearby families from what they considered revenge-seeking hordes. The Third Army blitzkrieg was over—at least for the time being.

Prior to Market-Garden's failure, however, the mood at SHAEF—hundreds of miles from the front—was decidedly optimistic. The war seemed like it would soon be over. So relaxed and confident was the mood, that groups of foreign Allies were given authorization to observe their counterparts. For instance, on September 16, as Montgomery readied the huge air and land operation, Patton wrote that a party of ten Soviets was due to visit the Third Army the next day—obviously part of SHAEF's continuing accommodation to the Soviets. But Patton had no intention of hosting them. "I won't be here," he wrote. "I decided to go to the front. I had a map prepared for them which showed exactly nothing in a big way," because, he wrote, "This is what they do to *us*."[28] His absence and lack of cooperation must have angered Ike and SHAEF—more proof to them of his intolerable obstinance, inability to be controlled, even insanity. *Tough*, would have been Patton's response. He was not going to kow-tow to soldiers he did not trust or respect. Besides, he was actually needed at the front, was happy to be there, and became involved in the actual fighting, directing attacks, sacking slackers, patting backs, and dodging bullets and artillery. An attack against Metz, the capitol of Lorraine and a heavily fortified town in front of the Siegfried Line, produced some of the toughest fighting of the Allied advance. Because of the weather, lack of replacements and supplies, almost impenetrable forts and the fanatical defense, it became a drawn out siege. These were hard days for Patton, who hated slow slog-fighting, believing it benefited defenders and cost casualties and, ultimately, victories.

With the failure of Market Garden, Patton returned to prominence. Eisenhower, with Bradley back in the fold, had, on Bradley's recommendation, decided on a more cautionary strategy of advancement into Germany—a broad line offensive stretching roughly from the North Sea down to Switzerland. The armies on the front would press roughly equally towards the Siegfried Line, thereby forcing the enemy to defend all parts of the line equally and not mass their forces. They would have to spread thin—or so Eisenhower thought. But he wanted a breech as well and learned with great relief that Patton was already out front and hammering. As part of the strategy, Eisenhower decided he wanted to maximize the effort to break through into Germany that began in early November and he authorized a bombardment to blast a passage through the Siegfried Line ahead of Patton so the Third Army could rush through. But the weather was getting worse; rain and increasing mud and cold hampered movement. Patton postponed the launch for several days. Finally, in the pre-dawn of November 8, he decided he could wait no longer. Despite the weather, he launched. "At 0745, Bradley called up to see if we were attacking," he wrote. "I had not let him know for fear I might get a stop order. He seemed delighted that we were going ahead. Then General Eisenhower came on the phone and said, 'I expect a lot of you; carry the ball all the way.'"[29] With the chips down, Eisenhower was counting on his star again, even encouraging him. It was all Patton, a loyalist if there ever was one, needed to get the job done. He was starved for recognition from his superiors.

Unfortunately, given the weather and fierce German resistance, it was not until November 22 that Metz, with its medieval-like defenses, finally fell. But so, too, did the snows of winter—a further hindrance to operations. Now the earlier Patton halt, failure of Market Garden, and relaxed optimism of SHAEF—all delaying the Allied time table for months—produced its fruit. But that fruit was for the Germans. And as Patton prepared a major assault on the Siegfried Line just beyond Metz, the Nazis, taking advantage of the overall slowdown to muster a major fighting force and sneak into position under cover of storm clouds through which Allied reconnoitering airplanes could only occasionally see, launched their last-ditch counterattack in the snow and cold-drenched Ardennes Forest—the infamous Battle of the Bulge. Patton, briefed by his able and worried intelligence chief, Oscar W. Koch, actually predicted the attack, just as he had, interestingly, the Japanese Pearl Harbor sneak attack years before it occurred.[*] But at SHAEF, Eisenhower disregarded the warnings. So unconcerned was SHAEF about the threat, according to Patton historian Charles Province, that they had set up a rest and recuperation area in the Ardennes.[30] And on December 16, fast-moving German tanks and infantry maintaining radio silence hit unprepared troops of the First Army in Belgium with such surprise that thousands of Americans were killed or captured as the salient quickly produced a large breakdown and "bulge" in the lax American line. In London, where Eisenhower and his surprised SHAEF officers—playing cards, as Province describes them—looked aghast at what was happening, it quickly became apparent that the Germans were driving to split the Allied forces along the line and cut off Antwerp

---

[*]He predicted the December 1941 attack in a 1937 paper he wrote while serving as an intelligence officer in Hawaii. D'Este in *A Genius for War*, 361–362, writes that the report was "chillingly accurate."

which had finally become operative as the hub of a network of new Allied supply depots. If they succeeded, the Allies would be cut off and possibly annihilated or thrown back into the sea, losing all territory they had won. It would be Dunkirk, Britain's 1940 defeat, all over again.

Desperate, Eisenhower again turned to Patton—the only one of his commanders convened at an emergency meeting to have an answer. Because Koch had warned him of the tenuous situation along the line, Patton, weeks before, had tasked his staff to come up with contingency plans for just such a surprise German assault. Although he was deep in the preparations for the earlier ordered attack on the Siegfried Line, he told the Supreme Commander he could redirect his huge war machine north in a matter of days and mount a rescue of paratroopers and others who had temporarily halted the German advance through the forest but were in desperate need of help. No one at the meeting could believe he could do it quickly enough. As Province writes, "The Third Army had to stop a full scale attack they had started to the east, pull back the entire army, swing around ninety degrees to the north and then begin another full scale attack on the southern flank of the German forces. Nothing like that had ever been done in the history of warfare."[31]

Patton did it. His troops arrived in a matter of days and were the crucial factor in pushing the bulge back into Germany. Snow and cold, added to a ferocious last-ditch effort by the Germans, extended the fighting in the area for a month, although once Patton's troops arrived, the issue was no longer in doubt. Overall, the U.S. suffered an estimated 81,000 casualties in the Battle of the Bulge, 19,000 of them dead—all as a result of Eisenhower's lax precautions.[32]

Luckily, Patton bailed him out again.

The irony, as Province points out—or perhaps better stated, the *portent of things to come*—was that Eisenhower never even thanked him.

CHAPTER SEVENTEEN

★ ★ ★ ★

THE CAR THAT ISN'T

The car Patton was traveling in the day of his accident could provide valuable clues about what happened to the general. It is in the Patton Museum of Cavalry and Armor at Fort Knox, Kentucky. The museum's website stated that it "has the finest collection of Patton artifacts in the world including his trademark ivory gripped Colt pistol and the Cadillac staff car in which he was fatally injured."[1] At last I could look at a tangible piece of evidence in this mystery—the veritable scene of the crime. Would there be blood stains? A dent or broken fixture which would show how he injured his head? I remembered a sudden insight I had while visiting the ancient Wailing Wall in Jerusalem. Jesus had actually walked by these huge stones. Patton certainly was not Jesus, but the principle was the same. It would probably be the closest I would ever get to my subject—if his writings were not that.

But then some preliminary research began to call the Cadillac at Fort Knox into question. Noting certain inconsistencies of the

Patton Cadillac in pictures right after the accident and pictures of the car at Ft. Knox, Doug Houston, a classic car expert, had written an article in 1980 in *Torque*[2] stating his belief that the Ft. Knox Cadillac was a 1939 model, not the 1938 in which it is known Patton had been injured. Certain "glaring discrepancies," such as different front bumpers and grill design, had caused him, he wrote in the article, to call Horace Woodring, Patton's driver, who, by 1980, was running a car dealership in Morganfield, Kentucky. "I asked Woodring if the display car is the Patton car, and he answered, 'No, and I've told [the museum] that it isn't.' It is the writer's feeling that the car should be billed as 'similar to the Patton car,'"—not the actual car itself—"but such is not the case."[3] I located Houston in Detroit and he verified what I had read. "The display car is a true '39 export model," he wrote in email exchanges with me. It had been a long time since he had been to the museum, he cautioned, but that was his belief based on what he had seen.

So the car at the museum might be a fake?

I contacted the museum's curator, Charles Lemons, who gave me what seemed to be a logical explanation. The car, he said, had been rebuilt shortly after the accident from the firewall forward, mostly with 1939 parts including the hood, bumpers, grill, ornaments, and lights. The engine was not original and the grill had been fashioned by a craftsman who got the details wrong—specifically, he did not know that the direction of the lines on the distinctive grill should be vertical rather than horizontal, as they are on the car at the museum. But everything else from the front windshield back, including the front driver's compartment, spacious rear passenger area where Patton and Gay sat, as well as the car's entire frame and chassis cementing body and wheels, was authentic. It was the original 1938 car, he said—"the one used by

General Patton on 9 December 1945," as a museum handout he sent me phrased it. The difference is it has been partially rebuilt. So Houston's observation is right, he acknowledged, but pertains only to the front third.

But then he began to hedge.

The car's history is spotty, especially immediately after the accident. It is known from pictures and newspaper stories at the time that the car Patton was injured in was a 1938 Series 75 Cadillac sedan. Cadillac exported them. A number were in Europe and this one, original owner unknown, apparently was captured from the Germans by Patton's troops as they sped across France after D-Day. In a letter to the museum, according to an eleven-page museum publication entitled "The 'Patton' Cadillac," Brigadier General William Birdsong wrote that while he was a major in Third Army, his battalion captured a "Cadillac limousine" during a fight for Chartres, France, August 17–18, 1944, and that the car was eventually sent to Patton at Third Army Headquarters via one of Birdsong's bosses, Major General LeRoy Irwin, 5ᵗʰ Infantry Division commander. Confirming receipt of the spoil, according to the museum, General Patton wrote back to General Irwin, "My Dear Red: You were very generous indeed to send me the lovely automobile captured by the Third Battalion, 11ᵗʰ Infantry Regiment under Major Birdsong.... Please express... my appreciation...."[4]

There are a few photographs of the car at various Patton headquarters following the war, two of them in the museum publication about the car. They show a 1938 Series 75 "Imperial" sedan, as do several other photos taken right after the accident. Then there is a dearth of information about the car at least for several months, if not approaching an entire year. Where did the car go immediately after the accident? They have no official records about that, said Lemons. As far as he knew, such records do not exist. However, formerly secret Seventh Army Public Relations documents I found regarding handling of information to the press during Patton's hospitalization reveal that "General Patton's car was taken to the military police motor pool and later turned over to the Seventh Army collecting point," whatever and wherever that was. What happened there? Was the car stripped of incriminating evidence? It is certainly possible.

Two later pictures in the museum publication show the car in what is listed as "the Salvage Yard." One photo is undated and the other is labeled "circa 1946." Both pictures show the front axle and wheels missing and damage to the front that occurred in the accident. Lemons believes these pictures show a stage of stripping or cannibalization—but does not know for sure. No pictures, pre- or post-accident, reveal the car's interior, which is its most important part in regard to searching for evidence of the cause of Patton's injuries. Following this "salvage yard" period, according to Lemon, the car was rebuilt with the 1939 front and a new engine which, interestingly, he says appears to be an M24 light tank engine, which he said was also built by Cadillac. From there it was put back in service as a car for the commanding general of the U.S. "Constabulary," the downsized, reorganized occupation forces charged with keeping the peace after the war fighting forces had left. "In 1951," according to museum records, "the car was rediscovered and arrangements were made to ship it to the Patton Museum, where it arrived in November of that year."

A further problem clouding the car's pedigree, conceded Lemons, was the fact that they had not been able to locate a Vehicle Identification Number, or VIN, on the car at the museum. The number, permanently placed on the chassis, and sometimes other surfaces, is unique to every car and gives specific information about it such as its maker and year produced. Law enforcement uses the VIN to establish automobile identity. Potential buyers of used cars can trace its damage history with the VIN. "We've scraped paint but so far nothing," said Lemons. "If we could find the VIN, we could find out a whole lot of things."

Obviously, the VIN was something I should look for. But I knew little about cars. I contacted General Motors and they referred me to their Cadillac history expert, Matt Larson, a retired Navy commander, member of classic car associations, author of at least one book on Cadillacs, and a onetime owner of a 1938 Cadillac Series 75 car just like the one Patton was injured in. Larson had actually visited the museum with a car group in 2001 and become suspicious of the Patton car himself. But they had not let him inspect it closer and he was skeptical that I would be able to do any better. But in the interim there had been a change of management, and the new museum director, Frank Jardim, assured me I would get access. He wanted to know the truth, too. So, although Larson lived in Detroit, he agreed to a lengthy drive down to Kentucky to meet me at the museum after I flew in from Los Angeles.

We met on a Saturday, which was good—visitor traffic was light. The museum staff was not harried. A young soldier, Owen Yeager of Rockford, Illinois, was assigned to be our escort. The car, cordoned off with ropes and a sign to keep others from touching it, was dark olive drab and well kept. Larson had brought a camera and set about a planned inspection. I went immediately to the rear passenger compartment and began checking the seat where Patton and Gay had sat. It stretched across the car's width and was a light tan or grey, as was the entire interior which seemed plush. The seat easily could accommodate three passengers. But in a letdown—at least to me—it was relatively clean and free of anything resembling bloodstains. Thinking about it later, I do not know why I had expected traces of the blood reported by

Woodring and others still to be there. If the car had later been used by Constabulary brass it most probably would have been cleaned up. Still, would not the Army or some entity have kept the stained upholstery for history's sake? I do not buy the argument frequently advanced that the accident was not important at the time. Patton's accident, and especially his death, was front page news throughout the world.

Nevertheless, no blood was the reality. And as I inspected the compartment, I could not find any evidence of Patton's head hitting and damaging anything in the car either. There was a light fixture on the roof of the compartment directly above the middle of the seat. It was about the size of a soap bar and appeared to be made of chrome and plastic—not very heavy or stable. But it was in perfect condition. For Patton to have hit it with his head he would have had to have flown almost directly upward and toward the middle of the roof which did not seem likely given the probable momentum in the crash. It would have carried him forward, not up.

In front of the seat, perhaps three to four feet ahead, was the partition that separated the two passenger compartments—front and rear. It had a full window in its upper half. The window was set in and surrounded by a thin, mahogany-like casing which had a small clock embedded at the base, roughly in the middle of the partition. Neither the clock nor the casing protruded very much. But either, I suppose, if hit, could have caused a cut. But if he had hit the window, it was not shatterproof, according to information Larson had sent me on the car. Patton most probably would have gone through the glass and cut himself even worse than he did. He likely would have stuck there, speared on a shard. But there was not any evidence of damage to any part of the partition, including the clock. In addition, below the window, embedded in the lower half of the partition, were two pullout seats. If employed, two more passengers could sit in the back. But if they had been employed, Patton could not have been catapulted forward. The seat would have been in his way.

By this time, Larson, deeply involved in his inspection, was coming to a conclusion which, if true, would affect much of my passenger compartment speculation. He told me he had seen enough of the car to begin thinking the entire vehicle was 1939—not just the front. He began showing me why. If the car was the original that had been in the accident, the chassis, which extends from back to front on the underside of the entire car and basically holds it together, would show evidence of damage and repair at the point where the car and truck collided—the right front bumper area. There was none. Furthermore, he said, the dashboard was 1939; as were the running boards, door handles, rear bumper, and tail lights. There were only so many differences between the 1938 and 1939 models, which look very much alike, he said, and he was covering most of them. Weeks later, after he had time to check Cadillac manuals and archives, he wrote to me that unequivocally he believed the car was entirely a 1939 Cadillac, not a rebuilt 1938: "On examination of the car in the museum, ALL [sic] of the visual difference cues are distinctly 1939 features, not 1938. . . . There are no visible signals of anyone making major changes." In addition to the similarities he had already pointed out at the museum, he further noted that the car's "instrument cluster" was 1939 and the "tan Weise cloth interior shows all signs of being original . . . it is not a replacement interior done during the 'restoration.'" The trunk handle, rear license plate mount, and hubcaps were 1939.

Most surprising were his findings about the VIN. Before we left the museum, he located what was left of it. It was down by the engine base on one of the flat surfaces behind the left engine mount. I had to stick my head under the hood and search hard with a flashlight while leaning over the bumper before I finally saw it—a short, flat strip of chassis metal barely visible—and for good reason. Most of the number had been crudely scratched out. You could see the haphazard striations on it going every which way. Only a few numbers were faintly showing. It was obvious someone had purposely tried to remove it. Why? In his later report, Larson wrote, "The serial number [VIN] of the museum car has intentionally been filed down at some time to obliterate it and render the car unidentifiable.... There is no mistaking that the serial number is intentionally obliterated."

In addition, he wrote, the "Body by Fisher" tag on the car was "phony." It was conspicuously displayed on the high left side of the cowl, the divider between the engine and the passenger compartments to which, among other items, the car's windshield and dashboard are fastened. The problem, he wrote, was that Fisher, a famous car body craftsman company, did not make the Series 75 bodies. Fleetwood did. "Cadillac Motor Car Company would not have shipped any Series 75 car with a Fisher Body tag—the prestige position of large series Fleetwood bodied cars was of particular importance and value to Cadillac Motor Car Company." So why had such a tag been affixed? Who had put it there? Even if Fisher *had* made the body, the identification number on the tag— "1034," designating it as the one thousand thirty-fourth such body manufactured—was "impossible." The specific 75 style of Patton's Cadillac was "7533"—one of the largest models made. Records show there were only 479 of that style body built in 1938. Further, the type of paint listed on the Fisher tag to be applied to the body—number "558"—did not exist for 1938 models. "Paint number 558 is not found in any 1938 record in the GM Heritage Center archives," he wrote.

Both Larson and I had hoped to examine museum records on the car as part of our visit. They might provide some answers. We had been told we could. But when we arrived that Saturday, the museum assistant, Ivon Bennett, informed us that the files were locked in a safe. We would have to return another day. We were out of luck on that score. We both had come very long distances on tight schedules and limited budgets and were leaving Kentucky that evening. Larson lamented not having access. Nevertheless, he wrote, "Although not proven, it appears that the Fisher body tag attached to the left side of the cowl...is an attempt to make the car appear to be a 1938 Cadillac Series 75." He found another number he believes is a VIN elsewhere on the body and said it was not unusual for VIN numbers to be affixed twice on a car. It is Larson's belief that that number 3290473—which belongs to a 1939 Series Cadillac shipped to Antwerp, Belgium on November 18, 1938*—identifies the Cadillac at the museum. I sent Larson's report to the museum, but so far have received no response. Apparently, unless the museum can provide compelling rebuttal, the car it advertises as Patton's is not Patton's. It is just a good facsimile. Larson put in his report that there were some simple chemical methods used by law enforcement on weapons with filed down serial numbers that could be used to resurrect the obliterated VIN should the museum wish to pursue it.

I do not think the museum has intentionally mislabeled its Cadillac. At some point in its history—before it got to the Constabulary motor pool—the real Patton car, the 1938 Cadillac, disappeared and the current fraudulent car apparently was substituted. Who gave it to the Constabulary? There may have been

---

*The museum also apparently knew about this car because the build sheet for it is referenced in their 11-page "The Patton Cadillac" publication.

records, but they are probably gone now—purged, in my opinion, just like the accident reports. By the time the Constabulary took possession, the car was already believed to be Patton's. No one, for whatever reasons, chose to investigate. And if they had, would they have found the filed down VIN? Or noticed the phony Fisher tag? It has eluded detection prior to my evaluation, judging from the fact that I am the first to mention it in print. Even the car's supposed "light tank" engine is in dispute. Contrary to what Curator Lemons told me, Larson says the motor's serial number—487620455—indicates "a 1948 engine manufactured for a Series 76 long wheelbase commercial chassis, as used for a hearse or ambulance"—not a tank. The first two numbers denote year. "I found none of the typical military features on the engine," he wrote. But at least we apparently now know when it was put in the car—approximately 1948 or after.

So why the VIN obliteration and the phony body tag? Was it just the result of some shady car switch deal on Germany's black market, a way to secretly sell the authentic car to a private collector, as historical artifacts sometimes are sold, and represent the substitute as real? If so, would not the real car have surfaced by now? One can only speculate, but it seems that like the missing accident reports, the accident car is missing too—and by design. Clearly deception was involved. Why? Did the car contain incriminating evidence?

★ ★ ★ ★

CHAPTER EIGHTEEN

PROBLEM CHILD

Following the Bulge victory, Patton was enthused. He wanted to take the Third Army into Germany and stab at its heart. He had the momentum. The Nazis were again reeling and, this time, definitely on their last legs. After Ardennes, they had few reserves left. But "he was told to cool it," wrote Farago.[1] Bradley delivered the news. "Unfortunately, 'higher authority' [Eisenhower and the joint chiefs of Staff led by General Marshall] had already decided to make the main effort elsewhere"—or at least, curiously (preposterously, when one thinks of his record), not to put their money on Patton. They were holding him back again. He was dumbfounded. He had just saved Eisenhower from catastrophic defeat. And it had not been the first time. "I'll be damned if I see why we have divisions if not to use them," he wrote. "One would think people would like to win a war... we will be criticized by history, and rightly so, for having sat still so long."[2] Defiant, and with Bradley's tacit but cautionary approval—because Bradley basically agreed with him—he decided to proceed on his own, cajoling, conniving, and sneaking forward as best he could. "What a war," he wrote. "I've never been stopped either by orders or the enemy yet"[3]—only by his own commanders.

In early 1945, Patton took the ancient German city of Trier, retorting to Eisenhower's order, received after the fact, not to attack it unless he had more troops with, "What do you want me to do? Give it back?" In Patton's mind, the gloves were off. The city was a key part of the Siegfried Line and conquering it yielded 7,000 prisoners.[4] Grateful for the breakthrough, "higher authority" decided to let him continue. Later that month—again without authorization—his troops were the first Allied soldiers to cross the mighty Rhine, the enemy's last natural defense. They had made it ahead of rival Montgomery, who, despite his recent failures nevertheless had been promoted to field marshal, the British army's highest rank. Montgomery had also officially been given the Rhine fording mission. Beating his rival again must have energized Patton, who, strangely, had *not* been promoted while Bradley and his other contemporaries had. As Farago describes it, "On March 23, 1945," as Bradley finished his morning coffee, "he took Patton's call and almost dropped the cup. 'Brad,' he heard Patton say, '-don't tell anyone but I'm across.' 'Across what?'.... 'Across the Rhine, Brad.' 'Well, I'll be damned!'"[5] To celebrate, Patton stopped in the middle of the pontoon bridge his engineers had hastily constructed and urinated in the enemy river, an act caught in a photo sent somewhat shockingly (for those times) around the world.[6] Summoned to Bastogne by Eisenhower, he thought he was going to be cashiered for his unauthorized advance—maybe even for stealing Montgomery's thunder again. But instead he was complimented—the first time ever by the supreme commander. As

Farago points out, "It was Ike who received the kudos for the 'unauthorized' campaigns west of the Rhine even as John Jervis was given the peerage and pension for Nelson's [19th Century Trafalgar] victory."[7]

But then he made a mistake, sending a too-lightly armored force into enemy territory near Hammelberg, Germany, to liberate American prisoners of war. (The territory was still in German hands.) One of the POWs was his son-in-law, Lieutenant Colonel John K. Waters, who had been captured by the Germans in Tunisia in 1943. Not only was the mission unauthorized, but the POW camp was destined to be overrun by Allies shortly. Worst of all, the raid basically failed, resulting in the deaths of 25 of the 294 rescuers and the wounding or capture of most of the rest—including the POWs it had been organized to liberate.[8] Waters was one of the lucky few who made it to freedom but was wounded badly. Patton maintained he was never sure his son-in-law was at the camp and that his main purpose was only to free the prisoners because he was close enough to do so and to occupy the Germans as he made stronger thrusts elsewhere. But few believed him. Detractors, including politicians at home, charged he was risking American lives for purely personal reasons—and it appeared they were right. It became worse when he tried to keep the story quiet by firing a censor who was going to let details be published. The move backfired since he lacked the authority. Eisenhower wrote General Marshall, "Patton is a problem child.... He sent off a little expedition on a wild goose chase.... The upshot was that he got twenty-five prisoners back and lost a full company of medium tanks and a platoon of light tanks." And oh, by the way, "his son-in-law was one of the twenty-five released," which, of course, looked terrible. "Foolishly, he then imposed censorship on the [raid].... The story has now been released and I hope the newspapers do not make too much of it"—a worry Marshall and Eisenhower always shared.[9]

But they did. Patton later admitted he had made a mistake, although the apology was mostly that he had sent too small a force. The damage, however, was done. Marshall, by now an open Patton detractor amongst his (Marshall's) intimates, was not happy. Eisenhower followed suit. "Eisenhower thought that a baffling change had come over Patton," wrote Farago. "Something was driving him into callous and arbitrary acts; he was arrogating undue privileges to himself; and he was behaving as if his assured place in history had filled him with reckless arrogance."[10] Farago, like most authors since, was following the assumed logic that Patton had finally gone too far and Eisenhower was reluctantly doing what he had to. But military historian Charles Whiting adds a larger perspective:

> The writing was on the wall. Now that victory in Europe was clearly in sight, Patton was no longer needed. His flamboyant style and unpredictability was becoming a liability; a liability that Eisenhower could not afford any more. Patton himself had already realized that Eisenhower had political ambitions after the successful conclusion of the war. Could he, Eisenhower, afford to associate himself too closely with a man, who, in the eyes of East Coast liberals and much of the press, was—admittedly—a war-winning general; yet at the same time, an autocrat who disdained the "New Deal" and everything that went with it? Indeed, there were some who maintained that one of the great democracy's leading generals was not a democrat himself.[11]

No, by this time, in the opinion of his growing number of enemies, he was a war-mongering, strident fascist[12]—Eisenhower's rabid attack dog, as General James Doolittle remembered he was regarded, unleashed when needed and then promptly muzzled.[13] But he was also a powerful renegade dangerously at odds with the Allies' cautious yet punitive strategies for defeating and burying Germany and also their growing deference to Stalin. The demand for unconditional surrender, for instance, in Patton's view, was causing fanatical resistance by the Germans who, because of it, saw no way out but to keep fighting. His men were dying needlessly because of the policy. Deference to the USSR and Stalin was allowing a loss of liberty across Eastern Europe that, in Patton's eyes, made a mockery of the Allies' soon-to-be victory. He saw the Russians as enslavers and wanted to fight them before it was too late. And, as he argued to Under Secretary of Defense Patterson, whose reaction was shock at Patton's outspokenness, the Allies had liberated Europe only to give it over to a new, more brutal conqueror, Russia. He was right—as the ensuing Cold War would prove. But almost no one in power at the end of the war agreed. They thought him out of touch with the "new reality," narrow-minded, and even crazy.

Yet the insanity was all around Patton.

When a report ordered by Roosevelt to determine responsibility for the murder of thousands of important Polish soldiers and civilians* determined the assassins to be the Soviet NKVD, Roosevelt himself suppressed it, banishing the author, a respected U.S. Naval officer, rather than making it public and condemning the Soviets. The massacre, in 1940, had been at the order of Stalin, according to a CIA report,[14] but Stalin and the Soviets had fervently maintained the Nazis were the killers. It was a shameless and calculated lie. They had committed the crime to eradicate

---

*Estimates vary from 14,000 to 22,000 in the Soviet Union's Katyn Forest.

Polish leadership and make the country a puppet. Not until the post-USSR Russian government admitted guilt and apologized in 1990 was the matter finally settled. Poland, bordering the Soviet Union on the west, was a vital part of one of Stalin's main World War II aims—to build a buffer of slave states between the motherland and Western Europe and thereby blunt any future invasions from that direction. The other aim was to spread communism. And Roosevelt, Patton's commander in chief, was complicit. He naïvely thought Stalin—"Uncle Joe," as he called him, one of the worst political mass murderers in history—was a man of peace and benevolence needed to keep the postwar world free of conflict.

So intent was FDR on maintaining good relations with the Soviets that he actually proposed that the Red army be given personal representation on the U.S. joint chiefs of staff, according to historian Bradley F. Smith in *Sharing Secrets with Stalin*. It would have been an unprecedented up-close intrusion. The joint chiefs were, with Roosevelt's consent, running the war. Not surprisingly—if for no other reason than they resented anyone, regardless of reason, interfering in their sacred sanctum—they nixed it.[15] Of course, there was little need on the Russians' part by that time to have such a representative. Through their many high-placed Soviet spies and informers, the Soviets knew almost everything important going on in the U.S. anyway. And even if they had not infiltrated the White House and OSS, among other key venues, the joint chiefs, while rejecting Soviet attendance at their secret meetings, were, in the person of their leader—General George Marshall—basically of the same mind as Roosevelt.

As early as 1943, as American military assignees went to Moscow in preparation for the first "Big Three" meeting in Teheran, joint chiefs' head Marshall had instructed his team "to do all in its power to cooperate with the Soviets," according to

Smith.[16] By January 1945, as Patton continued his unauthorized fight into Germany—Eisenhower reaping the accolades—and preparations for the important Yalta Conference, the next "Big Three" meeting, commenced. Marshall was, as were most of the other top administration officials, completely under the Soviet sway. Thus, on that score alone, they were on a collision course with Patton, the only high-ranking officer with the guts or audacity (depending on the view) to publicly challenge his superiors. "Marshall and Eisenhower 'were among the last to agree that we couldn't get along with Stalin,'" former White House correspondent Steve Neal quotes wartime U.S. ambassador to the Soviet Union Averell Harriman, a New Dealer himself, in *Harry and Ike: The Partnership That Remade the Postwar World*. It is one of the latest books on the crucial but little studied immediate-postwar period.[17] Other noted military historians and scholars agree.[18] Marshall was "primarily a military man" with "little knowledge of . . . the skill with which the communists pervert great and noble aspirations for social justice into support of their own diabolic purposes," wrote General Wedemeyer, Marshall's aide.[19] Marshall was concerned with Germany and Japan. Consequently, he was committed to FDR's policy of courtship and deference to Stalin. He saw it as his duty, wrote Wedemeyer, and by Yalta, February 4–12, 1945, Roosevelt was so sick—he would die within two months (on April 12)—Marshall was running the war, and because the war was America's overwhelming business, he was, in effect, running the country. Roosevelt had been fading since mid-1944, his mounting ailments putting him in stupors and clouding his judgment.[20]

While FDR figuratively presided at Yalta, Stalin, now heady with his armies' recent victories over the Nazis, ran the show. This was not only because of Roosevelt's ill health and fawning acquiescence, but because the U.S. desperately wanted the Soviet Union to declare war on Japan—a plum Stalin, prior to the introduction of the atomic bomb, dangled in front of them—and Stalin pulled no punches in making sure he would prevail. "Stalin was even better informed about his allies at Yalta than he had been at Tehran," wrote Christopher Andrew and Vasili Mitrokhin, in their books based on rare access to KGB archives.[21] The lavish Crimean castles Roosevelt, Churchill, and their staffs stayed in were bugged. The Russians heard all their private discussions. As if that was not enough, as earlier noted, Alger Hiss was part of the American delegation and was secretly briefing the Soviets regarding American positions. The "Cambridge Five," Britain's cadre of English-born, top-level Soviet spies—including Guy Burgess, Donald Maclean, and Kim Philby—were supplying Churchill's positions. Stalin, therefore, according to Andrew and Mitrokhin, was well aware of the importance the Allies put on having at least "some 'democratic' politicians [put] into the puppet Polish provisional government already [forced on Poland] by the Russians"— a token that would at least show concern for their subjugated ally. "On this point, after initial [fake] resistance [like a Poker player holding the winning hand], Stalin graciously conceded, knowing that the 'democrats' could subsequently be excluded [and probably later murdered]."[22]

When the Yalta meeting ended, Stalin had won almost everything he wanted. His only requirement was to give assurance that the Soviet Union would declare war on Japan three months after victory in Europe—an assurance that guaranteed him huge spoils, like Japanese territory, which he would hardly have to fight for since the U.S. had been the overwhelming force in the Pacific War. By Yalta, the outcome was already determined. Chief amongst Stalin's wins was formal acceptance by the U.S. and Britain of Soviet domination over Poland, Hungary, Romania, Bulgaria, half of Germany, and other sovereign areas that together would provide an unbroken half moon-like swath of territorial protection for the USSR. The swath stretched roughly from the Baltic Sea in the north to the Adriatic in the south, invasion buffer that it was. He also secured the agreement that all former residents of the vast and polyglot USSR, regardless of their wishes, would be returned to the Soviet Union. "The Allies understood that they were sentencing hundreds of thousands of men, and quite a few women and children, to death and misery," wrote Jonah Goldberg in the *National Review*. "Many of these refugees went to extraordinary lengths to end the war in British and American custody only to be forcibly— i.e., at gunpoint—returned to the Soviets for liquidation. Many killed themselves and their families rather than go back."[23]

It was these kinds of treacherous[24] giveaways that Patton objected to most. He was a fierce fighter, but he was not vengeful. He had pity for those who had suffered through the war and preferred freedom to the Gulags or worse, most because of their ethnicity or circumstances beyond their control, such as becoming POWs which Stalin considered treason. The treachery and shortsightedness of Yalta and the U.S. administration's deference to the Soviet Union came vividly home to Patton in the last months of the war when his mighty army was approximately fifty miles from Berlin, and Eisenhower, prompted by OSS reports, diverted him south to Czechoslovakia to chase what turned out to be a phantom Nazi force dubbed "Redoubt," a purported last-ditch mountain stronghold of die-hards. He saw the deference again in the very last days of the war when he and his army, fully capable of liberation, were within sight of Prague, Czechoslovakia, one of the grand old capitals of Europe, and its Czech citizens begged for help against a Soviet occupation, but Eisenhower, in contact with an angry

Soviet general demanding Patton's halt, again ordered him to stop. Stalin had successfully negotiated a line beyond which the other allies were not supposed to cross—but could have because of the vagaries of war. It conveniently left half of Germany, including Berlin, to the Soviets.

What really happened to keep the Western Allies from taking Berlin—as important a prize as, for instance, Baghdad in the 2003 American-Iraqi War—is still, more than sixty years later, a debated mystery. Eisenhower, upon whom the decision supposedly fell, maintained after the war that with victory all but assured, he had no intention of losing more Americans for a "symbol" that had, in his opinion, lost its "strategic importance." Yet, as late as September 1944, he had considered the German capitol his major objective, during which time he endorsed Montgomery's failed Market-Garden offensive, the ultimate objective of which was the capture of Berlin. Many of his commanders, such as General James M. Gavin, still thought as late as March 1945 that Berlin was the objective. That was the last Gavin had heard as he detailed in *On to Berlin*, his 1978 book. What had changed? One answer is Yalta. The meeting in the Crimea had served notice that Stalin and the Soviets were in charge—at least if the U.S. wanted their cooperation, as so many believed was essential, in beating the Japanese and building a better post-war world. They did not want the Western Allies in Eastern Europe. Eisenhower was so cautious not to offend the Soviets that he actually contacted Stalin to offer him Berlin, telling the Soviet dictator he did not think it was now important. The wily Stalin, seeing another Yalta-like coup dropped in his hands, pretended to agree, and then "within moments of [the] communication," according to Patton scholar Charles Province, "ordered five tank armies and 25,000 artillery pieces, all under the command of Marshal G. K. Zhukov, who would become a good friend of Eisenhower's and bring him to Moscow, to attack the German capital."[25] If Eisenhower did not think the city important, Stalin certainly did.

Some, like Province, think the failure to take Berlin may have been Eisenhower's "greatest error," if not "one of the greatest political blunders in history."[26] By adhering to the line of advance Stalin proposed at Yalta—the Oder River, west of Berlin—the Western Allies left themselves no routes to the city, which was the heart and soul of what had been fought for. They were to get occupation zones in Berlin, which would become part of free West Germany, but no way to get to them except through roads controlled by the Soviets. Berlin, in effect, was left an island in the midst of Soviet dominated Europe. The Soviets were therefore able to isolate the city and thus cause crises such as the one sparking the 1948 to 1949 Berlin Airlift, the Soviet attempt to starve the city's West Berlin inhabitants into submission, and to easily and brutally quell the 1956 Hungarian revolution. But had Eisenhower alone made the decision about Berlin? Or had it come from his superior Marshall, or even the ailing FDR? With new information emerging about the war, scholars continue to debate that question. Military historian Bruce Lee, for instance, citing newly unearthed formerly secret documents, says it was Marshall who ordered Eisenhower not to take Berlin and to confer with Stalin about all military matters concerning Europe. By that time, Marshall, primarily concerned with winning the war in the Pacific and counting on Stalin's help in fighting Japan, wanted Eisenhower to wrap things up as soon as possible in Europe and avoid angering the Soviets.[27] Lee says Marshall actually tried to cover up the fact that he had made the decision about Berlin.[28]

Whatever the truth, there had been major, inexcusable mistakes made in the European war. The reining of Patton, the failure to close the Falaise Gap and anticipate or detect the surprise German offensive leading to the nearly catastrophic Battle of the Bulge were huge errors. The war could have ended perhaps six months sooner had such mistakes not occurred. General Albin Irzyk lists twelve major high command mistakes in his *Gasoline for Patton*, including Eisenhower's continual choice of Montgomery and Bradley over Patton when Patton's record was better, "failure to plan for the deadly terrain" which slowed the Allied advance right after D-Day, Eisenhower keeping his headquarters far from the front instead of close to the fighting, and Eisenhower approving Montgomery's Market Garden plan as well as concurring in the mistakes Montgomery made leading to its failure.[29] Add to these the concession of Eastern Europe to Stalin, and these "blunders," as British correspondent Tom Agoston characterizes them,[30] can be attributed to the highest levels.

As the official announcement of the German surrender was made on May 10, 1945, there is some indication that such mistakes, unknown at the time to the public, were on Eisenhower's mind. On that date, Eisenhower hosted his top generals in a private lunch. Afterward, he made a speech "designed to coordinate their postwar accounts and assure that none of them would be talking out of turn." He "spoke very confidentially of 'the need for solidarity'" in case "any of them might be called before Congressional committees probing the conduct of the war."[31] General Irzyk writes he "strongly intimated that they should not criticize publicly the way the campaign in Europe had been fought."[32] After the meeting, Patton wrote that the speech "had to me the symptoms of political aspirations....It is my opinion that this talking cooperation is for the purpose of covering up probable criticism of strategic blunders which he unquestionably committed during the campaign. Whether or not these were his own or due to too much cooperation with the British, I don't know. I am inclined to think that he over-cooperated."[33]

And those already mentioned probably were not the only secrets Patton knew. General Irzyk concludes,

> Close friends of Patton like Dr. Charles Odom [his unit surgeon][34] and Gen. Geoffrey Keyes [fellow academy graduate and confidant] were convinced that if Patton had lived and returned to the States, he would surely have quickly resigned from the army. Once that occurred, he would have been free to open up. By written and spoken word, he undoubtedly would have been critical of...Eisenhower's conduct of the war, and would have pointed out the significant lapses of judgment...as well as the "Mistakes"...which he believed Ike made...Eisenhower, on the one hand, would have tried to suppress them, while Patton, on the other, would have endeavored to expose them.[35]

Patton, unlike others, would not have been cowed by a threat. Physically, he was fearless. This was around the time—war's end, as he railed against the Soviets and Stalin—that the "Polish" Spitfires jumped his Piper Cub, that he was almost decapitated in a strange jeep accident, and a "runaway" ox cart nearly gored him. He was a man of principal, who could not be swayed to compromise his beliefs. Independently wealthy, he could afford to eliminate his pension and could not be bought.

For pro-Soviets and Stalin, as well as those who had run the war, among them individuals with political aspirations, Patton was a big problem—and growing bigger.

Worst of all, he wanted to go to war with Russia.

★ ★ ★

In order to get a clearer picture of Patton's accident, I asked Toni Wolf, a Los Angeles Police Department investigator with over fifteen years of experience, to evaluate the pictures and stories I had accumulated. She said she would give me an opinion. Her subsequent report to me was not much help—which was no fault of hers. She said she could not tell much without official, professional accident reports and interviews done no later than forty-eight hours after the incident. "It has been proven that memory of a traumatic event lapses with the first twenty-four to forty-eight hours. If the interviews had been conducted within this time frame, with a qualified investigator, I believe that there would have been a clearer understanding of what transpired so many years ago," she wrote. Perhaps that was the reason the original reports are gone. They were the most truthful while the later ones—the recollections, memoirs, and author investigations that have survived—did not have the spontaneous, still-vivid verisimilitude that might incriminate.

The copies of photos I supplied of both the Cadillac and the larger truck caused particular problems. "None of [the photos] show the same damage," she wrote. They "were taken at angles which distort the amount of damage as well as the location of the damage done to both vehicles.... This can make the damage appear worse or less, depending on the angle" and "raises questions in my mind as to what the vehicle actually looked like just after the collision and why... the damage [varied] from photograph to photograph." Welcome to the club, I thought. The photos I supplied are the main ones found in every book or article that discusses the accident. There are not many. There just is no professional record of any kind—reports, photos, or interviews—available on which to base unequivocal, inarguable deductions about what happened on that German roadway December 9, 1945.

Nevertheless, she ventured a few opinions. The accident was *not* a "minor" collision. Stressing that there was no way, given the lack of official, competent data, to positively know the speeds of the vehicles involved, Wolf wrote, "If I assume the driver [Woodring] was indeed traveling at 30 mph [as most accounts indicate]," given "the average perception and reaction time for an experienced driver as 1 ½ seconds.... [Woodring] would have hit the much larger much heavier truck at a speed very close to 30 mph. At 30 mph I would expect to see significant damage and moderate to major injuries." Okay, that perhaps explains Patton, but what about Gay and Woodring? They escaped even moderate injury, unless Band-aids qualify. The car at the museum features hand grips by the back windows. Maybe Gay, although he never mentioned it, was holding onto one of those while Patton was not? But Woodring had no grips except the wheel he was holding. A trauma doctor I talked with said the natural inclination in such situations was to use the hands and arms for protection and throw them up to shield from injury. But none of them, including Patton, showed signs of that in the subsequent medical examinations.

In any case, most interesting to me in Wolfe's report was her evaluation of the forces in the car at impact. In all accounts—books, articles, and interviews—the speculation is always that Patton, sitting on the edge of the seat (an erroneous assumption if Woodring is to be believed),[36] is thrown forward in the passenger cab to hit either a fixture on the roof or a clock in the middle of the far partition directly behind the driver. Again, I use the word speculation because, as stated earlier, no one claims to have actually seen him hurtling forward or hitting whatever caused his injuries, nor is there ever mention in any account of the accident of a damaged fixture or clock.* But the speculation is frequent, sometimes stated as fact. The Patton Museum, for instance, stated emphatically on a plaque near the car that Patton "hit the clock

---

*Another reason why having the original car to examine is important.

mounted on the rear of the front seat." Wolfe, however, indicates that from what she can deduce, it is more likely that Patton was propelled at impact toward the door beside him—the one holding the window he was reportedly looking out of—rather than toward the farther partition.

As Wolf notes, the Cadillac did not strike the truck flush or head on; i.e., make contact with the Cadillac's entire front at a "90 degree angle." Rather, Woodring says he swerved left to avoid the collision and therefore first hit the truck with the Cadillac's right front bumper, where most of the car's damage in photos can be seen. It was at that instant that the occupants would have been propelled forward from their seats. But since the car was now shifted to the left, the trajectories of its rear passengers would not have been longitudinally down the entire length of the rear passenger compartment toward the partition, but actually right of that direction toward the right side of the car which, because of the left veer, was now more in front of them. Patton would have therefore hit the window he was looking out of or at least the area, including the door, which the side window was in. "If the General were on the right side of the vehicle when the collision occurred," she wrote, "he would move towards the direction of travel [i.e., towards the truck which stopped the Cadillac's movement at impact]. If his driver turned the wheel towards the left [thus turning the compartment surrounding Patton to the left relative to his motion], the General would have hit the window next to him and then fallen back towards the other rear passenger."

This was a new way of looking at what happened to Patton—at least what his probable trajectory causing his injuries would have been which rendered weak the speculation about him catapulting through the entire length of the rear compartment and hitting the mid-car partition or roof. This new information centered what happened to Patton around the window he was looking out of, and that, in my mind, brings his injuries closer to what Douglas Bazata said happened. It also offered a new potential explanation for why Gay was not injured. Patton hit the window and ricocheted back on top of Gay, stopping Gay's forward motion and pinning him. It even opened more the possibility that Patton was shot in the face by the unorthodox object Bazata claims was fired (thus possibly accounting for the odd nose-to-cranial laceration he had) and then was propelled back by that force to land on Gay—initially hard to believe, but now less improbable. Maybe even possible.

CHAPTER NINETEEN

★ ★ ★ ★

MARKED MAN

"**Emotional, and with a** tremendous capacity for dynamic action, Patton was an unusual type of military man who was not only physically courageous but also possessed the rare quality which the Germans call 'civil courage,' wrote General Al Wedemeyer, sent by General Marshall in 1943 to observe Patton preparing for Sicily. "He dared to speak his mind and act according to his convictions."[1]

Now that the war in Europe was over, Patton was even more vigorously displaying his penchant for frankness.

On the day the war in Europe officially ended, May 8, 1945, he addressed a press briefing in a manner that must have shocked leaders from Washington to Moscow. As War Correspondent Larry G. Newman recalled,[2] "Patton entered the room followed by his faithful English bulldog, Willie." He had his "twin pistols with the ivory grips on each hip, [four] stars on the shoulders of his battle jacket...four more on his shining helmet." Pointing to a map showing the Red Army in Poland, Lithuania, Latvia,

Estonia, Austria, Bulgaria, Rumania, Czechoslovakia and Germany, he began:

> This war stopped right where it started. Right in the Hun's backyard....But that's not the end of this business....What the tin-soldier politicians in Washington and Paris have managed to do today is another story you'll be writing for a long while.... They have allowed us to kick hell out of one bastard and at the same time forced us to help establish a second one as evil or more evil than the first....We have won a series of battles, not a war for peace...we'll need Almighty God's constant help if we're to live in the same world with Stalin and his murdering cutthroats.

With tears in his eyes, wrote Newman, Patton recalled those

> who gave their lives in what they believed was the final fight in the cause of freedom. I wonder how [they] will speak today when they know that for the first time in centuries we have opened Central and Western Europe to the forces of Genghis Khan. I wonder how they feel now that they know there will be no peace in our times and that Americans, some not yet born, will have to fight the Russians tomorrow, or ten, fifteen or twenty years from tomorrow. We have spent the last months since the Battle of the Bulge and the crossing of the Rhine stalling; waiting for Montgomery to get ready to attack in the North; occupying useless real estate and killing a few lousy Huns when we should have been in Berlin and Prague. And this Third Army could have been. Today we should be telling the Russians to go to hell instead of hearing them tell us to pull back. We should be telling them if they

didn't like it to go to hell and invite them to fight. We've defeated one aggressor against mankind and established a second far worse, more evil and more dedicated than the first.

All of this was "off the record," according to Newman, which apparently is why it is little known. I did not find it until uncovering
Newman's 1962 article in the National Archives.[3] But Patton had
many enemies in the press—which he fully knew—and his remarks, without question, were certainly forwarded to those who
were watching him and wanted to know what he was saying. That
had to include leaders in Washington, Britain, and Moscow. Patton concluded:

> [Winston] Churchill was the only man in a position of power
> who knew what we were walking into. He wanted to get into
> the Balkans and Central Europe to keep the Russians at bay.
> He wanted to get into Berlin and Prague and get to the Baltic
> coast on the North. Churchill had a sense of history. Unfor-
> tunately, some of our leaders were just damn fools who had no
> idea of Russian history. Hell, I doubt if they even knew Rus-
> sia, just less than a hundred years ago, owned Finland, sucked
> the blood out of Poland, and were using Siberia as a prison for
> their own people. How Stalin must have sneered when he got
> through with them at all those phony conferences."

And how Stalin, a murderer equal to if not surpassing Hitler, must
have seethed in anger when he heard Patton's remarks.

It was a few days later that Patton had shocked everyone—
mostly diplomats and military brass—at the Paris hotel gathering
he attended with his nephew, FBI agent Fred Ayer Jr., by saying basically the same things.

And that was only the beginning.

Asked to drink a toast with a Soviet general in Berlin, Patton told his shocked translator, "Tell that Russian sonovabitch that from the way they're acting here, I regard them as enemies and I'd rather cut my throat than have a drink with one of my enemies!" At first the Russian linguist refused to translate, but was ordered by Patton to do so. The Soviet general retorted he felt the same way about Patton, which amused Patton. The two ended up toasting.[4] In his diary, he wrote, "They [Russians] are a scurvy race and simply savages. We could beat hell out of them."[5]

Returning to the U.S. in June 1945 for his first leave home in nearly three years, Patton advocated to cheering crowds, among other controversial ideas, that the U.S., to contain the Soviets, continue the universal draft. The country would need it not only because it was "the simple duty of every man to serve" and "the strict discipline of two years of army life was a strengthener of personal and national character," but because the Soviet menace demanded it. "Just you wait and see," he told Ayer. "The lily livered bastards in Washington will demobilize. They'll say they've made the world safe for democracy again. The Russians are not such damned fools. They'll rebuild...if we have compulsory... military service...the world will know we mean what we say."[6]

The return-in-triumph speeches, reaching the world's capitols, caused another Patton controversy. Most Americans were tired of war. Without question, the world was. Among those protesting Patton's ideas were church leaders. Patton, a man of considerable one-on-one persuasive powers, according to Ayer, decided to meet with Archbishop (later Cardinal) Richard Cushing of Boston, his wife's hometown, in hopes of gaining the prelate's support. He asked his brother-in-law (his nephew's father), Fred Ayer, Sr., who knew Cushing, to set up a meeting, which he did, and, mindful of army requirements, informed the War Department of his intention. Suddenly, according to Ayer, he had to call it off. Phoning Ayer's father, he said, "Fred, if you've made that appointment with Cushing, cancel it. I've just been told to keep my mouth shut and that I'm a warmonger."[7]

The details of Patton's admonishment are not revealed by Ayer. But it was at this same time, according to Patton biographer Farago, that joint chiefs' head Marshall, in what Farago calls a "bizarre" move, tried to have Patton surreptitiously observed by a psychiatrist in order to possibly declare him insane. In response to reporters' requests that he clarify his draft statements, Patton had scheduled a press conference for June 14. Marshall, according to Farago, was afraid Patton might "go off the rocker." The chief of staff had found a Navy psychiatrist who had "treated several high-ranking officers . . . for nervous breakdown," writes Farago, and was ready to send him to the press conference. His plan "showed how seriously the Patton problem was considered by the superiors." But Secretary of War Stimson, for whom Patton had been a trusted aide years before, vetoed the idea, saying he would go instead and make sure his favorite general did not say anything he should not.[8]

Contrary to Marshall's expectations, the press conference went well. Stimson, according to Farago, handled the proceedings like a "combination master of ceremonies, interviewer, and censor." He asked most of the questions and gave most of the answers. Patton, according to Farago, "did not seem to mind." There were no further attempts to "evaluate" him—at least while he was still in the States. Regardless, like Eisenhower, Marshall was through with his outspoken and controversial subordinate. But curiously, he did not fire him. While Patton lobbied vigorously during his stay to go to the Pacific and fight the Japanese, his requests, which went all the way up the chain of command to a personal meeting with newly installed President Truman, were denied. Truman, in the dark about nearly everything important when Roosevelt died and trying to catch up, had vowed to continue his predecessor's policies. That included deference to the Soviets and letting Marshall run the war, which at that stage Truman was glad to do. Some have written that General Douglas MacArthur did not want Patton in the Pacific, which may be true. But it was Marshall, MacArthur's boss, who denied Patton his request—which appears to be one of the more curious decisions at the end of the war. Patton clearly was the United States' best fighting general. The atomic bomb was still just a possibility at this time, although a month later, a first test in the New Mexico desert would be positive. Marshall was faced with planning the greatest invasion in the history of the world, yet he rejected the one American commander he had who had run roughshod over the enemy? Biographers argue Patton was already slated for retirement and that his fast-moving type of lightning war using tanks was not appropriate for the Pacific. But the decision still makes little sense. At crucial times, one uses the best resources available. Rather, Marshall sent Patton back to a job for which he had no liking, training, or aptitude—occupation governor of Bavaria.

Why? Was something in the works?

Before he returned to Germany, Patton, waiting until his wife had left the room, told his daughters, Bee and Ruth Ellen, that he would not see them again. "What are you talking about?" Ruth Ellen and Bee protested. "The war is over. You'll be home in a few months for good." No, he retorted, "my luck has all run out. I've used it up...like money in the bank...I've had increasingly narrow escapes. It's too damn bad I wasn't killed before the fighting stopped, but I wasn't. So be it."⁹ He had always told them, Ruth

Ellen writes, that he would die on foreign soil. But this was very specific. He was not returning home. He was going to die when he returned to Germany. How could he know? Was it the result of Bazata's claim that he told the general about a plot?

Despite his fatalistic outlook, Patton was not about to stop his criticisms of Allied post-war policies nor warnings about the Soviets. He returned to Bavaria and quickly became involved in more controversy. He opposed the repatriation of "fascist traitors," Stalin's characterization of Soviet POWs and ex-patriots, which the Russian dictator had secretly gotten Roosevelt and Churchill to agree to at Yalta and which Eisenhower vigorously—brutally—enforced. "The roundup and mass deportation of some 2 million Russians, known as Operation Keelhaul, is one of the saddest chapters in American and British history," wrote John Loftus, a former Justice Department investigator who helped uncover the top secret American "Keelhaul" in the early 1980s. The majority of those repatriated

> were POWs who had cooperated with the Nazis merely to survive. Many were confirmed anti-Stalinists and passionately wanted to remain in the West. But, ignoring every tradition of asylum, the western Allies uniformly treated all Russians [including persons who considered themselves from other nationalities, like Ukrainians and Byelorussians] as "traitors" and forcibly loaded them into boxcars for shipment to the Soviet Union. Rather than return, some of the desperate Russians committed suicide by throwing themselves under the trains. Those who escaped execution were shipped to Siberia as slave laborers in the gulags.[10]

Eyewitness accounts are worse. Russo-British Historian Nikolai Tolstoy described what happened when four hundred former

Soviets kept at Dachau, Germany, formerly scene of an infamous Nazi concentration camp, were told they were being repatriated:

> The scene inside was one of human carnage. The crazed men were attempting to take their own lives by any means. Guards cut down some trying to hang themselves from rafters; two others disemboweled themselves; another man forced his head through a window and ran his throat over the glass fragments; others begged to be shot. . . . Thirty-two men tried to take their own lives. Eleven succeeded; nine by hanging and two from knife wounds. . . . Despite the presence of American guards and a Soviet liaison officer, six . . . escaped enroute to the Soviet occupation zone. More and more the repatriation of unwilling persons was coming to disturb bat-tle-hardened troops.[11]

Through his intelligence people and his own experience, Patton was acutely aware of this. He rebelled, letting some 4,500 Russian POWs escape, according to Dr. Mark Elliott, director of the Global Center at Alabama's Samford University and a Soviet affairs expert.[12] Such defiance must have angered Eisenhower, if not Marshall and Truman. One of SHAEF's major jobs was the enforcement of repatriation. But even worse to Patton's superiors and enemies, according to Farago, were Soviet charges, relentlessly pressed, that Patton was secretly hiding and husbanding former Waffen-SS units with which to later attack them.[13] The Soviets presented proof gathered by their numerous spies. With Eisenhower in Moscow at the invitation of his friend General Zhukov, "Hero of Berlin," where he unprecedentedly (for a non-Russian) joined Stalin for celebrations at Lenin's tomb, SHAEF generals sent investigators to check the charges. They returned shocked. Among other things, nearly 5,000 former German soldiers who should have already been discharged and sent home and made to plow fields under punitive occupation policies were being kept in readiness at a camp located at Garmisch-Partenkirchen, the alpine resort which hosted the 1936 Winter Olympics.[14] And there were other such enclaves being kept by Third Army officers under Patton. Some of the prisoners were hardened Nazis who should have been caged in war-criminal camps. "No explicit orders," writes Farago, "could be traced to document the scheme.... But the design was unmistakable," according to at least one of the investigators, Walter Dorn, an Ohio State University professor who had helped devise the administration's plans for denazification and saw the pattern as a major occupation violation.[15] Presented with the evidence, Major General Walter Bedell ("Beetle") Smith, Eisenhower's chief of staff whom Patton detested, exclaimed, "There is no rational explanation for what General Patton is doing. I don't doubt any longer that old George has lost his marbles."[16]

In fairness to Patton, writes Farago, Third Army had the best record in the occupation of discharging POWs and sending them home, a formidable task because of the large numbers. But to Dorn, who, according to Farago, was to "bring to bear" his "ingrained liberalism" in Bavaria, "this was a case of chronic insubordination. Patton was defying Ike, his commander, and in the process he was sabotaging the will of the government of the United States."[17]

In other words, in Dorn's opinion, he was committing treason.

Returning to SHAEF from Moscow, Eisenhower, incensed, ordered Patton to Frankfurt and reportedly screamed at him behind closed doors. "I demand that you get off your bloody ass and carry out the deNazification program as you are told instead of mollycoddling the Nazis," he's quoted as saying by Mark Perry, author of one of the latest books mentioning the incident. Eisenhower aides, writes Perry, "could hear their commander out in the hallway."[18]

Patton's response, while contrite, was basically to go hunting and continue publicly to state that Russia, not Germany, was the problem. At an August 27 meeting at SHAEF, he showed he was unrepentant. Exactly what he said may not be recorded. But afterward, he wrote,

> I attended the Military Government meeting at Frankfurt. There were a number of speeches by General Eisenhower and his various assistants . . . and in every case the chief interest of the speaker was to say nothing which could be used against him. It is very patent that what the Military Government is trying to do [with repatriation and deNazification] is undemocratic and follows practically Gestapo methods. [These] doctrines . . . promulgated by [Secretary of the Treasury] Morgenthau at the Quebec Conference [September 12 to 16, 1944] . . . with Roosevelt copying . . . stated that Germany was to be made an agricultural state [which is] patently impossible . . . . First, because there is not enough [fertile land?] in Germany for the country to feed itself on such a basis, and, second, because if Germany has no purchasing power [which was part of the Morgenthau Plan] we will not be able to sell our goods to her and, therefore, our markets will be very considerably restricted. If any [news]paper opposed to the Democrats should get hold of the stuff that is being put out by those in charge of the Military Government of Germany, it could produce very bad results for the Democratic government. I stated that in my opinion Germany is so completely

blacked out as far as military resistance is concerned, they are not a menace, and that what we have to look out for is Russia. This caused considerable furore [sic].[19]

On the same day, he wrote his wife, "If what we are doing is 'Liberty, then give me death.'"[20] Two days later he received the order from SHAEF to evict civilian Germans from their homes in order to give displaced Jews, many from concentration camps, better housing. Patton called General Harold R. Bull, Eisenhower's deputy chief of staff under Beetle Smith, to protest. "If for Jews, why not Catholics, Mormons, etc.?" he wrote, "and called [Bull's] attention to possible repercussions but got nowhere .... Naturally I intend to carry out the instructions to the limit of my capacity in spite of my personal feelings against them, and in spite of my fear that in doing such things we will lay ourselves open to just criticism. We are also turning over to the French several hundred thousand prisoners of war to be used as slave labor in France. It is amusing to recall that we fought the Revolution in defense of the rights of man and the Civil War to abolish slavery and have now gone back on both principles."[21]

As a result of his protest, charges that Patton was anti-Semitic began appearing in the press. There is no doubt that he saw Jewish New Dealers like Secretary Morganthau and some Jewish newspaper reporters as destructive and, at least in the case of the reporters, his enemies. His diaries, especially after he was fired, are peppered with criticism of Jews and belief that Jews, especially Jewish liberals, were plotting against him. But he was a complicated man, and such bias from him was as much directed at individuals as at a race or religion. As historian Victor David Hanson writes,

Patton's bombast supposedly proves that he was anti-Semitic, but a prominent trusted military aide, the intelligence officer Colonel Oscar Koch, was Jewish and beloved by Patton—as was his official biographer Martin Blumenson. Patton was reportedly racist, but more than most other commanders he admired black units ("I don't give a damn who the man is. He can be a nigger or a Jew, but if he has the stuff and does his duty, he can have anything I've got. By God! I love him"), in-sisted on the presence of some black officers as judges of mil-itary tribunals involving black defendants, and spent more time with his African-American aide, Sergeant Meeks, than with almost anyone else while in Europe, developing a rela-tionship of mutual respect that transcended that of a general and his valet.[22]

Many Jews served with him and won his loyalty—as he did theirs.

However, even before the issue of Patton's anti-Semitism became prominent, it appears officials at SHAEF decided he was an enemy. The supposedly secret army of Nazis he was keeping—never proved, but at least apparently wished for by Patton—seems to have been the deciding factor. Patton, above all others, had the moxie, ability, and will to use such a force. More importantly, So-viet leaders—as well as U.S. leaders—*believed* he might use them, which could mean World War III. Nobody but Patton wanted that. Patton was now viewed as a bonafide menace, and a threat to world peace in addition to being insubordinate, uncontrollable, and, in the eyes of some, treasonous. Appropriately, in view of what their investigations revealed, General Clarence Adcock, an-other of Eisenhower's staff, decided that Patton, as Eisenhower and Marshall had earlier come to believe, was indeed "mad, for he could offer no rational explanation for what the general was doing and saying."* He therefore, as Marshall had tried earlier, had a Medical Corp psychiatrist sent to Patton's headquarters "in the disguise of a supply officer to observe Patton as closely as possible." In addition, he ordered Patton's phones, including those in his residence, tapped. Not only did U.S. officials need this stealthy monitoring for their own purposes, writes Farago, but also, "it was assumed, from certain passages in the Russian communications to General Eisenhower that the Russians were also tapping and bugging Patton," so they wanted to know what threats the Russians were hearing in order to placate any Soviet reaction.[23]

Patton, obviously, was now a marked man. Everything he did and said privately would be known to American and Russian leadership. And to think the Russians were not also surreptitiously monitoring him is to think naively. They had spies in the White House, had bugged Allied leaders at Teheran and Yalta, and generally had made the U.S. and its soldiers among the most spied on in the world. Spying on Patton would certainly, in view of that, be expected and, in comparison with Teheran and Yalta, much easier. Skubik, in fact, told his son, Mark, that he had seen the Russians tapping U.S. phones in the area:

> [H]e was just driving to or from HQ [headquarters, not otherwise specified] one day when he spotted a couple of guys fooling with a telephone pole that serviced the HQ. Since his job was to prevent saboteurs and other insurgent activity by the remaining Nazi forces, he stopped to find out what was going on. That is when he found out they were Russians and arrested them. They were let loose against dad's will, and to

---

*According to Farago.

his amazement, he caught them again about a week later tapping the telephone line again.[24]

As Skubik's son relates, the Russians had the run of the American occupation zones with little fear they would be thwarted. They knew the American policy of appeasement in hopes of peace. The repatriation enclaves they established in Western zones were actually spy hubs used primarily for clandestine activities. They were off limits to U.S. authorities. General Davidov, whom Skubik accused of plotting against Patton, was officially head of repatriations from August 1945 until he disappeared shortly after Patton's death. Additional indication that Soviet intelligence was specifically targeting Patton is found in *The Haunted Wood,* Weinstein and Vassiliev's ground-breaking work on Soviet espionage in this period. It discloses that, interestingly, OSS's Donald Wheeler, an Oxford graduate and friend of Donovan aide, Duncan Lee, a Soviet spy, was passing to the NKVD "the monthly confidential report of the military governor in the U.S. occupation zone of Germany," as well as other secrets, at least through "October/November 1945."[25] The military governor up to October was General Patton, and although OSS was officially disbanded October 1, 1945, the organization, in fact, continued in operation for months afterward, and then simply changed names. Were they just interested in the military governor, or was it specifically Patton they were after?

Similarly, the American bug on Patton's phones was in operation at least through December 5, 1945. I found a three-page transcript of a conversation on that date between Patton and Beetle Smith at the Library of Congress. It shows, word for word, a discussion about Patton's plans to leave Germany on December 10—the day before his fateful accident. He asks for permission to take an unnamed aide and his orderly, Sergeant Meeks, with him, as well as for some other travel arrangements. Undoubtedly, the bug was in operation until at least after Patton was injured so his movements were easily monitored. And the Americans expected the line to be tapped, as one conversation with Patton proved.

General Joseph T. McNarney, an official who came after the war to be Eisenhower's replacement,* had called Patton to press him on "the Soviet complaint that he was too slow in disbanding" the SS troops he was believed to be harboring. "Hell," Patton exploded, "why do you care what those goddamn Russians think? We are going to have to fight them sooner or later....Why not do it now while our army is intact and the damn Russians can have their hind end kicked back into Russia in three months? We can do it easily with the help of the German troops we have if we just arm them and take them with us. They hate the bastards." McNarney could not believe what he was hearing. "Shut up, Georgie, you fool," he blurted. It was not only that he was shocked. He was fearful that the Soviets might be listening. "This line may be tapped and you will be starting a war with your talking." But Patton persisted. "I would like to get it started in some way. That is the best thing we can do now. You don't have to get mixed up in it at all if you are so damn soft about it and scared of your rank—just let me handle it down here. In ten days I can have enough incidents happened to have us at war with those sons of bitches and make it look like their fault."[26]

McNarney hung up.

What was the Soviet reaction?

---

*Eisenhower left Europe in November 1945—just weeks before Patton's accident.

McNarney reported the incident to Robert Murphy, Eisenhower's special political advisor, who called Patton to his office. Murphy, who found the statements just as shocking as McNarney, writes Patton did not tone it down a bit. "He inquired, with a gleam in his eye, whether there was any chance of going on to Moscow, which he said he could reach in thirty days, instead of waiting for the Russians to attack the United States when we were weak [following the troop drawdown which was in progress] and reduced to two divisions [in Germany]."[27]

Even without such provocation, Patton was already an avowed enemy of several Russian generals—a dangerous thing in its own right, according to Nicolai Khokhlov, a former NKVD/KGB operative. In 2007, I interviewed Khokhlov, widely reputed to have been a Soviet assassin. When we met, he corrected, "I was not an assassin. I was the director of many of them [assassinations], but not one myself." His story is unique and redemptive in that he eventually had a crisis of conscience over his dark work and consequently defected to the West in 1953, giving the CIA its first inside look at SMERSH (*Smert' Shpionam*—or "Death to Spies," that operated from 1943 to 1946, although elements carried on into the early Cold War period), the Soviets' most infamous murder unit.

Khokhlov was back in the news in 2006 and 2007 because of the bizarre death of former defected Soviet spy Alexander Litvinenko who, in November 2006, became the first known victim of polonium-210 poisoning, a particularly heinous Soviet means of assassination whereby the unsuspecting victim ingests lethal radioactivity. Khokhlov, himself, was an earlier victim of the same Soviet method, although from a different type of nuclear poison. Lecturing in Frankfurt in 1957, he accepted a cup of coffee laced with radioactive thallium, a mixture undetectable by taste but administered in fulfillment of the Soviet dictum that no one ever gets away with crossing the regime. "I suddenly felt very tired," he wrote. "Things began to whirl about me in the hall." Lights swayed, their rays doubling in his vision. Pain surged in his heart and stomach. What he had no way of knowing was that once ingested, the surreptitious thallium burned "through his stomach lining and entered the bloodstream," where, by the time its torturous physical effects began appearing on the outside of his body, it supposedly would have vanished from his system—the perfect undetectable poison. "Friends...rushed him to a hospital where severe gastric poisoning was diagnosed. His condition worsened. His face erupted in black, brown and blue lumps, his eyes oozed a sticky liquid and his hair fell out in handfuls. The blood in his veins was turning to plasma; his bones were crumbling...'my body was convulsed into a terrible struggle with some strange force'"—a new height in torture death.[28]

By the grace of God, he says, he only drank half the cup of coffee. He recovered. "I am a religious man. Someone up there can do something."[29] As often occurs in the spy trade, things go wrong with the best made plans, and a leading New York toxicologist, aided by Khokholov's knowledge of exotic Soviet poisons and the former spy's medical records, deduced what had happened. In hindsight, Khokhlov remembered the coffee and realized he never should have accepted it in the first place. Today, as a professor, he lives comfortably in Southern California, having been pardoned by Boris Yeltsin in 1992. He lost his wife and child over the defection, and there were other heartbreaks in his story. But for my purposes he ventured that if Patton had been assassinated—something he said he had no personal knowledge about—his best guess would be that it was done by Soviet generals. Patton "was very aggressive with Soviet generals. He probably offended some, even

Marshall Zhukov. And knowing some of these guys mentally, they would say he needs a lesson. He needs to be taught a lesson."

Not only had Patton offended Soviet generals, most notably at Prague and with post-war toasts, but he had indeed offended the mighty Zhukov himself. It had been Zhukov who had personally and vehemently pressed the charges against Patton about keeping and readying the SS troops. Zhukov "was one of the toughest individuals I had ever encountered," wrote General James M. Gavin, commander of the elite 82nd Airborne Division which had been dropped into Normandy in advance of D-Day. He met Zhukov, he wrote, when Eisenhower and the "Hero of Berlin" exchanged reviews of troops. Eisenhower, as a measure of his esteem, had presented the 82nd in full dress to Zhukov. Afterward, at a host's luncheon he arranged, Gavin was amazed to see another Russian general fearstruck when asked to step inside and join Zhukov and him for toasts. "I went out to talk to him through an interpreter, and when he learned that Marshal Zhukov was in the house, he actually trembled. He would not enter the house in any circumstances. With apologies he departed. When I went back into the house, I noticed that when Marshal Zhukov came into a room everybody disappeared....Such was the degree of fear that he seemed to cause among his subordinates. He apparently had the right of life or death and did not hesitate to use it."[30]

At a conference to plan a September 7, 1945, parade to celebrate the victory over Japan, Zhukov tried to tell Gavin "what to do." Gavin knew he had equal status. "I declined [his attempt to take over]. He then told me that he was going to get in touch with Eisenhower. I told him that was fine with me but I saw no reason to change my position. That was the end of the discussion. Several days later I received some very nice candid photographs taken during the conference, although no cameraman had been visible."

At the actual parade, which was to feature Zhukov and Patton together, things almost got comical if they did not foreshadow the tensions soon to become widespread. There had been a misunderstanding about who would lead the marchers, and when Zhukov, resplendent with medals hanging almost to his waist, jumped in a car to review the troops, Patton, who had not been told to wear his and was mad about it, had commandeered a car himself and ridden almost bumper to bumper with the perturbed marshal, making sure America was represented as well.[31]

Back on the parade stand, wrote General Lucius Clay, "the Soviet commander and his staff acted as if the review was theirs alone," crowding the Americans, British, and French back from the prominent center. Patton "sensed, as did most of us, that this was a deliberate Soviet effort to take sole credit for the capture of Berlin and major credit for the defeat of Germany.... But when the head of our marching column [the 82nd Airborne troops and 2nd Armored Division tanks] reached the stand...Patton whispered...'This is where you and I step forward'...we did so with great pride...."[32] Further, when Russian tanks emerged, Patton aide Major Van S. Merle-Smith told Fred Ayer, Jr., he overheard the following exchange: "My dear General Patton," Smith said Zhukov boasted, "you see that tank, it carries a cannon which can throw a shell seven miles." Patton [responded], "Indeed? Well, my dear Marshal Zhukov, let me tell you this, if any of my gunners started firing at your people before they had closed to less than seven hundred yards [less than half a mile] I'd have them courtmartialed for cowardice." It was the first time, said Smith, "I saw a Russian commander stunned into silence."[33]

It was less than a month later that Patton was fired as occupation governor of Bavaria and, perhaps more importantly, as commanding officer of his beloved Third Army. He was banished into obscurity, not just in terms of public profile, but into the relatively unprotected physical area of Bad Nauheim, and stripped of the major security and protection, such as bodyguards and the large intelligence apparatus, he formerly had that had always kept him advised of dangerous situations. Skubik wrote, "I have spoken to Bert Goldstein, one of Patton's bodyguards during that time.... Bert states that had the bodyguards not been removed Patton would not have been murdered. He is convinced that his favorite general was murdered."[34] I never could find Bert Goldstein, nor any list of Patton's bodyguards in order to verify this. But I do not doubt that at least the bodyguards existed. Generals, and especially someone as controversial and outspoken as Patton, often had them.

He was fired at the end of September for an off-hand remark about political parties that was seized upon by critical reporters who knew it would bring him trouble. As part of the deNazification controversy he was embroiled in, Patton had agreed to a press conference on September 22 to clarify his positions. Eisenhower's diplomatic aide, Robert Murphy, recalled, "Patton asserted that [the occupation government] would get better results if it employed more former [inconsquential] members of the Nazi party in administrative jobs and as skilled workmen." Otherwise, they would be hiring incompetents. One of the correspondents, detecting an opening for a sensational news story, asked a loaded question: "After all, General, didn't most ordinary Nazis join their party in about the same way that Americans become Republicans or Democrats?" The unsuspecting Patton replied, "Yes, that's about it." Within a few hours newspapers around the world were reporting: "American General says Nazis Are Just Like Republicans and Democrats!"[35]

An uproar ensued. Most accounts paint a similar picture of what had happened—a cabal of liberal, anti-Patton reporters, angry with what they felt were Patton's pro-Nazi, anti-Soviet, fascist views conspired to destroy him. Farago, however, wrote that the reporters were only pawns to "Eisenhower's inner circle. In the end," he wrote, "Patton was toppled . . . not by those 'itenerant' (sic) correspondents . . . but by a greater design devised by his own colleagues . . . [Gen.] Bedell Smith . . . [Gen.] Harold R. (Pinky) Bull, and [Gen.] Clarence Adcock . . . ."[36] Jeffrey St. John, Patton Society Research Library, concurs. "Fred Ayer Jr. [in *Before the Colors Fade*] provides considerable details on the press conference and concludes that the distorted press accounts were used by key U.S. officials to justify removing General Patton and ending his anti-Soviet campaign."[37] Patton's alleged anti-Semitism was injected in the controversy, arousing "the ire of American Jews such as Henry Morgenthau, [FDR advisor and financier] Bernard Baruch, and [Supreme Court Justice] Felix Frankfurter," adds Farago. Leftists and anti-Pattonists from every corner joined in and the overwhelming cry from the press became, "General Patton should be fired."[38]

Eisenhower was quick to comply—so quick that he unexpectedly phoned Patton after assuring him the reassignment would unfold gradually and said it would have to be immediate now because the news had somehow been leaked. The October 2 call prompted Patton to write, "Eisenhower is scared to death, which I already knew, and believes that a more prompt announcement of my relief than the one he had originally planned will be beneficial to him. The alleged leak is nothing but a figment of the imagination which is a euphemism for a damned lie."[39] Among those lauding the firing, and Eisenhower for doing so, was the now-Soviet controlled newspaper, *Berliner Zeitung*, according to a story by Russell Hill of the *New York Herald Tribune*. "The democratic peoples do not let the wool be pulled over their eyes, particularly in such a vital matter as the fight against Nazism," it proclaimed. "If there are American officers who believe they can make their own policies, they are taken to task for it. In its resolute stand against Patton's behavior, the American people showed a sure feeling for justice."[40]

Patton himself wrote:

> This conference cost me the command of the Third Army.... I was intentionally direct because I believed that it was then time for people to know what was going on. My language was not particularly politic, but I have yet to find where politic language produces successful government. The one thing which I could not say then, and cannot yet say, is that my chief interest in establishing order in Germany was to prevent Germany from going communist. I am afraid that our foolish and utterly stupid policy in regard to Germany [punishment and repression] will certainly cause them to join the Russians and thereby insure a communistic state throughout Western Europe.... At least I have done my best as God gave me the chance.[41]

Patton was now deposed, officially disgraced amongst his own, and banished to relative obscurity—making him that much easier a target should an assassination plot be afoot.

CHAPTER TWENTY

★ ★ ★ ★

INTO THE NIGHT

O f all the questions surrounding Patton's mysterious death, why he might have been assassinated is the easiest to answer.

Patton's Third Army ended the war by capturing the Nazi's hidden cave vaults laden with gold, priceless art, and other riches, as well as finding the Germans' secret weapons factories buried within vast mountain installations. Some of the recovered gold was stolen that summer in what the *The Guiness Book of Records* reportedly calls the greatest robbery on record.[1] It involved billions calculated at today's values. Rumors have connected the theft to Patton's demise. He was on the robbers' trail, they say. That was the basis for the plot of the 1978 movie *Brass Target*, which speculated that renegade U.S. officers stole some of the gold and featured an assassination attempt on Patton much like Bazata describes. The actual robbers have never been found.

Similarly, recent non-fiction books *Blunder* (1985), *The Hunt for Zero Point* (2002), and *Reich of the Black Sun* (2004) argue that Patton discovered futuristic Nazi secret weapons at Pilsen, Czechoslovakia, where the Third Army basically ended the war, and that fear that he would disclose the finds caused his assassination. These books' assertions about what was discovered, including undisclosed German nuclear research and fantastic sources of space propulsion, are based on little known facts, some of which are emerging in the continual unraveling of World War II secrets, and deserve more study. It is interesting to note that it was while Patton was in Pilsen that Skubik said the general "became acquainted with the Ukrainian Insurgent Army" and Stepan Bandera.[2] But Patton in his diary mentions Pilsen and the hidden factories several times and nowhere hints that he found anything worthy of special secrecy. Of course, if he were keeping it secret, why would he? Whatever the truth of the missing Nazi gold and recovered Nazi secret weapons, the secrets involving the conduct of the war Patton knew from his participation before and after he arrived at Pilsen are, in the opinion of military historian Charles Whiting, the "obvious" reasons to silence him.[3] These included the strategic and tactical blunders made by his superiors,* the resultant prolonging of the war and considerable loss of life estimated to have occurred because of them, and the appeasement of Stalin and the Soviets that allowed half of Europe to be enslaved at the conclusion of the war which resulted in the costly, 45-year Cold War. Such secrets were aspects of the conflict and its aftermath hidden in 1945 and are still little known except amongst scholars who debate them today.

---

*It should be noted here that mistakes are made in every war. Bad commanders are fired and replaced until sucessful ones emerge. Lincoln fired several until he found Grant. But Patton, even in success, was passed over for promotion and medals several times.

And there are still other, little-known motives.

For instance, thousands of Americans and European soldiers who were POWs when the Russians overran their camps never returned home.[4] John M. G. Brown, a former Vietnam War combat infantryman, has been studying the matter since the 1980s. In a two-part series of articles that appeared in the *New American* in 1990, he detailed a secret decision that is still largely hidden today: Roosevelt, Truman, and Marshall, "to avoid a 1945 military confrontation with Stalin over the thousands of American, British, and Commonwealth POWs under Soviet control" decided not to press Russia to return the Allied POWs because "Soviet participation in the United Nations and entrance into the Japanese war were seen as more important." Patton, according to Brown, was one of those who protested the decision in secret because of its classification. One of the reasons he was sent back to the U.S. in the summer of 1945, writes Brown, was to separate him from the policies that would leave so many in bondage for fear he would blow a whistle.[5] As a result of the cruel policy, according to Brown, many of the abandoned POWs spent the rest of their lives in the gulags working as slave labor for the USSR.

"General George Marshall issued the secret orders implementing the policy decision," wrote Brown. "In the last two weeks of his life Roosevelt stuck to the decision. From this point on, Stalin knew that the American leadership would back down" when he made demands. Stalin was using the POW "kidnapping," which amounted to holding hostages, to get the U.S. and Britain to agree to Soviet control of Eastern Europe. "Nearly a month later, as the European war drew to a close, a new president, Harry Truman, was briefed by [U.S. ambassador to the Soviet Union] Averell Harriman on the POW kidnapping.... Truman, however, also decided that the potential losses, both diplomatic and military, of open conflict with the Soviet Union were not worth the recovery of all U.S. prisoners in Soviet control. He too considered the United Nations and the Japanese war top priorities and endorsed Roosevelt's decision."[6]

As a result of Truman's decision, wrote Brown, who said he found details of the Soviet "blackmail" in declassified documents in the National Archives, "Marshall again issued the order forbidding the use of military force to recover American POWs.... U.S. and British intelligence reports and cables from General Marshall spoke of more than 15,000 Americans and some 8,500 British and Commonwealth prisoners in Soviet-occupied Austria alone." Many of those POWs, he wrote, had been identified by Patton's Third Army. "While the Soviets temporarily admitted their existence, they refused U.S. and British ... entrance into the camps" and eventually denied the POW's existence outright. "The crisis was kept secret from the American and British people, who were told on May 31, 1945 by Undersecretary of War Robert Patterson that substantially all their prisoners had been returned. Yet a classified SHAEF memo ... the day before states that an estimated 20,000 Americans and 20,000 British remained in Soviet hands." Robert Patterson was the same man who had vouched for Soviet spy Nathan Silvermaster when the FBI had questioned his loyalty and whom Patton had shocked by pleading, "Mr. Secretary, for God's sake.... Let's not give [the Russians] time to build up their supplies. If we do ... we have had a victory over the Germans [but] failed in the liberation of Europe."

Even beyond knowing such shocking secrets as the alleged betrayal of American POWs, Patton's public threats against the USSR and Stalin seem motive enough for the Soviets to target him. I have been told Stalin would never be so foolish as to try to kill

Patton—especially at that time. Things were going his way. He had Eastern Europe and U.S. policy in his hands. Why chance losing that? Such thinking, in my opinion, assumes Stalin was reasonable and hoped for peace like his Allies. He was not—although, incredibly, many viewed him that way. He was a paranoid, unhinged dictator who ruled by fear and murder; a ruthless, merciless killer who calculatingly marked enemies and friends alike for death on a list he penciled daily at his desk like a crossword puzzle.[7] The Katyn masscare showed what he thought of caution in international politics. He ordered every Polish military and civilian leader in Soviet captivity murdered in order to control resistance in Poland. Patton, with his influence and intentions, was a larger danger to the dictator than the Poles. And Stalin was not known to hesitate. Like "a spider at the center of a web," wrote Russian historian Donald Rayfield, one of the few who has documented the dictator's crimes, Stalin "was alert to any disturbance and could neutralize any threat."[8] "Assassination [was] an integral part of Stalin's foreign policy," wrote Vasili Mitrokhin, former KGB archivist.[9] At the end of the war, NKVD murder, often directly ordered and plotted by Stalin, was almost a daily occurrence. Other foreign notables whose fame and prestige matched Patton's—all military men—were marked for death by Stalin, including Hitler, General Franco of Spain, General Goering, General Tito, and Trotsky, the revolutionary, according to subordinates like his chief of assassination, Sudoplatov.[10] For various reasons,* his old rival Trotsky was the only one of those he was able to have killed. But he hatched assassination plots against all of them. Each was as prominent as Patton and most of them were

---

*Different plots failed.

capable of hurting him politically should his or the NKVD's fingerprints be discerned (Hitler and Goering being the exceptions)—but that never seems to have worried him.

Just how bizarre and international Stalin's plots could become is shown in the recent revelation that American icon John Wayne, the actor, was among his intended victims, according to British film historian and Wayne biographer Michael Munn. In the late 1940s, Wayne, a symbol of American independence and ruggedness, spurred by revelations of communist infiltration into the U.S. government, became an ultra-right anti-communist. He supported Senator Joseph McCarthy in denouncing communists, while most in Hollwood, where Wayne worked, attacked McCarthy and the blacklisting of Hollywood leftists which McCarthy was spawning. He was elected president of the Motion Picture Alliance for the Preservation of American Ideals and spoke frequently at "Crusade for Freedom" rallies where he denounced such films as *All the King's Men*, the 1949 Best Picture winner, which he felt "smeared the machinery of the country's government" and would "tear down people's faith in...the American way."[11]

According to sources Munn interviewed,* Sergei Gerasimov, a Soviet film director, was in Hollywood and became aware of Wayne's activism. Gerasimov returned to Russia to tell Stalin, who took an active part in Russian film making, about Wayne's crusade and influence in America. Stalin became convinced that Wayne "was one of the greatest enemies to the Soviet Union," and a major obstacle to world revolution.[12] In 1983, writes Munn, Orson Wells, no conservative, told him,

---

*Munn's sources included British actor Peter Cushing, movie legend Orson Wells, and American stuntman Yakima Canutt, a personal friend of Wayne's.

> I do not know if the name John Wayne was already known to...Stalin before 1949, but in 1949 he...came to hate it. He feared it. He felt that the name had become a major threat to him and his ideals....In Stalin's warped mind, the Americans had invented some new secret weapon, more subtle than a nuclear bomb, but just as destructive....Stalin was mad, of course...should have been put in a straightjacket. Only a madman like Joseph Stalin would have tried to have John Wayne killed.[13]

Wayne himself admitted as much—although he wanted it kept quiet because of a questionable stunt he pulled to scare some KGB assassins sent to kill him. Munn writes he and Wayne were in Wayne's trailer when Munn asked "Duke" if what he had heard about Stalin targeting him was true. Wayne was silent a few moments. "Then, in an almost hushed tone, he said to me, 'Once the genie's out of the bottle, how ya gonna get it back in again?...Kid, I've been criticized for years because I've made my feelings known about those pinko bastards....I'll be straight with you 'cos I like you, and you already know more than anyone should. This is between you and me. The communists have been trying to kill me since 1949.'"[14] The revered actor then told Munn a story involving a thwarted KGB attempt to kill Wayne. It "was at Wayne's office at Warner Bros., where he and Jimmy Grant [Wayne's frequent screenwriter] would be working on a script," writes Munn. The FBI had informed Wayne that the assassins were coming and would be masquerading as agents. When real agents arrived to set a trap, Wayne asked if he and Grant could teach the Russians a lesson. He wanted to show he was not afraid of them. He proposed using guns loaded with blanks to act out an execution on the assassins. The agents agreed. When the assassins arrived, they were arrested and taken in a car to a place up the coast of California. Munn concluded, "That's how John Wayne and James Grant came to be on a remote beach late into the evening, with guns aimed at the heads of two KGB agents, kneeling in the sand, and thinking their time was up."[15]

Having failed in their mission, the two assassins defected.

If Stalin targeted John Wayne, why not George Patton?

Banished to Bad Nauheim, where he would preside over the leisurely writing by a small group of soldiers and military historians of tactical lessons learned in the war, Patton was hurt, angry, and spied upon by the Russians and his own country. SHAEF's tap of his phone line meant he was being monitored by his superiors, who worried he might do something rash and hoped they would be alerted with enough time to stop him from any potential war-starting scheme. And the Soviets, watching him as well as listening to his phone conversations, were in a position to monitor his every move and react.*

Those listening in on the phone taps probably got an earful. They could have little doubt that Patton had no plans of remaining silent once free of his military fetters.

On October 2, Patton wrote to Charles Codman, his former aide-de-camp,

---

*Formerly classified U.S. intelligence documents I found at the National Archives, dated 30 November 1945, 4 December, 12 December, as well as others through March 1946, indicate there was heightened spy activity in Patton's general area and a belief on the part of the Russians by sources quoted in the documents, that "the Soviet is preparing for war and that in a Soviet-American war, America could not win." The Soviets were very bold at this time.

Today I am performing with my usual efficiency my duties as undertaker at my own funeral.... Actually, while I regret being relieved for what amounts to...lack of guts—not my part though—from the Third Army, it may all work out for the best because various rules and regulations imposed on us from Washington and elsewhere, chiefly at the behest of the press, are practically unsolvable....I am really very fearful of repercussion [from the policies he opposed] which will occur this winter and I am certain we are being completely hoodwinked by the degenerate descendants of Ghengis Khan. People who talk about peace should visit Europe where, as I believe the Lord said, I bring you not peace but the sword... .I could say a good many more things but even yet fear censoring, though it is not supposed to exist, so shall refrain until I see you. My new job in the Fifteenth Army is really literary rather than military and furthermore has the advantage of getting me out of the limelight.[16]

On or about October 13, Patton was involved in an auto accident in which he was only slightly injured. Details, strangely, are almost nonexistent. Blumenson mentions it fleetingly in the *Patton Papers*, as does Farago in *Last Days*, who attributes it to Patton's alleged propensity to be "accident prone," a belief which most Patton historians echo. A small newspaper story from the Independent News Service, datelined October 14, records, "Patton was reported in an automobile accident near his headquaters at Bad Nauheim" and "escaped serious injury." It is possible, since this accident is relatively close in time to the more fateful one on December 9, that some of the seemingly erroneous reports about December 9 are mixing the two. Was this preliminary October accident, innocuous as it seems by most accounts, an earlier assassination attempt?

★ ★ ★

On October 15, Patton penned to his wife, "Ike is bitten with the presidential bug and is also yellow.... He will never be president!... I will resign when I have finished this job which will be not later than Dec. 26. I hate to do it but I have been gagged all my life, and whether they are appreciated or not, America needs some honest men who dare to say what they think, not what they think people want them to think."[17] To retired Major General James Harbord, an old friend and advisor, he wrote:

> I think General Eisenhower is most pusillanimous in yielding to th[is] outcry... I shall prove even more conclusively that he lacks moral fortitude.... It is interesting to note that everything for which I have been criticized in the handling of Germans had been subsequently adopted: to wit—I stated that if we took all small Nazis out of every job, chaos would result. Military Government the other day announced that from two to five per cent of Nazis would be kept.... [W]hen I finish this job... I shall resign, not retire, because if I retire I will still have a gag in my mouth.... I should not start a limited counter-attack... but should wait until I can start an all out offensive.[18]

Much of Patton's short three months at Bad Nauheim was spent working on a book, later to be published as *War as I Knew It*, early chapters of which he was sending to various friends and relatives for advice and safe-keeping while stressing that it had to be kept secret. The book, based primarily on his diary, which itself was sometimes haphazardly kept on scraps of paper, eventually would be published posthumously by Houghton Mifflin in 1947.

Since word had gotten out that he kept a diary, the book was eagerly anticipated—with great trepidation by some of those he had served with or under who had reason to fear what it would contain. For instance, prior to publication, the Truman administration's Robert Patterson, who, by then, had become secretary of war, wrote Mrs. Patton, who apparently had sent him a copy, "There are many passages . . . that are fairly severe. . . . The general was entirely candid in speaking his mind and giving his impressions, even though they reflected unfavorably on individuals. . . . The inclusion of these critical reflections in a published book, I am convinced, would not only be contrary to his desires, but would lead to bitter controversies and recriminations. . . ." He urged her to purge the book, and she did edit it. While it generally, when published, gave his views, it was not as incriminating or shocking as Patterson implies. How Patton finished it is not clear, and one wonders what was edited out.[19] No unedited copies of the manuscript exist in any archives, but it is possible that Patton family members may have the original, although they do not mention it in their writings today.

He also spent time hunting, which he greatly enjoyed. Though some critics of the theory that Patton was assassinated charge that no one could have known he was going hunting that Sunday morning since it was a spur-of-the-moment decision, Patton was a frequent hunter. His driver, Horace Woodring said, "He [Patton] went hunting every Sunday morning."[20] Patton himself mentioned several hunting trips in November just weeks before his accident. In a letter to his wife on the 18th, a Sunday, he wrote, "I am going shooting at Hannon this P.M."[21] A day earlier, on November 17, he wrote Omar Bradley, "Since writing you I have been on a couple of other shoots in one of which I used the pump gun and in the other the over and under 16, which, as you recall,

I had made in Liege."[22] Patton was an avid hunter. Hunting was part of his routine; therefore, that certainly would have been taken into account by anyone planning to harm him.

Furthermore, it is unclear when the decision to go hunting was made. Some evidence indicates that the idea to go hunting that fateful Sunday was made only early that morning, thereby further shortening the time plotters had to get an assassination attempt together. But Colonel Robert S. Allen, one of Patton's close staff officers, wrote that the decision was made the previous night. "How about going out tomorrow?" he quoted Gay as asking Patton. Patton responded, "You arrange to have the car and guns on hand early tomorrow and we'll see how many birds we can bag." Allen was a famous journalist, author of several books and the syndicated column "Inside Washington." He was cognizant of the need to be accurate. Additionally, Patton's driver Woodring told Suzy Shelton, "The trip was a last-minute decision the night before."[23] He said the same to Brian Sobel for Sobel's book, *The Fighting Pattons*.[24] But to others like Farago and Fugate, Woodring indicated he did not learn about the trip until that morning. The witness of General Keyes, who was with Patton the night before the accident, can go either way.*

Even if the decision to go hunting was made that morning, foul play could still have been at work. There were spies all over, most of them Russian or working for the Russians. Bazata said he had

---

*Keyes had dinner with Patton and spent the night at Patton's headquarters but left early before seeing Patton, who Farago says was perturbed at missing him (p. 220). In the *Patton Papers*, p. 817, Keyes' reproduced letter to his wife the day after the accident says, "Had a fine visit with [Patton], and yesterday morning after breakfast I started home, and he and Hap Gay were to start for Mannheim...(omission Blumenson's) in a few minutes to go hunting." It remains to be determined whether he knew about the hunting trip from the night before or heard it from someone that morning before he left.

informants in Patton's headquarters, which is not hard to believe since everyone from professional military to cooks were engaged in supplying information if the price or cause was right. Bazata himself was nearby. As mentioned earlier, Patton's phones were tapped, certainly by the U.S., and most probably by the Soviets, as General McNarney and CIC's Skubik believed.

The only timeline for the beginning of the December 9 trip is provided by Farago from interviews he conducted. He said "Woody remembers" that when he went out to ready the Cadillac, after being woken to do so by a phone call from Patton's valet, Sergeant Meeks, a clock in the car "stood at three minutes to seven o'clock in the morning,"—6:57 a.m.[25] Presuming that is correct, that meant, allowing time for dressing and possibly eating, he had gotten the call fifteen to forty-five minutes before, say at 6:30 a.m. The few sources that discuss it indicate the hunting party—Patton, Gay, and Woodring in the Cadillac; Scruce, a hunting dog, and the guns in the open jeep—left Bad Nauheim anywhere between approximately 7:30 a.m. and 9:00 a.m.[26] (Farago says "between seven and eight"; Gay, in his memoir, says 8:50 a.m.) That gave any potential plotters between, roughly, a half hour to an hour and a half to get in motion; half a day, if they learned about the trip the night before. If they had been trying previously, as the many strange earlier accidents suggest, they already had the essentials in place—assassins, weapons, and method. It was just a matter of when and where. And if Douglas Bazata was the assassin, it is certainly relevant that he, as he and others who knew him stress, preferred quick action to lengthy planning. Speed and decisiveness were among his sought-after skills.

Scruce, according to Woodring,[27] left Bad Nauheim first and was to meet the Cadillac later at a checkpoint outside Mannheim—the one at which they supposedly transferred the dog to Patton's car. That means that if he had been in on any plot, he, too, had a chance to confer with conspirators in advance. But some suggest that the deviation from the autobahn by the later-leaving Cadillac to see the Roman ruins at Saalburg, another action believed to have been taken on the spur-of-the-moment, would make any possible plotters' task almost impossible, presumably because it would hinder their timing. Why? If assassins were tailing the car, as Bazata says, or, in other ways monitoring its progress, as an insider like the mysterious Scruce could have done, such a deviation could have been discovered and subsequently factored in to the plan. There was one standard route to Mannheim via the autobahn. The Cadillac would eventually have had to come back to the autobahn to pick up the route through Kaeferthal where the accident occurred. Plotters, ahead or in tail, easily could have monitored the route and had adjustments ready in case of deviation. They may have even, had things not gone their way, just abandoned the plot, and gone after him at the hunting spot, or on the way back, or just let him go, in which case there would not have been an accident. Such deviations in route and timing do not *a priori* nullify any assassination plot.

A new piece of information I found related to the fateful trip is a letter written home by General Gay's aide-de-camp, Lieutenant John A. Hadden. Addressed to his parents and dated November 27, 1945, it says, "This past Sunday General Gay and I went pheasant shooting down in our favorite spot south of Mannheim." In other words, Gay, an avid hunter like Patton, was a regular visitor to a hunting place which sounds much like where they were all heading that fateful Sunday. The letter, sent to me by his widow, Elaine Hadden, calls into question the often repeated details of Patton's last trip that the route to the hunting grounds was unknown to everyone in the caravan except Sergeant Scruce, and that Scruce pulled out ahead of the Cadillac at the railroad track because he was the only one who knew the way. Gay, it appears, knew the way. Hadden's letter may or may not be significant in the larger question of how Patton was injured, but in view of so many other mysteries regarding the accident, it needs to be considered too. Just how much of the standard accident story is true and how much is false? We do not really know.

Hadden, who died in 1994, also possibly sheds light on why Patton went to the Saalburg ruins in the first place, and how the legendary general's death could profoundly affect those even peripherally involved, like Hadden. A Cleveland, Ohio native, Hadden returned to his home after the war, where, in time, he became a prominent child psychiatrist and psychoanalyst, serving as staff psychiatrist for the Children's Aid Society there and for the Cuyahoga County Juvenile Court. He had hoped to write a psychological book about Patton and sometimes gave lectures about the general. His wife sent me a tape of one of the lectures. In it, he tells how Patton and Patton's younger sister, "Nita," were very close, wrote often, and that she had "stimulated his interest in some Roman ruins close to his headquarters." This, then, probably factored into the decision to make the detour—if it was not the main reason the detour was made. And since Hadden was aware of it, plans to make the detour may have also been known by others, such as those wanting to harm Patton.

Other bits of Hadden's letters and his lectures give a heretofore unseen, if small, snapshot of Patton's last days. As part of his job, Hadden sometimes ate dinners and breakfasts with the general whom he wrote "is a rather talkative individual," with a "prodigious memory," who needs only "a well directed question or two to keep him going." He was "anxious about the Russians and furious at Ike because he didn't let him take Berlin....Listening to him is ten times as interesting as a history [lesson] ever could be.... He announced he was going to retire* and run for the Senate himself from California."

There are other interesting snippets. Unfortunately, as the years passed, Hadden's memories, unlike his letters, must have blurred and he began to imagine himself in the front seat alongside Woodring when Patton broke his neck. Hearing that is why I contacted his wife. I eventually was sent a 1985 taped lecture in which he indeed said he had been in the Cadillac with Patton when it collided with Thompson's truck—in the front seat where the hunting dog was supposed to be. But a letter sent to his parents three days after the accident indicates he was not. Dated December 12, 1945, he wrote, "Such a lot has happened...Sunday morning I packed General Patton and General Gay off on the now famous hunting trip and settled down to moving my belongings from Gen. Gay's house to General Patton's house. Gen. P. had planned to leave early Monday morning and we were going to close our house and use only his....I finished moving by lunch time and we had sat down to lunch when the call came that the generals had had an accident...."

It is possible that other Patton stories which do not pan out were generated in the same probably well-meaning but confused way.

Hadden died of Alzheimers Disease.

---

*The use of "retire" instead of "resign" here is probably just a slip in word usage. Patton's writings show that although he wavered slightly while at Bad Nauheim, he had finally made up his mind before leaving to resign rather than retire.

Just weeks before his fateful accident, retired General Charles P. Summerall, former army chief of staff, wrote Patton, "Your success has aroused jealousy and made enemies of those who profited by your victories. They have finished with you and now seek to destroy you." On the same day as the date of that letter, November 24, 1945—which meant he probably received and read Summerall's letter near the final week he was at Bad Nauheim—Patton wrote in his diary,

> Admiral Lowry, the Navy member of the General Board, returned from a visit to Vienna. He was appalled at the utter destruction of the city and stated that in that portion of it under Russian control, the Russians are removing every movable article from the few remaining homes and that he personally saw a trainload of chairs, tables, bureaus, etc., en route to Russia and he also saw large numbers of Viennese from the Russian sector moving into the American and English sectors with nothing left but what they could carry on their backs. I advised him to spread the information when he gets home, as it is simply another evidence of the inevitable war with Russia and another evidence of our criminal folly in letting them take over any part of Western Europe.

By early December, Patton was making open arrangements to return home, had resolved his indecision about the future, and definitely was going to resign and speak out in what he indicated were going to be dramatic ways.[28]

The stage was set.

CHAPTER TWENTY-ONE

★ ★ ★ ★

ENIGMAS

No one can prove beyond a reasonable doubt that General Patton was assassinated—at least not currently with the evidence now available. Perhaps no one will ever be able to prove it, given the layers of secrecy and the propensity of government leaders and those in the clandestine world to destroy incriminating evidence. But a pretty good case could be made that Patton was murdered, or that at least one, if not many, attempts to murder him occurred, and a prosecutor probably could get an indictment for either. There are simply too many unanswered questions. Motives abound. The circumstances surrounding his accident and death are suspicious—in some particulars, highly so. And in the sixty-plus years since the general died, two credible witnesses—Bazata and Skubik—both in the clandestine world—have emerged from the murky World War II darkness to claim they were part of a hidden story involving Patton's death. Their witness is firsthand, not hearsay. What they say can be challenged, certainly, but cannot be summarily dismissed as has been done in the past by historians and the curious concerning other piecemeal and elusive rumors about the possibility of Patton having been assassinated.

Besides the two new witnesses, who, together, represent a much stronger indictment than either would alone, other circumstances indicate there is more to the story of why Patton died than is widely recognized.

All known reports at the scene of the December 9 accident, as well as investigations of it later, have vanished. If it were just a matter of one, or even two such records, one might easily think their disappearance is not out of the ordinary. Records get lost, misplaced, and accidentally destroyed. But the number of known, primary records about Patton's accident that are now missing is at least four, probably more. There could be even more we do not know about. Not a single one of the records known to be missing, according to numerous searches and official responses, can be found—only references to them survive. That suggests an intentional purge.

These known records include:[1]

1) "... [T]he official report of the accident from the 818 MP Battalion at Mannheim" referred to in a "10 Dec 45" memo "To: G-2" from Captain William R. Conklin, of the "7th Army, Western Military District, Public Relations Office."[2]

2) An "*informal probe*" launched by Patton's good friend, General Geoffrey Keyes, which Farago says included testimony by truck driver Robert L. Thompson that "could have been challenged in every one of his separate statements." (If Thompson's statements were written down, they, too, are missing.)

3) A *follow-up investigation* by the theater Provost Marshall mentioned in an "18 December 1945" memo by Seventh Army Chief of Staff, Brigadier General John M. Willems who himself was investigating why information about the accident was released to the press—a sign in itself of an initial cover-up.[3]

4) A documented *statement* given by Robert L. Thompson at the scene of the accident referred to in the December 18 memo by General Willems to have been taken by Lieutenant Hugh O. Layton of the military police.

5) The accident report by Lieutenant Peter K. Babalas, one of the MPs first on the scene.[4] Presumably, his report is the "official report" referred to in the Conklin memo above. But without either of the documents, nothing is certain.

6) Other reports and documents which surely would have been generated under normal conditions by various officials who are reported as being at the accident scene— such as the mysterious Lieutenant VanLandingham whom Woodring maintained in denying Babalas's presence at the scene, was the only investigator there.

What happened at the accident scene itself? Because of contradictory accounts and mysterious figures like Vanlandingham who have simply disappeared, the scene is still an enigma, and that includes how the accident itself occurred. No one disputes that the Thompson-driven truck abruptly turned without signal into the path of Patton's Cadillac—a seemingly incriminating act to begin with. But were the truck's occupants actually lying in wait for the Patton car before making the suspicious turn, as several of Woodring's accounts suggest?

What was Thompson doing there in the first place? That question has never been satisfactorily answered. Why was he supposedly whisked to London and away from questions—indeed, into total obscurity—immediately after the accident, as his friend and lawyer, Robert Delsordo, now discloses? What was the high-level concern which it would take to effect such an unusual airlift in ostensibly a nonfatal, essentially routine traffic accident? Patton was only injured, not dead. Thompson was a lowly T/5* truck driver, a "goofy" kid, as he was described at the scene, known for dealing in the black market and other shady practices. Why did authorities care? Why is there no record of that strange and unprecedented evacuation in Thompson's personnel file at the National Personnel Records Center in St. Louis? Why is nothing about the accident with General Patton mentioned at all? The records I obtained with help from his family show little more than name, rank, and serial number. Some of his records, of course, I was advised, were destroyed in the disastrous fire that ravaged the center in 1973.

What happened to Thompson's mysterious passengers? Where is Frank Krummer? *Who* was Frank Krummer? Is that a real name or a cover? Who and where is the third unnamed passenger? Both are mentioned as being in the truck with Thompson in the formerly classified Seventh Army PRO documents, as well as to a lesser degree in Farago's *Last Days*. Then they disappear. Were they also taken to London? One of them—it is not clear which—was described in the PRO documents as a "German civilian." It appears to be Krummer. What was a German civilian doing in an army truck?

---

*Technician 5th class.

Sergeant Scruce, part of the hunting caravan, is a further mystery. Gay, in his memoir, and others who have investigated the accident, such as Farago, state that it was only seconds after Scruce's jeep passed the Cadillac in order to take the lead that the accident occurred. Surely, at that minimal distance, he was aware of the crash right behind him and would have returned. He loved his hunting dogs like offspring, according to his daughter, and absolutely would have returned, she believes, solely out of concern for his dog alone. There are conflicting stories. Woodring, in one account, has Scruce crossing the railroad tracks just prior to the Cadillac having to stop, in which case he already would have been ahead of the Cadillac prior to its temporary delay at the railroad track. But then what did he do? Did he just drive on? Or did he pull over and wait, as would be expected of a sergeant charged with leading a four-star general to a destination? And if he went on, that meant the Cadillac's occupants knew the way and the notion that only Scruce knew is erroneous.

Such questions about Scruce occur because he, too, effectively disappears. He is only mentioned once after the accident, but not at the scene, nor afterwards in coverage of the accident and its aftermath. Lieutenant Hadden, Gay's aide-de-camp, presumably refers to Scruce in writing the following in a letter home on December 12: "Sunday afternoon [the day of the accident] I stayed at the house and was kept busy on the telephone. The driver of the car got back with the sergeant who was taking the Gens. hunting late in the afternoon and Col. Harkins, [Patton's] deputy chief of staff, and I talked to him to find out how the accident had happened. I don't know what the press reports said, but from all that I have heard about it, it was not our driver's fault. Gen. Gay was not hurt beyond a scraped knee and a wrenched wrist, which was fortunate."

That implies that Scruce did come back to the scene.

Where are the after-accident reports generated by interviewing him?

The information about Gay's wrist perhaps indicates that he was holding on to a safety strap in the car and that may have saved him from serious injury. In fact, Dr. Gerald Kent, who attended Patton and Gay at the hospital that day, wrote that is what happened.[5] But no more information about Scruce. He is a mystery. And I doubt if there ever will be more beyond what I was able to get from his military records which, like Thompson's, were damaged in the 1973 fire at the records center in St. Louis. One bright spot is that as a result of this story, Scruce's daughter, traumatically deprived of her father all her life, has been united with his family, including cousins, aunts, and uncles. She had no idea they had even existed. But their response when she visited them for the first time in 2007 was more of the same. Despite seeing him many times after the war, they knew nothing of Joe Scruce's involvement in the Patton accident. "I just don't think Joe ever told anyone of that fateful day," she wrote to me.

That is strange. One would think that the story would have been one of the highlights of his career—something for a career soldier, a Bronze Service Star awardee, a noncommissioned immigrant who served his new country so well to repeat, reflect upon, and be quoted about. Yet he kept it to himself. Some might say he kept it hidden. Why? He was not the silent type, according to his daughter. He was the opposite. Was he simply doing what was required of the clandestine, keeping silence about operations? Was he involved in a plot, however peripherally? He was there and had what could be crucial knowledge. At the very least, if I was an investigating officer that fateful day, I would have wanted to know what he had seen of the strange accident, if he remembered the truck waiting on the side of the road as he passed by—if that, in fact, is what happened. Where had he gone if he drove on? But he is never mentioned, at least with his name spelled correctly, except by Gay. And authors like Farago, who obviously did not talk to him, but got his name wrong from whatever source or sources they used, all but insured his anonymity after Patton's death as subsequent historians and researchers followed their lead and made the same mistake.

On the surface, Patton's death in the hospital seems natural. He had a broken neck, seldom an illness with a good prognosis. He died of complications from embolism, a danger to patients prone and immobile. He had suffered the same complication in a long hospital stay in 1937 (but recovered). Mysteriously, just before he died, he was doing so well that his doctors had decided he could go home to the states. Although that was a long and arduous trip in those days, travel arrangements were being made. Farago wrote, "[Patton's] progress became even more pronounced on December 18....Patton amazed his doctors with his basic health. Even under the enormous burden of his condition, his vital organs continued to function almost perfectly....Captain [Dr.] Kent said, 'The heart tones were good...no murmurs were audible. His blood pressure was 108 over 70'...was it just one of those typical Patton miracles?"[6]

Then came the sudden attack. He died alone. No autopsy was performed. But Mrs. Patton must have had second thoughts because her granddaughter, Helen Totten, an adult now, told Oliver North's *War Stories* that her grandmother hired detectives to investigate his death.[7] They found nothing, she said, which is not surprising given the levels of secrecy and deception that must have been used at that time to cover up any plot. What had caused General Patton to request a guard outside his room, as reported in early stories about his hospitalization? The reason was never explained—just that "he'd heard something he didn't like." What had he heard? What about the mysterious Russian colonel Mrs. Totten said approached her while she was abroad, claiming efforts had been made to induce pneumonia? She dismissed it on *War Stories*. Ultimately, it was the failure of Patton's lungs from embolism that killed him.

Curious, too, was something at the end of Dr. Spurling's long memoir about caring for Patton at the hospital—something I had missed at a first reading focused on Patton's condition: "General Marshall in Washington requested that a confidential medical report be sent to him daily. These confidential bulletins always told the stark truth and I am sure that there was never any question in Washington but what [sic] General Patton was done for. I always sent a copy of these reports to the Surgeon General of the Army." Spurling was sending back secret reports? Why? Was this just confidentiality to protect Patton's privacy? Or was there more to it than Spurling understood? The in-house medical reports were not released to the public. Would not those have sufficed to keep concerned colleagues like Marshall informed? Marshall, to put it mildly, in the words of one obituary writer, was a Patton "detractor."[8] It is hard to believe he was monitoring the situation out of personal concern. He was notoriously cool and distant toward his colleagues—and others, for that matter, save his family. Patton was certainly, after the accident, written off as a potential field general for military action. But he had already been written off *before* the accident. Basically, in Marshall's eyes, he was crazy. So why the clandestine reports? Neither Marshall nor Eisenhower attended Patton's funeral, nor did Truman, who did not care for Patton either.[9] Patton reportedly specifically asked his wife to keep Eisenhower's Beetle Smith from attending his funeral, although newspaper reports indicate Smith might have been there.

The Cadillac limousine in which Patton was injured is, in all this, a witness for the prosecution, albeit a silent, unfortunately inaccessible one. For decades, the car, repaired, was thought to be on display at the Patton Museum at Fort Knox, Kentucky. But Cadillac's expert determined along with obvious signs of fraud, including the crude obliteration of its identifying VIN number, that the car is a fake. It will never yield crucial answers. Why was this done? Was the filing down of the VIN and phony workmanship tags on the car at Fort Knox just to facilitate a Black Market swap? Or was it part of an assassination plot in order to get rid of crucial evidence? The real car might have answered key questions. How was Patton injured? Not only how had his neck been broken, but how had he gotten such a vicious gash on his face, the exact nature of which is still debatable? Did it start at the nose and rip a V-like patch of bone-exposing skin up to the top of the head? Or had it started on the top and ripped downward? The nature of his wound has some bearing on whether he might have been shot by a non-lethal object like Douglas Bazata claims.

The Soviets are among the most elusive part of this story. If Patton was murdered, it was most likely because he posed a political threat to the Soviets, as well as a personal and professional threat to some in his own camp who might therefore have participated or, just as easily, looked the other way. He also was hated by some in authority in the U.S. for his indiscretion and his desire for war with the Soviets, which very well could have sparked World War III. Given what is now known about NKVD-OSS cooperation and America's manipulation, if not near domination, by Stalin during the war and the U.S. administration's Left-led belief that the communist dictator's favor was essential for a peaceful and prosperous postwar world, it is not hard to imagine such factors combining to hatch a plot whose aims could morph from being purely non-lethal "Stop Patton" into a begrudging secret order for his "elimination."

Such an assassination scenario, of course, is speculation based on political and military realities from the still-emerging story of World War II. In the past, such speculation could not be substantiated beyond rumor. But now, in addition to the mysteries and questions that have emerged from studying Patton's accident and death—something not adequately done by prior historians—two members of the clandestine world, Bazata and Skubik, have added personal witness to the scenario. They are not kooks. Their testimony is not rumor. Bazata was at the heart of the clandestine assassination world during the war, and he was in Germany near Patton in the occupation. Skubik, while more policeman than undercover operative, worked for what could be called, in effect, the military's covert FBI—the CIC—during the war and in Germany when Patton died.

Both were there at the crucial time.

Bazata, after twenty-two years at the Mumm Estate and Baron Mumm's suicide, exited Europe abruptly around 1970,* some say under suspicious circumstances. Given the life he had led as a mercenary, head of his secret "Co-Op," and a flamboyant artist patronized by jet-setting European high society, rumors, hazy and impossible to check, were plenty. He and Marie-Pierre flew to Saigon to stay with, among others, William Colby, then a CIA official running the infamous "Phoenix" assassination program of counter-insurgency against the Viet Cong. He and Colby, who would soon head the CIA, had been Jedburghs together. Bazata's

---

*His papers and other documents show several dates within that time frame.

stated reason for the trip was to study Vietnamese art, specifically "lacquers," an ancient Asian technique using thick tree sap for paint. "The list of owners of [Bazata's] paintings reads like the Almanach de Gotha [royalty list], barons and princes galore," wrote Joy Billington, who profiled him later in Washington, D.C. Now he wanted to try a new way of painting, one he said was harder.[10] They spent some six months in Vietnam, Bazata spending time studying with local artists and playing a lot of poker at which he was said to be very good. But he also participated in Phoenix, which might also have had something to do with his going there. Phoenix was, in essence, a terror program, designed to counter Viet Cong insurgency. Later congressional hearings revealed that between 10,000 and 40,000 Vietnamese had died under the program. Suspected Viet Cong, for instance, were thrown alive from helicopters. "I participated lightly," Bazata told me. But he became "disgusted. It was kill, kill, kill. How could they tell who was guilty and who was innocent?" It was the beginning of a rift between Colby and him that never healed.

By the time he and Marie-Pierre left Vietnam, Bazata knew his days as a field-operating mercenary were over. The body can only take so much. He had lost an edge, although he still looked and seemed strong. He decided to come home and collect his due— what had been promised him, he said, by Donovan and others after the war who had told him that if he performed for them, he would be rewarded—a cushy job, good pay, no sweat. But it did not happen. Not only did it not happen, he was basically shunned. Who are you, he said upstarts at the agency asked when he tried to get a job there. When he told what he could of his past, they said prove it. Show us the records, which, of course, were mostly non-existent. Agents he had worked with were largely gone, retired, not inclined nor able to help. The agency, heavily hit by congressional and public outcry against intelligence abuses in the wake of President Kennedy's assassination, had begun purging operatives like himself and turning toward technology, such as satellites, for spying. Men like Colby, who could have helped, had lost their clout. Even if he had not, he and Colby were, by then, estranged, although they continued a tenuous relationship based on their OSS days. For all practical purposes, Bazata was out in the cold.

After a short, failed venture in Pennsylvania, he apparently began to reestablish some contacts, because he wrote of being offered jobs in "the clandestinity," which he refused. Probably, they demanded too much physically. However, he apparently accepted from the same people a job running a combination bird farm and hunting preserve in rural Maryland woods. It may have been a CIA-connected safe house because he wrote persons "under suspicion and surveillance" were involved. "Sportsmen" came to hunt and eat the birds. In June 1975, *Esquire* magazine featured him along with five other clandestines in a short piece titled "Declassified: Six Good Spies." A picture showed him looking hard-assed in front of a peacock, the caption reading, "PRESENT SITUATION: artist. Lives outside Washington, D.C. INTELLIGENCE DATA: Scored highest officer rating in the history of Fort Benning, higher than MacArthur and Eisenhower." That may have been a reference to his historic marksmanship, but he also claimed high scores in written tests. While at the farm, he said, there were attempts on his life because of what he knew. They continued for years, but he gave few details other than to say they were "amateurish" and he handled all of them. Much later, Marie-Pierre described one. She believed it was around 1975. "The peacocks were very good guard animals," she said. They would become noisy at the first sign of intruders. One night, late, the birds started making a ruckus. She turned on the light in their bedroom. Baz shouted to shut it off. As soon as she did, shots crashed through the window. Bazata had a pistol in his night stand. "He ran out and fired," returning shortly. Before she could inquire, he said "don't ask." She did not. She believed not knowing was for her own good.

Bazata and Marie-Pierre struggled. Money was scarce. Eventually his service-related wounds forced him to seek medical disability from the government. He had arthritis, stab and gunshot wounds that were giving him problems, a bad eye, mangled feet, the horrible groin wound, and an aching back and spine from so many parachute jumps. He even had "hitman anguish" he wrote, presumably jokingly, to one doctor. It had all occurred in service to his country. But when he went to the VA, they gave him the same treatment the CIA had. Where's the proof? He asked if he could sign an affidavit or take a lie detector test. No, they said. They had to have official records of which, again, in most cases, there were none. The work had been secret. No records had been kept. Their denials infuriated him. He spent two years fighting the VA. He had to write colleagues around the world asking them to supply letters attesting to his injuries and how he had gotten them. It was a bureaucratic nightmare for one who detested bureaucrats. In a final confrontation, he had to go before a three-doctor Board of Veterans Appeals. "Let me tell you of my entire body, part by part," he wrote in jesting preparation. I have the 54-page transcript of the session. In the end, they gave him 100 percent disability benefits.

It was immediately following this ordeal, which left him embittered, that Bazata made the public announcement at the OSS dinner that he had been asked by Donovan to kill Patton. Colby and other OSSers had been at the same table when he said it to reporter Joy Billington. He figured that would get some attention.

His disclosure led to the *Spotlight* articles, for which he was paid something in the neighborhood of $3,000, according to copies of checks I have seen. Did he need the money? Yes. Was that why he did it? Perhaps, but it is misleading to say that. He had been looking for a way to tell the story for years, urged on by what he thought was his own betrayal and by other World War II secrets that were being revealed. The OSS dinner came when he felt he could wait no more. He never asked me for money. Not once. Was it conscience? Anger? Duty? A little of all three, in my opinion.

He still could be lying. Some of his former Jedburgh friends do not believe him, but even they say he was not a liar and acknowledge that they themselves have no way of knowing the truth.

His diaries, for the most part, support his verbal claims. They provide volumes of agonized discussion of his involvement in the Patton plot. "I killed him. This is the truth....Why am I so evil?" On and on. I do not believe the diaries were written for somebody to find. Even to himself, he wrote in code. They are hard to interpret. There are notations which cause me to wonder. Was he, in writing them, practicing to pull the wool over someone's eyes? It is a possibility, but I do not think so. The diaries are not written as practice or sprucing up arguments. On the whole, they constitute a deeply remorseful confession and examination of a human life spent taking other human life, sprinkled with reluctant pride at how well he had done it. I think I was lucky, in terms of his willingness to talk, by coming to Bazata when I did when he was sick and his guard was down, his entire personality subdued. A year or two earlier, certainly before he had made his startling announcement, all I would have gotten would have been triple talk, or a noncommittal stare—if not intimidation. He never would have shown me those diaries. They are very private, very intimate. Only his stroke, in my opinion, loosed the bonds.

Impressive, I think, are the accounts Bazata wrote of the meetings he had with Donovan. They are very detailed and ring true, at least to me. Take the luncheon at London's Claridge Hotel: "He seemed very reticent and embarrassed," he wrote of Donovan. "I put him easy at once: with: 'General, Sir, you have an additional mission for me! You can trust me totally!'... 'Thank you, Douglas, I do indeed have a problem that we all must settle. It is the extreme disobedience of Gen. Geo. P. and his very very serious disregard of orders for the common cause.... He grows more violent daily and surely must be ill....'" Bazata did not talk like that. Or write like that. He usually wrote in complicated, almost undecipherable bursts. But someone like Donovan, broaching such a volatile subject as possibly assassinating one of their own—one so high up—may very well have talked like that. To me, it sounds like Bazata was recalling what he had lived. And Donovan's arguments for having to do away with Patton, as Bazata relates, follow what I have come to learn actually happened. They did think Patton was crazy. They did think he was out of control and resented him for it. They sincerely thought him a danger to postwar peace and their own pro-Soviet aims.

Bazata began the diaries when he first returned to the U.S. in the early 1970s. By the early 1980s, when President Reagan came to power, he went to work for Reagan's secretary of the Navy, John Lehman, whom he had met and impressed at parties held by former OSSers. Lehman told the FBI when they investigated Bazata for the government job* that he had first heard of Bazata from his cousin, Princess Grace Kelly of Monaco, who, because of his painting, talked about Bazata a lot. (Bazata had served under a

---

*Customary for someone applying for his position.

"Col. John Lehman" in American intelligence in the immediate post-war period, according to his letters, but it is not clear if the former secretary of the navy was related.) In a 1981 letter to Lyn Nofziger, assistant to President Reagan for White House Political Affairs, Lehman wrote, "During the course of the Reagan-Bush campaign [Bazata] was of invaluable assistance to the Reagan Defense and Foreign Policy Task Force." In effect, he became a close aide to Lehman, advising on anti-terrorism measures long before such U.S. activities became center stage following the September 11, 2001 attacks. Bazata had urged the formation of an aggressive anti-terrorist force. Unfortunately, he had little success. Also, because of his experience with the VA, he worked on Veterans Affairs issues under Lehman. Following his time with the Navy secretary, he served at the Department of Energy until his resignation in 1989 when the first Bush administration came in with new appointments.

If there is a chink in Bazata's story, it is the claim that he snuck up on the Cadillac while Patton and the others were examining the Roman ruins and inserted something in the mechanism of the Cadillac's back window to jam it so it would remain open for a shot when the accident was staged. If he had been tailing Patton, possibly even knew of Patton's intention to view the ruins, as General Gay's aide, Lieutenant Hadden, apparently did, he could have approached the car. But was the car unoccupied and did it continue on from the ruins with the window at least partially open in cold weather? These are hard questions to answer in favor of Bazata's account. General Gay probably walked up the snow-covered mountain with Patton to see the ruins, but Woodring, as most general's drivers would, most likely stayed in the car, which, in fact, is what Woodring told author D. A. Lande.[11] But did he stay in the car the whole time? For instance, might he have stepped out to relieve himself or wandered away somewhat just to break the monotony as he waited? If, in fact, he did not go with them to the ruins, how long did he have to wait? (Gay, in his memoir, says "some forty minutes.") They had to hike up a mountain and then inspect the castle, which probably was a lengthy trek. The entire trip from Bad Nauheim to Mannheim was approximately sixty-five miles—probably a little over an hour, assuming they drove straight through and with Woodring's and Patton's propensity for speed.[12] Since the accident happened at 11:45 a.m., and they left between 8:00 a.m. or 9:00 a.m., they could have been at the ruins for an hour or two. That is a long time to just sit and wait, even if it is cold. And since Lande's book was published in 2002, Woodring's recollection of not accompanying them was decades, if not half a century, removed. As Lieutenant Hadden's recollections prove, it is impossible to know for sure what happened there.

Patton, according to most accounts,[13] got in the front seat of the car for the next leg of the journey when they returned from the ruins. His boots were wet and the heater was up front. But maybe he did so because the back window was down, whether fully or partially.* Pictures of the car at the accident scene and after do not show the back window on the right side where Patton was sitting. It is impossible to tell whether the window was closed, open, or even partially open. When the Cadillac reached the outskirts of Mannheim, most accounts say they met Scruce at a checkpoint, and because Scruce's dog was cold, Patton got back in the right rear seat so the dog could be near the heater. If Scruce was part of a plot, one of his assignments might have been to get Patton to move to the rear because of the dog and thus be vulnerable to a shot.

---

*Bazata never clarified.

But Bazata said he tampered with the window. And before talking with me, he told the *Spotlight* that the shooter—not then identified as himself—had done the same. Given the now mounting indications of foul play and the varying accounts of what happened, who is to say he did not? That Bazata could make a shot into the car through an open window is not that hard to believe, given Bazata's world-class marksmanship. President Kennedy was a moving target at much greater range. With the way it is described, a professional shooter could have made the shot—with luck. And luck is part of any clandestine plot. If Patton was looking out even a half open window, a non-penetrating projectile such as Bazata describes could have caused the V-shaped injury to Patton's face and scalp, broken his neck, and pushed him onto Gay.

Other theories are just that—speculation. Nobody saw what actually happened. Patton himself, in the confusion of the accident, could have thought the injury was from something he hit in the car. He did not remember even whether he had been knocked unconscious or not, the shock of what had happened had been so great. And even if, for the sake of argument, we assume Bazata was lying, or confusing facts—at least in his talks to me because of his strokes—there is evidence enough to warrant a re-examination of what happened on that fateful December 9.

That evidence includes the credible witness of American CIC agent, Stephen J. Skubik, whose job it was to use Eastern European sources. He claimed that he uncovered an OSS-NKVD plot to assassinate Patton, and his efforts to stop the plot were thwarted by OSS officers, especially William Donovan, head of the OSS. Under Donovan's leadership, the OSS was documented to have been colluding with the NKVD. Not once, not twice, but three times, Skubik says he was warned by Ukrainians, who had spies in the NKVD, that Patton was marked for death by its assassins. These were no ordinary Ukrainians, but leaders of the Ukrainian resistance to communism. Stepan Bandera, for example, was deemed an asset, along with those he led, and, by 1946, he became an accepted part of the United States' spy network trying to penetrate the Soviet Union. Skubik was trained in and charged with evaluating such claims—and he believed them.

Second, there are too many missing documents. All pertinent records regarding Patton's strange auto accident on December 9, 1945 cannot be found and were most probably purged from U.S. files. At least five crucial records, including the official accident report, along with witness interrogations and follow-up investigations which were known to have existed, have disappeared.

Third, there is substantial evidence of malicious intent in what we do know of Patton's accident. Woodring repeatedly gave witness that, as he left the railroad tracks just prior to the accident, he saw the truck driven by Thompson waiting on the side of the road up ahead of him. It did not pull out and begin its journey toward him until he was in sight. And its trajectory ended, without signal, in the sudden swerve which caused the accident. His description indicates that the truck may have been lying in wait for Patton's car.

Fourth, the car alleged to be the one Patton was riding in when injured, which is at the Patton museum in Kentucky, has been proven to be a disguised and rebuilt replica by no less than Cadillac's vintage model expert. The museum purchased the car on the understanding that it was Patton's. What they did not know was that its identifying numbers were scratched out and misleading labels attached, which give rise to the suspicion that the fake was created to eliminate physical evidence.

Fifth, crucial witnesses and principals in the accident were allowed to disappear without adequate investigation. Those who were never sufficiently interrogated include Robert L. Thompson, driver of the truck which caused the crash, one or two passengers reported to have been with him in the truck in violation of army regulations, and Sergeant Joseph L. Scruce, an elusive member of the hunting party. As witnesses, all subsequently vanished—as did several military officials, like Lieutenant Vanlandingham, who, after he was mysteriously mentioned as being at the accident, never again surfaced, even in death.

Sixth, Patton had escaped injury in no less than three earlier accidents in the months prior to the one that claimed his life. All three occurred under suspicious circumstances. They began as he became increasingly more belligerent to the Soviets and attacked or undercut by his own press and superiors. The most suspicious "accident" occurred April 20, 1945, when the small Piper Cub aircraft Patton was traveling in was attacked by a supposedly rookie Polish Spitfire pilot, who mistook the clearly-marked Piper Cub for a Nazi warplane. He made repeated attacks as other Spitfires circled ominously. At that time, Poland was under Soviet domination. As the Soviets were known to use local assassins in their plots, and official records are missing, it seems likely that this was a failed assassination attempt that was foiled only by the quick action of Patton's pilot. The other two near-accidents occurred as Patton was driving—just as he was on December 9. Records on all three are missing.

There was a definite "Stop Patton" effort, tactics in which ranged from actually withholding his gas during his march toward Germany to attempting to have him surreptitiously observed in order to declare him insane. This effort could have been driven in large part by the personal ambitions of individuals—such as Eisenhower—or anyone else who stood to suffer from the revelation of any of the many secrets Patton undoubtedly knew from his wartime experience and high position. And he certainly did not hesitate to speak his mind or act on his own personal convictions—consequences be damned. That tendency invoked anger from the Soviets to their allies, the American hierarchy, who would eventually appease their way into the Cold War. It also marked him as a dangerous renegade who would not hesitate to use former Nazi troops in an attack on Russia.

Least speculative of all is the witness of recorded former OSS assassin Douglas Bazata. His claim to have been given the order to assassinate Patton, while currently unable to be proven, held up under a lie-detector test and is not contradicted by records of Patton's accident or subsequent death.

The evidence that something sinister happened multiplies.

★ ★ ★ ★

EPITAPH

The final days of the OSS were chaotic but lingering. While the intelligence organization was officially disbanded by President Truman in October 1945,[1] it continued to unofficially function in various places like Germany almost through the rest of the year as members transitioned to the official replacement organization, the Strategic Services Unit (SSU), and other government groups, such as the State Department's Research and Intelligence service. That transition did not happen overnight. In the midst of the slow death was Donovan, still exerting influence and power, desperate to revive his hopes of heading the eventual intelligence agency which he knew would emerge, which eventually became the CIA several years later. In that regard, he was keeping ties with agents, like Bazata and others, many of whom would be in the CIA, making secret deals to advise, help, and hopefully eventually lead those who would transition to the larger organization.

Among Donovan's last official war-connected efforts were those made in Germany while he helped with the preparation for war crimes trials at Nuremberg. He arrived at OSS headquarters near Berlin on October 2* and stayed in Germany at least through November.[2] His FBI report lists him arriving back in New York from Nuremberg on December 17, a week after Patton's accident.[3] He had flown to London prior to arriving in Berlin with British spy William Stephenson, according to National Archives documents.[4] So he was in a position to have met with Bazata in both London and Germany, as Bazata claims, although it has never been clear about exactly when the meetings took place. By the time he returned from Germany, after quitting the Nuremberg prosecution team over policy differences, Donovan was being "attacked from almost every quarter," according to historian E. H. Cookridge, and despite support from his friend Dwight Eisenhower (who, by then, had succeeded General Marshall as U.S. military chief of staff), "went into retirement, a bitterly disappointed man."[5]

Exactly what transpired in the furtive dealings of this covert man is one of the most hidden secrets of World War II and its immediate aftermath. It would be a monumental task, if it is even possible, to track his moves through extant records. Only vague references, events peripheral to his activities which can be dated, and various arrivals and departures from of his registered travel arrangements, are available. He kept his movements intentionally undisclosed. When the demise of the OSS was certain, Donovan and his personal administrative aide, young Lieutenant Edwin Putzell, a member of Donovan's law firm before the war, spent three nights frantically microfilming files and burning others outright. A National Archives publication about the purge says, "So

---

*According to Richard Dunlop, one of his biographers.

hastily did they work that their palm and finger prints appear on many of the [microfilm] frames." Persico wrote that Putzell was Donovan's trusted courier to President Roosevelt. Putzell said he would deliver Donovan's messages to FDR in a "locked leather briefcase with a strap that I wound around my wrist."[6] But FDR never gave Putzell messages to take back.

The documents that survived on microfilm stayed hidden until 1980, according to the National Archives, when a close Donovan associate gave them to Anthony Cave Brown for use in writing his Donovan biography, *The Last Hero*. They then became public. But the considerable amount of records that were outright destroyed in that three-day frenzy are lost forever.*

In addition to losing the OSS and not being given the directorship of the CIA, which biographer Brown says was one of the tragedies of his life,** Donovan's immediate post-war troubles quickly mounted around his alleged sympathies for communists, a charge his Republican background would seem to belie. But as his wartime record unfolded in 1946, his toleration of, if not collaboration with, communists brought him considerable grief. He had always been more of an opportunist than an ideologue. Charges of "fronting" for post-war Left-wing organizations, such as the American Institute of International Information, were leveled. He was accused of complicity in the "Amerasia" scandal, one of the first big anti-communist flaps following the war.[7] It did not help when his assistant Duncan Lee was accused of being a Soviet spy and fled. And when Donovan was called before a

---

*Some records may have survived the purge with Putzell. According to an OSS source I talked with, Putzell burned all of his papers just before he died in 2003. Their content, whether Putzell's or from the original purge, will never be known either.
**He had also lost a child earlier.

congressional committee investigating communists in the OSS, he lied about the backgrounds of four communist party members he had hired, according to Library of Congress historian John Earl Haynes and Emory University professor Harvey Klehr.[8] Admiral Roscoe Hillenkoetter, first director of the CIA, accused Donovan of being "a traitor to his country."[9] Others Donovan thought were in his camp followed suit and disowned him.

The forces that caused this vilification were not clear. Was it just a backlash from the opportunistic Donovan's "deal with the devil" attitude in an effort to help win World War II, or did the scorn, which included Truman's rebuff and dislike, indicate secret knowledge by high-placed officials of something damning but not revealed? In 1983, *Washington Post* writer Thomas O'Toole wrote, "Donovan was inclined to move boldly, even recklessly, in grasping what he felt to be the big chance."[10] It was never clear just how far he had gone. When Senator Joseph McCarthy began citing numbers of "Reds" in the government in the post-war "Red Scare," Donovan sided with those attacking the senator, which won him some favor with the Left but further alienated him from the Right. It was not until the early 1950s that he again began to be identified as a Right-leaning, anti-communist Republican. By then it was too late to revive his earlier ambitions to serve in the new intelligence agency with any hope of success. Truman, who had by then seen the truth about Soviet aims and was beginning to become an anti-communist himself, was long done with him. Donovan probably had influence in the CIA, maybe even worked for it unofficially, according to biographer Brown.[11] But he was politically weak and in debt, and the period began his decline.

In 1953, newly elected President Eisenhower, probably partly as a consolation to his ambitious friend, appointed Donovan U.S. ambassador to Thailand, a Southeast Asian nation bordering Vietnam with communist insurgents all through the region. William J. van-den Heuvel, later an assistant U.S. attorney with Robert Kennedy and deputy ambassador to the United Nations, was Donovan's assistant. In a diary vanden Heuvel kept, he recorded a slow deterioration of his boss. At first, well-experienced in insurgency, Donovan threw himself enthusiastically into the job. But it was a losing battle. In 1954, the U.S.-backed French were overrun in Vietnam at Dien Bien Phu in the next big defeat for the West following the fall of China to communists. The victors, known as the Viet Minh, were later to become the Viet Cong. As months went by, vanden Heuvel began having disheartening clashes with the ambassador. "He suffers from psychotic meglomania which afflicts us all . . . but his is of the malignant variety." One morning, he records, they disagreed and Donovan began hurling "goddamns" at him. "I am willing to serve him in every capacity, to do without question the work he wants done, but to be the victim of his temper and ego and enormous conceit is not part of the task." Run-ins with Donovan's "bad mood" increased, and vanden Heuvel considered leaving, even though he felt indebted to Donovan for a "fantastic opportunity. . . . It was the phoniness, the enormous conceit veiled in humility, the attack on virtually everyone in authority while pointing out his correctness over all these years." Mistakes made in World War II were apparently taking their toll. Was there something grating on his conscience? One can only speculate. He was America's first superspy and, according to Eisenhower, his final real backer, "the last great hero."

Donovan spent just one year in Thailand. When he went home, the tide of communist revolution in Southeast Asia was larger than when he had arrived. In 1957, he had a series of strokes and was confined to a nursing home, in need of constant care. He died in 1959, and whatever secrets he had went with him.

★ ★ ★

Fred Ayer, Jr., Patton's FBI agent nephew, immediately suspected murder when he learned of his uncle's accident. "Those communist sons of bitches killed him," he wrote he blurted upon receiving the news. Later, however, he had second thoughts. "One does not hit a car carrying the intended victim of assassination with a truck at low speed and from an angle. Nor does one choose a second vehicle as a murder weapon.... Also, I was told that the driver of the truck in question felt such deep remorse that he later attempted to commit suicide."[12] But Thompson's possible suicide attempt, if that occurred, could be viewed a different way—that he was distraught over having been part of a monstrous plot.

However, as noted in Chapter 13, the NKVD favored assassination-by-truck. Theodore Romzha, the canonized bishop killed by NKVD thugs in 1947, was hit by a Soviet truck being used as a weapon of assassination. And just as pertinently, he was taken, like Patton, injured—because the assassination was botched—to a hospital where he was poisoned by an NKVD assassin-nurse.[13] And that was not the first time the NKVD killed in a hospital. Stalin, according to his personal interpreter, Valentin M. Berezhkov, used traffic "accident" as a murder weapon. He had a truck stationed around a sharp curve on a mountain road, knowing that former Russian Ambassador to the U.S., Maxim Litvinov, whom he wanted eliminated, would be recklessly traveling the road. Litvinov, as planned, roared into the truck and was killed. Joe Lagattuta, an OSS officer in Europe at the time of Patton's demise and friend of Bazata, said he was nearly killed right after the war by a German truck purposely ramming his jeep and knocking him into a ravine. At the hospital, he said, Bazata, who quickly arrived and worried for his friend, asked him, "Shall I kill someone?"[14]

Maneuvering a potential victim into a hospital and killing him there—usually because of botched first attempts—was not a rare occurrence for NKVD assassins. They had a laboratory that specialized in undetectable poisons which induced natural causes of death like embolism. Skubik says Pavel Sudoplatov, NKVD head of assassinations at that time, was in Germany when Patton had his accident and died. The area, according to documents, was crawling with NKVD spies, who, in that very December, were communicating with great urgency about a secret event that U.S. military intelligence—rival to the OSS—tried with no success to decipher. While the U.S. was withdrawing troops, then, Stalin was gearing for war, which he, like Patton, believed imminent. As E. H. Cookridge, a British political journalist and wartime intelligence agent, notes, "Stalin had said at the Red Army's first victory parade, 'We are watching the plans of the capitalist reactionaries in London and Washington who are hatching plans for a war... against our socialist motherland. Constant vigilance is needed to protect the strength of our armed forces who may be called upon to smash a new...imperialist aggression.'"[15]

Retired Air Force Lieutenant General George E. Stratemeyer, a Patton contemporary, was so convinced that Patton had been murdered and that he, espousing that view, might suffer the same fate, that he wrote a letter to the FBI stating that they were not to believe it if he was found dead by his own hand. Stratemeyer, a 1915 graduate of West Point who had leadership jobs in World War II and Korea, wrote in 1960, "We have always been suspicious" of Patton's death, as well as of other anti-Soviet American officials, such as Secretary of Defense James Forrestal, who died in an apparent suicide under mysterious circumstance in 1949. "We have notified our lawyer that we have no intention of committing suicide. That if we are found dead under peculiar circumstances or should disappear, we want him to insist upon a thorough investigation."[16] Patton's own wife was not sure he had not been assassinated—as evidenced by her hiring detectives to investigate the matter.

Patton's accident and death is a bona fide mystery and it is time that fact is acknowledged. But someone like me can only scratch the surface. An official investigation should be launched, because if Patton was murdered, it is not only important history, but it is at the heart of a significant moral question. Should assassination be used by governments or leaders of governments to arbitrarily impose their will? If Patton was assassinated, he was not only the first major victim of the Cold War, but also of a World War II policy of assassinating enemy leaders that continued after the war and has included Mossadegh in Iran, Allende in Chile, and Diem in Vietnam—not to mention its use by nations like the former Soviet Union, now Russia, as shown by the recent murder of a Russian journalist* that has been tied to the KGB.

Ironically—or perhaps significantly—Eisenhower, who has to be examined closely in regard to Patton's fate, was probably one of the first practitioners of the World War II assassination policy by reputedly authorizing the murder of the Vichy French leader Darlan. Additionally, "President Eisenhower authorized the first CIA attempt on a [peacetime] foreign leader's life," according to Joseph J. Trento in *The Secret History of the CIA*.[17] That leader was Red China's Chou En-lai. Eisenhower is also alleged to have authorized the assassination of Cuba's Fidel Castro, and was president when the CIA reportedly conspired unsuccessfully to assassinate Congo's Patrice Lumumba.[18] Eisenhower's public image has been mostly that of a strong and kindly grandfather. But he was different than that. It was Ike who imposed—Patton enemies would say with good reason—starvation on German

---

*Investigative journalist Anna Politkovskaya was murdered in Moscow in 2006.

POWs during the occupation (a policy Patton opposed) and forced the repatriation of large numbers of Soviet subjects despite certain death and torture. He and Marshall tried to have many of their records destroyed, according to David Irving in *The War Between the Generals*.[19] He was also not above lying in a memo to cover himself, as when there was "inquiry" into "why the Ardennes [Battle of the Bulge] region had been so thinly defended."[20]

Eisenhower was "Machiavellian," wrote *U.S. News & World Report*'s Michael Barone in a review of *Harry & Ike*. "He violated the rules of personal morality for what he regarded, reasonably, as the good of the state .... He proceeded very much less than straightforwardly." He was "misleading and duplicitous... Truman was appalled that Eisenhower made appearances with Senators William Jenner and Joseph McCarthy—who had harshly criticized General George Marshall—and omitted from his speech in Wisconsin lines praising Marshall."[21] Eisenhower strangely found Patton's loyalty to him a weakness rather than a strength and bragged to Marshall of exploiting it, as he did many times when he relied on Patton to get him out of battlefield jams. Dr. Charles B. Odom, Patton's personal physician during the war and a noted New Orleans doctor following it, wrote, "If Patton had lived to write his book, one wonders whether Eisenhower would even have been nominated, much less elected President of the United States."[22] As it was, Patton's book that came out posthumously, *War as I Knew It*, was tamed by editing and omission, as were his diaries.*

---

*The originals were only seen by a few, such as his wife, who is dead. Although the Library of Congress has copies of the original penned pages up to March 24, 1945, they do not have originals after that. When I asked Daun van Ee of the library's staff where the later originals were, he said, "That's all we got.. ...The family has the originals and donors always withhold so we do not know what has been taken out or covered up."

Does that mean Eisenhower murdered Patton? Of course not. Eisenhower was human and had flaws like anyone else. He was a great diplomat, had a decisive hand in the European victory, and served America well for two terms as president in the 1950s. But no one with motive, given the evidence already known, should be beyond suspicion, especially when the circumstances of that time are taken into account. The world had just emerged from the worst war in history. The greatest fear was another war. Those in power in the West were determined to make the peace work. Death and dying, however, was everywhere in Europe. All the military forces were used to it—and not adverse to using it for their own purposes. Assassination was a convenient way of dealing with problems with no easy solution. The OSS used it. The NKVD used it. So did every clandestine service at work in post-war Europe. Patton was threatening to plunge the world into World War III. Even well-meaning, reasonable men shuddered at the thought of what the renegade general—one who had continually disobeyed orders and had demonstrated he was capable of acting on his beliefs—could do. And Patton, especially, was feared and hated. There was a vengeful element in the U.S. against him—not to mention Russian motive. It would not be hard for even good men to contemplate a final solution—as long as there was deniability—and turn the other way.

The possibility of another war alone would have been reason enough. The stakes were that high. The mounting complaints about Patton by the Russians would have given the situation urgency. Germany was a giant stage in 1945—a turning point for the world. Which way would it go? The Russians were paranoid and took matters into their own hands. As for America, early on, statements about Patton like Marshall's, "He needs a brake to slow him down," certainly furthered, if not initiated, the "Stop

Patton" movement.[23] Donovan, untethered, reporting only to the president and those he chose, would have become involved as the movement snowballed, with Patton making more enemies, angering higher-ups as he triumphed, slapped, disobeyed, and boldly spoke his mind through North Africa, Sicily, England, France, and Germany. Then, in the occupation, he became really dangerous. What would he do? What about when he returned home? He was admired. He could easily win public office. Add Donovan's turmoil at war's end and the pieces are there for a secret deal, a final solution. Such plots are not written down. The orders—"suggestions"—are verbal. Sometimes, they just evolve, or morph from original intentions, the originators not privy to the final machinations—and not wanting to be; only aware and glad once the problem finally goes away.

That is a dramatist's scenario for the most part, not backed by any proof in its darkest possibilities. But the evidence so far unearthed suggests that it *could* be true. There is fact in the scenario. It could have happened. Something is not right about what we, so far, know happened to Patton—as well as what we do not know. His accident and death need further investigation.

His remains should be exhumed and tested. In 1991, the remains of Zachary Taylor, twelfth president of the U.S., were exhumed to determine if he had been poisoned with arsenic back in 1850.*[24] If Taylor, why not Patton? Getting access to Russian documents will be difficult, if not impossible. The Russians, especially, do not like to air their dirty laundry, no matter how old. Eastern European archives, formerly under communist governments, will probably be easier to access. And there are many archives here, especially those connected to organizations and persons

---

*He had not.

paramount in this story—FDR, Marshall, Eisenhower, Donovan, Morgenthau, and the OSS and CIC, to name the most prominent—which might yield further information. And veterans from that era could come forward with valuable information once what we do know is published.

It seems clear that what really happened to Patton has been covered up. Until the truth is revealed, the rumors about his accident and death will persist, crucial history may be lost, and an enormous crime may have gone unpunished. Patton deserves better.

★ ★ ★ ★

POSTSCRIPT

OCTOBER 2010

More than a year after *Target: Patton* was published I was looking through my files and found something surprising. It was a three-page letter to me from the late Ralph de Toledano, the former *Newsweek* editor, author of twenty-five books (including best sellers), syndicated columnist, and journalist who had helped found William F. Buckley's *National Review*. Toledano was a revered investigative reporter. What was surprising was that I had not used his letter. It supports the evidence that Patton was assassinated.

I had contacted Toledano because of a 1999 column he had written about an early CIA plot to assassinate Chiang Kai-shek. During World War II, Chiang was an American ally and the leader of the Nationalist Chinese. Fighting Mao Zedong's Red Chinese right after the war, Chiang relocated to the island of Taiwan and established the Republic of China in opposition to the communist government on the mainland. Like Patton, he was anathema to the Truman administration which, like FDR's before it, favored

Soviet Russia early on. The CIA (formerly OSS) had proposed a "simple" solution: "Eliminate Chiang and Taiwan's will to resist the communist onslaught would end."[1]

(Further research shows this was not the only time a plan to assassinate Chiang had been proposed. During the war, President Roosevelt himself, who had broken many promises to his Chinese ally, had asked that a plan be made to "eliminate" Chaing, according to Colonel Frank Dorn, aide to General Joe Stillwell, US liaison to China in whose territory the plan would be carried out. Donovan's OSS is said to have devised a plot for an aircraft "accident." But FDR never gave final approval.[2])

It was incredible to me that we sided with Mao, not only a communist but probably the twentieth century's greatest mass murderer.[3] But we did. A CIA hit team, led by a U.S. Army colonel, was budgeted $3 million for the mission. But Chiang, now leery of his "ally," found out about it before they could act. Vice President Richard Nixon, about whom Toledano was writing a book when he heard of the failed plot, confirmed the earlier mission and added that Syngman Rhee, the anti-communist leader of South Korea, had also been the target of a CIA murder attempt.[4] (Patton, remember, was anti-communist.) At the end of the column—prompting me to contact him—Toledano wrote he'd learned of a plot to assassinate Patton.

Reading over the 3-page letter, I realized why I'd probably buried it. Preceding a certain mid-letter disclosure, he'd admonished, "For obvious reasons, the following must in no way be attributed to me or to anyone else, and can be used as coming from an anonymous source." I don't like to use anonymous sources; thus I probably had put the letter aside to either return to it later or find sources I *could* quote—as I did. But apparently—stupidly—I'd forgotten about it. It was dated "3 January 2005."

Since Toledano, an OSS agent during the war, died in 2007, I see no reason now not to quote from it.

Here are the pertinent parts:

> I have been cudgeling my brain and recollections and can offer you the following partial list of those who told me that Patton had been assassinated by OSS.
>
> **Raymond Murphy**, head of State Department security during and after the war years. Ray was the one who recommended me to OSS for a parachute drop behind the Italian lines. That I was kicked out saved my life, since those who parachuted and had the wrong [i.e., anti-communist] politics were killed.[5]
>
> **John A. Clements**, Hearst VP for public relations and one of my best friends. He was part of a very secret Marine Corps Intelligence operation which even penetrated the Kremlin, and I did a few jobs for them. Jack, who was murdered by the GRU-NKVD in a New York hotel in the 1970s, told me that Patton had been murdered by an OSS-Rote Kapelle (Red Orchestra, the chief Soviet Intelligence operation in Germany) team. His group kept an eye not only on the Soviets but on CIA which it distrusted heartily.

This reinforces one of the main ideas in this book: that the assassination was a joint OSS-NKVD operation.

Toledano continues:

> I was the first newsman to interview Lieutenant **Igor Gouzenko**, the Soviet code clerk who broke up Soviet atomic espionage.[6] After my interview [Gouzenko] told me some things on my promise to keep them secret until after his

death . . . .He mentioned the Patton case just as something he had picked up, with no details.

In talks with **Richard Nixon** (for many years I was close to him and wrote two books about him)* [he] casually men-tion[ed] OSS as being involved in the murder of Patton. So did **Louis Nichols**, defacto second-in command [to long-time director J. Edgar Hoover] of the FBI. [Nixon also confirmed the assassination attempts on Chaing and Syngman Rhee].

Toledano's admonition to me not to quote him came in regard to something **Lieutenant General Albert C. Wedemeyer** confided to him. (Wedemeyer, now deceased, whose book, *Wedemeyer Reports* Toledano helped get published, is the same I quoted earlier in this book.)

What Wedemeyer confided, wrote Toledano, "came in strictest confidence. . . . Never a friend of the top Pentagon brass but very much in the know, Wedemeyer told me that Marshall Zukov had put pressure on General Eisenhower to 'get rid' of or 'remove' Patton. He had heard, but could not vouch [for] it that Noel Field (OSS liaison in Zurich with the Rote Kapelle) had reported similarly to Allen Dulles [OSS chief in Switzerland and later head of the CIA]. Eisenhower had passed on Zhukov's 'message' to the Pentagon."

This, too, underscores what I had learned about Zukov, the powerful Russian general.

General Alexander Barmine (GRU [Russian intelligence] de-fector who worked with various U.S. wartime Intelligence services), **Whittaker Chambers** [*Time* magazine editor who outed Alger Hiss as a Soviet spy and] (who secretly worked

---

*Nixon confirmed the assassination attempts on Chaing and Syngman Rhee.

with ONI [Office of Naval Intelligence] during WWII), **General Bonner Fellers** (of General MacArthur's WWII staff who gave me copies of files on the Sorge spy ring in the Far East),[7] and **Robert Morris** (ONI and counsel to the Senate Internal Security Subcommittee) were all certain that Patton had been assassinated by or on orders from OSS.

Senator Joe McCarthy (a source who often turned to me for help), told me before the Army-McCarthy circus that his investigators had been working on the Patton murder and that he was planning hearings. He saw it as an OSS-MI-6 (the Charles "Dickie" Ellis-Burgess-MacLean wing) plot,* with General George C. Marshall, Ike's superior and rabbi, having some input. McCarthy was put out of business, and after the 1960 election, the Senate Permanent Investigations subcommittee was taken over by the Democrats, with Bobby Kennedy as counsel, and many files "disappeared."[8]

These leads apart, the history and structure of OSS are of tremendous significance in arriving at conclusions. In the early days of U.S. involvement in WWII, FDR realized that America's Intelligence structure was woefully inadequate and he turned to the British. They had consolidated their secret services under Sir John Hay Drummond.... The British supplied Dickie Ellis, second in command of Intrepid's** operations, who had been collaborating with the GRU's Richard Sorge and the Frankfurt School [neo-Marxists named for their origin in Frankfurt, Germany] since the late 1920s. It was Ellis who selected Donovan ... to head OSS, who organized it, and who kept a finger on its operations. Donovan was politically

---

*Notorious Soviet spies working inside British intelligence.
**Sir William Stephenson, the British intelligence chief instrumental in getting Bill Donovan appointed head of the OSS.

naïve, full of wildly romantic plans, and could by-pass those restraining hands by going directly to [President Roosevelt]. The [OSS] Central European desk was turned over to [German Marxist] Herbert Marcuse and the Frankfurt School...

Significantly re Patton: In the last days of the Nazis and after their surrender, Marcuse and the OSS Central European desk moved to the ETO [European Theater of Operations] and completely won over General Lucius Clay, Gauleiter of the U.S. occupation [who had succeeded Patton, after Eisenhower had fired Patton from the job]. Marcuse's efforts were (1) to undercut anyone of importance who was anti-Soviet and (2) to eliminate anti-Nazi-anti-Communist leaders like Konrad Adenauer from any role in the rehabilitation of postwar Germany.

That's what Toledano had written me.

I caution that none of these good leads has been corroborated. I have only recently revisited the letter. But given Toledano's reputation and background, I give them strong credence. As veteran journalist Wes Vernon wrote in his May 7, 2007 eulogy of Toledano—titled "Hard-nosed investigative reporting: a giant has left us"—"Ralph had covered the political landscape of the 20th Century. He was a walking encyclopedia. Mention almost any historical figure and Ralph had either interviewed him or covered him as a newspaperman." His "shoe-leather detective work... shed...light on...dark corners where certified scoundrels and plotters of all kinds of mischief dwell."

The Toledano letter is one of many responses I've had to my research. But it was the only one of note previously not mentioned that came *before* the book was published. Many have come since. I had hoped that more people with firsthand knowledge of the plot would contact me. But that hasn't happened so far. Anyone involved, even if they'd been in their teens, would be over eighty today. Any crucial higher ups would be well over 100. And any plotters would have to deal with the possibility of prosecution or revenge, not to mention facing the implications within their own consciences of what they'd done. Most likely, those actually involved, like Bazata and Skubik—regardless of participation or innocent witness—are now dead.

Nevertheless, I've received lots of reaction, some of it tantalizing in terms of possibly shedding more light. For instance, a German interpreter/typist at U.S. military headquarters in Munich when Patton was injured wrote that she and her coworkers and U.S. bosses suspected a cover-up. "Our superiors at that time had appeared equally puzzled as to the murky situation that was sparingly reported by the official press. Powerful agencies directed from on-high must have [had] ways to lose or destroy any firsthand factual reports about the accident near Mannheim. The very strict rules and regulations for military reports could not have been disregarded otherwise. This accident would never have been classified as a trivial fender-bender. It was deliberately misrepresented to deceive the rest of the world of what had actually happened."

Another reader wrote that he knew Arlis Vanlandingham, probably the mysterious "Vanlandingham" young Horace Woodring, Patton's driver, said was the only investigating officer he saw at the scene of Patton's accident. Although not closely acquainted, the reader said he and Arlis, now deceased, had attended the same church twenty-five years ago. "I was never aware that he had served in the military. One day in a conversation I mentioned that my dad had served in Patton's Third Army and that he considered old blood & guts to be the best general in the entire army [and that he] thought there was something fishy about Patton's 'accidental' death. At that comment, Arlis looked as if he was about to become ill and quickly left the group. After that, I noticed that he always seemed to avoid me, and we soon lost contact." Did that indicate guilt? When I contacted the reader, he could provide no more but said, "I realize this evidence is sketchy but...I believe he was."

The son of an Oregon personal counselor advised, "You might be interested to learn that my deceased mother was a confidante of General Bedell Smith," Eisenhower's "bull dog" assistant whom Patton disliked and distrusted. "When the movie 'Patton' came out decades ago, [she] mentioned that Patton had been assassinated to prevent a confrontation with the USSR. There is no corroborating evidence that would render what I say as being more than anecdotal. I do however have my mom's photograph of Bedell Smith which was inscribed to her by him. I could send you a photocopy...to...verify my mom's knowing Smith."

A post-war nationalized Canadian woman who grew up in Mannheim and was there when Patton was injured wrote:

> So the rumours flying around in my hometown...might be true after all. To the people of Mannheim, Germany, there was no mystery, but rather a well-timed assassination plot. It was said that General Patton's car had traveled on an isolated country road that morning without any other vehicle on the horizon. When it approached an intersection, an army truck came barreling down the other road aiming for Patton's car and crashing into it. This is what I remember people saying

back in 1945. They also said Patton wanted to take on the Russians and that did not sit well with his top brass.

While the official story is that the hospital in which Patton died was not equipped to do an autopsy—and that was why no autopsy was performed—a former orderly there at the time of Patton's death wrote, along with sending me pictures of the place, that the 130th Station Hospital in Heidelburg "was very capable of performing autopsies."

So why didn't it?

These are witnesses who were there at the time or who have personal knowledge bearing on the issue. Reading more of Bazata's seemingly endless diaries about his clandestine life, I came upon this stream of consciousness which seems appropriate with which to end. To get to the point quickly and succinctly, which Bazata seldom did in his secretive, long-winded, often-coded writings, I'll paraphrase:

> What really matters? Not so much the individual scandal of the Patton saga—that is only a closeted skeleton surrounding a great and total soldier. Rather, it is man's evil. Patton's murder is but an episode in a continuing saga—important mostly because it shows how this evil works: good intentions corrupted then betrayal. I've seen once brave and courageous men become the enemy because of petty greed, power grabbing and protectiveness. Patton had to be killed in Germany so it would look like a hostile people had done it. It was hoped the brutal Germans would be blamed....It was the easiest and safest place to do it because of the chaos there. It had to be done before he returned to the U.S. and launched

real trouble as president or policy maker and great exposer of
Ike, Monty, Winny (Churchill), FDR, Truman and "Milly"
(Donovan) of OSS.[9]

Who knows the full truth? Where there is smoke there is fire. And
there is a lot of smoke here.

★ ★ ★ ★

ACKNOWLEDGMENTS

I **wish to thank** my wife, Bego, children, Robert and Amaya, and my cousins Tim Wilcox and Bobby Russell. The idea grew as a family affair. My agent Jim Trupin, JET Literary Associates, placed the proposal with Doug Grad, now an agent himself, and then Anneke Green, both of whom edited the manuscript. Harry Crocker brought it to Regnery.

Once the research commenced, Stephen Skubik's children, especially Mark Skubik and Harriet Hanley, were helpful, as were former OSS agent Rene Defourneaux, Peter J. K. Hendrikx, Denver Fugate, Christine Sample, Elizabeth Rettig, and Betty McIntosh, also a former OSS agent.

At the National Archives, John Taylor, Lawrence H. McDonald, Will Mahoney, David VanTessel and David J. Mengel aided. Helping with the CIC and military intelligence research were former CIC agent Duval Edwards, Conrad "Mac" McCormick, and Col. John H. Roush, Jr. (Ret.). At the Library of Congress, Historical Specialist Daun van Ee provided documents and at Ft. Knox's

Patton museum, Director Frank Jardim took photos I needed. Curator Charles Lemons and librarian Candace Fuller also contributed.

Others worthy of special mention were Dr. Ferdie Pacheco, the famous "fight doctor," novelist Fredrick Nolan, Schluchtern (Germany) resident Christa Krucker, Gloria Pagliaro, Matt Logan, Toni Wolf, and Marie-Pierre Bazata who was always helpful whenever I asked.

In addition, I wish to thank the following (in alphabetical order): Jim Adams, Thomas Allen, Jeff Bagwell, Rich Baker, Sam Baker, Tom H. Black, Nancy Campbell, Susan M. Catlett, Prof. Stephen Cohen, Lev E. Dobriansky, Bill Dial, Jeff Flannery, Jeff Fletcher, Bill Foley, Bonnie Gillis, Catharine Giordano, James Graff, Mitch Hamilburg, John Haynes, Ronald Janeczko, David Keough, Steven Kippax, Prof. Harvey Klehr, Beth Knobel, David Krall, Heidrun Kruce-Krebs, Myron Kuropus, Dr. Gerald Looney, Lt. Col. Tom Lynch, Anita MacFarlane, Edwin R. Motch III, Tom W. O'Connell, Ron Pantello, Clark Perks, Charles M. "Mike" Province, Charles Pinck, Sammy Popat, Pierre Rinfret, Andrei Robotnov, Val Ruffo, Alan F. Rumrill, David Russi, Jonathan Sanders, Duane Schulte, John D. Shank, Richard Sommers, Jenifer Stepp, Taras Szmagala, Gary A. Trogdon, Steve Uanna, Cyd Upson, Eric Voelz, Jules Wallerstein, David Woll, Joseph Robert White, Ernie Wolf, and Jim Zobel.

★ ★ ★ ★

SOURCES

Sources used but not explicitly cited. For a complete list of sources (including a list of those interviewed), go to www.targetpatton.com

BOOKS:

Stephen E. Ambrose, *Citizen Soldiers: The U.S. Army from the Normandy Beaches to the Bulge to the Surrender of Germany* (Touchstone Books, 1997).

Army Times, editors, *Famous American Military Leaders of World War II* (Dodd, 1962).

Albert Axell, *Russia's Heroes 1941-45* (New York: Carroll & Graf Publishers, Inc., 2001).

Robert L. Benson and Michael Warner, editors, *VENONA: Soviet Espionage and the American Response* (1939-1957; CIA, 1996).

Jim Bishop, *FDR'S Last Year: April 1944-April 1945* (William Morrow, 1974).

Martin Blumenson, *The Battle of the Generals: The Untold Sstory of the Falaise Pocket* (William Morrow, 1993).

Martin Blumenson, *Mark Clark: The Last of the Great WWII Commanders* (New York: Congden & Weed, 1984).

B. E. Boland, *Patton Uncovered: The Untold Story of how the Greatest American General Was Disgraced by Scheming Politicians and Jealous Generals,* (Voorhees: Melody Publishing, 2002).

Anthony Cave Brown, *The Secret War Report of the OSS* (Berkley, 1976).

George Capozi Jr., *Red Spies in the U.S.* (Arlington House, 1973).

George C. Chalou, *The Counter Intelligence Corps in Action* (New York: Garland, 1989).

CIA Public Affairs, *The Office of Strategic Services: America's First Intelligence Agency,* preparation directed by Michael Warner, CIA History Staff, 2000.

417

Gen. Mark Clark, *Calculated Risk* (New York: Harper & Brothers, 1950)

Nick Cook, *The Hunt for Zero Point: Inside the classified world of antigravity technology* (New York: Broadway Books, 2002).

Ed Cray, *General of the Army: George C. Marshall: Soldier and Statesman* (Touchstone, 1990).

Joseph P. Farrell, *Reich of the Black Sun: Nazi Secret Weapons & The Cold War Allied Legend* (Adventures Unlimited Press, 2004).

Richard F. Fenno, Jr. (editor), *The Yalta Conference: Problems in American Civilization*, (Boston: D.C. Heath Co., 1955).

Corey Ford, *Donovan of OSS: The Untold Story of William J. ("Wild Bill") Donovan and America's Top-Secret Agency forIintelligence, Espionage, and Unorthodox warfare in World War II* (Little Brown, 1970).

Roger Ford, *Steel From the Sky: The Jedburgh Raiders, France 1944* (London: Weidenfeld & Nicolson, 2004).

Howard Frazier (editor); *Uncloaking the CIA* (The Free Press, 1978).

Alan Furst, *Night Soldiers*, (New York: Random House, 2002).

Michael Green, *Patton's Tank Drive: D-Day to Victory* (Motorbooks International, 1995).

Gen. Paul D. Harkins, *When The Third Cracked Europe* (Army Times Publishing Company, 1969).

Wilhelm Hoettl, *Secret Front: Nazi Political Espionage 1938-45* (Enigma Books, 2003).

Brig. Gen. Oscar W. Koch and Robert G. Hays, *G-2: Intelligence for Patton* (Shiffer Military History, 1999).

Capt. Peter Mason, *Official Assassin* (Williamstown: Phillips Publications, 1998).

John Mendelson, *The History of the Counter Intelligence Corps* (New York: Garland, 1989).

————, *OSS-NKVD Relationship, 1943-1945* (New York: Garland, 1989).

Robert J. Moskin, *Mr. Truman's War: The Final Victories of World War II and the Birth of the Post War World* (University of Kansas Press, 2002).

Patrick K. O'Donnell, *Operatives, Spies, and Saboteurs* (Free Press, 2004).

Ferdie Pacheco, *Who Killed Patton* (Author House, 2004).

Ira Peck,, *Patton* (New York: Scholastic Book Services, 1970).

Edward Radzinsky, *Stalin* (Anchor Books, 1997).

Gayle Rivers, *The Specialist: The True Story* (Charter Books, 1985).

Harry H. Semmes, *Portrait of Patton* (Paperback Library, 1964).

Ronald Seth, *The Executioners: The Story of SMERSH* (New York: Hawthorne Books, 1967).

Thomas Parrish, The Simon And Schuster Encyclopedia of World War II (New York: Simon and Schuster, 1978).

Harris R. Smith, *OSS: The Secret History of America's First Central Intelligence Agency*, (Berkeley: University of California, 1972).

Strategic Services Unit, *War Report of the O.S.S.* (prepared by History Project, Strategic Services Unit (successor to the OSS), published by Walker Publishing Co., Wash., D.C., 1976).

Thomas F. Troy, *Donovan and the CIA: A History of the Establishment of the Central Intelligence Agency*, Volume Two; CIA Intelligence Institute, 1975, declassified version, obtained from CIA website

Unstated, *History of the Counter Intelligence Corps* (30 vols., uncensored, April 1960 United States Army Intelligence, Fort Holabird, Baltimore 19, MD, accessed at NARA, College Park).

Nancy Wake, Nancy; *The Autobiography of the Woman the Gestapo Called 'The White Mouse'* (Melbourne: Sun Books, 1986).

Charles Whiting, *Death on a Distant Frontier: A Lost Victory 1944* (New York: Sarpedon, 1996).

Earl F. Ziemke, *The U.S. Army in the Occupation of Germany 1944-1946* (Washington DC: Army Historical Series, Center of Military History, 1975).

ARTICLES:

Robert S. Allen, "Patton's Secret: 'I am Going to Resign From the Army,'" *Army 21* (June 1971): pp. 29-33.

Anonymously authored 2000 treatise entitled *Belarusian Nazi during the World War II and their work for the Cold War*. It discusses Nazi collaborators from Belarus, a country formerly under Soviet domination, and their use by the US after the war, especially by the CIA. It is on the net at www.geocities.com/dudar2000/Bcc.htm?200532 and the author says it is taken primarily from *The Belarus Secret* by John Loftus.

Anonymously authored 1964 CIA memorandum prepared for the Warren Commission investigating President Kennedy's assassination. It is titled, "Soviet Use of Assassination and Kidnapping," obtained at NARA, College Park, from the CIA CD available from computers on the third floor library—A4

Robert L. Benson, "The Venona Story," NSA website.

Joy Billington, "Douglas Bazata—A Many-Faceted Man," *The Sunday Star and Daily News*, Wash., D.C., September 17, 1972.

Jeffrey Burds, "Ethnicity, Memory, and Violence: Reflections on Special Problems in Soviet & East European Archives," an article in "Archives, Documentation, and the Institutions of Social Memory: Essays from the Sawyer Seminar, 2000-2001," University of Michigan Press, Ann Arbor, forthcoming November 2005.

George Fowler, "Patton and Son," an interview with Maj. Gen. George S. Patton discussing his father, the famed World War II commander: *The Barnes Review*, January 1995.

——————, "Patton: A 'New Realism'," *The Barnes Review*, January 1999.

Pat Hammond, "Ex-Agent: Patton's Death No Accident," (Manchester) *New Hampshire Sunday News*, January 9, 1994.

Andrew S. Harding, "Two General Apart: Patton and Eisenhower," Senior Thesis for Manchester College found on MilitaryHistoryOnline.com.

John Earl Haynes and Harvey Klehr, "In Denial: Historians, Communism & Espionage," *Insight Book Review*, October 10, 2003.

Peter Kirsanow, "Patton & Preferences II: Competence is colorless," *National Review* Online, February 11, 2004.

Robert D. Novak, "Stalin's Agents," The Schwarz Report, reprint from *The Weekly Standard*, December 25, 2000, pp.40-42.

Eric Pace, "Douglas DeWitt Bazata, Artist And O.S.S. Officer, Dies at 88," August 22, 1999, *New York Times*.

Michael E. Parrish, "Soviet Espionage and the Cold War," *Diplomatic History*, Volume 25, Issue 1, found on *www.politcalreviewnet.com*—A31 (its in my "Donovan Communist Sympathies" file.

Martin Price, "Who Killed Patton?," *The Spotlight*, October 15, 1979.

Rorin M. Platt, "Red Care or Red Menace?," *News & Observer* (Raleigh, NC) January 31, 1999.

Ronald Radosh, "Redhanded: Venona comes to PBS," *Weekly Standard*, February 4, 2002.

Stephen J. Skubik, "A German synagogue 39 years later," *The Keene (New Hampshire) Sentinel*, July 6, 1984.

"The Press and General Patton," Patton Society Research Library.

Jeffrey St. John,,"Reflections of a Fighting Father," Patton Society Research Library, 1985.

★ ★ ★ ★

NOTES

Chapter One: The Last Ride

1. With Korea, Vietnam, and their aftermath factored in.

2. Woodring had been driving Patton for a few months.

3. He believed in reincarnation and that he had fought in major battles in previous lives before. See *The Unknown Patton*, 247–259, for a poem he wrote, "Through a Glass, Darkly," telling of his past warrior lives. It begins, "Through the travail of the ages, Midst the pomp and toil of war, Have I fought and strove and perished, Countless times upon this star. . . ."

4. Hammelburg, Germany. His son-in-law was Lt. Col. John Waters. Richard Baron, Abraham Baum, & Richard Goldhurst, *Raid!: The Untold Story of Patton's Secret Mission* (Dell Publishing: Random House), 1981.

5. Ladislas Farago, *The Last Days of Patton* (Berkley, 1981), 31.

6. Francis Sanza, interview by the author, July, 2005.

7. Patton diaries, August 18 and August 27, 1945. Library of Congress.

8. Christopher Andrew and Vasili Mitrokhin, *The Sword and the Shield: The Mitrokhin Archive and the Secret History of the KGB* (Basic Books, 1999), 147–148. It describes how FDR and Stalin laughed together at a "scowling" Winston, making fun of him, who then had to join in. FDR said he and Stalin were "like brothers."

9. As evidenced by many of the social programs of Roosevelt's "New Deal" policies, such as government-subsidized jobs and Social Security. Roosevelt's two-term vice president and secretary of commerce, Henry Wallace was a socialist champion of the Soviet Union and ran for president against Democrats in 1948 on the Progressive ticket.

10. Patton diaries, August 8, 1945.

11. James D. Sanders, Mark A. Sauter, & R. Cort Kirkwood. *Soldiers of Misfortune* (National Press Books, 1992); Barrett Tillman, "Whatever Happened to Harley Hall," *Tailhook*, summer 1999.

12. Particularly those from Eastern Bloc countries under Russian rule.

13. Patton diaries, August 29, 1945.

14. Robert S. Allen, "Patton's Secret: 'I am Going to Resign From the Army,'" *Army* 21 (June 1971): 29-33. Allen served with Patton.

15. Patton diaries, May 6 and August 27, 1945.

Chapter Two: A Curious Crash

1. Mason King, "Gumshoe family ducks cloak-and-dagger stereotypes," *Indianapolis Business Journal*, September 30, 1996.

2. Ladislas Farago, *Patton: Ordeal and Triumph* (Dell, 1970).

3. Ladislas Farago, Omar Bradley, Francis Ford Coppola, & Edmund North. *Patton*, directed by Franklin Schaffner. Twentieth Century-Fox Film Corporation, 1970.

4. Ladislas Farago & William Luce. *The Last Days of Patton*, directed by Delbert Mann. Entertainment Partners, 1986.

5. Ladislas Farago, *The Last Days of Patton* (Berkley, 1985).

6. Ibid.

7. Ibid.

8. Nick Longworth interview by the author, Fall, 1996.

9. Ibid.

Chapter Three: The Jedburgh

1. Ben Parnel, *Carpetbaggers: America's Secret War in Europe* (Austin: Eakin Press, 1993).

2. Robert R. Kehoe, "Jed Team Frederick 1944: An Allied Team with the French Resistance," CIA Archive, (https://www.cia.gov/library/center-for-the-study-of-intelligence/kent-csi/docs/v42i5a03p.htm).

3. Col. Aaron Bank, *From OSS to Green Berets: The Birth of Special Forces* (Presidio Press, 1986); Col. Aaron Bank & E. M. Nathanson, *Knight's Cross* (Birch Lane Press, 1993).

4. In later years Bazata would refer to himself as "one of Donovan's original 38." Gordon Chaplin, "I Learned to Keep a Secret," *Potomac* magazine, *Washington Post*, June 6, 1976.

5. Occidental records, among others, show that he captained both the football and baseball teams, was a star at track, and was voted Southern California "Athlete of the Year" in 1903, a fact repeated in his *New York Times* obituary October 1, 1951.

6. Written in a formerly "secret" OSS "Interviewer's Report," dated "19 Feb 45" and signed by "John A Kneipp, 1Lt., MC, AUS." Douglas Bazata's CIA file.

7. Douglas Bazata, interviews by the author, September, 1996.

8. Ibid.

9. Douglas Bazata's FBI file.

10. Now in the possession of the author with copies distributed to others for safekeeping.

11. Ibid.

12. Douglas Bazata to "Xistian" not further identified, 16th July, probably, but not for certain, 1974.

13. The marines didn't have an official champion. The designation was simply agreed upon by officials involved in the various fights.

14. According to his letters and diaries. Chicago papers confirm that Baer, Sharkey and Johnson were at the fair and exhibitions were fought.

15. The injury is attested to in his Veteran's Administration records and was viewed by the author.

16. A May 9, 1942 story in the *Washington Post* tells how "eyes popped" as he scored 298 hits out of a possible 300 at a firing demonstration at Ft. Meade, Md.

17. Bernard Knox, *Essays Ancient and Modern* (The Johns Hopkins University Press, 1990).

18. Ibid.; William Colby, *Honorable Men: My Life in the CIA* (Simon & Schuster, 1978), 35.

19. Marie-Pierre Bazata, interview by the author, September 1996.

20. Lt. Col. H.W. Fuller, U.S.M.C. R., Douglas Bazata CIA file.

21. In all, Bazata gave me over 35 diaries. Some have hundreds of handwritten pages. In my system of filing, I call them "Ledgers." This came from Ledger 11, pages 7-8. In a private letter addressed to "Cher Rochard" (not otherwise identified) and dated "30 August 1980"—one of many letters he also gave to the author—he wrote the same claim more succinctly: "I first went into the USA professional killing trade via the Marines."

22. See Adm. Freeman's biography (http://www.arlingtoncemetery.net/ cfreeman.htm). He died in 1969.

23. *Carpetbaggers*; Lt. Col Will Irwin, *The Jedburghs: The Secret History of the Allied Special Forces* (France 1944) contain details of the mission, as does Thomas L. Ensminger's Carpetbagger website at (http://home.comcast.net/ ~801492bg.historian/MainMenu.htm). Used to recreate the mission was Bazata's own OSS after-action report, The U.S. National Archives; and George Millar, *Maquis: The French Resistance at War* (first published in Great Britain by William Heinemann, 1945).

24. This exceptionally low figure comes from two letters written by Bazata which include details of the drop. One is addressed to a "Jack S," not otherwise identified, and dated "3 Mar '79." The other is from the last page of a three page letter unfortunately separated from its first two pages and identified only by "June 21st" on the top.

25. *Carpetbaggers*, 69-70.

26. Two letters by Bazata about the jump dated "3 Mar 79" and "June 21." Bazata indicates this happened as he hit a telephone or electric wire close to the ground.

27. Douglas Bazata to Bill Colby, December 15—probably written in the 1970s. Bazata and Colby had a deep relationship that hit rocky ground in their later years. Colby mentions Bazata fondly in his 1978 autobiography, *Honorable Men*.

28. Bazata letter, December 15.

29. CEDRIC daily summaries, U.S. National Archives.

30. *Maquis*, 316.

31. The fact that Bazata used it to treat his wound is in a 16 December 1944 OSS medical report about him.

32. Bazata letter to Richard Floyd dated 12 December 1977.

33. "Report of Jedburgh Cedric," National Archives, RG266(OSS)E169, Box 1, Folder 3.

34. Ibid., 4,

35. *Maquis*, 327.

36. Douglas Bazata's CIA File, 20 January 1945. Forgan's last name is not clear on the document and could be something similar, like Porgan. Bazata got the award.

37. Report of Jedburgh Cedric, 4.

38. *Maquis*, 330.

39. After action report, Report of Jedburgh Cedric, 5.

40. *Maquis*, 332.

41. Bazata's after action, 5; *Maquis*, 337.

42. After action, Report of Jedburgh Cedric, 6.

43. Ibid.

44. The quotes come from a letter written by Bazata and dated only "10 August," but probably, because of references in it, 1973. Both Bazata's after action report and Millar's *Maquis* contain versions of the incident.

45. *Maquis*, 343.

46. Ibid., 351.

47. Ibid.

48. Ibid.

49. His after action report and an outline he wrote for a book he gave the author, dated "2 Aug 75."

50. *Maquis*, 353.

51. "11 Sept 44" dispatch from Cedric, U.S. National Archives.

52. Douglas Bazata, interview by the author. September 1996. While VA records indicate it could be one of his 8 noted wounds, it is not mentioned in the after-action report or in *Maquis*.

53. After-action, Report of Jedburgh Cedric, 6.

54. Both the recommendation and actual citation can be found in Bazata's CIA file and in records on Bazata at the National Archives.

55. Douglas Bazata's CIA file. Recommendation by Lt. Colonel Charles E. Brebner, OSS European Theater Operations executive officer.

56. The two page, signed and single-spaced statement was obtained by the author from Bazata's files and is written on Pietsch's stationary and dated September 15, 1977.

Chapter Four: A Meeting with Donovan

1. Anthony Cave Brown, *The Last Hero: Wild Bill Donovan* (Vintage, 1984).

2. The article appeared, according to the *Spotlight*, in the September 26, 1979 edition of the *Star*.

3. Bazata's relationship to the CIA is murky, as are many such relationships. He had a long, rocky friendship with fellow Jedburgh William Colby, CIA director from 1973 to 1975, and friendships and working relationships with other CIA per-

sonnel. He was also a critic of the CIA. The agency released to me under an FOIA request 316 pages from their file on him. Many pages had redactions and some had references to withheld pages. Bazata always said he had gotten 600 pages from his CIA file in the 1970s and that he never was in the CIA, but was a "contractor" to them.

4. They are controversial and it is unclear from the records—so far—exactly what happened on them.

5. Alan Haemer to Douglas Bazata, June 1976. Haemer was a long-time intelligence associate and professor at an Oregon college. It was occasioned when the FBI visited Haemer to interview him in a routine background check on Bazata who was applying for a government job. Haemer, who had known Bazata since their days at Syracuse University, had vouched for Bazata's "honesty and loyalty" in the FBI report which I additionally found in other sources. Haemer told the agents, "Bazata was never known to be dishonest."

6. Bazata considered Grace a friend.

7. A painting of his at Oregon State University prompted this letter from the Dean of Humanities and Social Sciences, Prof. Gordon W. Gilkey: "dear Douglas, The magnificent 'Green Crab Or Portrait of Anthony Peter Smith' arrived today and I hasten to say that the painting is a visual treat and a most welcome addition to our collection...."

8. A photo of the two together allegedly ran with the *New York Times* obit when Bazata died July 14, 1999. He wrote about the painting in several letters I have, lamenting the fact that he had lost the work.

9. Phil Chadbourne, interview by author, December, 1997. I was to meet and interview Chadbourne shortly before he died in 2000.

10. Bazata diaries, ledger number 11 in my scheme.

11. My notes on this last point leave room for interpretation. What they say is, "The nails, which have never grown back, still look painful." There is the possibility of a little nail left or grown back, but not much.

12. George Millar, *Maquis: The French Resistance at War* (first published in Great Britain by William Heinemann, 1945), 342-343.

13. Eight meetings is the figure he gave to both me and the *Spotlight*. That number includes meetings after he retuned from Cedric.

14. *Spotlight* staff, "I Was Paid To Kill Patton," the *Spotlight*, October 22, 1979. Bazata Diaries, Ledger 40, 25b.

15. According to many sources, Donovan took orders directly from the president and/or the War Department.

16. See D'Este's *Genius For War*, 660-664; Axelrod's recent *Patton*, 141-144. Or, for a view from inside Patton's forces, Allen's *Lucky Forward*, 103-114.

17. Patch's attitude was told to me by Bazata in our interviews. Millar does not mention Patch in *Maquis*.

18. Bazata Diaries, Ledger 38.

19. Austen Lake, *Boston Record American*, February 21,1963.

20. This is stated in several documents unearthed at the National Archives,

including Bazata's "Recommendation for Award of Oak Leaf Cluster to Purple Heart Medal," 23 May 1945, which is part of his CIA file.

21. Douglas Bazata to Bernie Knox, undated. He said one of his secret missions in France was to kill two communist "chiefs" for the Free French, headquartered in London. He did it, he writes, and "wisely refused any decoration that might surface stupidly." Bernie Knox was a fellow Jedburgh; the letter is undated but appears to have been written around 1976.

22. Bazata Diaries, Ledger 16, 53-56. ("The Crow Flew Freely!")

23. The italics are mine to try and convey the meaning of his words as best I understood them.

24. According to conversion tables readily available on the Net.

25. At times it seemed he was talking about one window, at other times, two.

26. He said both at different times in our interviews.

27. Bazata never mentioned the depot or the entrance.

Chapter Five: Vanished Archives; Secret Writings

1. Gordon Chaplin, "I Learned to Keep a Secret," *Potomac* magazine, *Washington Post*, June 6, 1976.

2. Long after it was over, Bazata continued to be angered by the 1945 accusations, saying and writing that the very fact they were brought was evidence of an ungrateful U.S. government—a fact which in itself was one of the reasons, he said, he was now telling his story.

3. He always claimed he was the most decorated Jedburgh, including in formal VA hearings during his late-life fight to get 100 percent disability. That claim was never challenged.

4. RG 338, 7th U.S. Army, Box 12, in or around file "VIP."

5. Ibid.

6. Van Ee's email to me is dated 12/7/2005. The D'Este reference is on page 787 of the Harper Collins paperback edition.

7. Archivist Mahoney's personal Patton file.

8. Ladislas Farago, *The Last Days of Patton* (New York: Berkley, 1981), footnote, 277.

9. Ibid., 278.

10. Record Group 338, Stack Area 290, Row 66, Compartment 5, Shelf 1, Box 12, "Seventh Army G-2 Subject File, VIP."

11. National Archives, Record Group 165, Box 1749, Patton 201 file, OPD Decimal File 1942–45.

12. Colonel Starbird of the European Section.

13. National Archives, Record Group 165, Box 1749, Patton 201 file, OPD Decimal File 1942–45.

Chaper Six: Clandestine

1. There may be more but that was near the number I carried away.

2. An apple brandy from the French region of the same name.

3. The 3rd member of Bazata's team, the Frenchman, Cap. F. Chapel, was housed in another safehouse. Bazata had particular affection and protective feelings for 18-year-old Floyd whom he regarded as "this excellent chap... a happy virgin... very devout Catholic."

4. The Jedburghs, although a pet project of Donovan's, were trained and controlled by the British, who had the expertise from a long history in commando operations. Therefore, Bazata was reporting back to the British, not the U.S., although certainly the U.S., i.e. OSS, was kept advised—at least in a general way. His reference to keeping the U.S. in the dark about this particular part of his mission underscores the complexity of clandestine activities, as well as the hidden agenda he carried into France. Apparently he had missions from various governments during Cedric and one master didn't know about the other. As Bazata says, it was a devious and dirty business with even allies spying on each another.

5. Transcript of hearing on Bazata's petition before the Board of Veterans Appeals, March 29, 1979, 8.

6. Typed statement "To Whom It May Concern," signed by La Gattuta and dated 14 October 1978.

7. The order was from "Headquarters, United Kingdom Base, APO 413, U.S. Army" and dated "1 June 1945."

8. Eventually OSS did mount such a mission with Green Beret founder Aaron Bank in the lead. But the war ended before "Operation Iron Cross" could be launched. There may have been other such missions to kill Hitler.

9. Throughout his writings, Bazata takes the view that OSS, especially in its beginning, was amateurish, and that the British, who mentored OSS, and the Russians, were much better at spy craft.

10. Diary-journal 38 in my numbering system.

11. Diary-journal 2 in my numbering system.

12. *A Man Called Intrepid*, 1976 autobiography by William Stevenson (who, despite the similarity in names, is no relation). Intrepid was Stephenson's British codename.

13. Thomas Troy, *Wild Bill and Intrepid: Donovan, Stephenson, and Origin of CIA*, (Yale University Press, 1996).

14. Anthony Cave Brown, Henry M. Hyde, (OSS spymaster and author of *The Quiet Canadian*,) and Thomas Troy.

15. Brown, 166; *Wild Bill and Intrepid*, 130.

16. *Wild Bill and Intrepid*, 186.

17. *Last Hero*, 167.

18. Based on what he says Donovan said to him.

19. Various facts within the different discussions of the meeting indicate it could have been held both before Cedric or after.

20. Most of these three-dot (...) insertions between sentences are Bazata's; as are the 2, 5 and 6 dot (.. ....) insertions. Only a few are mine which I will indicate simply with a footnote "My dots." I am editing very little from this, only lines which I consider irrelevant and/or confusing.

21. One of London's oldest and finest, established in 1898. It was a favorite of "visiting statesmen" during the war, according to its website, and is just a block or so from Grosvenor Street. Bazata indicates that he went there often with friends, implying that going to the hotel might have been his suggestion, not Donovan's.
22. My dot insertions.
23. My dots.
24. My dots.
25. My dots.
26. My dots.
27. My dots.
28. Interview with Longworth 9/3/05.

Chapter Seven: Hit List

1. Best estimate based on a witness, Frank Theubert, who was there that day and other data I've gathered in tracking down the Skubik story.
2. Transcript of speech at Keene, New Hampshire, Skubik tape November 1984. His daughter Harriet has the tape and allowed me to transcribe it.
3. Douglas Botting and Ian Sayer, *America's Secret Army: The Untold Story of the Counter Intelligence Corps*, (London: Fontana Publishers, 1990); Duval A. Edwards, *Spy Catchers*, (Red Apple Publishing, 1994).
4. Douglas Botting and Ian Sayer, *America's Secret Army: The Untold Story of the Counter Intelligence Corps*, (London: Fontana Publishers, 1990), 232.
5. Norman Naimark, *The Russians in Germany: A History of the Soviet Zone of Occupation* (Harvard University Press, 1995).
6. According to his son Mark and indicated in *America's Secret Army,* 232. References to Hammitzch are few. Secret Army, in recounting the suicide, spells his last name "Hammitzch." Others spell it Hammitsch or Hammitzsch. He was the second husband of Hitler's half-sister, Angela.
7. These experiences are a combination of things described to me by his son Mark who had heard them from his father, and Skubik's own recollections in the Keene Library tape.
8. The team was part of a larger unit of 12 to 15 men designated "960/69", which was part of the larger 960th CIC Detachment under the Twelfth Army in the American Zone.
9. According to Skubik.
10. Stephen Skubik, Speech; "Aberman synagogue 39 years later," *Keene Sentinel,* July 6, 1984.
11. Ibid.
12. Email from Theubert to Mark Skubik dated July 8, 2006.
13. The encased numbers here are mine.
14. His service record, obtained at the National Personnel Records Center, St. Louis, says he was born October 3, 1915 in Linden, N.J., and both his birth parents had been born in Austria-Hungary.
15. Obituary, *Ukrainian (National) Weekly*, October 6, 1996. Also confirmed by his family.

16. Information on this is scarce because it was such a secret program. But one source which talks about it is *The Friends: Britain's Post-War Secret Intelligence Operations* by Nigel West, (Wiedenfeld and Nicolson, 2005), 66–68. I obtained the formerly CIA-classified book at the National Archives under their new CIA-sponsored program which allows researchers to look up subjects on CIA-controlled computers. See also Peter Grose, *Operation Rollback: America's Secret War Behind the Iron Curtain* (Houghton Mifflin, 2000).

17. Skubik, op. cit., 16.

18. CIA "Studies in Intelligence," Vol. 19, No. 3, Fall, pages 2–8, available at National Archives.

19. Ibid., 107-108.

20. Ladislas Farago, *The Last Days of Patton* (New York: Berkley, 1981), 50.

21. Bryan J. Dickerson, "The Liberation of Western Czechoslovakia 1945," (http://www.militaryhistoryonline.com/wwii/articles/liberation1945.aspx).

22. Martin Blumenson, *The Patton Papers 1940-1945* (Boston: Houghton Mifflin, 1974); *Last Days,* 59-60, among other sources.

23. *Patton Papers,* 441.

24. For a concise, impartial look at this controversy see Alan Axelrod, *Patton: A Biography* (Palgrave Macmillen, 2006), 127-129.

25. Fred Ayer Jr., *Before the Colors Fade* (Dunwoody: Norman S. Berg, publisher, 1971).

26. Stephen J. Skubik, *Death: The Murder of General Patton*; (Bennington: self published, 1993), foreword.

27. Anthony Cave Brown, *The Last Hero: Wild Bill Donovan* (Vintage, 1984).

28. *The Murder of General Patton,* 35.

29. Ibid., 16.

30. Ibid., 22-25.

31. Gay Diary, April 20, 1945, Carlisle Barracks.

32. Col. Charles R. Codman, *Drive* (Atlantic-Little Brown, 1957), 293.

33. George S. Patton Jr., *War as I Knew It* (New York: Bantam, 1980), 290.

34. *Patton's Last Battle,* 166.

35. Patton diary entry for "April 20, 1945," Library of Congress.

36. Gay Diary entry for April 20, 1945, U.S. Army War College center, Carlisle, Pa.

37. Ladislas Farago, *Ordeal and Triumph* (Dell, 1970), 787.

38. Emails from Maciej Stanecki, a graduate student at both Warsaw University and Poland's National Academy of Defense.

39. Communication from Rene J. Defourneaux, former OSS officer and author, who forwarded the information from a current RAF-USAF representative in France.

40. See the recently declassified article, "Soviet Use of Assassination and Kidnapping," in the Fall 1975 issue of CIA's *Studies in Intelligence,* for one.

41. His diary was unclear about the location of the incident.

42. *War as I Knew It,* 305.

43. *The Murder of Patton,* 113,117.

44. *Patton's Last Battle,* 183-184.

45. Pavlov Shandruck, *Arms of Valor* (Robert Speller & Sons Publishers, Inc., New

York, 1959), with an introduction by Roman Smal-Stocki. Available on the Net at (http://galiciadivision.org.ua/lib/shandruk/).

46. *Death: The Murder of General Patton,* 17.

47. *Arms of Valor,* Chapter 30, paragraph 2.

48. *Death: The Murder of General Patton,* 17.

49. Ibid., 7-14.

50. Ibid., 14-15.

51. Ibid., 18-19.

52. Ibid., 26-31.

53. John O. Koehler, *STASI: The Untold Story of the East German Secret Police* (Westview Press, 1999), 36-45.

54. *The Murder of Patton,* 20-22.

55. Ibid., 34–38.

Chapter Eight: Strange Bedfellows

1. Allen Weinstein, and Alexander Vassiliev, *The Haunted Wood* (Modern Library, 2000), 238-239. Vassiliev is a former KGB agent. He and Weinstein had access to Russian intelligence archives which were briefly opened to certain researchers during the 1990s.

2. Ibid., 89.

3. On microfilm at Carlisle Barracks.

4. Edward Jay Epstein, *Dossier: The Secret History of Armand Hammer* (Da Capo Press, 1999).

5. Armand Hammer to Bill Donovan, September 11, 1941.

6. Bradley F. Smith, *Sharing Secrets with Stalin: How the Allies Traded Intelligence, 1941-1945* (University Press of Kansas, 1996), 78 & 116; Bradley F. Smith, *The Shadow Warriors: OSS and the Origins of the CIA* (Basic Books, Inc., 1983), 339.

7. Anthony Cave Brown, *The Last Hero: Wild Bill Donovan* (Vintage, 1984), 417-418 for FDR's pro-Soviet views and Donovan's adherence to them.

8. The secret interoffice memo is from "William A. Kimmel" and addressed "Colonel Donovan." Another discussing the same thing is dated 1/15/43 and is addressed to "Major David Bruce," who would head OSS's London office, from "Calvin B. Hoover." Microfilm, Carlisle Barracks.

9. May 4, 1943 OSS "office memorandum" from "Emmy C. Rado" to Donovan. Microfilm, Carlisle Barracks.

10. Christopher Andrew and Vasili Mitrokhin, *The Sword and the Shield: The Mitrokhin Archive and the Secret History of the KGB* (Basic Books, 1999), 143.; Joseph Persico, *Piercing The Reich: the penetration of Nazi Germany by American secret agents during World War II.* (Ballantine Books, 1979), 209.

11. "Memorandum of Conversation at the Commissariat for Internal Affairs," December 27, 1947; John Mendelsohn, *The OSS-NKVD Relationship 1943-1945,* (Scholars Review, 1987).

12. David E. Murphy, Kondrashev, Sergei A.; Bailey, George; *Battleground Berlin: CIA vs KGB in the Cold War* (New Haven: Yale University Press, 1997), 3–4.

13. Available in a variety of sources including Mendelson's "OSS-NKVD Relationship" and on the CIA website under "OSS-NKVD Liaison."

14. Herbert Romerstein and Eric Breindell, *The Venona Secrets: Exposing Soviet Espionage and America's Traitors* (Washington, DC: Regnery, 2000).

15. *Mitrohkin*, 782, footnote 40.

16. *The Haunted Wood*, 249.

17. Ibid., xxiii.

18. Elizabeth Bentley, *Out of Bondage*, (Ballantine Books, 1988). She tells about becoming disillusioned with the communists.

19. For more on the D-Day revelations see *The Haunted Wood*, 258.

20. Robert Novak, "Stalin's Agents," *The Weekly Standard*, December 25, 2000.

21. FBI report on Donovan, File #: 77-58706, Part 1c, page 47. Available at (http://foia.fbi.gov/donovan/donovan1c.pdf).

22. A Russian intelligence report quoted in *The Haunted Wood*, 242-243.

23. Joseph Persico, *Roosevelt's Secret War*, (Random House, 2001), 291.

24. *The Last Hero*, 228-230, for an account of the break-in.

25. *Roosevelt's Secret War*, 292.

26. Ibid., 143.

27. Footnote 9, in a 9 March 1944 "Memorandum for the President"; Studies in Intelligence, Vol. 7, no. 1, Winter 1963, 63-74, with the ftnt on page 70.

28. Ibid., 170.

29. Memo found amongst the Donovan papers at Carlisle Barracks.

30. "Memorandum for the President," 349-351.

31. Ibid., 351.

32. OSS-NKVD Relationship, document 102, Letter from Maj. Gen. John R. Deane to NKVD Col. A.G. Grauer, 9 January 1945.

33. Ibid., document 106, Letter from Lt. Gen. P. M. Fitin to Maj. Gen. John R. Deane, 15 February 1945.

34. Ibid., 354.

35. OSS-NKVD Relationship, document 108, Letter from Lt. Gen. P..M. Fitin to Maj. Gen. John R. Deane, 26 February 1945.

36. Ibid., document 110, Letter from Lt. Gen. P. M. Fitin to Maj. Gen. John R. Deane, 9 April 1945.

37. Ibid., documents 111-114, letters involving various, including Fitin, 14 – 18 April 1945.

38. Ibid., document numbers 115-116, letters from Kennan dated 12 and 18 May 1945 respectively.

39. CIA brief titled "Background of Dr. Wilhelm Hoettl," 5 August 1949, National Archives.

40. CIA "special collections" document "Dr. Wilhelm Hoettl" acquired at the National Archives. This one is 10 pages and has "Nazi War Crimes Disclosure Act 2000" stamped on it.

41. Page 753. Cave-Brown, obviously pro-Donovan, sounds like he's making excuses here.

42. Ibid.
43. "11 July 1945 PRIORITY" cable to "US EMBASSY MOSCOW for DEANE from DONOVAN OSS." It is Document 117 in OSS-NKVD Relationship.
44. Document 130 in OSS-NKVD Relationship. The italics are mine.
45. *The Haunted Wood*, 248.
46. OSS-NKVD Relationship, Document 124.
47. Ibid. Document 132.
48. *The Last Hero*, 754.
49. OSS-NKVD Relationship, Document 132.
50. Summer 2003, 6.
51. *The Last Hero*, 627.
52. Volume Two, 369.
53. For more on the Park report, see *The Last Hero*, 792-793.
54. Ibid., 468.
55. FBI File #: 77-58706, Part 1, WFO (77-44319) 14 (obtainable at FBI website).

Chapter Nine: Dancing with the Devil

1. C.R. McCormick to author, email August 2, 2005. U.S. Army Intelligence Museum, Ft. Huachuca, Ariz. Mr. McCormick writes, "A roster of 970th CIC Det personnel, 7 Dec 1945, shows Skubik as a Sgt., date of rank 3 Nov 1945." I was later to find the roster myself at the National Archives.
2. Stephen J. Skubik, *Death: The Murder of General Patton;* (Bennington: self published, 1993). Foreword and 111.
3. Skubik, op. cit., 32–34.
4. Ibid., 37.
5. Ibid., 36-42

Chapter Ten: NKVD

1. Stephen J. Skubik, *Death: The Murder of General Patton*; (Bennington: self published, 1993).
2. It's a 1935 model 853. It is at the Moscow Museum of Antique Cars & Motorcycles and has "starred in 25 films." Other references say Goering owned a 1938 Horch.
3. Skubik op. cit., 384.
4. This was another of those newly deposited papers obtained by the archives from Ft. Meade and/or the CIA. This one was declassified through the recent "Nazi War Crimes Disclosure Act" and has on its front "This dossier is continued from the last reels," indicating it comes from microfilm and there is earlier material I do not have. My notes on the back identify the file as, "Davidov, Alexander D035079. CIC-CIA"
5. Dr. Mark Elliott, "The Soviet Repatriation Campaign," Wsevolod W. Isajiw, Yury Boshyk, and Roman Senkus, eds., *The Refugee Experience: Ukrainian Displaced Persons after World War II* (CIUS Press, 1995).
6. A document in the "Davidov, Alexander Do35079. CIC-CIA" file dated "15 Feb 46" and signed by an agent "Fiedler" (it is impossible to make out the faint first ini-

tials) from the "Weiden Sub-Regional Office."

7. This report is repeated in several different documents I found, the earliest of which seems to be 4 December 1945, Headquarters Seventh Army." My note on the back gives the following citation: RG 319, IRR Impersonal Files, Box 50, "Subversive Activities of USSR Officers," ZF011636.

8. "19 January 1946, USFAT G-2 Division, Counterintelligence Branch" report from RG 319, IRR Impersonal Files, Box 50, "Subversive Activities of USSR Officers," ZF011636.

9. Letter in the "Davidov, Alexander D035079" file.

10. Ibid.

11. I received it from David Mengel of the archives' FOIA staff in response to an FOIA request I made.

12. Skubik, op. cit., 42–44.

13. Ibid., 36,55, 102.

Chapter Eleven: Mystery at Mannheim

1. According to its official history, dated "30 January 1946," National Archives.

2. 24 August 1945, according to its unit history.

3. Ned Snyder, "Death of Patton—II Army doctor at accident scene," December 1987, an article Snyder published in *Military* magazine; Ladislas Farago, *The Last Days of Patton* (New York: Berkley, 1981), 228.

4. Ibid.

5. This article was in *Military's* August 1987 edition. Staats's story was authored by John Enigl, a contributor to the *Milwaukee Journal Sentinel*.

6. The assertion is in Sawicki's December 17, 2001, obituary in the *Buffalo News* and was confirmed to me by his family who had heard the story many times.

7. Lester Gingold, interview by author, Winter, 2005.

8. Gerald T. Kent, M.D., *A Doctor's Memoirs of World War II* (The Cobham and Hatherton Press, 1989).

Kent made his claim in a 1989 book, *A Doctor's Memoirs of World War II*.

9. *Last Days*, 277.

10. Ibid., 817. Blumenthal's "statement" by Woodring carries no date but the book was published in 1974. Early newspaper stories about the accident also said two trucks were involved.

11. Bazata infers they were on opposite sides, the disabled truck on the side into which the traveling truck would turn, the traveling truck waiting on the opposite side.

12. *Last Days*, 78.

13. While Denver Fugate, a historian who visited the site of the crash in Germany, believes Thompson was turning into a quartermaster depot, (see Denver Fugate, "The End of the Ride: An Eyewitness Account of George S. Patton's Fatal Accident," *Armor*, November-December 1995), Farago in *Last Days,* who also researched there, does not. (See 226-227).

14. In some interviews, Woodring says the speed was 30 miles per hour.

15. John Woodring's former wife, Anne Woodring, confirmed these views in a

separate interview, May 2005.

16. I had a copy of the manuscript entitled, *Horace L. Woodring: The True Story of "The Last Days of Patton,"* sent to me by Peter J.K. Hendrikx, a Patton admirer and researcher in the Netherlands. While I've not been able to contact Shelton, members of Woodring's family say she is related, although they are not sure how. The manuscript, which Hendrikx thinks might have been written as a thesis, states that the interview was made on November 11, 1986.

17. This is shorter and different from the quote Farago attributes to Gay in *Last Days*, page 226. But since it's much closer to the accident, I give it more credit.

18. Undated and unsigned, the statement was sent to me by Daun van Ee, Historical Specialist at the Library of Congress. The citation van Ee gave is "Patton Papers, Box 14, Chronological File, December 2-18, 1945." Portions of the statement, including the "Look!" references referred to here are in early press reports about the accident.

19. Seventh Army Public Relations Office (PRO) documents sent to me from the National Archives. Sources of the documents are not identified other than a folder labeled "Very Important Persons, Pro. Sec., 10 December 45 – 1 Feb 45."

20. Both mentioned in the Gay statement.

21. Brian M. Sobel, *The Fighting Pattons* (Dell, 1997), 79.

22. Peter J.K. Hendrikx, "An Ironical Thing," Patton Appreciation Society Newsletter, UK, December 1995.

23. The article is in an undated New Jersey newspaper story about the crash. "In an INS dispatch," it says, "Sgt Armando DeCrescenzo, of George Road, Cliffside Park . . . and three other soldiers rushed to the scene and gave treatment to the general . . . ." This meshes with Woodring's statement in *Fighting Pattons* about the first "ambulance."

24. "The End of the Ride," Denver Fugate

25. *Last Days*, 227.

26. An MP headquarters that records show did exist.

27. See Woodring's interviews in the articles by Hendrikx, Fugate, and Shelton.

28. Obtained from Old Dominion.

29. "18 December 1945" memorandum by "Brig. Gen. John M. Willems," Seventh Army Chief of Staff, in whose jurisdiction the accident took place. Its subject is "Accident investigation" and is addressed to "Provost Marshal." It says information on the Patton accident came from a report signed by 1Lt. Peter Sabalas (sic) of the 818th Military Police Company, Mannheim. Obviously the "S" is a mistake.

30. *Last Days*, 9-10.

31. United Press (UP) dispatch from Mannheim, dated December 10 (1945). No press have been reported at the scene so such stories were probably written from second hand reports.

32. Stars and Stripes Frankfurt bureau report, dated December 9.

33. Babalas's biographical sketch in Old Dominion University, Norfolk's, special collections section which has his papers, as well as news stories such as "Legislator 'Upset' by Landbank's Rates," *The Virginian-Pilot*, Sept. 19, 1990.

34. Ibid.

35. The book was co-written by former assistant Deputy FBI Director Anthony E. Daniels.
36. See Hendrikx and Shelton.
37. Originally published in Britain as *The Oshawa Project.*
38. In separate interviews.
39. I have a copy of the story given to me for other reasons by Bazata.
40. Since service numbers are much longer, the 7340 is either part of a service number or more likely a phone number.
41. On the 90th's website.
42. *Last Days*, 278.
43. As his military record, eventually unearthed, would show.
44. The declassified document is a typewritten release from "Conklin, acting PRO Seventh Army" to "Information Room PRO USFET" giving Gen. Patton's condition at the hospital the Thursday after the accident.
45. *Last Days*, 226-227.
46. Signed by Brig. Gen. M. Willems, it concerns the "Provost Marshal Accident Investigation" and is dated 18 December 1945."
47. Kingsbury Smith, Camden, N.J. *Courier-Post.* It was Thompson's hometown paper.
48. This deviation is also in Seventh Army Public Relations Officer documents quoting an alleged statement Woodring gave at the scene. But it does indicate changing details in his story as Woodring has retold it through the years.
49. *The Fighting Pattons*, 79.
50. See the Conklin PRO memo.
51. Ibid., 277.
52. When asked, neither the army nor the Post-Tribune could shed any new light on this.

Chapter Twelve: The Last Bullet

1. Ball states the time in a letter to Esther E. Rohlader, historian at Walter Reed Medical Center, who apparently requested his recollection for the Center's records. The letter is dated October 19, 1964.
2. "12 December 1945 Case Summary of General George S. Patton Jr." which is part of his medical records.
3. Hill's recollection is in another letter addressed to Walter Reed Medical Center's Rohlander. It's dated October 21, 1964. Kent's is in a book, *A Doctor's Memoirs of World War II,* published in 1989.
4. This quote is widely attributed to Patton and can be found in, among other sources, Ladislas Farago, *The Last Days of Patton* (New York: Berkley, 1981), 233 and Robert H. Patton, *The Pattons: A Personal History of an American Family* (Brassey's, 2004), 280.
5. The description of his injuries here is from a variety of notes written on hospital forms predominately by Dr. Hill upon Patton's admittance. They are labeled variously "History of the Present Illness'," "Chief Complaint-Condition on Admission,"

"Physical examination',' "Progress Notes',' and "Operation Report." All are dated "9 Dec 1945."

6. The description of Patton's head wound comes from Hill's memoir to Walter Reed historian Rohlander as well as several of the hospital forms already footnoted.

7. *Last Days*, 232.

8. "History of the Present Illness," dated "9 December, 1945" and initialed by Hill. Names of the witnesses are not given.

9. *I Was With Patton,* 274 The italicized "ever" is Lande's.

10. In terms of the available record.

11. Gerald T. Kent, M.D., *A Doctor's Memoirs of World War II* (The Cobham and Hatherton Press, 1989), 88.

12. The summary I have is only one page long. There may be more pages to it that might have an author's signature.

13. Hospital records.

14. Ibid.

15. The time is found in two of the hospital documents already cited and the place is in *Last Days*, 233.

16. This probably was Cobb, whom Gay writes in his memoir drove him to the hospital.

17. Letter from Hill to Walter Reed Historian Esther Rohlader, dated October 19, 1964.

18. *A Doctor's Memoirs of World War II,* 90.

19. Hill letter to Rohlader.

20. Morphine sulphate shows up periodically on Patton's day-to-day medical charts.

21. *Last Days*, 235-236.

22. *Death of Patton*, op. cit.

23. The story, datelined "Mannheim, Dec. 10 (UPI?)" and headlined "Both Drivers Called Careless in Auto Crash',' does not have a byline. Dr. Kent also discusses the guards outside Patton's room.

24. *Last Days*, 252-253. The story is quite famous for it got the nurse in trouble. The fact was that Patton was not as hard a drinker as often portrayed, although certainly not a teetotaler.

25. This number is contained in a memoir by Dr. R. Glen Spurling, Patton's chief neurosurgeon, which appears to be from where Farago obtained it. The memoir comes from a 30-page talk he gave approximately a year after treating Patton. He sent the speech to Mrs. Patton in August 1950, according to a letter that accompanies it.

26. *Last Days*, 252-253.

27. A packet of nine pages, including letters and memos, titled "Outgoing Classified Message," dated variously 9 and 10 December 1945, with Col. Alfred D. Starbird listed as the "preparing" officer.

28. *Last Days*, 255.

29. *Patton Diary*, October 13, 1945.

30. Ibid., 17.
31. Ibid., 17-18.
32. Hospital records.
33. *Last Days*, 266.
34. Ibid., 265.
35. Cable to "Lt. Col. Michele De Bakey," of later heart surgery fame, at the surgeon general's office. It was marked "priority" and "restricted" and signed by Gen. Keyes.
36. *Last Days*, 265.
37. According to his medical records.
38. The "Certificate" is dated February 16, 1938, Fort Riley, Kansas." Attached is his 1939 annual army physical which reiterates the same information.
39. The summary, handwritten on a hospital "Progress Notes" form is for "Patton" and says, "20 Dec Last night suddenly developed acute attack of dysnea with . . . " The rest is unintelligible because of the poor quality of the copy.
40. *Last Days,* 268.
41. Ibid., 269.
42. "Progress Notes" for George S. Patton, "21 December, 1945. Summary."
43. *Last Days*, 268.
44. Spurling in "Patton Bulletin No. 4," one of the updates on Patton's condition issued periodically by "Headquarters, U.S. Forces, European Theater, Public Relations Division." This one was the final one issued after his death.
45. Spurling memoir. Phlebitis could have been an alternative cause.
46. Nurse's Notes.
47. *Last Days*, 271.
48. "Progress Notes," dated "21 December 1945."

Chapter Thirteen: Murder by Truck

1. Form 52-1, The Adjutant General's office, Washington, D. C., 24 December 1945.
2. "Progress Notes," dated "21 December 1945" and signed by Dr. Hill.
3. Spurling memoir.
4. Ladislas Farago, *The Last Days of Patton* (New York: Berkley, 1981), 2.
5. Ibid.
6. Gen. James M. Gavin, *On To Berlin* (New York: Bantam, 1979), 296.
7. George Nicholas, "Murder No Shock To Spooks," the *Spotlight*, October 15, 1979.
8. Conein, now dead, is known from Church Committee hearings as one of those involved in the assassination of South Vietnam premier Diem.
9. Safely dispersed with others.
10. The diagrams, hand drawn pictures each, are attached to both Dr. Ball and Dr. Hill's remembrances composed for Walter Reed Hospital.
11. Judyth Sassoon, "Biochemical Assassination Weapons," *Encyclopedia of Intelligence,* Gale Group, 2004. (http://www.espionageinfo.com/Ba-Bl/Biochemical-

Assassination-Weapons.html.

12. John Barron, *KGB: The Secret Work of Soviet Secret Agents* (Bantam Books, 1974), 419.

13. CIA memorandum entitled "Soviet Use of Assassination and Kidnapping", prepared in February 1964 for the President's Commission on the Assassination of President Kennedy and declassified in 1971; obtained at the UCLA Library.

14. Richard Camellion, *Assassination: Theory and Practice* (Paladin Press, 1977), 139.

15. Robert Johnson, "A Study of Assassination," appears to have been written as a graduate paper at Community University, Brooklyn N.Y. George Washington University National Security Archive.

16. Email response to my *Military* advertisement. Col. Roush, a current outdoors and military writer, said he had been near the Patton accident when it had occurred "but had no firsthand knowledge. We were all appalled to learn of the event."

17. Conquest is one of the deans of Soviet watchers.

18. Pavel Sudoplatov and Anatoli Sudoplatov, with Jerrold L. and Leona P. Schecter; *Special Tasks: The Memoirs of an Unwanted Witness—A Soviet Spymaster* (New York: Little Brown and Company, 1994), 252-253.

19. Ibid., 249.

20. Ibid., 270.

21. Stephen J. Skubik, *Death: The Murder of General Patton*; (Bennington: self published, 1993), 118.

22. Valentin M. Berezhkov, *At Stalin's Side: His Interpreter's Memoirs From the October Revolution to the Fall of the Dictator's Empire* (New York: Birch Lane Press, 1994), 315-316.

23. Ibid., 316-318.

24. Don Isaac Levine, *The Mind of an Assassin* (New York: Farrar, Straus and Cudahy, 1959). *The Mind of an Assassin* is the story of confessed Trotsky murderer Ramon Mercader, who used every subterfuge, including love and friendship, to gain access to Trotsky and then, when opportunity presented itself, plunge an ice-axe into his head. His mother, a devout Stalinist, put him up to it.

25. Christopher Andrew and Vasili Mitrokhin, *The Sword and the Shield: The Mitrokhin Archive and the Secret History of the KGB* (Basic Books, 1999).

26. *Sword and Shield*, 74-76.; John Barron, *KGB: The Secret World of Soviet Secret Agents*, (New York: Readers Digest Press distributed by E. P. Dutton & Co., 1974), 416 says the undercover NKVD aide was with Ledov in the hospital. Donald Rayfield, *Stalin and His Hangmen: The Tyrant and Those Who Killed for Him* (New York: Random House, 2004), 335, names the NKVD assassin.

27. "Murder No Shock to Spooks"; *Last Hero*, 721-727, 804-816. The Holohan case became a national sensation when first publicized in 1953. *Time*, among other magazines, ran continual stories about it.

28. *Death: The Murder of General Patton*, 44-46.

29. Ibid., 44, 118–120.

30. This is another of the vagaries of the accident scene. Without the reports to hopefully establish definite time lines, no one really can say conclusively who did what when. Skubik infers that there was an unnecessary delay, given Patton's obvious serious condition, between Snyder's arrival at the accident and the ambulance's departure.

31. *Death: The Murder of General Patton*, 133-137.

32. Records obtained from the National Personnel Records Center, St. Louis, confirm this.

33. Skubik writes that he was given a Bronze Star which is not in his available military records.

34. *Death: The Murder of General Patton*, 47.

35. Ibid., 47-48

36. *Death: The Murder of General Patton*, 49.

37. While I was successful in locating many of those discussed in Skubik's manuscript—or at least verifying their existence—my efforts to find Col. MacIntosh and Maj. Stone have been fruitless and it's possible they are among the few names Skubik changed. However, Skubik's family is very familiar with "Stoney" whom they say their father often talked about.

38. *Death: The Murder of General Patton*, 50-51.

39. Ibid., 51.

40. *Ukrainian Weekly,* obituary, "Stephen Skubik, consultant to Republican National Committee," October 10, 1996.

41. Harriet Skubik Hanley, email to the author, August 18, 2004.

42. Assistant director of health policy development for a state's health services department.

43. *Death: The Murder of General Patton*, Foreword and 52.

44. Stephen J. Skubik & Hal E. Short, *Republican Humor.* (Acropolis Books, 1976). Foreword by President Gerald Ford and Introduction by Vice President Nelson A. Rockefeller.

45. Harriet Skubik Hanley, email to the author, August 18, 2004.

46. Mark Skubik, emails to author, July, 20 2004 and August 24, 2005.

Chapter Fourteen: A Soldier, Not a Diplomat

1. Patton's diaries from this time confirm this.

2. Robert Murphy, *Diplomat Among Warriors* (Pyramid Books, 1964), 174.

3. Thomas Fleming, *The New Dealers' War: F.D.R. and the War Within WWII* (Basic Books, 2001), 190-191.

4. *Diplomat Among Warriors*, 173.

5. *New Dealer's War,* 165-170.

6. *Diplomat Among Warriors*, 175-176.

7. Anthony Cave Brown, *The Last Hero:Wild Bill Donovan* (Vintage, 1984), 262.

8. Robin Winks, *Cloak and Gown: Scholars in America's Secret War* (London: Collins Harvill, 1987), 183–184.

9. *The Last Hero*, 269.

10. Ibid., 270.

11. Stephen E. Ambrose, *Ike's Spies: Eisenhower and the Espionage Establishment* (University of Mississippi Press, 1999) (originally published by Doubleday 1981), 54-55.

12. David Irving, *The War between the Generals* (Congdon & Weed, 1993).

13. Ibid., 14–15.

14. Ibid., 15.

15. February 3, 1943 letter, in *The Patton Papers*, 168.

16. Patton's Diaries, February 5, 1943 entry, Library of Congress.

17. *New Dealer's War*, 174.

18. Fred Ayer Jr., *Before the Colors Fade* (Dunwoody: Norman S. Berg, publisher, 1971), 209-210.

19. *Diplomat Among Warriors*, 261.

20. Allen Weinstein, and Alexander Vassiliev, *The Haunted Wood* (Modern Library, 2000), 23; Jerrold Schecter and Leona Schecter, *Sacred Secrets: How Soviet Intelligence Operations Changed American History* (Washington DC: Brassey's, 2002), 156-160.

21. See the March 29, 1943 issue of Life magazine on the Soviet Union featuring a glowing centerpiece article by Davies for a glimpse of the distorted view Americans received. Donald Rayfield, *Stalin and his Hangmen: The Tyrant* and those who killed for him (New York: Random House, 2004). According Rayfield, Davies reported show-trial victims guilty when it was obvious to the world at large they were innocent. S.J. Taylor, *Stalin's Apologist* (Oxford University Press, 1990).

22. Christopher Andrew and Vasili Mitrokhin, *The Sword and the Shield: The Mitrokhin Archive and the Secret History of the KGB* (Basic Books, 1999), 107; also Sacred Secrets, 156-160.

23. *The Last Hero*, 417.

24. Joseph E. Persico, *Roosevelt's Secret War: FDR and World War II Espionage* (New York: Random House, 2001), 299-300.

25. *Sword and Shield*, 112. The authors cite Henry Kissinger, Diplomacy (Simon and Schuster, 1995).

26. Diaries, *The Patton Papers*, 157.

27. *The Patton Papers*, 168.

28. A new book, M. Stanton Evans, *Blacklisted By History: The Untold Story of Senator Joe McCarthy* (New York: Crown, 2007), director of the National Journalism Center and a former commentator for CBS, argues McCarthy has been wrongly vilified by the Left and stories used to impugn him are untrue.

29. Stephen J. Sniegoski, "The Reality of Red Subversion: The Recent Confirmation of Soviet Espionage in America," *The Occidental Quarterly* Volume 3, Number 3. shows how large was the infiltration.

30. Pavel Sudoplatov and Anatoli Sudoplatov, with Jerrold L. and Leona P. Schecter; *Special Tasks: The Memoirs of an Unwanted Witness - A Soviet Spymaster*, (New York: Little Brown and Company, 1994), 227.

31. *Sword and Shield*, 133
32. *Sacred Secrets*, 131
33. Jonah Goldberg, "Recovering Yalta," *National Review*, May 11, 2005
34. Herbert Romerstein and Eric Breindell, *The Venona Secrets: Exposing Soviet Espionage and America's Traitors* (Washington DC: Regnery, 2000),153.; also *Roosevelt's Secret War*, 374.
35. Harvey Klehr, "Spies Like Us," *The Weekly Standard*, July 8, 2002.
36. Ibid.
37. Craig's remark was made in an address at the International Spy Museum, Washington, D.C., broadcast on C-Span2 July 15, 2004.
38. *Sword and Shield*, 130. See the footnote as well.
39. *The Last Hero*, 438–442.
40. FBI message from "Boardman" via "Thornton" to "Director" marked "Urgent" and dated "June 30, 1953." It can be found in Donovan's file with the FBI.
41. *Venona Secrets*, 211-215.
42. See Sharing Secrets with Stalin, Sword and Shield, Special Tasks, and Sacred Secrets, each of which discusses this.
43. *Haunted Wood*, 14.
44. Ronn M. Platt, *News & Observer*, "Red Scare or Red Menace?" (Raleigh, NC) January 31, 1999.
45. *Haunted Wood*, 140–150.
46. For a list of some of the material, including communications to and from Eisenhower, Roosevelt, Morganthau, Truman and other high-level Allied leaders, see *Haunted Wood*, 270-271.
47. Venona specifically references 349 people in the government, industry and media as being "engaged in clandestine activities" or "approached" to be Soviet spies, John Haynes and Harvey Klehr, Venona: *Decoding Soviet Espionage in America*, (Yale University Press, 2000), 339. Fleming in *New Dealers' War*, 459, writes, "Roosevelt had no less than 329 communist spies in his administration."
48. Douglas Botting and Ian Sayer, *America's Secret Army: The Untold Story of the Counter Intelligence Corps*, (London: Fontana Publishers, 1990), 42–47.
49. *Before the Colors Fade*, 184.
50. Gen. Albert C. Wedemeyer, *Wedemeyer Reports* (New York: Henry Hold & Company, 1958), 87-88, 140, 345.
51. John Barron, *KGB: The Secret World of Soviet Secret Agents*, (New York: Readers Digest Press distributed by E. P. Dutton & Co., 1974), 228.
52. *The Haunted Wood*, 283-284
53. Several books, including Persico's *Roosevelt's Secret War*, include this alarming fact. *Sword and Shield* authors Andrew and Mitrokhin attribute it to historian Harvey Klehr, who answered my emailed query thusly: "The comment on White is found in a newspaper article written by Malcolm Hobbs, 'Confident Wallace Aides Come up with Startling Cabinet Notions,' an Overseas News Service Dispatch of April 22, 1948 that is reprinted in the McCarran Committee Hearings, 'Interlocking Subversion in Government Departments.' My notes have it in volume 20, 2529-

2530." He said he was "absolutely sure" about the Duggan projection but couldn't find the citation in his notes and so had left the story out of his own writings.

54. Patton diary, April 12, 1943, Library of Congress.
55. Eric Ethier, "General George S. Patton's Race to Capture Messina," *American History Magazine*, April 2001.
56. Carlo D'Este, *A Genius For War* (HarperPerennial, 1996), 539.
57. General Eisenhower to Patton, August 17, 1943, reprinted in *Patton Papers*, 329-330.
58. *Genius For War*, 540-541.
59. *Last Days of Patton*, 23.
60. Ibid., 536.
61. Charles Whiting, *Patton's Last Battle* (New York, Stein and Day, 1987), 39.
62. *Genius For War*, 543.
63. *The Patton Papers*, 340-341, 380-381.
64. November 28, 1943.
65. *The Patton Papers*, 440.
66. Ibid., 441.
67. Stanley P. Hirshson, General Patton: A Soldier's Life (Harper Perennial, 2003), 460.
68. Ibid.,461.
69. *The Patton Papers*, 449.
70. Ibid.
71. *Genius For War*, 590.
72. *The Patton Papers*, 452.
73. Ibid., 451.

Chapter Fifteen: A Tale of Two Drivers
1. Fred Ayer Jr., *Before The Colors Fade* (Cherokee Publishing Company, 2007), 261.
2. Denver Fugate, "The End of the Ride: An Eyewitness Account of George S. Patton's Fatal Accident," *Armor*, November-December 1995.
3. Alice Thompson to the author, August 2005.
4. "Woman, gunman die in shootout," *Philadelphia Inquirer*, December 9, 1982,
5. Beck could not remember its name.
6. For example, a UPI story on the accident, datelined "Mannheim, Dec. 10," was headlined "Both Drivers Called Careless in Auto Crash." There were others.
7. Stars & Stripes told him they no longer had the picture or the files that would give them the information.
8. This history is based on what Angela told me, personal papers and documents of his she has, and records I found in U.S. repositories.
9. It can be found on Lonesentry.com.
10. Brian M. Sobel, *The Fighting Pattons* (Dell, 1997), 77.
11. At least they did before the current era of Islamic terrorism.
12. In a 28 May 1952 "Request For Army Information" in his file, the exact word-

ing is, "There is no record on file in this office of autopsy report or any indication that an autopsy was performed." Why and by who the request was made is not stated.

13. National Personnel Records Center, St. Louis.

14. Emphasis hers.

15. Dated 18 December 1945 and addressed "To: Provost Marshal" (sic), National Archives.

Chapter Sixteen: Stop Patton!

1. Charles Province, *The Unknown Patton* (Bonanza, 1983), 60; For Patton's pre-use discussion of the plan, Martin Blumenson, *The Patton Papers 1940-1945* (Boston: Houghton Mifflin, 1974), 482.

2. George S. Patton Jr., *War as I Knew It* (New York: Bantam, 1980), 89.

3. Col. Robert S. Allen., *Lucky Forward: Patton's Third Army* (Manor Books, 1947, 1977), 86. Allen was co-author with Drew Pearson of the book and subsequent column, Washington Merry-Go-Round, and Washington bureau chief for *The Christian Science Monitor* before his death in 1981.

4. Albin F. Irzyk, *Gasoline To Patton: A Different War* (Oakland: Elderberry Press, Inc., 2005), 101; Gen. James M. Gavin, *On To Berlin* (New York: Bantam, 1979), 129.

5. Ibid.

6. *The Unknown Patton,* 50.

7. Richard Rohmer, *Patton's Gap, An Account of the Battle of Normandy 1944* (Beaufort Books, Inc., 1981), 176.

8. William B. Breuer, *Death of a Nazi Army: The Falaise Pocket* (Scarborough House, 1985), 295.

9. Martin Blumenson, *The Patton Papers 1940-1945* (Boston: Houghton Mifflin, 1974), 508, 511.

10. Fred Ayer Jr., *Before the Colors Fade* (Dunwoody: Norman S. Berg, publisher, 1971), 151-152.

11. *Gasoline To Patton,* 117-118.

12. Ibid., 110.

13. *The Patton Papers,* 530.

14. *Before the Colors Fade,* 190.

15. *Gasoline To Patton,* 127; *On To Berlin,* 136.

16. OSS Reports to the White House, Jan-April 13, 45, Carlisle Barracks.

17. *On To Berlin,* 137.

18. *War as I Knew It,* 116; *The Patton Papers,* 531.

19. Stephen E. Ambrose, *Ike's Spies: Eisenhower and the Espionage Establishment* (University of Mississippi Press, 1999) (originally published by Doubleday 1981), 135.

20. *The Patton Papers,* 556; David Irving, *The War Between the Generals* (Congden & Weed, 1981), 282.

21. *On To Berlin,* 139.

22. *Gasoline To Patton*, 123.

23. Diary entry September 17, 1944, found in *Patton Papers*, 550.

24. *On To Berlin*, 137.

25. *Patton Papers*, 548.

26. Ibid., 531.

27. *War as I Knew It,* 121.

28. Ibid., 549; also *War as I Knew It*, 127. The italics are mine.

29. *War as I Knew It*, 158-159; *Patton Papers*, 571.

30. Charles M. Province; "The Third Army in World War II," Patton Research Library. (http://www.pattonhq.com/textfiles/thirdhst.html).

31. Ibid.

32. Thomas Parrish, *Simon and Schuster Encyclopedia of World War II,* (Simon and Schuster, 1978), 91.

Chapter Seventeen: The Car That Isn't

1. Http://www.knox.army.mil/PattonMuseum/, accessed October 7, 2008.

2. A quarterly magazine published by Triumph Motorcycles.

3. Doug Houston, "General George S. Patton: A Tale of Two Classics," *Torque*, March-April, 1980.

4. These letters are contained in the museum publication, "The Patton Cadillac."

Chapter Eighteen: Problem Child

1. Ladislas Farago, *The Last Days of Patton* (New York: Berkley, 1981), 30.

2. Martin Blumenson, *The Patton Papers 1940-1945* (Boston: Houghton Mifflin, 1974), 644-645.

3. Ibid., 648.

4. Ibid., 649.

5. *Last Days,* 29. Farago took the scene from Omar N. Bradley, *A Soldier's Story* (Modern Library, 1999), 521

6. Nothing explicit was visible in the photo, though he was standing in a likely position, hands below the waist.

7. Ibid., 32.

8. Richard Baron, Major Abe Baum, and Richard Goldhurst, *Raid! The Untold Story of Patton's Secret Mission* (Dell, 2000), 250.

9. *The Patton Papers*, 675-676

10. Ladislas Farago, *Patton: Ordeal and Triumph* (Dell, 1970), 778.

11. Charles Whiting, *Patton's Last Battle* (New York, Stein and Day, 1987), 149.

12. See anti-fascist Dwight Macdonald's "The Ordeal of George Patton," The New York Review of Books, December 31, 1964; Orville Prescott, "Books of the Times," *New York Times,* February 27, 1946.

13. William R. Wilson, "Jimmy Doolittle Reminiscences about World War II," *American History Magazine*, August 1997.

14. Benjamin B. Fischer, "The Katyn Controversy: Stalin's Killing Field," (www.cia.gov/csi/studies/winter99-OO/art6.html).

15. Bradley F. Smith, *Sharing Secrets with Stalin: How the Allies Traded Intelli-*

gence, 1941-1945 (University Press of Kansas, 1996), 164.

16. Ibid., 166.

17. Steve Neal, *Harry and Ike: The Partnership that remade the Postwar World* (Touchstone, 2001), 53. The period, the end of the war until early 1946, is crucial because it led to 50 years of Cold War.

18. Bruce Lee, *Marching Orders: The Untold Story of World War II* (New York: Crown, 1995); Robert Murphy, *Diplomat Among Warriors* (Pyramid Books, 1964); and Victor Davis Hanson, "What Would Patton Say About the Present War?," *Imprimis*, October 23, 2004.

19. Gen. Albert C. Wedemeyer, *Wedemeyer Reports* (New York: Henry Hold & Company, 1958), 370.

20. For details see *FDR's Last Year, The New Dealers' War,* or *Roosevelt's Secret War,* among others.

21. Christopher Andrew and Vasili Mitrokhin, *The Sword and the Shield: The Mitrokhin Archive and the Secret History of the KGB* (Basic Books, 1999); *The Mitrokhin Archive: The KGB in Europe and the West* (Penguin Press, 1999).

22. Ibid. 133-134 and 175-176 respectively.

23. Jonah Goldberg, "Reconsidering Yalta," *National Review* Online, May 11, 2005.

24. To the friendly countries and innocent and unfortunate people sacrificed.

25. Charles M. Province, "More Than a Tank General," Patton Society Research Library, (http://www.pattonhq.com/textfiles/morethan.html).

26. Ibid.

27. *Marching Orders,* 368-369, 391-393.

28. Ibid., 392.

29. Albin F. Irzyk, *Gasoline To Patton: A Different War* (Oakland: Elderberry Press, Inc., 2005), 243.

30. Tom Agoston, *Blunder!: How the U.S. gave away Nazi Supersecrets to Russia* (Dodd, Mead & Co., 1985).

31. *Last Days,* 61.

32. *Gas To Patton,* 242.

33. *The Patton Papers,* 702.

34. Charles B. Odom, General George S. Patton and Eisenhower Word Picture Productions (New Orleans: 1985).

35. *Gas to Patton,* 242.

36. As discussed in Chapter 12, D. A. Lande quotes Woodring in *I Was With Patton* (274) that Patton "rarely ever [italics Lande's] sat on the edge of his seat."

Chapter Nineteen: Marked Man

1. Gen. Albert C. Wedemeyer, *Wedemeyer Reports* (New York: Henry Hold & Company, 1958), 222.

2. Larry G. Newman, "Gen. Patton's Premonition: An account of a press conference at which the General sounded a grim warning," *The American Legion* magazine, July 1962.

3. D'Este covered it, too.

4. Charles Whiting, *Patton's Last Battle* (New York, Stein and Day, 1987), 196.

5. Martin Blumenson, *The Patton Papers 1940-1945* (Boston: Houghton Mifflin, 1974), 712.

6. Fred Ayer Jr., *Before the Colors Fade* (Dunwoody: Norman S. Berg, publisher, 1971). 240.

7. Ibid., 241.

8. Ladislas Farago, *The Last Days of Patton* (New York: Berkley, 1981), 84-85.

9. Ruth Ellen Patton Totten, *The Button Box: A Daughter's Loving Memoir of Mrs. George S. Patton* (University of Missouri Press, 2005), 349.

10. John Loftus, *The Belarus Secret* (New York, Alfred A. Knopf, 1982), 48.

11. Charles Lutton, "Stalin's War: Victims and Accomplices," *Journal of Historical Review*, 4, Vol. 20, 2001. (http://www.vho.org/GB/ Journals/JHR/5/1/Lutton84-94.html).

12. Mark Elliott, *Pawns of Yalta*, (University of Illinois Press, 1982), 106; Douglas Botting and Ian Sayer, *America's Secret Army: The Untold Story of the Counter Intelligence Corps,* (London: Fontana Publishers, 1990), 338-339.

13. Ladislas Farago, *The Last Days of Patton* (New York: Berkley, 1981), 129-130.

14. Ibid., 143.

15. Ibid., 188. Dorn's background is on page 184.

16. Ibid., 149.

17. Ibid., 150.

18. Mark Perry, *Partners In Command: George Marshall and Dwight Eisenhower in War and Peace* (New York: Penguin Press, 2007), 369.

19. Patton Diary, August 27, 1945, Library of Congress.

20. *The Patton Papers,* 743.

21. Patton Diary, August 29, 1945.

22. "Footnotes to Greatness: A Review of Patton: A Soldier's Life"

23. *Last Days,* 191-192.

24. Mark Skubik, Email to author, August 6, 2005.

25. Allen Weinstein, and Alexander Vassiliev, *The Haunted Wood* (Modern Library, 2000), 255.

26. *Last Days,* 192-193; also Carlo D'Este, *A Genius For War* (HarperPerennial, 1996)., 763-764.

27. Robert Murphy, *Diplomat Among Warriors* (Pyramid Books, 1964), 329-330; E.H. Cookridge, *Gehlen: Spy of the Century* (New York: Pyramid Books, 1973), 197.

28. From an edited passage of Khokhlov's 1959 book, *In the Name of Conscience*, printed in *The Times of London*, December 1, 2006.

29. Ibid.

30. Gen. James M. Gavin, *On To Berlin* (New York: Bantam, 1979), 293.

31. Ibid., 294 - 295.

32. Lucius D. Clay, *Decision in Germany,* (New York: Doubleday & Co., 1950), 104 -105.

33. *Before the Colors Fade,* 245.

34. Stephen J. Skubik, *Death: The Murder of General Patton;* (Bennington: self published, 1993), Foreword.

35. Robert Murphy, *Diplomat Among Warriors* (Pyramid Books, 1964), 330.

36. *Last Days,* 176-179

37. Jeffrey St. John, "The Press and General Patton," Patton Society Research Library.

38. *Last Days,* 176-179.

39. *The Patton Papers,* 789-790.

40. Russell Hill, "Patton Removal Praised in Red Zone of Berlin," *New York Herald Tribune*, October 5, 1945.

41. George S. Patton Jr., *War as I Knew It* (New York: Bantam, 1980), 366.

Chapter Twenty: Into the Night

1. Ian Sayer & Douglas Botting, *Nazi Gold: The Sensational Story of the World's Greatest Robbery—and the Greatest Criminal Cover-Up* (Mainstream Publishing, 2003); I was unable to confirm with Guiness.

2. Stephen J. Skubik, *Death: The Murder of General Patton;* (Bennington: self published, 1993), 6.

3. Charles Whiting, *Patton's Last Battle* (New York, Stein and Day, 1987).

4. See *Soldiers of Misfortune: Washington's Secret Betrayal of American POWs in the Soviet Union* by James D. Sanders.

5. M.G. Brown, "Mikhail Gorbachev, Let Our People Go," Parts 1 & 2, *The New American,* May & June 1990.

6. Ibid.

7. Donald Rayfield, *Stalin and his Hangmen: The Tyrant and Those Who Killed for Him* (New York: Random House, 2004), 313.

8. Ibid., 201.

9. Christopher Andrew and Vasili Mitrokhin, *The Sword and the Shield: The Mitrokhin Archive and the Secret History of the KGB* (Basic Books, 1999), 355.

10. Pavel Sudoplatov and Anatoli Sudoplatov, with Jerrold L. and Leona P. Schecter; *Special Tasks: The Memoirs of an Unwanted Witness—A Soviet Spymaster*, (New York: Little Brown and Company, 1994). Includes plots for all but Franco, whose death sentence is reported in *Sword and the Shield* as well as a November 14, 2001 article in the *London Times* by Joanna Bale.

11. Michael Munn, *John Wayne: The Man Behind the Myth* (New American Library, 2005),124.

12. Ibid.,127.

13. Ibid., 27, 5.

14. Ibid., 4.

15. Ibid., 145-146.

16. Patton Collection, Library of Congress.

17. Martin Blumenson, *The Patton Papers 1940-1945* (Boston: Houghton Mifflin, 1974), 798.

18. Patton Papers, 799-800.

19. Patterson's declassified letter—it was "confidential" by the Department of Defense apparently until 1994, is dated May 7, 1947, and is written on War Department stationary. Unfortunately, I didn't mark where I obtained it but I believe it was the Library of Congress.

20. *The Patton Papers,* 818.

21. Patton Collection, Library of Congress.

22. Ibid.

23. Suzy Shelton, "Horace L. Woodring: The True Story of 'The Last Days of Patton,'" December 2, 1986. (Unknown where this appeared. It was sent to me by Peter Hendrikx, Netherlands.)

24. Page 88.

25. *Last Days,* 223.

26. Ibid.

27. Denver Fugate, "The End of the Ride: An Eyewitness Account of George S. Patton's Fatal Accident," *Armor,* November-December 1995.

28. "I'm going to resign. Quit Outright, not retire." Robert S. Allen, "Patton's Secret: 'I am Going to Resign From the Army,'" Army 21 (June 1971): 29-33.

Chapter Twenty-One: Enigmas

1. All italics in this listing of missing documents are mine.

2. Sent by National Archives.

3. Sent by National Archives.

4. Including Farago and a *New York Times* story dated December 14, 1945.

5. Gerald T. Kent, M.D., *A Doctor's Memoirs of World War II* (The Cobham and Hatherton Press, 1989), 88.

6. Ladislas Farago, *The Last Days of Patton* (New York: Berkley, 1981), 266.

7. Cyd Upson & Michael Weiss, "War Stories with Oliver North: The Remarkable Life and Mysterious Death of General Patton," 2006. DVD. FOX News, 2007.

8. Robert E. Laughlin, "Patton: The December Days," (undated newspaper article post-1981).

9. Steve Neal, *Harry and Ike: The Partnership That Remade the Postwar World* (Touchstone, 2001), 206.

10. *The Sunday Star.*

11. D.A. Lande, *I Was With Patton: First-person Accounts of WWII in George S. Patton's Command* (MBI Publishing Co., 2002), 272-275.

12. *Last Days,* 221-223.

13. Charles Whiting, *Patton's Last Battle* (New York, Stein and Day, 1987), 236, says they left the ruins with Patton in the rear seat.

Chapter Twenty-Two: Epitaph

1. His dissolve order was for 20 September 1945 but problems issuing it pushed the date to early October.

2. Richard Dunlop, *Donovan: America's Master Spy* (Chicago: Rand McNally & Co., 1982), 479.

3. Available at the FBI site (http://.foia.fbi.gov/foiaindex/donovan.htm).

4. RG 226, Entry 169a, Box 26, Folder 1129, U.S. National Archives.

5. Reinhard Gehlen, *The Service: The Memoirs of General Reinhard Gehlen* (World Publishing, 1972), 204.

6. Joseph E. Persico, *Roosevelt's Secret War: FDR and World War II Espionage* (New York: Random House, 2001), 163.

7. Amerasia involved the publication of formerly secret OSS documents favorable to the Chinese communists. Donovan's lax attitude toward communists in OSS was said to have facilitated the publication. Truman, siding with Leftists, called the divisive issue a "red herring."

8. John Earl Haynes and Harvey Klehr, *Venona: Decoding Soviet Espionage in America* (New Haven: Yale University Press, 2000), 192-193.

9. Donovan's declassified FBI file, Part 1d, 35 (or 190 on the page).

10. Thomas O'Toole, "Another Spy Story is in From the Cold," *Washington Post,* June 7, 1983.

11. Anthony Cave Brown, *The Last Hero:Wild Bill Donovan* (Vintage, 1984), 826.

12. Fred Ayer Jr., *Before the Colors Fade* (Dunwoody: Norman S. Berg, publisher, 1971), 260-261.

13. Vadim Y. Birstein, *The Perversion of Knowledge: The True Story of Soviet Science* (Basic Books, 2001) 132.

14. Joe Lagattuta, interview by author, November, 2004.

15. *Gehlen: Spy of the Century*, 210.

16. A copy of the letter was sent to me by Cyd Upson, a producer for Oliver North's *War Stories,* who acquired it from the General Douglas MacArthur Memorial, Norfolk, Va.

17. Joseph J. Trento, *The Secret History of the CIA* (New York: Crown Forum (Random House), 2001), 194.

18. Larry Devlin, *Chief of Station, Congo* (Public Affairs books, 2007), 94–97; Evan Thomas, *The Very Best Men: Four who Dared: The Early Years of the CIA* (Touchstone, 1995), 226–230.

19. David Irving, *The War Between the Generals* (Congden & Weed, 1981), 413-414.

20. Ibid., 358.

21. Michael Barone, "Understanding Harry & Ike: The Uneasy Friendship of Truman and Eisenhower," *The Weekly Standard*, April 1, 2002.

22. Charles B. Odom, General George S. Patton and Eisenhower Word Picture Productions (New Orleans: 1985), 80.

23. Stephen E. Ambrose, *Comrades: Brothers, Fathers, Heroes, Sons, Pals,* (Simon & Schuster, 1999), 57.

24. "President Zachary Taylor and the Laboratory: Presidential Visit From the Grave," *Oak Ridge National Review*, Vol. 25, Nos 3 and 4, 2002.

Postscript: October 2010

1. The column, "Were U.S. Allies in CIA Sights?" was datelined February 15, 1999,

and distributed by News World Communications, Inc. In fact, this was not the first time the U.S. had contemplated assassinating Chiang. See Dorn's "Walkout With Stillwell," pp. 75-79.

2. See Frank Dorn, *Walkout: With Stillwell in Burma* (Thomas Y. Crowell, 1970), 76–82, and Stanton Evans, *Blacklisted by History* (New York: Crown Forum, 2007), 417–22.

3. Most estimates say he was responsible for between 40 and 60 million deaths.

4. For more on these plots see veteran broadcast journalist Wes Vernon's article about Toledano, "Hard-nosed investigative reporting: a giant has left us," published May 7, 2007, at RenewAmerica.com. It should be noted that at this time—in the early period right after WWII—there was an on-going struggle in the CIA, as in all branches of government, between pro and anti-Soviet factions. It wasn't until later when the Russians, U.S. allies in WWII, revealed themselves clearly as an enemy that the anti-Soviet faction prevailed and the Cold War began in earnest.

5. As already explained in this book, the OSS was riddled with communists, including agents working directly for the Soviets. There were suspect "accidents" to agents dropped behind enemy lines. Douglas Bazata believed someone had tampered with his parachute resulting in the injury he received jumping into France. In Toledano's *New York Times* obituary (February 6, 2007), the obit writer says about his planned but cancelled OSS parachute drop, "Despite a crash course in Italian, he was rejected for covert work in Italy because he was deemed too anti-Communist to work with Italian leftists."

6. Gouzenko defected from the Soviet Embassy in Canada in September 1945.

7. Richard Sorge, a Soviet Journalist, has often been called Stalin's greatest spy. Toledano wrote extensively about him.

8. As I've already implied earlier in *Target: Patton*, I'm convinced Senator McCarthy, whatever his personal faults, has been wrongly portrayed by a largely biased leftwing press and Hollywood whose distortions have left an impression on ordinary Americans that McCarthy was a bullying, lying, demigod. The truth is he was correct and a patriot in his accusations that the immediate post-war Truman government was rife with communists. His information was coming from those running the ultra secret Venona project which had access to secret Soviet communications which the U.S. was secretly reading. But even he didn't know that. Venona didn't become public until just recently. For a more balanced and updated look at McCarthy see *Blacklisted by History* by M. Stanton Evans.

9. In my numbering of them, this is from Bazata diary 40, pp. 45b–46b, 80b–81b.

★ ★ ★ ★

INDEX